INTRODUCTORY READINGS IN

CANADIAN

GOVERNMENT

& POLITICS

SECOND EDITION

Introductory Readings in

CANADIAN

GOVERNMENT

& POLITICS

SECOND EDITION

Edited by

ROBERT M. KRAUSE
R.H. WAGENBERG

University of Windsor

Copp Clark Ltd.

Toronto

© Copp Clark Ltd., 1995

 work covered by the copyrights hereon may be
ns—graphic, electronic, or mechanical—with-
e publisher.

, taping, or for storing on information and retrieval
directed in writing to CANCOPY (the Canadian
Copyright Licensing Agency), 6 Adelaide Street East, Suite 600, Toronto, Ontario,
M5C 1H6.

ISBN: 0-7730-5440-5

Editor: Barbara Tessman
Executive editor: Jeff Miller
Proofreader: Sarah Robertson
Design: Sharon Foster Design
Cover photo: Courtesy Canadian Government Travel Bureau
Typesetting: Carol Magee
Printing and binding: Metrolitho

Canadian Cataloguing in Publication Data

Main entry under title:
Introductory readings in Canadian government & politics
2nd ed.
Includes bibliographical references and index.
ISBN 0-7730-5440-5

1. Canada - Politics and government. I. Krause, Robert M. II. Wagenberg, R.H., 1939–

JL65 1991.I68 1995   320.971   C94-932818-9

Copp Clark Ltd.
2775 Matheson Blvd. East
Mississauga, Ontario
L4W 4P7

Printed and bound in Canada

   2 3 4 5   5440-5   99 98 97 96

CONTENTS

PREFACE

Constant change is the hallmark of the Canadian political system, and thus a periodic updating of any book in this field is required if the material is to continue to be relevant or even accurate. Since this book of readings first appeared in 1991, not only have there been the normal reforms and refinements of various aspects of Canadian politics and government, but there have also been some rather crucial events. Of these, the proposed Charlottetown Accord, and its rejection in the referendum of October 1992, and the federal election of 1993, which not only put the Liberal Party into power but also dramatically changed the landscape of party politics, have had the most impact. Our contributors have endeavoured to make their various chapters as contemporary as possible. The election of the Parti Québécois in Quebec in September 1994 occurred after chapters of this edition had been revised and, in any case, the consequences of that victory will not be apparent for some time.

The basic aim of this collection remains the same as in the first edition. We have directed the readings specifically toward students who are in their first year of studying Canadian politics and government. The chapters are meant to supplement and complement introductory textbooks used in first-year courses. Contributors have constructed their chapters around questions that stimulate students' thought, interest, and discussion.

We have been fortunate in being able to recruit first-rate scholars from across Canada to create this book. Those contributors whose work appeared in the first edition have thoroughly revised and updated their chapters. In addition, Guy Lachapelle, Peter Aucoin, and Peter Woolstencroft have given us new chapters on Quebec, the prime minister and cabinet, and political parties respectively. Two subjects that were not covered in the first edition have now been addressed by the contributions of Kathy Brock on Aboriginal self-government, and Linda Trimble on women in Canadian politics.

As was the case with the original text, we do not seek to present any unified theoretical approach. As a consequence, we have a book that will expose students to the variety of approaches that scholars apply to the analysis of Canadian politics and government.

The order in which the essays appear is meant to approximate as much as possible the way in which topics are dealt with in introductory courses. Undoubtedly, because there is no rigid uniformity in the teaching of those courses, or the texts that are used in them, students may not necessarily be asked to read these chapters consecutively. Flexibility in assigning the readings is facilitated by the fact that each of the contributions stands on its own.

Our thanks in preparing this book go first to our co-essayists. They were remarkably easy to work with and produced what we consider to be first-rate work in a timely fashion. Jeff Miller of the Copp Clark team made the sometimes trying process of getting a book to its readers a surprisingly stress-free enterprise. We would like to thank Sharon Foster for a fine design and Barbara Tessman for her perceptive editing.

Val Allard and Barbara Faria of the Department of Political Science at the University of Windsor provided superb secretarial assistance in preparing our own essays. The staff of the word processing centre at the university, under the supervision of Lucia Brown, made it possible for us to deliver our manuscript to the publisher on time and in good shape. After all of this help, any imperfections in the presentation of these essays must be on our editorial heads. The merits, however, reside in the contributions of each of our essayists.

Neil Nevitte

THE DYNAMICS OF CANADIAN POLITICAL CULTURE(S)

T he goal of this chapter is to explore some of the central character-istics of the Canadian *political culture*. The discussion will consider four broad topics. The first section outlines what factors were crit-ical in making Canadian political culture during the formation of the Canadian state. The next section provides an overview of the major interpretations of why Canadian political culture turned out the way it did. The third part examines the dynamics of Canadian political culture, and the conclusion suggests what kinds of challenges will likely face Canadian political culture in the future. Before we turn to those spe-cific tasks, however, we need to step back from the particulars of the Canadian experience and to set the stage by making some general obser-vations about the nature of political culture itself.

The first point to note is that there is a vast literature dealing with the subject of political culture; definitions of the concept abound. Some schol-ars view political culture as "a system of beliefs about patterns of interac-tion and political institutions."[1] Others suggest that political culture includes "all politically relevant orientations of a cognitive, evaluative, and expres-sive sort."[2] Still others take political culture to include "attitudes, beliefs and sentiments that give order and meaning to the political process and provide the underlying assumptions and rules that govern behavior."[3] The sheer number of definitions creates the impression that there is a great deal of confusion about what political culture means. But for the most part the differences among definitions are a matter of emphasis. If we compared them all, we would find substantial agreement about the core meaning of the concept. In a nutshell, political culture refers to how citizens are oriented toward their political community.

We can get a more concrete sense of the central ideas included in so broad a definition by considering what kinds of questions students of political culture usually explore. For our purposes, we can list those questions under four broad headings:

1. Attitudes toward political symbols and institutions.

How strongly do citizens feel about such political symbols as the flag and the national anthem? Do citizens believe that their government institutions—parliament, the courts, the bureaucracy—are effective? Can government, the prime minister, and elected and appointed officials be trusted to do the right thing? What kinds of duties and obligations are implied by the idea of *citizenship*? Is the constitution fair?

2. Attitudes toward others in the political system.

Do citizens have strong loyalties to particular groups or regions? With what and with whom do citizens identify? How tolerant should majorities be of minority groups? Should citizens be tolerant of those who are critical of the political status quo? What types of protest behaviour are appropriate? How important is freedom of speech?

3. Political knowledge, values, and evaluations.

How much do citizens know about politics, about the workings of institutions, policy making, and political leaders? What kinds of beliefs, values, and sentiments do citizens have? How widely are they shared? What is the proper role of government in society and the economy? How should resources be distributed? How much support should be given to such disadvantaged groups as the old, the poor, the disabled, and minorities?

4. The acquisition and transmission of political beliefs.

Where do beliefs and expectations about political life come from? How are they learned? How effectively are they transmitted from one generation to the next? Are citizens' beliefs becoming more coherent, more ideological? Or are citizens becoming more "issue driven"?

Clearly, this list illustrates that an enormously broad range of topics falls under the general umbrella of political culture. Before we consider the specifics of the Canadian setting, two other general observations are worth noting. First, political cultures are dynamic: they are not set down once and for all; they are subject to change. The broad configurations of the Canadian political culture may well have been set in motion in the distant past, but conditions change, populations are replaced, and remote historical episodes can easily fade from collective memory. The second point is that, although political culture places emphasis on the subjective aspects of political life, it is a variable in explaining political behaviour. Thus political culture plays an important role in our understanding of how citizens vote, the ways political parties work, the effectiveness of political institutions, the formation of foreign and domestic policies, the behaviour of interest groups, and the workings of the constitution. Many of these topics are considered in detail in other parts of this book, and a reading of those chapters will provide a much fuller appreciation of the concrete ways in which Canadian political culture is played out. In this chapter we will paint in very broad strokes to highlight general themes.

THE MAKING OF CANADIAN POLITICAL CULTURE: AN OVERVIEW

Some distinctive aspects of Canadian political culture are very easy to recognize. The Canadian flag and the national anthem, for example, provide Canadians with unique *political symbols* that function as common points of reference, foci for communal loyalties. As such, they evoke a variety of feelings. For some, they signify pride in the past; they symbolize a history of collective achievements. For others, they may symbolize imperialism or exploitation. For yet others, they represent a set of common aspirations for the future. The mix of feelings may well differ but the symbols are nonetheless unique to Canada.

Isolating the precise ways in which Canadian orientations toward collective political life are unique is a much more difficult task. Canada stands as one of the world's oldest continuing democracies, and the essential components of Canadian political culture are much the same as those of other long-standing democracies. Canadian political values are rooted in the Western tradition and, like other states, the essential liberal elements within that tradition have been modified by democratic practices that have evolved since the eighteenth century.[4] Consequently, Canadian political culture embraces such values as equality before the law, the right to hold private property, the right of free speech and assembly, and the right to vote and to run for office. Unquestionably, these values are widely shared and occupy a central place in Canadian orientations toward collective political life, but they do not set Canadian political culture apart from the political cultures of many other advanced industrial liberal-democratic states. In other words, it is useful to recognize that Canadian political culture can be placed within the broader framework of other advanced industrial states. To see what makes Canadian political culture distinctive we must make finer distinctions.

To come to grips with the unique elements of Canadian political culture we have to consider how geographic, economic, cultural, and political factors combined to shape the formative experiences of the country. First, the sheer geographic size of Canada has had an enormous impact on the structure of political life. After Russia, Canada ranks as the largest country in the world. It sprawls across the northern half of an entire continent, occupying some 3.8 million square miles and spanning seven time zones.

Second, relative to land size, the Canadian population is small. Furthermore, that population is unevenly distributed. About 80 percent of all Canadians live within one hundred miles of the American border; 60 percent reside in Ontario and Quebec. The cultural distribution of the population is also uneven. Eighty percent of all francophones live in Quebec, and Canada's Native peoples form majorities in the sparsely populated Yukon and Northwest Territories.[5]

The physical expanse of the country, the harsh climate, and the size, make-up, and distribution of the population posed unique problems of communication and governance particularly during Canada's early years. The decision to adopt a federal political framework can be seen as an institutional response to these problems; federalism aimed to make government less remote to a far-flung and diverse population.

Third, the presence of a substantial linguistic minority concentrated in one part of the country also sets the Canadian political culture apart from that of other Anglo-American democracies with which it is most frequently compared. The rifts between anglophones and francophones had a profound impact upon Canadian political life from the start and continue to influence Canadian culture, politics, and economics in fundamental ways. The origin of contemporary conflicts can be traced to the British conquest of Quebec in 1759. Early attempts on the part of the British to assimilate the vanquished francophone Catholics failed, but the memory of those efforts lives on. The Quebec Act of 1774 reflected a shift in policy, inspired partly by American attempts to recruit Quebec's population in a joint effort to rid North America of the British. The British colonial authorities gave the francophones of Quebec guaranteed rights to language and religion in exchange for their loyalty to the British Crown. Those rights have remained intact. They lie at the root of Canada's linguistic duality and have worked as the chief instruments of the survival of Canada's francophone community. It might also be argued that those rights, in conjunction with the expanding shield of provincial government, have formed the historical basis of Quebec's political self-definition as a "nation" and, by extension, its claim to national self-determination.[6]

A fourth factor that has significantly influenced the evolution of Canadian political culture is the country's proximity to the United States. In some senses, the relationship between Canada and the United States is a curious one. As Seymour Martin Lipset observes, "these two peoples probably resemble each other more than any other two nations on earth."[7] That fact, coupled with geographic proximity, has consistently represented a challenge to Canadian national identity. The reach of the American media means that American cultural messages are easily transmitted across the Canadian–American border. For that reason, Canadians are continually faced with the challenge of sorting out how their culture differs from that of their southern neighbour. As Andrew Malcolm notes, "Canadians agree on very few things but they can agree on what they are not—Americans."[8]

Some historical background is necessary to understand why the United States has preoccupied Canadians concerned about national identity and their ability to develop and maintain a distinct political culture. The American Revolution was a decisive political event in the early formation of both countries, launching them into very different political trajectories. The revolutionaries rejected not only British colonial rule, but the idea of strong central government as well. Instead they embraced individualism and republicanism. Many of those on the losing side of the revolution left the United States and settled in Canada as the United Empire Loyalists. These political refugees became influential shapers of Canada's early political culture. The Loyalists brought to Canada "counter-revolutionary" values that, by most accounts, included a concern for maintaining ties with Britain, a willingness to accept bureaucratic and political leadership, a distaste for disorder, and a preference for a collectivist style of conservatism that placed less emphasis on the rights of the individual and a greater emphasis on group rights.

Sustained hostility between Britain and the United States and the ideological differences between the revolutionaries and the Loyalists go some distance toward explaining why the two countries adopted different political institutions. Canadians grafted the logic of British parliamentary practice—responsible cabinet government and the fusion of legislative and executive powers—onto a federal framework while keeping a constitutional monarch. In other words, early Canadians' political instincts directed them to employ tradition and convention as a guide. Americans did not; they learned different lessons from British colonial experience. It has also been suggested that the ideological differences between the revolutionaries and counter-revolutionaries continue to influence the political belief systems and values of the two societies.

INTERPRETATIONS OF CANADIAN POLITICAL CULTURE

There is widespread agreement that geographic size, population distribution, the presence of dual cultures, and proximity to the United States all contributed to the early formation of the Canadian polity. But how? It is easy to see that when all of these factors are considered together, they must have presented significant obstacles to the development of a single, clearly focused political culture. Several different interpretations have been offered to explain how these factors combined to give Canadian political culture its unique hue.

One interpretation, outlined by the American historian Louis Hartz, in *The Founding of New Societies*,[9] has been particularly influential. Hartz argues that "new societies," such as Canada, Australia, and the United States, are profoundly shaped by the values carried to those societies by early settlers and immigrants. The explanations for variations in the prevailing ideologies of new societies, according to Hartz, depends upon what kinds of answers history gives to three types of questions: First, what was the nature of the "founding fragment?" Or, more precisely, from what specific segment of the originating cultures did the founding fragments come? Second, what was the point of departure? Or, at what moment in the ideological evolution of the originating culture did the founding fragment leave? And third, what was the point of congealment? When did the values of the new society take on a distinctive and self-sustaining character?

From the Hartzian perspective, the prevailing radical working-class ideology of Australians is explained, for example, by the fact that Australia was peopled predominantly by segments of the English working class who left Britain after the Industrial Revolution had taken hold and after they had been exposed to English-style socialism. By contrast, Canada and the United States were settled earlier and largely by English middle classes. Both countries therefore reflect the middle-class values of liberalism and conservatism. Similarly, settlers to New France were rural Catholics from pre-revolutionary France, and the prevailing values of the colony reflected collectivist and anti-materialist beliefs.

The fine points of the Hartzian hypothesis have been vigorously debated, and they have been extended in a variety of intriguing directions. Gad Horowitz, for example, argues that, in its original application, the Hartzian approach tended to understate the differences between Canadian and American political cultures.[10] Unlike the United States, Horowitz contends, Canada developed a significant British and non-Marxist strand of socialism because of the presence of Toryism and because of the influence of immigrants from Britain who flowed into the country in the nineteenth century. This mixture of elements helps to explain not only Canada's historic attachment to the British Crown and deference to elites but also its acceptance of a larger role for government in society and the economy.

A second and complementary interpretation of Canadian political culture has been advanced by Lipset.[11] Lipset emphasizes the importance of formative events by drawing attention not only to the British conquest of Quebec, the American Revolution, and the role of the Loyalists, but also to the impact of the Rebellions of 1837–38 and the Riel Rebellion of 1869–70. According to Lipset, Canadians are more accepting of authority than Americans, because of these formative events. They are more likely to give governments a larger role in society and the economy, and they are more risk averse than their American counterparts. After sifting through a great deal of comparative evidence, Lipset concludes that Canadian society is less open and there are fewer opportunities for upward social mobility. At the same time, the Canadian version of the welfare state is more fully developed: there is universal access to health care and a variety of social supports, and the safety net for the casualities of free enterprise is more expansive and generous than in the United States.

A third line of interpretation focuses upon the central role that elites play in Canadian society. John Porter's pathbreaking book, *The Vertical Mosaic,*[12] is a study of how power is organized and exercised in Canadian society. The book provides a provocative analysis of the ways in which Canadian elites, both anglophone and francophone, exercise far more influence over Canadian society than is typical of elites in similar advanced industrial states. These elites, Porter contends, are crucial gatekeepers who exercise control over the economy, the bureaucracy, elected officials, the media, and intellectual and religious life. All societies have elites, but

Porter argues that Canadian elites are particularly powerful because they are small, relatively closed groups whose influence reaches across many aspects of social, political, and economic life. Moreover, because such small groups wield influence over such wide domains, they have been able to deflect attention away from class divisions in Canadian society and toward ethnic, religious, and regional divisions.

Porter's analysis has inspired a spate of studies, most of which extend and elaborate his central findings in greater detail. Some focus on corporate elites, others on political and bureaucratic elites. Most conclude, along with Porter, that the ability of these elites to act as power brokers has been greatly facilitated by a widely held political cultural value—the preparedness of the Canadian public to defer to figures of authority.

No review of interpretations of Canadian political culture can fail to consider the perspective provided by the influential political economist Harold Innis.[13] Innis argues that a full appreciation of the forces that shaped Canadian political culture requires an understanding of the importance of economic factors, particularly the historical significance of such staples as fish, fur, minerals, and wheat. From the outset, these primary resources formed the very core of the Canadian export economy, which has been directed toward the markets of other advanced industrial states. To a substantial degree, one's place in society is determined by the workplace and the kinds of rewards that the workplace brings. Consequently, Innis suggests, Canada's collective psyche, its culture, can be understood as having been conditioned by a preoccupation with the export of staples into world markets. The significant point is that Canada does not and cannot control the global economic factors that create the demand for Canadian staples: markets are subject to large fluctuations in supply and demand. As a result, the economic benefits of exporting staples have frequently been only marginal. Thus Canadians, Innis contends, have developed conservative, cautious, and even pessimistic or fatalistic attitudes largely because they have not been able to control their own economic destiny.

A careful consideration of these four broad interpretations of Canadian political culture suggests that they do not reach fundamentally different conclusions. In fact, the conclusions complement each other. The differences among the interpretations is a matter of emphasis: where Hartz emphasizes founding peoples, Lipset focuses on founding events. Porter's analysis of elites is narrower in scope, and his findings might well be interpreted as a result of cultural, social, and economic forces that Hartz, Lipset, and Innis place in a more sweeping historical context.

THE DYNAMICS OF CANADIAN POLITICAL CULTURE

In exploring the making of Canadian political culture we have stressed how a variety of underlying factors worked to influence the early development of the Canadian polity. When we turn our attention to more recent developments, it would appear that the task of forging a single harmonious national culture is far from complete. Divisive ongoing debates about constitutional change, Senate reform, Aboriginal rights, language rights, and multiculturalism all point to deep fractures within Canada. In fact, these divisions might well be interpreted in terms of conflicts between different political cultures. From that standpoint, it might be argued that cultural differences in Canada are getting stronger. Why has Canadian political culture become so fragmented? To provide a complete answer to that provocative question would require a separate study, but we can briefly point to three dynamics that appear to be crucial to these developments—transformations within Quebec, the new vitality of regionalism, and the pull of continentalism.

The Quebec Dynamic

The fundamental issue facing Quebec after the British conquest was how to sustain a viable francophone culture under British rule. As we have already indicated, the early solution to that problem emerged from a deal struck between the political elites of Quebec and the British colonial administration: francophones exchanged loyalty to the British administration in return for guaranteed language and religious rights. Francophone concerns for "nationhood," clearly, have very deep historical roots and have been an enduring feature of Quebec's political landscape. But the ways in which those concerns have been expressed have changed in quite dramatic ways and those changes, in turn, can be traced to profound social transformations within Quebec itself.

Prior to the 1960s, Quebec's traditional form of nationalism revolved around the idea of *survivance*. *Survivance* was an anti-liberal ideology; it idealized collectivist, rural, and largely anti-materialist values that were reinforced by three institutions: the parish, the school, and the family. The fact that these traditional values and institutions held sway in Quebec well into the middle of the twentieth century is remarkable, given the vitality and individualism of North America. It might be partly explained by the barrier of language, the enormous power of the Roman Catholic

Church in the province, and perhaps, by anglophone and francophone elite preoccupations with the importance of stability. But the long-term consequence of *survivance* resulted in the cultural isolation of Quebec. Traditional forms of Quebec nationalism took on a "culture under siege" quality. French Canadians were under-represented in Canada's powerful federal institutions; the Quebec economy was increasingly dominated by anglophone interests; and, by the 1950s, demographic trends were pointing to the eventual disappearance of a francophone society. The future looked bleak.

The tide turned by the 1960s. The death of long-time premier Maurice Duplessis in 1959 and the electoral defeat of Quebec's last traditional nationalist party, the Union nationale, marked the political turning point. As described in chapter 5, the social turning point was captured by the phrase the *Quiet Revolution*. The Quiet Revolution symbolized a reorientation of Quebec society in two related respects. First, it represented a willingness of Québécois to participate more fully in modern industrial society. Second, it entailed a new confidence in the vitality of Quebec's francophone culture and a search for new strategies to promote that culture. In short, the Quiet Revolution signified a transition from an old Quebec to a new Quebec. That transition was accompanied by the development of new political strategies aimed at maintaining and advancing the Quebec nation.

The 1960s was a period of considerable political turmoil. New nationalist parties emerged on both the left and the right. They held in common the view that the Canadian system of federalism was an obstacle to the flowering of Quebec's aspirations. They also believed that political independence from Canada was Quebec's best response to this obstacle. But their views of Quebec's future were quite different in other respects. The Alliance laurentienne, for example, wanted a new state that would promote such values as French humanism and Catholic fundamentalism. By contrast, the parties of the left saw economics at the root of Quebec's problems. They denounced anglophone Canadians as "colonialist ogres" and called for the "proletarian national liberation of French Canadians" to end "the exploitation of Quebec."[14] The political origins of modern Quebec nationalism can be traced to the policies of the Rassemblement pour l'indépendance nationale (RIN). The RIN foundered on the rocks of internal disputes, and the Parti Québécois (PQ), led first by René Lévesque, later by Jacques Parizeau, inherited the mantle of modern Quebec nationalism, a nationalism that has changed the course of both Quebec and Canadian politics since the 1970s.

The dramatic victory of the PQ in the provincial election of November 1976 marked a critical turning point in the political dynamics of Quebec in several ways. First, the victory indicated that a fundamental political realignment had taken place. Like many other parties that had emerged in the 1960s, the PQ started life by attracting a hodgepodge of supporters—young Québécois, intellectuals, artists, and those of the disaffected left. Unlike the other parties, the PQ's bases of political support broadened and deepened. It attracted the new middle classes, professionals, francophone business interests, and organized labour. In many ways, the victory of the PQ was the culmination of the social forces unleashed during the Quiet Revolution.

Second, the PQ came to power with a mandate to accomplish social change. At the heart of that program was the idea of economic reorganization. The PQ argued that, with new political leadership, Quebec's economic dependence could be reduced through a greater participation by francophones in the direction and management of the economy. The PQ saw the Quebec government as the political instrument for advancing the economic and social interests of Québécois: they saw the Quebec government as a "state in waiting."

Third, the PQ carried a platform for independence, and it developed blueprints for a social democratic progressive state. The strategy for independence was a gradual one. The PQ believed that independence could be achieved in gradual stages—*étapisme*. The viability of a politically independent Quebec and the precise forms that it might take were, and are, hotly debated. The significant point is that, between 1976 and 1985, the PQ established itself as a credible political party that could effectively govern by harnessing the substantial nationalist aspirations of broad segments of Quebec society.

In retrospect, it might be argued that Lévesque's PQ ultimately failed. They were defeated in the 1980 referendum, which would have given Lévesque the opportunity to seek sovereignty-association, and in the 1985 provincial election they were defeated by Robert Bourassa's Liberals. That view, however, is short-sighted and fails to take into account the very significant role that the PQ played in transforming Quebec politics in the last two decades. The PQ was the vehicle for the political modernization of Quebec nationalism. State intervention was the instrument of that transformation and, through the efforts of a PQ government, francophones moved decisively to improve their position in Quebec society and the economy. Furthermore, the credibility of the PQ as a political alternative to the Liberals is well entrenched, and the consistently strong level of public support for the PQ has had a significant impact upon constitutional discussions aimed at reshaping Canadian federalism, even when the PQ was not in office.[15]

The 1993 Canadian federal election provided yet more evidence of the resilience of modern Quebec nationalism. In that election, Quebec voters were presented with the opportunity to vote for a new federal party, the Bloc Québécois, the chief platform of which was to prepare the way for Quebec independence. They seized that opportunity with considerable enthusiasm. The Bloc Québécois took fifty-four seats in the province and became the official Opposition in the House of Commons. The politics of Quebec's cultural aspirations, then, have not receded; they have taken different forms and continue to play a critical role in the political life of the country.

The Regional Dynamic

Describing Canada as two nations within a single state focuses attention upon the historic role that anglophone–francophone conflicts have played in the evolution of the Canadian polity. Quebec counts as a region because 80 percent of Canada's francophones live in the province, but in the past twenty years it has become increasingly clear that other relevant regional divisions also shape the collective lives of Canadians in significant ways. Indeed, some observers have gone so far as to suggest that Canadian politics *is* the politics of regions.[16]

Evidence of the political importance of regions takes many forms. There is a long-standing tradition of taking regional considerations into account in the recruitment of ministers to the federal cabinet. The conflicts between regional and national interests are routinely displayed at federal–provincial conferences. Debates about the distribution of economic resources and social services typically take on a regional hue, and regional considerations shape the ways in which political parties are organized. In one sense, those regional differences are hardly surprising. After all, Canada is a federal state, and federalism, as a principle, acknowledges that there are differences among parts of a country. Indeed, federalism aims to accommodate those differences.

Two underlying factors contribute to Canadian regionalism: population and economics. More than most countries, Canada has relied upon immigration as a population source, and the patterns of immigrant settlement have resulted in an uneven cultural distribution of the population. The Atlantic provinces, Quebec, and Ontario were settled first, largely by immigrants from Britain and France. The Prairie provinces were settled much later and to a much greater extent by German, Dutch, Scandinavian, Polish, Ukrainian, and American settlers. In 1931, only about half of the prairie population was of British or French origin, compared to more than 80 percent for Canada as a whole. Ethnic, linguistic, and religious diversity gives the Prairies a distinctly multicultural quality that, in turn, helps to explain why, according to one observer, western Canadians tend to view French Canadians as simply another minority.[17]

Economic historians, following Harold lnnis, have argued that regional differences in economic development and in the modes of economic production contributed to the development of regional political cultures.[18] In the industrialized regions of Ontario and Quebec, the occupational mix of working populations is quite different from that of populations in the other regions—Atlantic provinces, the Prairie provinces, or British Columbia—which rely heavily on extractive and resource-based enterprises. Increasingly, all economies are exposed to the rigours of world markets, but regional economies fluctuate at different rates and times depending upon the particular economic base of the region. Thus while some regions enjoy prosperity, others falter, and the uneven performance of different segments of the Canadian economy aggravates regional political differences.

The cultural and economic features of various parts of the country certainly make Canada's five regions look very different from each other, but are these regional political cultures? Or, to put the matter more precisely, do regional populations have different basic orientations toward political life *after* these other differences have been taken into account? A substantial body of evidence suggests that they do. Simeon and Elkins,[19] in a now classic study, demonstrate significant differences across the regions with respect to two sets of orientations that are central to political culture. These are *political trust*, or, the extent to which individuals feel they can trust governments, and *political efficacy*, the extent to which individuals feel that they count politically. Analyzing data from the 1965 and 1968 national election studies, Simeon and Elkins show that British Columbians, Manitobans, Ontarians, and anglophone Quebeckers tend to have high levels of political trust and efficacy. By contrast, people from Newfoundland, New Brunswick, and Nova Scotia tend to have much lower levels of trust and efficacy.

Scholars have discovered variations in other aspects of political culture as well. Roger Gibbins, for example, demonstrates significant provincial differences in the communal identifications of Canadians. In 1983, he asked a national sample of Canadians whether they identified first with their country or with their province. These data show, not surprisingly, that most respondents (73 percent) first thought of themselves as Canadians. But the evidence also points to remarkable regional variations in identifications. The proportion of respondents identifying with their province was highest in Newfoundland (47 percent), Prince Edward Island (38 percent), Quebec (34 percent), and Nova Scotia (30 percent).[20] By contrast, only 5 percent of Ontarians identified with their province first, a finding that supports the contention that Ontarians tend to equate the interests of their province with the interests of the country.[21]

If, as we have indicated, there are strong regional differences in economic interests and political cultures, how does the regional dynamic play in contemporary Canadian political culture? A strong case can be made to suggest that the regional dynamic continues to frustrate the development of an integrated Canadian political community in a variety of ways. First, there is the rugged political arithmetic of the electoral system. The simple fact that about 60 percent of Canada's population resides in two provinces, Ontario and Quebec, means that voters in these two provinces carry enormous electoral weight; they can make or break nationally elected governments. Voters in regions outside of Ontario and Quebec have economic interests that are different from those of the industrial heartland and fewer reasons to be confident that their concerns will occupy a central place in the national agenda. If the homily "the one who pays the piper calls the tune" has any political application, then the federal government has a strong incentive to listen to the concerns of Ontario and Quebec.

Second, it has been argued that Canada's particular style of federal parliamentary institutions tends to aggravate rather than moderate regional divisions. All federal political systems have upper and lower houses. Typically, lower houses are based on representation by population while upper houses represent regional concerns. Does the Canadian Senate do a good job of representing regional concerns? Probably not. If population size is the benchmark, it is clear that some of the small provinces are indeed over-represented in the Senate. But others, such as Alberta and British Columbia, are under-represented. A more significant point stems from the fact that the Senate is an appointed, not an elected, body. The appointment process is often highly politicized: some appointees are placed in the Senate as a reward for service to the party. The perception is that the Senate lacks broad legitimacy, and the reality is that it has little power to challenge the House of Commons, although it has tried to do so on a number of occasions, including the Canadian–American Free Trade Agreement and the Goods and Services Tax (GST). Nevertheless, the Canadian Senate appears much weaker than the upper chambers in other federal states. Advocates of stronger regional representation argue that the Senate must be reformed, that it should be an elected body, and that it should have more power. The problem is that political power is a zero-sum game, and persuading others to give up powers is a difficult business.

Party discipline is a third institutional practice that frustrates greater regional representation at the national level. In the parliamentary tradition, party discipline is central to the workings of responsible government. MPs may lobby for regional concerns in caucus, they may press regional issues in private, but they have few opportunities to place the interest of their region over those of the party. The same applies to cabinet ministers. Despite the fact that there is a long-standing tradition of regional representation within federal cabinets, cabinet conventions of secrecy and collective responsibility tend to obscure evidence of regional representation from public view.

Thus the majoritarianism of the electoral system, the weakness of the Senate, and the workings of party discipline, it might be argued, are points of tension that combine to frustrate a national representation of regional concerns.

In the past twenty-five years, the emergence of provincial premiers as the champions of regional interests in national political life has presented one face of the shifting dynamics of regional political cultures. Another significant, and more recent, face of that change is evident in the shifting loyalties of voters. In the 1993 Canadian federal election, for example, regionally rooted federal parties became far more prominent than in the past. In that election, the Bloc Québécois took 54 out of 75 seats in Quebec. In the same election, another new party, the Reform Party of Canada, won 46 out of a possible 58 seats in Alberta and British Columbia. The regional dynamic, it appears, has not become less relevant with the passage of time. If anything, it seems to have become more vibrant.

The Continental Dynamic

Linguistic duality and regionalism are dynamics that appear to undermine the development of a clear, single political culture. These domestic sources of fragmentation combine with Canada's continental location to further obscure the evolution of a powerful and easily identifiable political culture. John Redekop assesses the impact of Canada's continental position as follows: "The overall American impact on Canada," he says, "is the most important single fact for Canada and the main key to understanding Canada's emergence, development, and current situation."[22] Redekop is referring, of course, to the multiplicity of ways in which the United States dominates the North American continent—by its population size, the power of its economy, and the vitality of its cultural institutions.

The extent to which Canada's economic fortunes are tied to those of the United States are well documented elsewhere[23] and require no detailed elaboration here. Canada and the United States have the largest single trading relationship of any two countries in the world. Since the Second World War, American direct and indirect investment in Canada has grown to account for more than 75 percent of all foreign investment in the country. Furthermore, American control of a variety of key industrial sectors—fossil fuels, chemicals, rubber, transportation, to name but a few—is remarkably high. According to one estimate, American enterprises account for about 60 percent of Canada's manufacturing sector.[24]

The American penetration of the Canadian economy is a mixed blessing. There is little doubt that Canadians enjoy a good standard of living in large part because of high levels of American investment. By the same token, the level and type of American interest in Canada has limited the ability of the Canadian government to exercise complete control over domestic economic policy making. It has been argued that, with the progressive integration of Canada into the continental economy, Canada has become little more than a branch plant of the United States. Left to the mercy of an "open" marketplace dominated by American policy, the Canadian economy will remain "in service" to its American parent. According to this view, the Canadian–U.S. Free Trade Agreement provides an institutional framework that authorizes the continuation of that process. Furthermore, the continentalization of the economy undermines Canadian political sovereignty and remains a constant challenge to the distinctiveness of Canada's social and cultural fabric.

Economics undoubtedly does have important political, social, and cultural consequences, although the extent of these is not very well understood. Nor is it possible to precisely measure the extent to which Canadians have absorbed American values. But there is no doubt that proximity, population distribution, and shared language mean that American cultural industries have easy access to the majority of Canadian households through the print and electronic media. Data show that Canadian consumption of American TV, film, and print media is very high indeed.[25] From time to time, Canadian governments have attempted to stem the flow of American culture into Canada and to encourage domestic cultural industries as a way of protecting Canadians from Americanization and of fostering a distinct Canadian identity.

In some respects, the record of government involvement in domestic cultural industries is a rather remarkable one. Clearly, the opportunities available to the American cultural industries for penetrating Canada are unique. The motive is also clear: Canada provides those industries with an additional marketplace. But if a crime has been committed—the Americanization of Canada's culture—then Canadians must be counted as accomplices. Evidence shows, for example, that anglophone Canadians consistently prefer American to Canadian TV programming. In 1976, the Canadian Radio-televison and Telecommunications Commission (CRTC) ordered Canadian FM cable companies to drop American stations in favour of Canadian ones. The angry public response forced the CRTC to cancel its Canadianization policy barely three months later.[26] The economic reality is that Canada is a small market, and its size presents serious obstacles to the development of strong domestic publishing and electronic cultural industries. For these reasons, cultural nationalists remain apprehensive about the long-term implications of sustained exposure to American media and the values they impart.

Given Canada's proximity and exposure to the United States, it is remarkable that we know so little about what impact American cultural exports have on the kinds of political values that Canadians acquire. The sketchy evidence that does exist indicates rather mixed results. One study, which examined the impact of exposure to American television on Canadian children's recognition of American and Canadian authority roles, found that Canadian children could correctly identify the American flag more often than they could correctly identify the Canadian flag. Furthermore, many children confused authority roles: a significant proportion of younger children identified the American president as the prime minister of Canada.[27] These data, while intriguing, do not provide us with sufficient grounds for drawing firm conclusions about the long-term impact of American values on Canadian political culture. Regardless of the quality of systematic evidence, however, observers of Canadian–American relations are united on one point: the impact of the United States upon Canadian political cultural life has been enormous.

THE CHALLENGES FACING CANADIAN POLITICAL CULTURE

The major themes that we have addressed in this chapter all point to the conclusion that Canadian nation builders, from the outset, confronted significant obstacles in pursuing the task of developing a single coherent political culture. The challenges are still formidable, for it would seem that, unlike that of the United States, Canadian political culture does not project a single powerful image. Canada has no equivalent to "the American way." Instead, the prevailing image of Canada is one of a "community of communities." Diversity has produced further diversity, and Canadian political institutions and leaders expend a great deal of energy simply managing that diversity. In this sense, it appears to be more accurate to speak of Canada's multiple political cultures.

Are there any particular characteristics that set Canadian political culture apart from those of other advanced industrial states? There is a combination of characteristics about which most analysts would agree. First, most social scientists have come to expect social class to play a significant role in shaping such political behaviours as voting. A long-standing puzzle of Canadian politics has been the apparent absence of a strong, consistent relationship between class and vote. Jon Pammett's exhaustive analysis of national election data from 1974 and 1979 found that only 4 percent of the Canadians sampled thought of themselves in terms of class, and most of those thought of themselves as middle class.[28] A second significant finding that sets Canadian political belief systems apart from others is the apparent weakness of left–right orientations within the population. John Meisel's analysis of 1965 and 1968 data indicates that Canadians saw almost no class or ideological differences between the two major political parties—the Progressive Conservatives and the Liberals—and that the differences between those two parties and the New Democrats were very slight.[29] Unlike people in other industrial states, a very high proportion of Canadians do not think of themselves or political parties in terms of "left" or "right." Other studies have also noted the comparative weakness of ideology in Canadian political life.[30]

To these findings we can add other evidence that is central to the analysis of political culture. Canadians exhibit levels of political trust that are similar to those found in the United States and in Western European democracies. More than half of all Canadians believe that people can be trusted, although the level of interpersonal trust among Quebec francophones is substantially lower. When it comes to political trust more specifically, Canadians have a high regard for those who govern, at least they did in 1979, 1983, and 1984. That finding dovetails with the observation that Canadians are more likely than Americans and citizens in other industrial states to defer to the political authority of leaders. Studies conducted in 1983 and 1984 indicated that the Canadian public is much more likely to comply with what government does or asks of them. Canadians are much more interested in politics than are people in Western Europe, and on this score there is little difference between Canadians and Americans. Canadians, however, are quite different from Americans when it comes to preferences about the role of government in society and the economy. Canadians have a much more positive view of the state. Unlike Americans, they want the state to "do more."[31]

What these findings suggest is that, despite the difficulties of linguistic and regional differences, despite the substantial obstacles to the development of a potent and easily identifiable national political identity, and despite the powerful pull of continental forces, a distinctive combination of political values is discernible in Canada. Whether those values that make up Canadian political culture will remain distinctive depends, of course, on a variety of factors. Two—population replacement and value change—are of particular note and both have enormous implications for the future character of Canadian political identity.

Throughout this chapter, we have emphasized that political cultures are dynamic. Part of the dynamics relates to patterns of population replacement and the nature of political socialization. In the past twenty-five years, Canada has experienced two trends that indicate marked departures from the traditional patterns of population replacement. First, fertility levels have fallen to the point that the Canadian population cannot replace itself by natural increase alone. The burden of increase, in other words, has shifted almost entirely to immigration. Between 1956 and 1960, Canadian immigrants coming from traditional European sources outnumbered those coming from non-European sources by a ratio of 15 to 1. By 1980, immigrants from non-traditional countries outnumbered those from traditional sources by a ratio of 2 to 1. The long-term implications of this change are enormous. Canada is far more culturally diverse than ever before; it is less "European." How will new immigrants be politically socialized to Canadian life? Will Canada's largely European founding experiences be meaningful to them? Answering these questions will undoubtedly be a major challenge. How they are answered will have a substantial impact upon Canada's future political culture.

The second challenge to the Canadian political culture has to do with the very substantial value changes that have swept across all advanced industrial states in the course of the last two decades. A large body of evidence indicates that these changes are transforming the political dynamics of these states in similar ways; new politics are replacing old politics. The importance of class and religion is declining. Citizens are less deferential to elites, and their ties to traditional political parties are weakening. Citizens are more outspoken, and they are more likely to engage in direct forms of political action. There have emerged new movements concerned with such issues as protection of the environment, the status of women, the rights of minorities, and the quality of life.[32] Publics are better informed about politics; they are better educated and more interested in political life.

There is a good deal of evidence indicating that this "new politics" is also under way in Canada.[33] All of these changes imply that the future of the Canadian political culture will not just be shaped by a particular cluster of domestic forces and tensions, or even by Canada's proximity to the United States. It will also be shaped by the larger forces that are sweeping across the entire postindustrial world.

Global change entails a variety of transformations. On the economic front, for example, it has become increasingly clear that countries are more interdependent now than ever before. Economic prosperity, particularly in advanced industrial states like Canada, increasingly relies upon exports and access to world markets. Gaining access to other markets, as the North American Free Trade Agreement illustrates, usually means giving others more access to our own market. Global change also involves the rapid development of technologies and the emergence of worldwide communications networks that have led to an information revolution. And all these have helped to quicken the pace of economic interdependence. Borders between countries have become more porous, and national boundaries are less relevant than they once were. Consequently, the task of forging coherent and unifying political cultures has not become easier. If anything, it may have become more difficult.

NOTES

[1] Gabriel Almond and G. Bingham Powell, *Comparative Politics: A Developmental Approach* (Boston: Little, Brown, 1966), 50.

[2] Sidney Verba, "Comparative Political Culture" in Lucian W. Pye and Sidney Verba, *Political Culture and Political Development* (Princeton, NJ: Princeton University Press, 1966), 518.

[3] Lucian W. Pye, *Aspects of Political Development* (Boston: Little, Brown, 1966), 1045.

[4] Richard Van Loon and Michael Whittington, *The Canadian Political System* (Toronto: McGraw-Hill Ryerson, 1981), ch. 2.

[5] Allan Kornberg, *Politics and Culture in Canada* (Ann Arbor, MI: Center for Political Studies, 1988), 4.

[6] François-Pierre Gingras and Neil Nevitte, "The Evolution of Quebec Nationalism" in *Quebec: State and Society*, ed. Alain G. Gagnon (Toronto: Methuen, 1984), 2–14.

[7] Seymour Martin Lipset, "Canada and the United States: The Cultural Dimension" in *Canada and the United States: Enduring Friendship, Persistent Stress*, ed. Charles F. Doran and John H. Sigler (Englewood Cliffs, NJ: Prentice-Hall, 1985), 109.

[8] Andrew Malcolm, *The Canadians* (New York: Times Books, 1985), 69.

[9] See Louis Hartz, *The Founding of New Societies* (New York: Harcourt Brace, 1964).

[10] Gad Horowitz, "Conservatism, Liberalism and Socialism in Canada" in *The Canadian Political Process*, ed. Orest M. Kruhlak et al. (Toronto: University of Toronto Press, 1965).

[11] Lipset, "Canada and the United States," 110–18.

[12] John Porter, *The Vertical Mosaic: An Analysis of Social Class and Power in Canada* (Toronto: University of Toronto Press, 1965).

[13] Harold A. Innis, *Essays in Canadian Economic History* (Toronto: University of Toronto Press, 1956).

[14] Gingras and Nevitte, "Evolution of Quebec Nationalism," 4–10.

[15] For an account of these changes, see Kenneth McRoberts, *Quebec: Social Change and Political Crisis*, 3rd ed. (Toronto: McClelland & Stewart), chs. 5–8.

[16] See Richard Simeon and David Elkins, "Regional Political Cultures in Canada" in *The Canadian Political Process*, ed. Richard Schultz, Orest M. Kruhlak, and John Terry (Toronto: Holt, Rinehart and Winston, 1979), 15.

[17] Roger Gibbins, *Conflict and Unity*, 2nd ed. (Scarborough, ON: Nelson Canada, 1990), 118–20.

[18] See, for example, David J. Bercuson, *Canada and the Burden of Unity* (Toronto: Macmillan, 1977), and Larry Pratt and John Richards, *Prairie Capitalism: Power and Influence in the New West* (Toronto: McClelland & Stewart, 1979).

[19] Richard Simeon and David Elkins, "Regional Political Cultures in Canada," *Canadian Journal of Political Science* 8, 3 (Sept. 1974): 397–437.

[20] Gibbins, *Conflict and Unity*, 139.

[21] François-Pierre Gingras, "Ontario" in *The Provincial Political System*, ed. David J. Bellamy, Jon H. Pammett, and Donald C. Rowat (Toronto: Methuen, 1976).

[22] John H. Redekop, "Continentalism: The Key to Canadian Politics" in *Approaches to Canadian Politics* (Scarborough, ON: Prentice-Hall, 1978).

[23] See, for example, Kari Levitt, *Silent Surrender: The Multinational Corporation in Canada* (Toronto: Macmillan, 1970).

[24] Redekop, "Continentalism."

[25] See *Report of the Task Force on Broadcasting Policy* (Ottawa: Ministry of Supply and Services, 1986), 17–18.

[26] Redekop, "Continentalism."

[27] Donald Higgins, "The Political Americanization of Canadian Children" in *Foundations of Political Culture: Political Socialization in Canada*, ed. Jon H. Pammett and Michael Whittington (Toronto: Macmillan, 1976), 251–64.

[28] Jon Pammett, "Class Voting and Class Consciousness in Canada," *Canadian Review of Sociology and Anthropology* 24 (1969): 269–89.

[29] John Meisel, *Working Papers on Canadian Politics* (Montreal: McGill-Queen's University Press, 1973).

[30] Neil Nevitte and Roger Gibbins, *New Elites in Old States: Ideologies in the Anglo-American Democracies* (Toronto: Oxford University Press, 1990).

[31] Kornberg, *Politics and Culture*, 20–24.

[32] See, for example, Claus Offe, *Contradictions of the Welfare State* (Cambridge: MIT Press, 1984), and Ronald Inglehart, *Culture Shift in Advanced Industrial Society* (Princeton, NJ: Princeton University Press, 1990).

[33] Herman Bakvis and Neil Nevitte, "In Pursuit of Postbourgeois Man: Postmaterialism and Intergenerational Change in Canada," *Comparative Political Studies* 20 (1987): 357–89, and Neil Nevitte, Herman Bakvis, and Roger Gibbins, "The Ideological Contours of 'New Politics' in Canada: Policy, Mobilization and Partisan Support," *Canadian Journal of Political Science* 22, 3 (1989): 475–503.

SUGGESTED READING

Almond, Gabriel, and Sidney Verba. *The Civic Culture*. Princeton, NJ: Princeton University Press, 1963.

The pioneering cross-national study of political culture.

Doran, Charles, and John Sigler, eds. *Canada and the United States*. Englewood Cliffs, NJ: Prentice-Hall, 1985.

A collection of essays that provide an overview of the economic, political, social, and cultural dynamics between the two countries.

Dumont, Fernard. *The Vigil of Quebec*. Toronto: University of Toronto Press, 1974.

An accessible and sensitive account of Quebec's transformations and its hopes.

Gibbins, Roger. *Conflict and Unity*. 2nd ed. Scarborough, ON: Nelson Canada, 1990.

A perceptive analysis of how the interactions between cultural, regional, institutional, and continental factors have shaped domestic politics.

Hartz, Louis. *The Founding of New Societies*. New York: Harcourt Brace, 1964.

Sets out the logic of how founding fragments are crucial to the shape of political culture in new societies.

Levitt, Kari. *Silent Surrender: The Multinational Corporation in Canada*. Toronto: Macmillan, 1970.

A classic analysis of the economics and politics of dependence and the roles of multinational corporations.

Porter, John. *The Vertical Mosaic*. Toronto: University of Toronto Press, 1965.

A definitive study of class, status, and power in Canada.

Simeon, Richard, and David Elkins. "Regional Political Cultures in Canada." *Canadian Journal of Political Science* 8, 3 (Sept. 1974): 397–437.

Provides detailed empirical evidence of regional political cultures in Canada.

IDEOLOGIES

M ost studies of ideology begin with a definition of the term. An *ideology* is a set of ideas that is neither scientific nor philosophical, but that has a cognitive content—that is, it involves a kind of knowledge. Sometimes a total ideology, or world view, is distinguished from a partial ideology, such as a political ideology. In this chapter, we confine our attention to political ideology.

There are two basic approaches to political ideology: the cognitive approach and the ethical approach. The *cognitive approach* stresses ideology as a perspective, vision, or representation. Quite simply, it is a way of looking at the political world. Such an ideology may present a more or less adequate picture of reality, depending on the extent to which it reveals or conceals certain aspects of social and political situations. The *ethical approach*, which is action-oriented, uses ideology to provide grounds for accepting laws and policies, thus giving direction to decision making and offering arguments for particular positions and policies. Both approaches are necessary since ideology is about knowledge *and* action.

The functions of an ideology are *representation*, *justification*, and *recommendation*. Some critics would argue that another function of ideology is concealment. For instance, Marxists claim that liberals hide the power and exploitation underlying economic relations by emphasizing freedom of contract.

What is called *representation* in a political doctrine involves a view of the social and political world, a view of the social configuration and its political consequences. Clashes among ideologies are rooted in differing perspectives on this configuration.

An ideology involves a *justification* for doing or not doing something, for maintaining a state of affairs or trying to change it. When an attempt is made to persuade others of the desirability of a particular course of action, arguments will be employed and appeals will be made to the values people hold, the interests that motivate them, and the goals that they share. While a philosophical argument is primarily an appeal to reason, a rhetorical argument, the kind that predominates in the public forum, is more than an appeal to reason. It is an appeal to passions and interests as well.

A political ideology leads to *recommendations* and directives. It has an orientation, be it toward change or conservation, toward revolution or reform, toward social reconstruction or adjustments to preserve an established order.

This chapter concentrates on three political ideologies that are particularly relevant to Canadian politics in the late twentieth century: liberalism, neoconservatism, and socialism. Later in the chapter, we briefly look at populism and nationalism and explain why these terms are not given more prominence in this chapter. Another significant ideology in the late twentieth century is feminism. There is not just one feminist ideology, but a set of ideologies, commonly divided into liberal, socialist, and radical feminism. Gender plays a more fundamental role in radical feminism than it does in liberal or socialist feminism. This chapter concentrates on liberalism and socialism out of which liberal and socialist feminism emerge.

LIBERALISM

In the nineteenth century, Canada developed in a manner that was similar in many ways to other liberal societies. In the first half of the nineteenth century, groups opposed oligarchies of privilege like the Family Compact and Château Clique, the Canadian counterpart of an aristocracy that owed its predominance not to achievement in a competitive framework but to the efforts of non-elected groups to maintain their power and prestige. Not as dramatic as the revolutions that brought down the old nobility in Europe, the struggle against these groups nevertheless had certain analogies with the revolutionary struggle. In the 1830s and 1840s, Canada went through a protracted period aimed at establishing responsible government, embodying the liberal ideas that the legislature must be supreme and the executive subordinated to it. Liberals had consistently fought for the division of power, even though they condoned cabinet government, which combines legislative and executive power, because those who exercised power in such governments were elected. Eventually an evolution took place from a liberal regime to a liberal-democratic one. During the Confederation debates, there were a number of manifestations of anti-democratic sentiment, but a generation later, Canada, like Great Britain and the United States earlier, became a liberal democracy. Like other liberal societies, Canada passed through a period of national self-assertion in the nineteenth century, even though it was somewhat diluted: while control over domestic affairs was in Canadian hands, the exercise of external affairs was still under British control. Full-blown political independence was achieved in the twentieth century, and true democracy was fully realized only when women were included in the federal suffrage during the First World War.

Liberal ideology has been the predominant ideology in Canada. Perhaps in the nineteenth century, the liberalism of the philosophic radicals, who were concerned with economic, political, and legal reforms, was more influential than the natural rights philosophy articulated in the American constitution and the French Declaration of the Rights of Man and the Citizen. In the twentieth century, though, Canadian liberalism has been preoccupied with the political protection of rights, first in a federal bill of rights, then in the Charter of Rights and Freedoms. It is customary to distinguish between civil rights and liberties and political rights and liberties. The former concern freedom of religion, association, assembly, speech, and the press. Political liberties bear directly on political participation—that is, the right to vote and to hold office.

Liberalism has been identified with constitutional government and the rule of law. An important part of this is the attribution of the power to the judiciary to review the laws passed by Parliament. While the power of the Supreme Court of Canada once seemed confined to the task of ascertaining whether or not a particular piece of legislation was properly in federal or provincial jurisdiction, the Charter of Rights and Freedoms considerably extends judicial purview. The Canadian political system now seems to be closer to the American political system, in the limitations it places on legislative, or parliamentary, supremacy. Liberals are sometimes criticized for a non-democratic reliance on judicial decision making, presumably relying on the wisdom of judges in contrast to the folly of elected assemblies. However, liberals have endorsed both parliamentary supremacy and extensive judicial review. That the two come into conflict is basically a dilemma within liberal ideology, which we will deal with below.

Clearly, there is a strong legal cast to liberal ideology with its emphasis on constitutional law, government under law, human rights, and rules of procedure. Let us contrast liberal ideology with a politics of power. The latter is a political doctrine concerned solely with evaluating in terms of success or failure how one acquires, maintains, increases, and exercises power. The name of Machiavelli, generally considered a bad influence by

English-speaking countries, is often associated with this kind of politics. While the proto-liberals of the seventeenth century, notably Thomas Hobbes and John Locke in England, were also concerned with power, they were mainly interested in the process by which power became legitimized. Unlike Machiavelli, they did not examine technical prescriptions about how to seize power, but rather principles that limited power and rendered its possession and exercise rightful. They developed consent theories of government, in which governments are legitimately constituted by the consent of the governed, to explain why the possession of power by certain people was justifiable. Such theories also set down guidelines for the use of that power. It may well be the case that the original concern with power has somewhat faded in liberal ideology with the success of its basic principles of government.

Liberal ideology not only has a strong legal cast to it but has developed certain conceptions about justice as well. Since questions of justice concern equality and inequality, we can best grasp the liberal conception of justice by examining the forms of equality that it endorses or disdains. In terms of competition, the liberal stresses equality of opportunity or equality of access. As in a race in which all begin at the same mark, the unequal results will be justified by the fact that the starting line is the same for all. Thus liberalism is associated with equal opportunity, but not equal results or outcomes. In terms of procedures, liberals advocate equal treatment and abhor special treatment by which privilege enters the picture. Liberals support equality before the law. It may in fact be difficult to achieve either equality of opportunity or equal treatment, but they remain norms of justice for liberals. Liberals approach the issue of distributive justice with the criteria of merit and need. They see merit, or desert, as the appropriate basis upon which to award a professional position, for example. Likewise, they see the criterion of need as determining who should receive social assistance. Some liberals give priority to desert, while others stress need and may even reject the notion of desert as a criterion.

A liberal is a person who gives primacy to freedom as a leading value, so it is understandable that some liberals may want to speak of justice as equal liberty. However, it is not evident that all questions of justice can be translated into issues of freedom. Conflict between freedom and justice is possible. Does this mean that liberals will prefer freedom in such a contest? That seems to be a reasonable assumption.

Among the basic freedoms of the liberal creed is freedom of association. The presence of this freedom has led to a proliferation of groups of various kinds and, indeed, the social perspective of the liberal is pluralistic. In contrast to socialists, who maintain that society should be understood as an arena of class conflict, liberals do not give priority to socioeconomic groups in their social vision. Of course, such groups are among the multiplicity of intermediary bodies between the individual and the government, but they are not necessarily front and centre, except in conflicts between labour and management. In some situations, ethnic groups may be given special attention, in other instances religious or professional groups. The widely held view that we live in a broadly middle-class society may account for the depreciation of class concerns. There are the rich and the poor at the opposite ends of the social spectrum, but a broad middle rank is a significant feature of society.

Intermediary bodies, or interest groups, are an important feature in the process of government. Many of them exercise pressure on parties and on government at various levels to achieve their aims (thus an interest group becomes a pressure group). Some of them—the medical profession, for example—have authority delegated by the government. The process by which particular interests attempt to influence policy is considered legitimate in Canada, assuming that it does not involve the corruption of public officials. Realistically, one has to face the fact that conflict of interest is a constant problem for democratic governments.

Liberal societies pride themselves on being pluralistic not just in terms of freedom of association, but in regard to the different values people adopt. For instance, liberals are considered to be more permissive than conservatives about what people read or view; they thus oppose censorship. Liberals take a pro-choice view on abortion. The standard liberal form of secularism views religion as a private matter and resents the "intrusion" of religious groups in politics. However, interest-group liberalism, far from negating this "intrusion," sanctions it.

Earlier, several tensions within liberal ideology were identified: parliamentary supremacy and extensive judicial review, the criteria of desert and need in distributive justice. This section will end with a discussion of other dilemmas within liberalism. The first concerns affirmative action; the second concerns the management of the economy.

As we have seen, liberal ideology has advocated equality of opportunity as opposed to equality of outcome. The liberal meritocratic approach held that selection should be based on desert in a situation of equal opportunity. To eliminate irrelevant and unfair criteria, liberals pushed for prohibitions against discrimination on the basis of factors like age, race, gender, or national origin. Recently, a conception that appears to run counter to the meritocratic approach has received liberal endorsement. Alternatively labelled affirmative action or reverse discrimination, depending on one's perspective, this approach ostensibly gives priority to women and minority groups in an effort to address historical inequalities. The inconsistency with liberal theory is clear: one cannot be both colour-conscious and colour-blind; one cannot be both gender-conscious and gender-blind. One cannot maintain equality in competition and then give preferential treatment, no matter how expedient it seems to be. It is not easy to see how this dilemma can be overcome. Either it is wrong to use such factors or it is not. In the former case, non-discrimination predominates. In the latter case, non-discrimination is discarded. The issue may be stated in another way. Sociologists contrast the liberal emphasis on achievement with the pre-liberal emphasis on ascribed status. The current stress in certain aspects of social policy on what you are (your status) rather than on what you have done (your achievement) indicates a shift toward what was once considered a pre-liberal, if not anti-liberal, viewpoint. The departure from the primacy of achievement or merit in hiring thus marks a movement away from a long-standing feature of liberal ideology.

Another source of division within liberal ideology concerns the management of the economy. It is worthwhile employing the distinction between egalitarian liberalism and libertarian liberalism to make the point.[1] The former kind of liberalism may mean staunch support for the welfare state—the use of taxation and allocations to achieve greater equalization in the economic system. It favours selective state intervention in the marketplace. By contrast, libertarian liberalism objects to any attempt by government to achieve some pattern of social equality, though it might accept the idea of a social minimum. The government should leave the marketplace alone. Egalitarian liberals have accepted the mixed economy; libertarian liberals are opposed to it. Egalitarian liberals may support wage and price controls; libertarian liberals would not. Another way of referring to libertarian liberalism is to use the term neoconservatism.

NEOCONSERVATISM

During the Great Depression of the 1930s, the government, influenced by the economic theories of John Maynard Keynes, adopted a policy of intervention in the economy. One of the most important of these policies was that of pump-priming: the government attempted to stimulate demand by pouring money into the economy through deficit spending, so that buyers would have the funds to purchase goods and services.

It was assumed that the absence of effective demand, meaning demand with resources, was a contributing cause of the economic crisis.

The government's intervention in the economy increased during the Second World War and continued thereafter with the extension of welfare state provisions. A challenge to Keynesian policies came about because of the failure of government to control inflation. In fact, contrary to expectation, inflation and economic stagnation occurred simultaneously, producing what became known as "stagflation." In the 1970s, the aim of controlling inflation led to the imposition of wage and price controls, both at the federal level and, later, in the province of Ontario.

These essentially liberal approaches to government management of the economy did not go unchallenged. The growth of the interventionist state, the cost of its operation, the increasing deficits generated by its policies, and a perception that aspects of the welfare state had failed gave rise to a reaction against the prevailing policies. This reaction, which occurred first in the United Kingdom, then in the United States, and about the same time in Canada, has become known as *neoconservatism*.

Even when Keynesianism was in vogue, there had been a dissenting view, expressed notably by Friedrich Hayek, which became known for the thesis that the development of the interventionist welfare state was leading down "the road to serfdom."[2] But where Hayek had once been considered to be a marginal defender of laissez-faire (letting the economy alone), his ideas, and those of his disciples, were suddenly at centre stage. This school of thought is described by economists as *libertarian*. Among political scientists, it is more customary to refer to it as neoconservatism.

The focal point of neoconservatism is the relationship of the state to the economy. The main tenets of the ideology have been formulated by economists who take a rather narrow focus on politics. If the drift must be away from the interventionist state to a greater reliance on a relatively free market economy, then it makes sense to deregulate that economy. If the government is involved in areas that belong in the private sector, then it makes sense to privatize Crown corporations. Indeed, the initial attempt (rescinded and then later renewed) to privatize Petro-Canada seemed to be the opening volley in the privatization battle. Subsequently, such public entities as Air Canada, de Havilland, Polysar, and Teleglobe Canada have been placed on the auction block by the federal government. In Saskatchewan, there has been an ideological dispute concerning the provincial government's proposal to privatize the Crown-owned natural gas monopoly. The potash corporation had already been privatized in that province.

One of the leading neoconservative assumptions is that governments cannot operate enterprises as effectively as private industry can. Nonetheless, there has not as yet been any serious attempt to privatize the Canadian medicare system. Nor has the government proposed a privately run system of postsecondary education, although it expects a certain portion of the budgetary needs of such institutions to come from the contributions of private individuals and groups. There have been some proposals for private universities, but the initiatives have not been governmental.

Another component of the neoconservative approach is to aim at a balanced budget or, at least, to sharply reduce the public debt. In the United States, there have been legislative requirements to balance budgets; in Canada, there has been a set of governmental proposals to do so. These include raising new revenues to increase assets and reducing government programs in order to decrease the debt.

Unlike that in the United Kingdom and the United States, the neoconservative trend in Canada has not adopted some of the monetarist policies usually associated with neoconservatism; that is, it has not depended primarily on manipulation of the money supply to achieve its goals, although the recent maintenance of high interest rates by the Bank of Canada fits the pattern. Obviously, any government in Canada must be attentive to the value of the Canadian dollar on the world market and to the prime interest rate, since these factors have so much importance in foreign trade, most of which takes place with the United States. When the interest rate is maintained at a certain level for other purposes, that suggests a neoconservative strategy.

In this context, something should be said about the ideological significance of free trade. The advocacy of free trade, aside from pragmatic considerations of relative economic advantage in tariff reduction, is basically a nineteenth-century liberal conception. Free trade was a central feature of liberal internationalism in the nineteenth century and a corollary of a generally pacific view of international relations. The most notable instance of this in Canadian history was Wilfrid Laurier's endorsement of what was then called reciprocity. For some today, the development of trading blocs, particularly the European Union, has made free trade a necessity rather than an ideological preference. Nevertheless, it was originally a liberal idea.

The impression has no doubt been given that neoconservatism is a narrow kind of ideology. With deregulation, privatization, and balanced budget proposals, the emphasis has been on economics alone. What of the neoconservative view of social programs? Most nonconservatives call for the reduction, but not the dismantling, of the welfare state. They adopt the minimalist notion of the state as providing a safety net. This metaphor implies that life is a kind of high-wire act and the state will ensure that people who fall (the unemployed, the sick, the destitute) will be minimally provided for. They are wary, however, of encouraging laziness, and they believe that there should be incentives for people to work or disincentives for those who do not.

Neoconservatism in its more developed forms has a theory of law rather than a theory of justice. Neoconservatives are critical of any kind of preference given to special interests. While liberal ideology legitimizes interest-group activity, neoconservatives, though not wishing to impose restrictions on freedom of association, tend to view interest groups negatively and castigate those interests that look for public support for their causes, such as labour unions seeking legislation against strikebreakers, businesses seeking guaranteed loans, farmers demanding subsidies. Neoconservatives may also be wary of ethnic, racial, or gender advocacy groups. Thus what liberal ideology views as normal and legitimizes, neoconservative ideology views as abnormal and tries to counter.

It is possible that in placing the "public interest" over special interests, neoconservatives may indeed conceal support for some interests over others. Still, when the government becomes involved not only in supporting the demands of special interests, but in giving grants to organizations such as feminist lobbies, consumer advocacy groups, industry associations, and labour councils, the legitimization process seems to go too far for neoconservatives. So there is a marked contrast between the liberal view of interest groups and their political activities and the neoconservative view.

The notion of justice in neoconservative ideology is more problematic. Patterns of distribution produced by the operation of the free market are not considered just, or unjust for that matter. Neoconservatives believe that the results of voluntary contracts should be considered fair. That means that fairness is reckoned in terms of the fulfilment of certain conditions of exchange and not in terms of the results of the transaction. Neoconservatives would strongly oppose efforts by government to affect socioeconomic patterns by the redistribution of income and transfer payments. The legally acquired goods of individuals and organizations should be respected, and force and fraud in the marketplace condemned. Need is addressed by ensuring a basic minimum. To sum up, neoconservatives seem to be more notable for their attacks on the concept of social or distributive justice than for any original or distinctive theory of justice of their own.

It would not make sense to refer to neoconservatives as libertarian liberals unless they accepted the idea that the basic political value is freedom.

But what type of freedom is this? We should recognize that everyone is interested in particular kinds of freedom. Journalists are particularly interested in freedom of the press; artists and writers in freedom of expression. Dissidents, perhaps, are most concerned with freedom of association; university teachers with academic freedom; and certain religious minorities with religious freedom when their beliefs collide with the law. Liberals are criticized because they are concerned with civil and political freedoms, while restricting economic freedom. Neoconservatives, on the other hand, are often preoccupied with the issue of economic freedom. It is not freedom of choice in regard to art, literature, and entertainment (or abortion and pornography), but freedom of choice in the economic sphere that holds the neoconservative's attention. The freedoms we enjoy do not have the same kind of importance for us as do the freedoms we are denied.

The neoconservative conception of freedom is the absence of coercion for entrepreneurs and consumers. The economic freedom of the workers is not considered important. Neoconservative ideologists are anti-union, frequently arguing against such organizations as a form of labour monopoly. The worker is presumably free to choose where to work, though this may require the person to move elsewhere to find employment. The ideology must include all economic categories, such as management and labour, producers and consumers, in the exercise of economic freedom. Suffice it to say that workers have not been the usual clientele of neoconservatism. The neoconservative rejects the identification of freedom and power. The worker will be more concerned with relative power in the marketplace than with a frequently elusive freedom to choose a place of employment.

For neoconservatism, the real enemy is not so much interventionist liberalism, but socialism. At a time when capitalism seems to have the upper hand over a declining socialism, it is important to understand what the socialist ideology has been in Canada and how it stands in regard to liberalism and neoconservatism.

SOCIALISM

Two conceptions of socialism have been influential in the formation of socialist ideology in Canada: *democratic socialism* and *Marxism*. To the extent that society is viewed in terms of class conflict between the proletariat (industrial working class) and the bourgeoisie (those who own the means of production, distribution, and exchange), the two conceptions share the same general perspective. The Marxist vision, however, holds that class conflict will be resolved only by the political and social dominance of the working class. With the replacement of capitalism by socialism, primarily by public ownership of the means of production, distribution, and exchange, a classless society will develop. This is in contrast to the democratic socialist view where socialism is presumed to come about through peaceful electoral means, with an emphasis on public control of the economy rather than complete public ownership. Observers have argued that democratic socialism, in Sweden for instance, has made its peace with capitalism since control over the economy does not entail a significant amount of public ownership. However, the goal of social equality is given priority. Perhaps a useful way of differentiating this kind of democratic socialism from Marxism in economic terms is to say that the former is a socialism of distribution and the latter is a socialism of production.

Unlike liberalism and neoconservatism, the socialist value system accords priority to equality over freedom; more specifically, social equality is accorded priority over economic freedom. Socialism respects civil and political freedoms, as liberalism does. Still, the aim of a more just—that is, more equal—society requires redistribution, effected through tax policies and social welfare programs to ensure social justice, another name for distributive justice. The main criterion of distributive justice is need. If basic needs are the same, the outcome of distribution according to need should be a more egalitarian society.

The main emphasis in democratic socialism is on distribution rather than production, on government policies to achieve social equality rather than on public ownership. Nonetheless, democratic socialists may be in favour of strategic nationalization, or public ownership of key aspects of the economy such as investment banking. By and large, this kind of socialism combines a general acceptance of private ownership with government intervention to ensure greater equality through tax policy, welfare policy, and transfer payments.

Historically, Canadian democratic socialism began with an emphasis on nationalization, in the famous Regina Manifesto of 1933. After a recital of the evils of the capitalist system, it states: "We believe that these evils can be removed only in a planned and socialized economy in which our natural resources and the principal means of production and distribution are owned, controlled and operated by the people."[3] Democratic socialism has moved away from this emphasis on public ownership and, since 1970, has limited itself to distributive concerns, to achieving greater equalization within Canadian society. To that extent it, like Swedish socialism, has come to terms with capitalism; it offers to its adherents a form of socialist capitalism.

Along with the call for a planned economy and the notion of a co-operative commonwealth—aimed at transforming the competitive capitalist system into a co-operative economic system—Canadian socialism has expressed the ideal of an *industrial democracy*. The term specifically refers to the movement toward greater worker self-management in the workplace, as opposed to the perpetuation of the adversarial relations of management and labour. More often, the term is used indiscriminately to indicate that socialism means better housing, better health care, provision for the elderly, greater access to higher education, and a reformed system of taxation that will force the rich to pay their fair share. The goal is to realize in the socioeconomic sphere the kind of equality presupposed in the democratic principle of universal suffrage.

To accomplish these goals, a strong central state with an extensive bureaucracy is required. Bureaucratic socialism is not an accident or a distortion of the socialist ideology, as Marxists might say, but the inevitable outcome of the social service state. Of course, the bureaucracy even in the liberal welfare state is already quite extensive. The state simply cannot offer public provision and attempt to bring about redistribution of income without extensive public agencies.

Whatever may have been its former radicalism, democratic socialism in Canada now appears to pursue a prudent policy of reform, more radical no doubt than that of the liberals, yet scarcely close to Western Marxism. It has little of the internationalism of European democratic socialism and, in fact, is strongly nationalistic. It is increasingly concerned about the American penetration of the Canadian economy, particularly since the Canadian–U.S. Free Trade Agreement and NAFTA.

NATIONALISM

Nationalism will not be treated as a separate ideology in this chapter, for there are various conceptions of Canadian nationalism that are conditioned by the particular ideology one endorses. There is the nationalism of Conservatives like John Diefenbaker, of Liberals like Walter Gordon, and of New Democrats like Ed Broadbent. For some nationalists, the focus is political—the pursuit of an independent foreign policy. For others it is primarily economic or cultural. For some it may entail a national vision, such as Canadian unity or a planned economy; for others it is mainly negative, expressed in anti-Americanism. And we can hardly ignore Quebec nationalism, now present at the federal level in the form of the Bloc Québécois after the parliamentary election of 1993. Historians often refer to clerical nationalism in Quebec prior to the Quiet Revolution of the 1960s because of the prominence of the clergy in articulating a vision of Quebec tied to the land and traditional religion. The current kind of nationalism is secular, articulated by intellectuals and publicists, and reflects a vision of modern industrial Quebec. The former kind did not pursue political independence, while the latter does.

An observer of the federal elections in Canada and the United States in 1988 would have concluded that nationalism was on the left in Canada (meaning the NDP and the Liberals) and on the right in the United States (meaning the Republican Party). Nationalism in Canada has three dimensions—political, economic, and cultural—and to an extent all three of these dimensions were at stake in the free trade debate. If nationalism in Canada bears on the whole country, populism has usually been a regional concern in Western Canada.

POPULISM

Populism once flourished in Canada but has gradually disappeared as a significant ideological movement. Populist ideology originated in the Prairie provinces and had links with the American populist movement, mainly because of the large number of farmers who immigrated from the United States. The ideology appealed to the common people and defended western interests against the alleged oppression of eastern interests, particularly financial ones. It advocated an egalitarian democracy and the capitalism of small producers.[4] Indeed, there are still populist attitudes, and populist measures like the privatization of the British Columbia Resources Investment Corporation through its sale to people in the province.[5] However, such occasional manifestations and the durability of populist appeals to a democratic electorate do not constitute the kind of pattern discernible in liberalism, neoconservatism, and socialism. Still, the campaign of the Reform Party in Alberta for an elected Senate may indicate a resurgence of populism, for it too began as a western protest against dominant eastern interests and now plays a prominent role at the federal level in Parliament. However, there are significant differences between the old western populism and Reform Party populism. The older brand had both an economic and a political side. The Reform Party does not embody economic populism—its program has a neoconservative resonance—but rather political populism. Thus, its program emphasizes measures such as an elected Senate, a delegate conception of representation, an empowered constitutional convention, the use of the referendum (particularly to ratify constitutional amendments), free votes in Parliament, and the use of popular initiatives and voter recall. All of these measures are designed to remove power from political parties and elites and return it to the people.

CONCLUSION

Ideologies vary in their longevity. Liberalism is surely the most durable ideology in Canada, principally because it has evolved to suit the times. Populism, on the other hand, has waxed and waned. The current prominence of neoconservative ideology may be short-lived. In Eastern Europe, it may have a future denied to it in North America. Ideologies once thought dead and buried have had a second life, while communism, one of the most powerful ideological influences in Western history, is in a state of rapid decline. Perhaps the most surprising aspect of the ideological phenomenon in the modern period is not that ideologies are mortal, but that certain ideologies have survived repeated announcements of their demise.

NOTES

[1] Michael Sandel, ed., *Liberalism and Its Critics* (New York: New York University Press, 1984), 4. W. Christian and C. Campbell speak of the distinction between negative (business) liberalism and positive (welfare) liberalism in *Political Parties and Ideologies in Canada* (Toronto: McGraw-Hill Ryerson, 1983), 58.

[2] F.A. Hayek, *The Road to Serfdom* (London: Routledge and Kegan Paul, 1944).

[3] H.D. Forbes, ed., *Canadian Political Thought* (Toronto: Oxford University Press, 1985), 241.

[4] W.L. White, R.H. Wagenberg, and R.C. Nelson, *Introduction to Canadian Government and Politics*, 6th ed. (Toronto: Holt, Rinehart and Winston, 1994), 93–96.

[5] See Michael Bliss, *Northern Enterprise: Five Centuries of Canadian Business* (Toronto: McClelland & Stewart, 1987), 574n.

SUGGESTED READING

Brooks, Stephen J., ed. *Political Thought in Canada: Contemporary Perspectives.* Toronto: Irvin, 1984.

This wide-ranging collection of essays examines such issues as religion and politics, social and political democracy, French Canada, liberalism, and federalism.

Christian, William, and Colin Campbell. *Political Parties and Ideologies in Canada*. 3rd ed. Toronto: McGraw-Hill Ryerson, 1990.

What has been and is now the influence of different ideas or ideologies on Canadian party politics? The authors identify four ideologies: liberalism, conservatism, socialism, and nationalism. They argue that the three major parties combine ideological elements and that recent Canadian politics has seen an ideological shift to the right.

Horn, Michiel. *The League for Social Reconstruction: Intellectual Origins of the Democratic Left in Canada 1930–1942*. Toronto: University of Toronto Press, 1980.

This valuable historical study tells us about the left-leaning intellectuals of the League, their ideas and their influence on social reform in Canada.

Marchak, M. Patricia. *Ideological Perspectives on Canada*. 2nd ed. Toronto: McGraw-Hill Ryerson, 1981.

This study examines various aspects of Canadian society in view of the confrontation between the dominant ideology (liberalism) and the counter-ideology (Marxism). Shortcomings are discerned in both of these ideologies.

Qualter, Terence H. *Conflicting Political Ideas in Liberal Democracies*. Toronto: Metheun, 1986.

The author identifies three major ideologies in Canada: the Liberal Mind, the Tory Tradition, and the Socialist Faith. Democratic ideology is also discussed in an analysis that indicates the influence of the late C.B. Macpherson, an eminent Canadian political theorist.

3

THE LIVING CONSTITUTION

Questions of constitutional reform and amendment play a major role in contemporary Canadian politics. Canada is unique in this respect. While other Western democracies debate such issues as taxes and social services, Canada's political agenda has been frequently pre-empted by the more fundamental challenges of national unity and major structural and institutional reforms. Quebec separatism, western alienation and Senate reform, the Charter of Rights (1982), the Meech Lake (1987) and Charlottetown (1992) accords—these are the issues that have engaged the energy and skills of Canadian leaders for the past twenty years.

Constitutional issues such as these cut to the very core of Canadian politics. They address not the question of what laws to make, but the prior and more fundamental question of who shall make the laws and how. While there is unanimous agreement that "the people" shall govern, there is no agreement on who constitute the people. Is Canada a single nation state or a community of communities encompassing two (or more) distinct societies? Which level of government—federal or provincial—should be more powerful? Should Quebec enjoy special status different from that of the other provinces? Should Canada's two founding races—the French and the English—enjoy a higher constitutional status than the many other ethnic groups that make up the Canadian mosaic? Should Aboriginal peoples be accorded a similar "First Nations" status? Are individual rights more important than provincial rights? Should the Supreme Court be allowed to overrule legislatures in the name of rights? Or should legislatures be able to overrule the Supreme Court in the name of democracy?

Answers to these questions shape the structure, the powers, and the institutions of Canadian political life. Currently, there is no consensus on these fundamental constitutional issues. Yet how they are answered will determine Canada's future, perhaps even its existence. This chapter introduces some of the important constitutional issues as Canada enters the 1990s.

THE CONSTITUTION: LAW AND CONVENTION
The Living Constitution

We must first clarify what we mean by the constitution. The constitution defines the structure of the state, its major institutions, their composition and powers, and their relationships to one another and to the citizens and groups who make up society. It is tempting to say that Canada's constitution consists of the British North America Act, 1867 (BNA Act, now known as the Constitution Act, 1867) and the Constitution Act, 1982 (which includes the Charter of Rights and Freedoms). These are indeed the two most important documents in Canada's written constitution,[1] but to stop here would reduce the constitution to a formal set of documents to be dickered over by lawyers and judges. The written constitution is complemented and brought to life by a rich and complex set of constitutional conventions and traditions, which constitutes the unwritten (or informal) constitution. The unwritten constitution operates independently of the courts and judges and ultimately shapes and limits the practical meaning of the written constitution and judicial decisions. The unwritten constitution has been formed and maintained by successive generations of Canadian leaders, and ultimately by the loyalties, beliefs, and practices of the Canadian people.

We will discuss below the important elements of both the written (formal) and unwritten (informal) constitution, but it is important at the start to be clear that Canada's constitution consists of both elements. This allows us to understand that the constitution is not some century-old document, a static nineteenth-century code, but rather, as Alan Cairns has written, a living institution. "To view the constitution in terms of what the Fathers [of Confederation] intended and immediately achieved fails to see that the constitution is in continuous creation. It contributes too much deference to the constitution as it existed in 1867, and too little attention to the contribution of subsequent generations to its evolution."[2] This "living constitution" is very much rooted in the BNA Act. But many provisions of the founding pact are now "dead letter" and without effect, just as there is much of the "living constitution" that is new and cannot be traced to 1867. Thus, "in a practical sense, the constitution is always contemporary."[3] It is a process of continuous renewal, rejection, and addition, on which each generation leaves its mark. By understanding the constitution as a living constitution, we can better understand both the historical origins of the constitutional challenges that face Canada today and our own generation's responsibility for meeting these challenges.

Constitutional Law

The BNA Act was the act of union that created Canada out of the British colonies of the United Province of Canada (consisting of Canada East and Canada West, which became Quebec and Ontario), New Brunswick, and Nova Scotia. Although drawn up by Canadian leaders, the act was enacted by the British Parliament in Westminster. Its preamble declares the intention to create a constitution "similar in principle to that of the United Kingdom"—that is, a system of parliamentary democracy. The BNA Act created the office of the governor general, the House of Commons, and the Senate, and specified the composition and powers of each.

The BNA Act also established a federal structure for the new Canadian state. Federalism denotes a state in which the legislative (law-making) powers are divided between the national government and the provincial governments. This was a deviation from the British model, made necessary by the distinctive and independent character of the four founding provinces. None of the provinces—especially French-speaking Quebec—wanted to lose control over local matters to a new and distant legislature in which its representatives would be a minority. Thus sections 91 to 95 of the BNA Act allocated the legislative powers of the state to the two different levels of government. Section 91 gave the new federal government the power to make laws for the "peace, order and good government of Canada" (hereafter referred to as the "POGG power"), including such specific matters as trade and commerce, taxation, currency, navigation and shipping, national defence, and criminal law. Section 92 gave the provinces jurisdiction over such matters as "property and civil rights" and "all matters of a merely local or private nature." Needless to say, the boundary line between these two spheres of jurisdiction is not clear and has been a source of dispute ever since. Section 93 conferred jurisdiction over the sensitive issue of education to the provinces. However, section 93 also guaranteed a separate system of Protestant schools in Quebec and a separate Catholic system outside of Quebec and gave the federal government power to intervene if a province failed to respect these education rights.

The federal form of the new constitution reflected the fact that the new Canadian state encompassed two distinct societies—one anglophone and largely Protestant, the other francophone and largely Catholic. This dualism was explicitly incorporated in several important provisions of the new constitution. In addition to the section 93 education guarantees, section 133 made French and English the official languages of both the federal and Quebec governments. It required that both languages be allowed in legislative debates and in the courts and that the records and statutes of each government be published in both languages. This dualism subsequently gave rise to a version of the "compact theory" of Confederation—that Canada was formed by a pact between its two founding "races." This version of the compact theory provided the basis for Quebec's claim—as the representative of the French people—to a right to constitutional veto over any amendments to the BNA Act. This right—if it ever did exist—was lost with the proclamation of the Constitution Act, 1982. The Meech Lake Accord would have restored it.

The Constitution Act, 1982, capped the political career of Prime Minister Pierre Elliott Trudeau and changed the original constitution in several important ways. First, it severed Canada's constitutional connection to the United Kingdom and provided a made-in-Canada amending formula for all future constitutional amendments. Prior to 1982, once the federal and provincial governments had agreed to an amendment, Ottawa had still to ask the British Parliament to enact it. The new amending formula requires the approval of both houses of Parliament and seven of the ten provinces with at least 50 percent of the population. This "7/50" amending formula means that a proposed amendment can be defeated by the combined opposition of Quebec and Ontario, since between them they have more than 50 percent of the population. This arrangement did not satisfy the government of René Lévesque, which believed that it stripped Quebec of its traditional right of constitutional veto.[4] For this reason, Quebec refused to approve the Constitution Act, 1982.

The Constitution Act also added the Charter of Rights and Freedoms to Canada's written constitution. The Charter enumerates a long list of individual and group rights against both levels of government. The Charter specifically authorizes judicial review; that is, it empowers the Canadian courts to interpret and to enforce the Charter, and to declare laws invalid if they violate these rights.

Constitutional Conventions

The other component of the Canadian constitution is convention. Constitutional conventions are not written: they can be understood as political traditions that everyone agrees must be followed. A convention usually restricts the way in which a legal power may be exercised. The fact that constitutional conventions are not in the form of written law means that they cannot be enforced by the courts, but this does not make them less important than the written constitution. Some of the most important principles of the constitution are in the form of conventions. For example, nowhere in the written constitution is there any mention of the prime minister, the cabinet, responsible government, or votes of no confidence. Indeed, a foreigner (with no knowledge of our unwritten constitution) who simply read the BNA Act would think that Canada is autocratically ruled by the British Queen and her appointed representative, the governor general.

The truth, of course, is much different. In practice, the governor general of Canada and the lieutenant-governors of the provinces are honorary heads of state who basically follow the "advice" (i.e., instructions) of the prime minister (or premier) and the cabinet. The cabinet, in turn, exercises such authority only so long as it commands the support of a majority of the members of the House of Commons or provincial legislature. If the government loses a vote on an important bill, it must resign and (normally) new elections will be held. Thus, link by link, "responsible government" and Canadian democracy is formed. The Crown is responsible to the prime minister, who depends on the members of the House of Commons, who must submit to general elections at least every five years.

All of this and more is implied by the simple preamble to the Constitution Act, 1867—that Canada shall have a government "similar in principle" to that of the United Kingdom. In addition to parliamentary supremacy and responsible government, the preamble imports the entire British common-law tradition into Canada's unwritten constitution. This includes the rule of law and the independence of the judiciary upon which the rule of law is founded. It also embraces such practices as religious and racial tolerance and the freedoms of speech, press, association, and assembly without which parliamentary democracy cannot properly function.[5]

Constitutional convention is thus as important as the written elements of the constitution to the proper functioning of Canadian democracy. Both ultimately are founded in public opinion, in the collective consciousness, customs, and morals of the Canadian people. To explain by way of metaphor, Canada's written constitution can be thought of as the skeleton and body of the Canadian state, while convention is akin to the soul. Without the animating spirit of its many conventions, the written constitution would be a dull and lifeless corpse.

FEDERALISM AND THE POLITICS OF REGIONALISM

Legally speaking, federalism can be defined as the section 91–95 division of the law-making powers between the federal government and provincial governments. It would be wrong to think of federalism as simply a technical or legalistic feature of the constitution. Like democracy, federalism reflects the character of Canadian society. A non-federal Canada is just as unthinkable as a non-democratic Canada. Federalism responds to and channels regionalism, one of the strongest forces in Canadian society. Regionalism denotes Canadians' strong sense of regional identity and the long tradition of provincial governments—especially in Quebec—trying to protect and promote this identity by maximizing provincial powers and autonomy.

The politics of regionalism manifests itself in two basic ways: either by seeking influence within the institutions of the federal government or by minimizing federal influence in the conduct of provincial governments. Examples of the former can be seen in attempts by the regions to place their MPs in key cabinet posts and thereby to favourably influence the awarding of federal contracts, economic subsidies, transfer payments, and the like. There is a perception—especially in the West—that Quebec leaders have excelled at this activity. This perception in turn has nurtured western alienation, a sense that western interests are chronically under-represented in the House of Commons.

This approach of trying to increase regional influence within the federal government has clear limitations. The enforcement of strict party discipline makes it political suicide for an MP to vote for regional interests against party policy. Also, the sheer numerical dominance of Central Canada—Quebec has 75 MPs and Ontario 99—makes it difficult for MPs from the western (86) and Maritime (32) provinces to exercise much collective influence. One symptom of this problem has been the recent push to reform the Senate to give each province more equal and more effective representation in the upper chamber. A reformed Senate, with each province having an equal number of votes regardless of its population, would give the Maritime and western provinces a greater voice in the governing process. Despite such future possibilities for increasing regional influence, up to the present most provinces have invested considerable effort and resources in the alternative approach of maximizing provincial powers against Ottawa.

With the passage of time, the forces of industrialization, urbanization, and the mass media have eroded many of the cultural differences that once distinguished the various regions of Canada. Even Quebec, while still the most distinctive regional culture, is much more like the other provinces than several generations ago. If federalism were simply a reflection of society, then it should have declined as regional cultural differences declined. This is what has occurred in the United States. In Canada, however, the opposite has happened. This has given rise to the theory that in Canada federalism is as much a cause as an effect of political regionalism. Federalism seems to have taken on a life and logic of its own. Provincial governments and provincial politicians have a vested interest in promoting their own powers and indulging in "fed bashing" when things go wrong, blaming the provinces' problems on the distant and allegedly insensitive government in Ottawa. This province-building activity takes both legal and political forms. Because the federal–provincial divisions of powers is part of the written constitution, it has been subject to legal interpretation—judicial review—by the courts.

Judicial Development of Federalism

Judicial review has become widely accepted as a necessary corollary to federalism. For a federal distribution of powers to be functional, there must be a mutually acceptable process for settling the inevitable disputes over where one government's jurisdiction ends and the other's begins. The need for a neutral umpire to resolve such disputes has been met through judicial review by a final court of appeal. Other federal states— the United States, Australia, and Germany—also use judicial review to resolve jurisdictional disputes.

The Judicial Committee of the Privy Council (JCPC) in London served as Canada's final court of appeal for constitutional issues until 1949. During this time, the JCPC gave a decidedly decentralist interpretation to sections 91 and 92 of the BNA Act. The federal government's broad residual power to make laws for "the peace, order and good government of Canada" was whittled away to almost nothing by the JCPC's "emergency doctrine," which restricted Parliament's power to legislate under the POGG power to "emergency" situations such as war. The federal government's unrestricted power to make laws for "the regulation of trade and commerce" was gradually reduced to the much narrower power to regulate only "interprovincial" and international trade and commerce. During this same time, the JCPC developed an expansive interpretation of the section 92 powers of the provinces to make laws with respect to "property and civil rights" and "all matters of a merely local or private nature."

The net effect of the JCPC's federalism decisions was to shift a considerable degree of legislative power from the federal to the provincial side of the ledger. Criticism of the JCPC's performance peaked during the 1930s when it struck down a series of new federal laws intended to alleviate the economic hardships caused by the Great Depression. Critics maintained that the JCPC's decisions had made it impossible for the Canadian government to effectively manage a modern, industrial economy.

This dissatisfaction led to the abolition of appeals to the JCPC in 1949. Critics hoped that the Supreme Court of Canada, liberated from the JCPC's supervision, would develop a bold centralist jurisprudence. These hopes were partially realized. From 1950 to 1976, the Supreme Court did not strike down a single piece of federal legislation. While the court did not abandon the emergency doctrine, it developed an alternative interpretation of the POGG power—the *national concern* doctrine. This test extends the federal government's jurisdiction under POGG to include new, unanticipated policy areas that are of importance to the entire country and are incapable of being dealt with by a single province. Examples include the regulation of aeronautics, telecommunications, and environmental protection. This new approach to POGG has the potential to expand federal jurisdiction significantly and to shrink provincial powers correspondingly.

A surge of judicial activism in the late 1970s saw both federal and provincial laws declared invalid. The court appeared to try to strike a balance between Ottawa and the provinces, but this did not prevent loud protests of bias from the provinces. Most of the federal laws invalidated during this period were relatively old and of limited importance. The court upheld the one new federal policy initiative —the Trudeau government's 1976 Anti-Inflation Act—as a legitimate exercise of the emergency doctrine, the first time it had ever been used successfully during peacetime.[6] By contrast, almost all the nullified provincial laws involved recent policy initiatives considered important by their respective governments. Alberta and Saskatchewan[7] saw their taxes on natural resources declared invalid, while Quebec's attempt to regulate cable television was also struck down.[8] Although the Supreme Court's federalism decisions during this period were relatively balanced, the provincial perception was one of a judicial bias in favour of Ottawa.

The new national concern doctrine, combined with the provinces' perception of a federal bias, made many provincial leaders wary of the Supreme Court. This suspicion was further compounded by the adoption of the Charter in 1982, which armed the court with a new and expanded set of constitutional restrictions to enforce against the provinces. This provincial perception of the Supreme Court as a centralizing force and a threat to provincial rights explains the provinces' insistence on the section 33 "legislative override" as a precondition for accepting the Charter. It is also behind their more recent demand in the Meech Lake (1987) and Charlottetown (1992) accords to acquire the power to nominate Supreme Court justices.

Non-Judicial Development of Federalism

While British and Canadian judges have shaped the evolution of Canadian federalism, politicians and civil servants, acting outside the courtroom, have been even more influential. For example, the federal government's powers to unilaterally nullify provincial legislation—the powers of disallowance and reservation—have been rendered impotent by the constitutional convention of non-use. These two powers were placed in the BNA Act by centralists such as Sir John A. Macdonald, who favoured "legislative union" and feared that under a system of "pure" federalism the provinces would be too strong. Disallowance and reservation were clearly intended to subordinate the provinces to the new federal government.

In the decades following Confederation, their coercive use by Ottawa provoked such a negative reaction from provincial governments that they came to be viewed as illegitimate federal intrusions into provincial matters. Legally, Ottawa still possesses these powers, but it has not exercised them since the 1940s. Public opinion is such that there is no likelihood of their being used again. The development of this convention of non-use significantly enhanced provincial powers in the equation of Canadian federalism.

Another important constitutional convention governing federal–provincial relations concerned the amending formula. The founders who drew up the BNA Act did not provide for a general amending formula. They simply assumed that future amendments would be made the same way the BNA Act itself was enacted—by the British Imperial Parliament. A convention was quickly established that the British Parliament would not change the BNA Act except at the request of the government of Canada. The role of the provinces in the amending process was not so simple to define. If Parliament could unilaterally amend the division of powers laid out in sections 91–92, the provinces would be at the mercy of the federal government. To prevent this, a practice developed that for amendments directly affecting provincial powers, the consent of all the provinces would have to be obtained before any request was sent to England.

The precise status of this practice—whether it was a constitutional convention or merely a political courtesy on the part of Ottawa—was never clear. Provincial rights proponents insisted that it was a fundamental element of Canada's unwritten constitution. This claim was based on the compact theory of Confederation, which held that the BNA Act was essentially a contract between self-governing colonies, and that the new federal government was the product of this compact. Since it was the colonies who had made the contract in the first place, it could not be amended without their consent. As noted above, Quebec leaders developed their own version of the compact theory, which held that Quebec in particular had a right to a unilateral constitutional veto. In principle, Ottawa never conceded either of these claims, but in practice it usually followed the convention until 1982.

This issue came to a head in 1981 when Prime Minister Trudeau, having failed to win the consent of the provinces, claimed that he could and would proceed unilaterally with a request for constitutional amendments—the Charter and a new amending formula. Eight provinces challenged the constitutionality of Trudeau's actions. In the most important decision it has ever made, *The Patriation Reference*,[9] the Supreme Court ruled that provincial consent was not required "as a matter of law," but that a "substantial degree" of provincial consent was required "as a matter of convention." Both sides felt vindicated, and further negotiations ensued, which resulted in the agreement of all but Quebec.

What the federal government lost in disallowance, reservation, and amending powers, it made up through the explosive growth of its spending power and conditional grants after World War II. The federal government's ability to raise and spend money far outstrips that of the provinces. In the decades after World War II, the federal government effectively co-opted large chunks of provincial jurisdiction by initiating over one hundred new social programs on a conditional, shared-cost basis. Billions of dollars of federal money were made available to the provinces for health, education, and welfare programs on the condition that the money be spent according to federal guidelines. While provincial leaders resented adopting policies and spending priorities made in Ottawa, they were even more reluctant to forego the large federal grants. Little by little, the federal government thus

bought its way into large areas of provincial jurisdiction without any formal amendments to the constitution. This provincial grievance was one of
the issues addressed by the Meech Lake Accord.

Executive federalism and its most visible event, the first ministers conference, have become mainstays of contemporary Canadian politics but are
nowhere mentioned in the written constitution. *Executive federalism*
denotes the systematic meetings of federal and provincial administrators
and politicians to co-ordinate national policies that straddle both levels
of government. Executive federalism has developed independently of the
courts and is generally viewed as a better way to settle federal–
provincial disputes, especially disputes involving complex economics and
large sums of money. The uncertainty and zero-sum ("winner take all")
character of litigation has led many politicians to prefer negotiation and
compromise. While judicial review is unlikely to disappear, it is basically
a complement to executive federalism, and certainly not a replacement.

To summarize, regionalism is the oldest but still most vital force in
Canadian politics. It is expressed and channelled primarily through the
various institutions of federalism. Provincial governments pursue their interests both within the federal government and also against it. Courts have
played a significant role in shaping the federal–provincial balance of
power. The JCPC's work contributed to the decentralization of Canadian
federalism. The modern (post-1949) Supreme Court of Canada has
favoured a more centralist interpretation of the BNA Act. Non-judicial
developments have been even more important. The decline of disallowance and reservation, the explosive postwar growth of the federal
government's spending power, the development of executive federalism
and first ministers conferences—all attest to the continued vitality of
Canadian federalism. The most recent and most dramatic development
in this evolution is the 1982 Charter of Rights and Freedoms.

THE CHARTER OF RIGHTS AND FREEDOMS

All liberal democracies are based on the twin principles of liberty and
equality. The principle of innate equality means that no person (or group)
has a right to govern another without that other's consent. In the eighteenth century, the principle of political equality was used to overthrow the
historical claims of priests and kings to rule on the basis of alleged natural
superiority. In the twentieth century, it rejects the legitimacy of both left-
and right-wing dictatorships, including the "dictatorship of the proletariat"
as practised by communist regimes. In practice, political equality means

government based on the consent of the governed and thus some form of majority-rule democracy. Political equality constitutes the democratic element of liberal democracy.

The principle of liberty denotes the natural rights of individuals: the rights to life, liberty, and security of the person and property. All men and women are understood to possess these rights by nature—that is, independently of any specific statute or government. The purpose of government is to protect these rights, and no just government can violate them. The principle of liberty—of individual rights—represents the liberal element of liberal democracy.

There is a tension between equality and liberty at the core of liberal democracy. Equality demands that government be based on the consent of the governed—majority rule. Liberty requires that this same government respect the natural rights of all its citizens. The tension arises when majority rule produces policies that do not respect the rights of individuals or groups who are not part of the majority. The balancing of majority rule and minority rights is a practical problem that confronts all liberal democracies.

There have been two principal approaches to giving institutional expression to the principles of equality and liberty in modern liberal democracies: the British parliamentary model and the American separation of powers model. Because of two major differences between the parliamentary and American systems, the courts in each system have very different functions and characteristics. The American model is ultimately based on and organized by a single basic document—a written constitution. By contrast, the Westminster model is based on an unwritten constitution—a combination of historically important statutes, the common law tradition, and numerous unwritten conventions and usages. The second difference is that the written constitution of the Americans includes an enumeration of the fundamental rights and liberties of the individual against government, known collectively as the Bill of Rights. While individuals enjoy basically the same rights and freedoms under the British parliamentary model of democracy, they are not spelled out in any single basic document of government—that is, they are not constitutionally entrenched. The result of these two differences is that in the American model of democracy, the courts, and especially the Supreme Court, play a much more explicit and influential political role.

At Confederation, the government of Canada was basically modelled after the British parliamentary system. The important exceptions were the federal form of the union of the Canadian provinces and the defining of the forms and limits of this union in a single written document. These aspects of Canadian government are important because they thrust upon the courts the function of judicial review, or umpire of the federal system. Federalism aside, both levels of government in Canada were formed after the parliamentary model, which meant legislative supremacy within their respective spheres of jurisdiction.

Accordingly, Canada until very recently followed the British approach to the protection of civil liberty: parliamentary supremacy, the rule of law, and the conventions that support them. The proximity of the United States has prompted constant comparisons. One of the most eloquent and forceful defences of the Anglo-Canadian approach to protecting civil liberties was given by the dean of Canadian political science, R. MacGregor Dawson. Dawson argued that unwritten constitutional conventions backed by public opinion are a more reliable support for civil liberties than a written bill of rights.[10] He was probably thinking of the American experience, where the constitutional requirement of "equal protection of the laws," embodied in the Fourteenth Amendment adopted in 1868, had failed to prevent a century of mistreatment of and discrimination against Blacks in the American South. Similarly in Canada, the constitutional protection of French-language rights in the province of Manitoba was ignored by provincial governments for eighty years. Written constitutional rights appear to be more secure because their violation can be challenged in the courts. But the courts have no means to enforce their own decisions. Dawson's insight was that even the effectiveness of judicial protection of rights depends ultimately on public opinion. Without such support, constitutional guarantees become mere parchment barriers, without real effect.

In the wake of World War II and the revelation of Nazi and Communist atrocities, Canadian political leaders became increasingly attracted to the American approach to protecting civil liberties. In 1960, the Diefenbaker government enacted the Canadian Bill of Rights. It took the form of a statute, not a constitutional amendment, and applied only to the federal government and not to the provinces. Partly because of dissatisfaction with this document and partly in response to the threat of Quebec separatism during the 1970s, the Trudeau government undertook a program of constitutional reform in 1978. Prime Minister Trudeau's constitutional agenda included patriating the BNA Act, developing an amending formula, and writing a Charter of Rights that applied to both levels of Canadian government. After a year and a half of political manoeuvring, confrontation, and, finally, compromise all three objectives were achieved.

The adoption of a constitutionally entrenched Charter of Rights fundamentally altered the Canadian system of government by placing explicit limitations on the law-making power of both levels of government. Parliament was no longer supreme; the constitution was. Or almost. Trudeau failed to have the Charter adopted in its original "pure" form. Attachment to the tradition of parliamentary supremacy, combined with provincial suspicion of a centralizing Supreme Court, were too strong and forced an important compromise—the section 33 legislative override. Section 33 allows a government (federal or provincial) to protect a statute from judicial nullification by declaring that it shall operate "notwithstanding" certain sections of the Charter.[11] Section 33 thus preserves a qualified form of parliamentary supremacy.

The Legislative Override Controversy

Section 33 was—and remains—controversial. Its critics contend that it undermines the Charter. What is the point of constitutionally entrenching fundamental rights and freedoms, say the critics, if a government can violate them by simply invoking section 33? This criticism is valid if we assume that section 33 applies directly to specific Charter rights. While true in theory, in practice this assumption is problematic, because it ignores the crucial role of judicial interpretation in giving effect to the Charter. The Charter is not self-interpreting. While the core meaning of most of the various rights are well established, their peripheral meaning is not. Since it is highly unusual for any Canadian legislature to violate the core meaning of these rights, almost all Charter litigation involves questions of peripheral meaning. Judges must choose among competing interpretations. Unfortunately, different judges often choose different—even contradictory—interpretations. Section 33 critics thus make two false assumptions: that the true meaning of Charter rights is either self-evident or can be discovered, and that judges are infallible in discerning this meaning.

The problem of ambiguous Charter meaning and judicial discretion is well illustrated by the most famous Charter cases to date—*Morgentaler v. The Queen*,[12] and its counterpart, *Borowski v. The Queen*.[13] Both Morgentaler and Borowski challenged the validity of Canada's 1969 abortion law, but for opposite reasons. The 1969 law prohibited abortions except when the pregnancy threatened the "life or health" of the mother, as determined by a committee of doctors at an accredited hospital. Dr Morgentaler argued that the prohibitory section of the law violated the woman's right to liberty and security of the person. Mr Borowski argued that the permissive section of the law violated the right to life of the fetus. Both men based their arguments on section 7 of the Charter, which states: "Everyone has the right to life, liberty and security of the person and the right not to be deprived thereof except in accordance with the principles of fundamental justice." In other words, both men relied on the same section of the Charter to support completely opposite conclusions. Which argument is correct?

In 1988, Morgentaler won, but not for the reasons he wanted. The Supreme Court ruled 5–2 that the abortion law violated the procedural fairness protected by section 7. Only one justice—the sole woman on the court—ruled that section 7 gave women a constitutional right to abortion. The two dissenters pointed out that abortion is not mentioned in section 7 and that judges are not free to add unintended meaning to the Charter. A year later, the Supreme Court dismissed the Borowski appeal for technical reasons without deciding the substantive issue of whether a fetus is a "person" and thus protected by section 7.

The division of the court in the *Morgentaler* case illustrates how it is the discretion of the judges and not the actual language of the Charter that often determines the result. When constitutional language is vague and the court is divided, it is the judges who are speaking, not the constitution. When, in addition, the outcome significantly affects important public policy, there is no reason to consider the constitutional issue permanently settled by the decision of nine (or five) unelected, unaccountable judges. In the absence of a clearly worded constitutional requirement, it would make no more sense to allow the court to prohibit all restrictions on abortion than it would to allow the court to prohibit abortions altogether. This would be to allow constitutional supremacy to degenerate into judicial supremacy. A society that allowed an appointed court to impose either of these options would cease to be self-governing, or governed by the consent of the governed.

Viewed in this light, section 33 seems more positive. It is not a direct attack on rights but a check on the judges' interpretation of the Charter—a sort of legislative review of judicial review. Just as judicial review serves as a check on legislative error or excess, so the legislative override serves as a check on judicial error or excess. Thus, section 33 places joint responsibility for protecting constitutional rights on legislatures and the courts. The Canadian people, armed with the power of the vote, remain the ultimate judges of the outcome of this partnership.

Canada thus finds itself today almost equidistant between the British and American models of liberal democracy, with their differing approaches to civil liberties. The debate over which form of liberal democracy is best designed to protect the liberties of its citizens remains very much alive. The truth of this debate most probably lies somewhere between the two contending positions, for, as Dawson pointed out, "Written law and the conventions will normally complement one another, and each becomes necessary to the proper functioning of the other."[14]

The Charter at Work

The immediate effect of the Charter was not the creation of new rights but a new way of making decisions about rights, in which the courts play a more central and authoritative role.[15] Most of the rights and freedoms enumerated in the Charter existed in the form of statutes, convention, or common law prior to 1982. The fundamental freedoms (section 2) and legal rights (sections 7–14) reflect similar rights in the 1960 Bill of Rights, which in turn codified the conventions and common law inferred by the preamble to the BNA Act. What the Charter did was to transfer primary responsibility for the articulation of these rights to the courts.

This transfer explains one of the most important effects of the Charter: the creation of a new forum for interest-group activity. Historically, Canadian interest groups have concentrated their lobbying activities at the cabinet and senior levels of the bureaucracy and have rarely used litigation as a political tactic. This was predictable. The absence of constitutionally entrenched rights deprived the courts of any supervisory role over legislative policy making, except for assuring that the limits of federalism were respected. Because of Canada's strong historical attachment to the practice of parliamentary supremacy, attempts to change laws through the courts were viewed as illegitimate. With the advent of the Charter, all this has changed. Interest groups that fail to achieve their policy objectives through the traditional political party and bureaucratic channels can now turn to the courts.

Interest-group use of Charter litigation as a political tactic can take several different forms. The most direct is for the interest group to turn its cause into a case and go to court itself. This was the approach used by Operation Dismantle, a coalition of peace and anti-nuclear groups that challenged—unsuccessfully—the government's decision to allow the United States to test the cruise missile over Northern and Western Canada.[16] A successful example of direct litigation was the Charter challenge, undertaken by the National Citizens' Coalition, to the "anti-PAC" clause of the Canada Elections Act.[17] An Alberta Court of Queen's Bench ruled that the act's restrictions on election expenditures by "political action committees" unaffiliated with any political party violated the freedom of expression of these groups.

A second way for interest groups to participate in Charter litigation is to pay the legal expenses of individuals who are willing to challenge laws that the groups would like to see nullified. In the two major abortion cases discussed above, both Borowski and Morgentaler had the financial backing of interest groups on opposing sides of the abortion issue. Campaign Life and the Canadian Abortion Rights Action League (CARAL) spent over $350 000 each to allow their respective champions to fight their way to the Supreme Court. A national feminist organization founded in 1985, LEAF (Women's Legal Education and Action Fund), pursues an active strategy of supporting Charter litigants in cases involving sexual equality issues. Until 1992, the federal government's Court Challenges Program provided funds to groups who litigated minority language rights and equality issues under the Charter.

The third and final way for interest groups to participate in Charter politics is to intervene in appeal court hearings. An intervenor is a third party (other than the Crown and the actual litigant) that the court permits to present legal arguments. Acting as intervenors, interest groups can put forward arguments and evidence that support their interpretation of Charter rights. LEAF is a frequent intervenor in section 15 equality cases. The Canadian Civil Liberties Association (CCLA) also frequently intervenes in cases raising Charter issues that it considers important. The presence of intervenors is usually a good indicator that the case involves political issues that transcend the legal dispute before the court. In the abortion cases, for example, there were intervenors representing both positions on the issue.

As recently as 1975, one of Canada's leading historians could accurately state that Canadian "judges and lawyers, supported by the press and public opinion, reject any concept of the courts as positive instruments in the political process. Political action outside the party–parliamentary structure tends automatically to be suspect—not the least because it smacks of Americanism."[18] The extensive interest-group use of Charter litigation—much of it actually financed by government—shows how much has changed since 1982.

Interest groups such as LEAF and the CCLA have also been pleased by another Charter-induced change—a dramatic surge in judicial activism. In a sharp reversal of pre-Charter practice, Canadian judges, led by the Supreme Court, have been much more willing to override legislative decisions and to declare federal and provincial laws invalid. Under the 1960 Bill of Rights, the Supreme Court had exercised great self-restraint—the opposite of judicial activism—nullifying just one (quite insignificant) statute in 22 years. By contrast, the Supreme Court nullified 41 statutes (26 federal, 15 provincial) in the first ten years under the Charter. Another good index of judicial activism since 1982 is the number of victories for Charter litigants before the Supreme Court: 65 (in 195 decisions) compared to just 5 victories (in 35 cases) under the 1960 Bill of Rights.

The main policy impact of the Charter has been in the area of criminal law enforcement, accounting for two-thirds of all Charter decisions. The Supreme Court has given a broad interpretation to the right to counsel (section 10b) and the right against unreasonable search and seizure (section 8). In a sharp reversal of pre-Charter practice, the court has established a policy of excluding evidence from a trial if it was obtained in a manner that violated the rights of the accused, no matter how good the evidence. The effect of the court's activism has been to substantially enhance the procedural defences of those accused of crimes, a result applauded by civil libertarians. The cost has been a proportional decrease in the efficiency of law enforcement and crime control, a trend that worries others.

Beyond the criminal law field, the policy impact of the Charter has been random. Reference has already been made to the Supreme Court's two abortion decisions, as a result of which there is still no criminal regulation of abortion. The Mulroney government introduced a revised abortion law that was approved by the House of Commons but defeated by a tie vote in the Senate. Likewise, as a result of the successful challenge to the Canada Election Act by the National Citizens' Coalition, there is still no regulation of non-party expenditures during federal elections. This turned out to be important during the November 1988 elections, as it allowed pro–free trade groups to spend millions of dollars on political advertising in the closing weeks of the campaign. This support certainly helped Prime Minister Mulroney achieve his subsequent electoral triumph. In another contentious policy area, the Supreme Court's two Sunday closing decisions[19] have contributed to the significant increase in Sunday shopping across Canada.

Quebec has been the province most affected by the Charter. As soon as the Charter was adopted, the Quebec Protestant School Board challenged the education provisions of Bill 101, the Charter of the French Language. The education sections of the bill restricted access to English-language education within the province. In 1985, the Supreme Court of Canada struck down these restrictions as a violation of the section 23 language education rights of the English-speaking minority in Quebec.[20] Because section 23 is excluded from the scope of the section 33 legislative override, Quebec had no alternative but to accept the court's decision.

Three years later, the Supreme Court struck down another section of Bill 101—the "French only" public signs requirements.[21] This provision prohibited the use of English in commercial signs and billboards, storefront advertising, and the like. Quebec anglophones, especially the 650 000 living in Montreal, considered the provision oppressive and humiliating and challenged it as a violation of the Charter right to freedom of expression. Quebec nationalists considered the "French only" rule essential to preserving the "French face" of Quebec, and they harshly denounced the Supreme Court's decision. The recently elected Liberal government of Robert Bourassa—contrary to promises it had made to anglophone voters in the 1985 election—gave in to nationalist sentiment and invoked the section 33 legislative override to reinstate the public signs policy. This override infuriated many people in English Canada and put in jeopardy the ratification of the Meech Lake Accord.

The *Quebec Protestant School Board* decision realized Quebec nationalists' worst fears about the Charter. Coming on the heels of the loss of its traditional constitutional veto, the decision further isolated Quebec from the rest of Canada. To protest its exclusion from the Constitution Act, 1982, the Quebec government boycotted all subsequent first ministers conferences dealing with constitutional issues. Quebec's absence was not only regretable in itself but also prevented any progress on other constitutional issues such as Senate reform, much to the dismay of its supporters. It was generally recognized that no Quebec government would consent to the Constitution Act, 1982, until the province regained, among other things, its control over the language of education within the province. Concern over Quebec's growing isolation and the desire to bring it back within the constitutional fold led to the Meech Lake Accord of April 1987.

THE MEECH LAKE ACCORD

The Meech Lake Accord was a set of constitutional amendments proposed by Prime Minister Mulroney in the spring of 1987. It was the result of a first ministers conference held at the federal government's facilities at Meech Lake near Ottawa. The prime minister had gained the consent of all ten provincial premiers (a rare feat!) for a document whose primary purpose was to gain Quebec's endorsement of the Constitution Act, 1982, and thus end the province's political isolation. This process became possible after 1985 with the election of Robert Bourassa as premier of Quebec. His government made a number of constitutional proposals that provided the basis for negotiation. As Prime Minister Mulroney triumphantly observed when he announced the accord, "Tonight Canada is whole again, the Canadian family is together again, and the nation is one again."

The initial reaction to Meech Lake was one of national celebration, especially in Quebec. Quebec Premier Robert Bourassa hailed it as "one of the greatest political victories of [Quebec] history." The accord was quickly approved by Parliament when it was endorsed by both the Liberals and the New Democrats. Eight of the ten provinces quickly followed suit, but this initial burst of enthusiasm soon dissipated, as a growing chorus of critics attacked the accord. The basic thrust of this criticism was that the prime minister had bargained away too many of the powers of the federal government, mainly to Quebec but also to the other provinces. The result, according to the critics, would be an enfeebled federal government incapable of co-ordinating national policies or protecting the rights of individuals and minorities. Former prime minister Pierre Trudeau, the architect of the Constitution Act, 1982, came out of retirement to spark the attack on Meech Lake: "Those Canadians who fought for a single Canada, bilingual and multicultural, can say goodbye to their dream. We are henceforth to have two Canadas each defined in terms of its language."[22]

Trudeau's stinging attack served as a catalyst for mounting opposition to Meech Lake. The ratification juggernaut was slowed down when new provincial governments with leaders opposed to Meech Lake were elected in New Brunswick and Manitoba. Meanwhile, the chorus of critics was growing. Feminists, ethnic groups, French minorities outside of Quebec, the English minority within Quebec, human rights activists, civil libertarians, and supporters of Senate reform all found fault with the accord.

The amending process ground to a complete halt in December 1988, when the Bourassa government invoked the section 33 power to override the Supreme Court's decision in the French-only public signs case. The premiers of the two remaining holdout provinces, New Brunswick and Manitoba, abruptly cancelled scheduled legislative hearings on Meech Lake and announced that they would not reconsider the accord until Bourassa repealed this measure. Subsequently, the newly elected Liberal premier of Newfoundland, Clyde Wells, announced that he intended to repeal that province's earlier approval of the accord. As the three-year deadline for ratification—23 June 1990—approached with continuing deadlock, both Mulroney and Bourassa issued dire warnings that national unity would be threatened if Meech Lake was not approved. Nonetheless, Elijah Harper, a Manitoba MLA of Native ancestry, was able to use the rules of the legislature to prevent ratification before the deadline, and in Newfoundland the necessary vote was also not taken. The amendment thus failed.

Opposition to the Meech Lake Accord

The controversy over Meech Lake was about both how it was made and what it would do; that is, critics objected both to its process and its substance. Objections to the process by which the accord was reached focused on its closed, secretive, and undemocratic character. There was no hint prior to the announcement of the accord that the first ministers were considering significant amendments to the constitution. There was thus no prior public discussion or input from interested groups. Once the accord was announced, public discussion was irrelevant, as all eleven first ministers rejected the idea of any changes, describing the accord as a "seamless web," to be accepted or rejected as an indivisible "package." While the approval of each legislature was required, this was initially considered little more than a formality, as each premier could invoke party discipline to ensure passage. It was basically a deal struck in private between the eleven first ministers without any public input either before or after. Meech Lake was presented to the Canadian people as a "done deal," to be accepted gratefully or otherwise.

While this approach to constitution making was consistent with the past practice of executive federalism, it did not sit well with the new, more democratic political spirit ushered in by the Charter of Rights. The Charter had the effect of conferring new rights, new status, or both, on a number of groups in Canadian society. These new "Charter Canadians" felt they had an important stake in the constitution, and they were angry that it was going to be changed without any input from them. This anger was heightened by their perception that the substance of Meech Lake threatened their recently acquired rights and status.

The substance of the accord reflected the five demands set forth by the Bourassa government as a condition for Quebec's acceptance of the Constitution Act, 1982. These five conditions were constitutional recognition of Quebec as a "distinct society"; restoring Quebec's historical constitutional veto power; the right to opt out of new federal spending programs in areas of exclusive provincial jurisdiction, with full financial compensation; a role in the appointment of Supreme Court judges; and greater control over immigration into the province.

In its final form, Meech Lake met all five demands but extended the last four to the other nine provinces as well, due to their jealous resistance to any special status for Quebec. Thus the agreement would have produced a decidedly more decentralist form of federalism. It would have meant that no province could be forced to accept a new federal spending program or a constitutional amendment to which it objected. This obviously would have made amending the written constitution more difficult. The provincial power to nominate Supreme Court judges would have made it more difficult for the federal government to exercise any indirect influence over the court's jurisprudence through the appointment of centralists or Charter activists.

The provinces' new power over immigration would probably have been significant only for Quebec, which would try to encourage a high percentage of French-speaking immigrants. The practical effect of the accord's recognition of Quebec as a "distinct society" with the right "to protect and to promote" this distinctness was uncertain. Its meaning would ultimately have depended on judicial interpretation. Quebec nationalists claimed that it would have produced the opposite outcome in the two Charter cases nullifying the education and public signs sections of Bill 101. Critics of the "distinct society" clause—especially Quebec anglophones—were against it for this very reason.

Opposition to Meech Lake clustered around several related issues. The most widely shared criticism was that Meech Lake would fatally weaken the federal government by transfering too much power to the provinces. This criticism was pervasive among groups who favoured or benefitted from a strong central government and uniform national policies. This group overlapped considerably with a second bastion of anti-Meech sentiment—the feminist, ethnic, linguistic, and other minorities who have been the primary beneficiaries of the Charter of Rights. These Charter Canadians looked to the courts for policy leadership and distrusted legislatures, especially provincial legislatures. They felt threatened by the enhanced powers of Quebec and the other provincial governments, not least of all because of the control that Meech Lake would have given them over the nomination of Supreme Court judges. They also objected to the distinct society clause, which they claimed would undermine the practical value of their sections of the Charter.

A third and distinct source of opposition to Meech Lake came from the supporters of "triple-e" Senate reform. This movement wants the Senate to be "elected, equal and effective." *Equal* refers to an equal number of representatives from each province, similar to the United States Senate. *Effective* means that the reformed Senate would be a meaningful part of the law-making process. Supporters of Senate reform believe that it is the only way that the less populous provinces from the West and Atlantic Canada can achieve fair representation and influence in the federal government. A Senate based on equal representation for each province would mean a significant reduction in the proportion of senators from Quebec and Ontario. Currently, Senate reform is possible under the "7/50" amending formula. Meech Lake would have required unanimity. Senate reformers feared that if Meech Lake had been adopted Quebec would no longer have had any incentive to give up its large quota of senators and would have used its new veto to block Senate reform.

THE OLD CONSTITUTION VERSUS THE NEW

The Meech Lake affair can be interpreted as two different constitutions battling for control of the Canadian state.[23] One is the old constitution, with its roots in Confederation. The other dates only from 1982. The old constitution is the constitution of the compact theory—the constitution of governments, federalism, and French–English dualism. Since this constitution belongs to the governments, it can be changed by the governments, by first ministers' conferences. Under it, constitutional politics is mainly a process of bargaining among political elites. This old constitution has always implicitly recognized the special status of Quebec. Meech Lake made this recognition explicit through the distinct society clause.

The new constitution is the constitution of the Charter. It is concerned with individuals and their rights and freedoms. It is also concerned with group rights, but not in the old sense of only the French and English. The new constitution is multicultural and asserts the equal status of ethnic Canadians and Aboriginals with the two founding peoples. Since this new constitution belongs to the people, it cannot be amended without their participation and consent.

Meech Lake was made by the partisans of the old constitution. It was attacked primarily by partisans of the new constitution. Charter Canadians objected to Meech Lake not only because of its content but also because they were excluded from the process. A constitution that belongs to the people, they argued, should not be amended unilaterally by eleven first ministers. The fate of Meech Lake suggests just how powerful this new constitutional vision has become. Ten years earlier, it would have been unthinkable that a proposal endorsed by all the first ministers, plus the leaders of both opposition parties, could not become law. In 1990, the unthinkable became the new reality.

THE CHARLOTTETOWN ACCORD

The defeat of the Meech Lake Accord cast the country into renewed constitutional crisis. Quebec now felt twice rejected and withdrew from further constitutional discussions. Within Quebec, support for sovereignty soared. The Quebec government organized two separate task forces to re-examine Quebec's relationship with the rest of Canada. The results—the Bélanger-Campeau and Allaire reports—staked out new minimum constitutional claims for Quebec, which far surpassed what had been offered in Meech. Premier Bourassa set 26 October 1992 as a date for a referendum for Quebeckers to vote on their future relationship with English Canada. The date served as a challenge and a deadline for Ottawa and the nine other provinces to produce a better offer to Quebec. The result of this new round of constitutional struggle was the Charlottetown Accord and the national referendum of October 1992.

The Mulroney government was determined not to commit the same mistakes as in Meech. Procedurally, the result was openness with a vengeance. The English-Canadian public was assaulted by government consultation initiatives: the Spicer Commission, the Beaudoin-Dobbie Committee, and five regional constituent assemblies. With respect to substance, the results were predictable. By broadening the process, Mulroney had also opened up the constitutional agenda. There was something for everyone. The contents of the Charlottetown Accord were characterized as "Meech plus," meaning that it contained everything present in the Meech Lake Accord plus concessions to all the aggrieved interests from that earlier round.

Westerners (and Newfoundland) won Senate reform, although not of the pure "triple-e" variety. Social democrats, having missed the Charter bandwagon the first time around, now demanded a social charter, the constitutional entrenchment of social welfare rights. They too received some, but not all, of what they originally demanded. The biggest winners were Aboriginal groups. They received extensive and explicit commitments to the "inherent right to self-government" and were mentioned three times in the Canada clause. Most of the Charter Canadians also received new recognition and reaffirmation in the Canada clause, although not enough to appease some.

The contradictory and disorderly character of the Charlottetown Accord was captured in the convoluted logic of the Canada clause. The Canada clause was the successor to the distinct society clause in Meech. It was an interpretive clause that was intended to guide judicial interpretation of the constitution. Under the Canada clause, Quebec retained its recognition as a distinct society and the separate power "to protect and to promote" its distinctness. However, this recognition was now balanced by a second "fundamental constitutional characteristic"—the commitment of all governments to the "vitality and development of official language minority communities throughout Canada." Aboriginal rights and self-government received prominent recognition, but this too was hedged by the principle of respect for human rights and especially the "equality of male and female persons." This kind of balancing was pervasive. Individual rights were paired with collective rights; parliamentary democracy with respect for rights; the diversity of the provinces with the equality of the provinces.

A major problem with the Meech-plus approach was that there was really nothing new for Quebec, except the permanent guarantee of 25 percent of the seats in the House of Commons, regardless of Quebec's future population. This was intended to compensate Quebec for its relative loss of seats and influence in the reformed Senate, but it was something Quebec had never wanted to begin with. Similarly, the distinct society clause was now hedged in with so many other countervailing fundamental characteristics that its practical value in constitutional litigation now seemed dubious to many Quebeckers.

The final details of the accord were agreed to by all eleven first ministers at Charlottetown at the end of August 1992. The accord was also supported by the leaders of both opposition parties in Parliament, the premiers of the two territories, the Assembly of First Nations (whose president, Ovide Mercredi, had been actively involved in negotiating the accord), the Canadian Chamber of Commerce, and the Canadian Labour Congress. In short, the accord enjoyed overwhelming elite support from across the political, social, and economic spectrum. The only nay-sayers at the outset were the Parti Québécois/Bloc Québécois and the fledgling Reform Party from Western Canada. As in the case of Meech, the prospects for adoption of the new accord seemed overwhelmingly positive.

There was one other important difference between the Meech and Charlottetown accords: the method of adoption. Quebec had already committed itself to considering "Canada's final offer" by way of referendum. Not to be "outdemocratized" by Quebec (and to avoid being burned again politically as they were by Meech), the Alberta and British Columbia governments had also committed themselves to decision by referendum. This groundswell of participatory democracy proved too powerful for Ottawa to resist. The Mulroney government enacted legislation authorizing a national referendum in the rest of Canada to coincide with the referendum in Quebec. The new constitution was to be accepted or rejected directly by the people. If anyone still doubted the political sea change in the Canadian polity since the adoption of the Charter, here was the final proof: vox populi had replaced consociational democracy, where communities accept agreements arrived at through elite accommodation, as the preferred means of constitutional adaptation. Whatever happened in the referendum, Canadian constitutional politics would never be the same.

At the outset of the referendum campaign, elite support was matched by popular support. Polls indicated a 60:40 support ratio, with weaknesses only in Quebec and British Columbia. Despite such an auspicious launch, not everyone loved the Charlottetown Accord. The critics were as diverse as their criticisms. The Reform Party complained about the special status conferred on Quebec and Aboriginals, and decried the abandonment of the principle of equality of all citizens. Some members of the Charter Canadians coalition also came out against the accord. Deborah Coyne, an adherent of the Trudeau vision of Canada, organized a no campaign, charging that Charlottetown's preference of group rights over individual rights would weaken the Charter and the courts. This latter criticism was echoed by the National Action Committee on the Status of Women (NAC), which also condemned the accord for subordinating women's rights to those of Quebec and Aboriginals. From the other side, PQ/BQ critics lambasted the accord as less than Meech: the original purpose of the distinct society clause had been diluted by the omnibus new Canada clause; Senate reform effectively reduced Quebec's power in Ottawa; and Quebec received nothing more in terms of the devolution of powers or constitutional veto than all other provinces.

Notwithstanding these criticisms, the opponents seemed too diverse and too divided among themselves to effectively resist the Charlottetown juggernaut. This scenario changed dramatically on 1 October when Pierre Trudeau once again broke the silence of his retirement and publicly denounced the accord. As the architect of the Charter and himself a

Quebecker, Trudeau's authority immediately legitimized and mobilized the hitherto diverse and divided criticisms of the accord. Support for the yes side tumbled dramatically and never recovered.[24] When the votes were counted on 26 October six provinces—including Quebec—had rejected the accord. Only in the Atlantic provinces did the yes side win decisively. In the four western provinces, the accord was defeated by a decisive margin of 60–40. Even in Ontario, the yes forces mustered a margin of victory of less than 1 percent. In Quebec, the accord was decisively rejected by 58 percent of the voters.

The results of the referendum may be interpreted at both a political and a constitutional level. It was clear in retrospect that the architects of the Charlottetown Accord made some serious political miscalculations. In adopting the strategy of something for everyone, they failed to gauge accurately whether what each interest received gave them sufficient satisfaction to offset their dissatisfaction with what their opponents received. Richard Johnston has described this as an "inverted logroll."[25] Instead of every party being satisfied by their net share of the dole, everyone was dissatisfied. To take one important example, triple-e reformers' dislike of the 25 percent "quota" for Quebec outweighed their support for the proposed Senate reform, while many Quebeckers felt that they lost more than they gained through this same exchange.

To interpret the outcome of the referendum as simply the result of political miscalculation, however, would be to miss a deeper and more troubling dimension. Contrary to appearances, the Charlottetown Accord was at base an attempt to preserve the constitutional status quo rather than to change it. That is, the accord proposed what its supporters hoped would be the minimum changes necessary to preserve the status quo. (This explains why all the various elites supported the accord. Since when do those who are privileged by the status quo want to fundamentally change it?)[26] In the same sense, two of the leading proponents of the no coalition—the PQ/BQ nationalists and the Reform Party—opposed the accord because they perceived it as shoring up a constitutional status quo that they deemed no longer acceptable. The problem was that the change they wanted was in opposite and mutually exclusive directions. As the Mulroney government was painfully learning, any attempt to appease the one alienated the other.

In 1992, this fundamental conflict between Reform sympathizers and Quebec nationalists was papered over by their mutual opposition to the Charlottetown Accord. Exactly one year later, in the 1993 federal elections, this constitutional chasm became painfully obvious. The governing

Conservatives were all but wiped out. Their seat total in the House of Commons dropped from 170 to 2. Their western base fell to the surging Reform Party, which captured 52 seats (all but one from the West) and became the "unofficial" opposition of English Canada. The Campbell Tories were also wiped out in Quebec, but on this front by the separatist Bloc Québécois. The BQ won 50 percent of the vote and 54 of the province's 75 seats, making it the official Opposition. The Liberal Party won a majority government but did so without carrying Quebec, a historical anomaly. Indeed, the Liberal support base was heavily regionalized, based almost entirely in Ontario (98 out of 99 seats) and Atlantic Canada (31 out of 32 seats). In short, the regional voting patterns in the 1993 election nearly mirrored those of the referendum, but with the no vote of 1992 now divided between the BQ in Quebec and the Reform Party in the West.

The results of the 1993 federal election have been described as "partisan balkanization of the worst kind."[27] In the past, the basic French–English constitutional cleavage underlying the Canadian polity was brokered by centrist political parties competing for electoral support in the voter-rich Quebec–Ontario centre. This cleavage has now been replicated in the partisan make-up of the House of Commons. Rather than having an incentive to broker the Quebec–Canada divide, the regionally based Reform and BQ actually have an interest in exploiting it.[28] This balkanization of the House of Commons further complicates the challenge of national unity in post-Charlottetown Canada. The Liberal government of Jean Chrétien is under considerable pressure to make new concessions to Quebec to counter the surge of nationalist sentiment. Yet any attempt to do so is likely to be sharply denounced by the Reform Party as a betrayal of English-Canadian interests.

CANADA'S UNRESOLVED QUESTION: WHO SHALL GOVERN?

In the wake of the defeat of the Meech Lake and Charlottetown accords, Canada faces constitutional challenges perhaps more daunting than those that confronted the founders over a century earlier. Some of these are genuinely new issues, but most are new versions of the issues that shaped Confederation. The challenge of Canadian federalism—the quest to strike an acceptable balance between the provincial and federal governments—remains central. This challenge is inextricably linked to the status of Quebec. How distinctive is Quebec, and how should this be recognized in terms of special powers and privileges? In theory, the issue of Senate reform is the question of how best to represent the interests of the less populous provinces within the workings of the federal government. In practice, it is really a question of how much of its current influence in Parliament Quebec is willing to give up.

Ironically, these problems have been aggravated by the democratization of Canadian politics associated with the advent of the Charter of Rights. It is clear that under the old way of conducting political business in Canada—through a closed circle of elite accommodation—both the Meech Lake and Charlottetown accords would have been approved. But this is no longer an option. One of the strongest legacies of the Charlottetown process is that any future attempt at mega-constitutional change will again have to be submitted to the Canadian people by way of referendum. There is no turning back the clock.

The Charter may have had the effect of making Canada a more liberal, more individualistic, and more democratic nation. A more democratic Canada, however, risks being a more divided Canada. Because it is individualistic, the new constitution attaches less value to provincial rights. Its emphasis on multiculturalism erodes the preferred status of the English and French cultures. To the extent that it is more participatory, it is less capable of the compromise and accommodation that has kept Canada together for over one hundred years. This more democratic style of politics is likely to reject proposals like Meech Lake and Charlottetown and to insist that Quebec be treated like the other provinces. These defeats have in turn rekindled the fires of Quebec independence.

Canada's constitutional odyssey thus continues.[29] Generation after generation, Canadian leaders have tried to negotiate acceptable compromises on such issues as the federal division of powers, an amending formula, national institutions, and fundamental rights and freedoms. Beneath this institutional restlessness lies a more fundamental and unresolved question: who should govern, and for what ends? This is really *the* constitutional question for every country. Once it is settled, the institutional questions can be more easily resolved.

Unlike the United States, Canada has been spared a violent revolution and a bloody civil war. In one sense, this is a blessing. But in another, it has deprived Canada of a genuine "founding" and a shared sense of common purpose. As Peter Russell has written, "Canadians have not yet constituted themselves as a people: they have not yet accomplished that profound but essential act of a constitutionally self-governing people—to agree on what they are and want to be as a people."[30]

Unlike other modern democracies, Canada has not chosen the "one state, one nation" model. From the start, we have remained one state, two nations. Whether this arrangement can be sustained remains to be seen. This is the constitutional challenge of the 1990s, the next phase of Canada's living constitution.

Notes

[1] Other acts included in Canada's written constitution are Manitoba Act, 1870; Rupert's Land and North West Territory Order (1870); British Columbia Terms of Union (1871); Prince Edward Island Terms of Union (1871); Alberta Act (1905); Saskatchewan Act (1905); Newfoundland Act (1949); Parliament of Canada Act, 1875; and the Statute of Westminster, 1931. See the Schedule to the Constitution Act, 1982, for a complete listing.

[2] This quotation and this theme are taken from Alan Cairns, "The Living Canadian Constitution" in *Constitution, Government and Society in Canada: Selected Essays by Alan Cairns*, ed. Douglas E. Williams (Toronto: McClelland & Stewart, 1988), 31.

[3] Ibid.

[4] Under section 41 of the Constitution Act, 1982, certain types of constitutional amendments continued to require unanimous support, thus giving each province a veto. These areas included the offices of the Queen, governor general, and lieutenant-governor; the right to a minimum number of MPs; language rights; and the composition of the Supreme Court.

[5] The 1982 Charter of Rights entrenched all of these "fundamental freedoms" and democratic rights in the written constitution. It is important to realize that these freedoms existed and flourished prior to the Charter. What the Charter changed was that these rights and freedoms are now subject to judicial interpretation and enforcement.

[6] *Reference re Anti-Inflation Act*, [1976] 2 SCR 373.

[7] *CIGOL v. Saskatchewan*, [1978] 2 SCR 545; *Central Canada Potash Co. Ltd. and Attorney-General of Canada v. Saskatchewan*, [1979] 1 SCR 42.

[8] *Public Service Board v. Dionne*, [1978] 2 SCR 191.

[9] [1981] 1 SCR 753.

[10] R. MacGregor Dawson, *The Government of Canada*, 4th ed. (Toronto: University of Toronto Press, 1963), 70.

[11] The section 33 "notwithstanding" clause can be applied only to the following Charter rights: fundamental freedoms (s. 2); legal rights (ss. 7–14); and equality rights (s. 15). It cannot be used against democratic rights (ss. 3–5); mobility rights (s. 6); language rights (ss. 16–22); or minority language education rights (s. 23).

[12] [1988] 1 SCR 30.

[13] [1989] 1 SCR 343.

[14] Dawson, *Government of Canada*, 71.

15 This is the central theme of Peter Russell, "The Effect of a Charter of Rights on the Policy-Making Role of the Canadian Courts," *Canadian Public Administration* 25 (1982): 1–33.

16 *Operation Dismantle v. The Queen*, [1985] 1 SCR 441.

17 *National Citizens' Coalition v. A.-G. Canada*, [1985] WWR 436.

18 Kenneth McNaught, "Political Trials and the Canadian Political Tradition" in *Courts and Trials: A Multi-Disciplinary Approach*, ed. M.L. Friedland (Toronto: University of Toronto Press, 1975), 137–61.

19 *The Queen v. Big M Drug Mart Ltd.*, [1985] 1 SCR 295; and *Edwards Books and Art Ltd.*, [1986] 2 SCR 713. *Big M* struck down the federal Lord's Day Act, while *Edwards Books* upheld Ontario's secular "day of rest" Sunday closing law. Notwithstanding the legal result, the latter decision did nothing to stop the trend toward Sunday shopping in Ontario and other provinces.

20 *Attorney-General of Quebec v. Quebec Association of Protestant School Boards*, [1984] 2 SCR 66.

21 *A.-G. Quebec v. Ford*, [1988] 2 SCR 712; *Devine v. A.-G. Quebec*, [1988] 2 SCR 790.

22 *Toronto Star*, 27 May 1987.

23 This is the thesis developed by Alan Cairns, "The Limited Constitutional Vision of Meech Lake" in *Competing Constitutional Visions: The Meech Lake Accord*, ed. K.E. Swinton and C.J Rogerson (Toronto: Carswell, 1988), 247–62.

24 For this and the data that follow, see Richard Johnston, "An Inverted Logroll: The Charlottetown Accord and the Referendum," *PS: Political Science and Politics* (March 1993): 43–48.

25 Ibid.

26 See F.L. Morton, "Judicial Politics Canadian-Style: The Supreme Court's Contribution to the Constitutional Crisis of 1992" in *Constitutional Predicament: Canada After the Referendum of 1992*, ed. Curtis Cook (Montreal: McGill-Queen's University Press, 1994).

27 Neil Nevitte, "Electoral Discontinuity: The 1993 Federal Election" (unpublished paper, 1994).

28 Ibid.

29 Both this concept and the analysis that follows are developed by Peter Russell, *Constitutional Odyssey: Can Canadians Be a Sovereign People?* 2nd ed. (Toronto: University of Toronto Press, 1993).

30 Ibid.

Suggested Reading

Cairns, Alan. "The Living Canadian Constitution." In *Constitution, Government and Society in Canada: Selected Essays by Alan Cairns*. Ed. Douglas E. Williams. Toronto: McClelland & Stewart, 1988, 27–42.

Cairns presents a more sophisticated and detailed analysis of many of the themes and subjects covered in this chapter. Written in 1970, it does not cover the Charter of Rights or the Meech Lake and Charlottetown accords.

Cook, Curtis, ed. *Constitutional Predicament: Canada after the Referendum of 1992.* Montreal: McGill-Queen's University Press, 1994.

A useful collection of essays that analyzes the referendum on the Charlottetown Accord and the consequences of its failure.

Gibbins, Roger, ed. *Meech Lake and Canada: Perspectives from the West.* Edmonton: Academic Printing and Publishing, 1988.

A collection of essays that captures the various perspectives—both pro and con—on the Meech Lake Accord.

Grant, George P. *Lament for a Nation.* McClelland & Stewart, 1965.

The most insightful and interesting investigation of Canada's struggle for political self-definition.

Knopff, Rainer, and F.L. Morton. *Charter Politics.* Toronto: Nelson Canada, 1992.

Knopff and Morton analyze and describe how the Charter has changed the practice of politics in Canada since 1982.

Monahan, Patrick. *Meech Lake: The Inside Story.* Toronto: University of Toronto Press, 1991.

The best history and analysis of the politics associated with the Meech Lake Accord.

Morton, F.L. *Morgentaler v. Borowski: Abortion, the Charter and the Courts.* Toronto: McClelland & Stewart, 1992.

A case study of the best known and most controversial Charter case thus far.

Romanow, Roy, John Whyte, and Howard Leeson. *Canada Notwithstanding: The Making of the Constitution, 1976–1982.* Toronto: Carswell-Methuen, 1984.

A good history and analysis of the politics that resulted in the Constitution Act, 1982.

Russell, Peter. *Constitutional Odyssey: Can Canadians Be a Sovereign People?* 2nd ed. Toronto: University of Toronto Press, 1993.

This is the best historical overview of Canada's ongoing quest to sustain the "one state, two nations" arrangement.

Agar Adamson

4

THE ATLANTIC PROVINCES: HOPE DEFERRED?

tlantic Canada might well be described as a conundrum, or at least as a labyrinth of complexities. On the one hand, high rates of unemployment, outward migration, rural poverty, the decline of the fishery, and the need for federal grants have all contributed to the formation of a rather conservative, cynical society in a region that may already have experienced its most productive economic days. In other words, Atlantic Canada is a region that for some time has not participated fully in the economic growth of the nation.

On the other hand, Dalton Camp, paraphrasing from the *Report of the Royal Commission on Canada's Economic Prospects* (the Gordon Report of 1957), writes that although Atlantic Canadians "could never expect to have it quite so good as Canadians elsewhere, there were compensations. These were listed as (1) the close proximity of fishing holes, duck blinds and curling rinks, and (2) the historic, hard-earned right not to work overly much. Gordon's observations outraged Maritimers, and rightly so. They did not wish that kind of information given out."[1] Reality, as this essay endeavours to illustrate, lies somewhere between these two poles.

THE SETTING

In other regions of Canada, politics is a fact of life that, like death and taxes, must be endured. But in Atlantic Canada politics is the very bread of life. Nowhere else in Canada, with the exception of the

Territories, are the inhabitants as dependent upon government for employment and social welfare as they are in this region. Similarly, the four provincial governments in Atlantic Canada are, per capita, more dependent on the federal government for assistance than are the other six.

Atlantic Canada needs financial assistance from Ottawa. In fact, federal money in one form or another—Atlantic Canada Opportunities Agency (ACOA) grants, equalization grants, Established Program Financing (EPF), Department of Regional Economic Expansion (DREE) grants, other federal grants, military bases, public works, old age pensions, unemployment insurance, and so on—accounts for more than half of the economy of the region. Consequently, Atlantic Canada is deeply affected by federal policy, as was witnessed by the reaction to recent federal budgets. Cutbacks—base closures, changes in ACOA's budget and certain federal grants, subsidies to VIA Rail, capping of EPF and equalization payments—have had a greater per capita impact on the Atlantic provinces than elsewhere in the nation.

Historically, governments in the region were reluctant to openly confront the federal government. Similarly, the electorate for some time did not wish to bite the hand that fed it. In fact, 65.6 percent of respondents to a questionnaire distributed to voters participating in the 1992 Nova Scotia Liberal leadership selection process thought that it was more beneficial for that province to have the same party in office in Halifax and Ottawa than to have different parties in power.[2] Despite this fact, something of a conundrum is apparent when one looks closely at recent election results. It is true that in 1993 the Liberals swept the region in the federal election and won provincial elections in Newfoundland, Prince Edward Island, and Nova Scotia, setting the Progressive Conservatives back to 1935 levels of electoral support. Nevertheless, an inspection of recent Atlantic Canadian election results illustrates that residents of these provinces, like those elsewhere in Canada, do elect governments that differ from those in Ottawa. For example, the Liberals won in Newfoundland in 1989, in Prince Edward Island in 1986, and in New Brunswick in 1987. The Conservatives won in Nova Scotia from 1978 to 1993 and in Prince Edward Island in 1982.

It appears that provincial elections are fought on local issues. This certainly was the case in New Brunswick in 1987 and Prince Edward Island in 1986. Moreover, premiers in this region, like those elsewhere in Canada, are not indisposed to a little "fed bashing," if running against Ottawa will ensure their election. Certain premiers, most notably Brian Peckford but also Frank McKenna, Clyde Wells, and Joe Ghiz, have openly challenged the federal government's stance on a number of issues including natural resource development, free trade, and the Meech Lake Accord. Others, like Richard Hatfield, John Buchanan, Catherine Callbeck, Robert Stanfield, and J.R. Smallwood, preferred quiet diplomacy no matter the colour of the federal government of the day. With a Liberal government in Ottawa, the Liberal premier of Newfoundland, Clyde Wells, is becoming a member of the silent co-operative school. Which policy has been most effective is open to debate.

HISTORY

Demographic realities, historical and current, have helped to shape Atlantic Canada. Although this region was settled very early, it has not benefitted from overseas immigration during the twentieth century. Consequently, the Atlantic provinces are home to an established citizenry, many of whom can trace their roots back several generations within the same community. This pattern has led to fiercely maintained local loyalties that in many ways belie the notion of Atlantic Canada as a single region—witness the area's reluctance to promote the positive aspects of Maritime union.[3]

Such settled communities do not mean that the population is static. The region has seen many of its inhabitants migrate to other areas of Canada or to the United States. "Going down the road" is a fact of life in Atlantic Canada, fed by the lack of employment opportunities within the region. Since the late 1970s, there has been a reversal of this trend: people are returning, bringing with them new ideas for a more open society, an end to patronage, and an acceptance of bilingualism. Within the region, as elsewhere, there has been a shift from rural areas to urban cores. Internal migration has led to the growth of the Halifax metropolitan region, Saint John, and St John's.

Atlantic Canada has not been blessed with an overabundance of natural resources. Historically, the principal resource industries have been the fishery, pulp and paper, base metals, lumber, coal, agriculture, and—in the case of New Brunswick and Labrador—hydro-electric power. Except for the latter, these resources have been buffeted by world markets and fluctuating prices. (The discovery of hydrocarbons off the coasts of Newfoundland and Nova Scotia briefly gave those provinces hope that there was to be an economic eldorado in their future, but to date these resources are only in the development stage, with some production now coming from the fields near Sable Island.) The fishery has always been the most important natural resource, and its rise and fall can be compared to the rise and fall of wheat in the West. On the Prairies, poverty is noticeable when the wheat crop fails. In Atlantic Canada, the poverty is of a less spectacular nature, but it is more constant and grinds down the inhabitants.

Such poverty has not always been the case. In 1867, Nova Scotia was considered to be a "have" province. A combination of political and technological factors changed this status. Steam replaced sail, and oil and natural gas replaced coal. Transportation costs, coupled with Sir John A. Macdonald's tariff policies, made it difficult for regional products to be competitive in Central Canadian markets. At the same time, the Maritimes lost many of their pre-Confederation markets. W.A. Mackintosh wrote that "in the Maritime Provinces the effect [of the tariff] was in the direction of accelerating the contraction of exports and of accentuating falling population and declining value of resources in those export industries which could not turn to the domestic market."[4] Climatic, technological, and political considerations led to the decision to keep the St Lawrence River open year-round to Montreal, thus damaging the economies of Halifax and Saint John. The construction of the St Lawrence Seaway injured the Maritime economy. Unlike Central Canada, the three Maritime provinces did not benefit from the opening of the northern and western territories.[5] Moreover, they were not compensated for the admission of new provinces. Nova Scotia and the other Maritime provinces became dependent on federal government fiscal transfers, as they had nothing to replace the industries lost as a result of the changes that ensued after Confederation.

In addition to economic setbacks, the Maritimes lost much of the political clout that they had had in 1867. The growth of the Canadian population, particularly west of the Ottawa River, meant proportionately fewer Maritime representatives in the House of Commons and less influence in the Senate, the Supreme Court of Canada, and the federal public service.

The strains on Canadian unity accompanying the rise of nationalist fervour in Quebec have prompted recent federal governments to earmark increased regional development funds for that province. Thus scarce resources badly needed in Atlantic Canada have been diverted to shore up the federal presence in Quebec.[6]

ECONOMIC DEVELOPMENT

The issue of economic development is the mainspring of politics and public policy in the four Atlantic provinces. Collectively, these provinces have the highest rate of unemployment in Canada, an average income below the national level, and a cost of living as high or higher than the national norm.

A 1989 study revealed that wage disparity between the Atlantic provinces and the wealthiest Canadian provinces had not improved in the past twenty to thirty years. The unemployment gaps in 1989 between the Atlantic region and the more prosperous provinces were greater than they had been for twenty years.[7] This was in spite of millions of federal dollars in economic aid. The recession of the 1990s has only exacerbated these trends.

According to the Gordon Report,

> An objective of economic policy should be to integrate and improve the basic economic framework of the Atlantic region, including, in particular, the transportation facilities of the area with a view to facilitating and encouraging economic growth within the region. This is not likely to be accomplished by a multiplicity of uncoordinated measures. . . . In fact, . . . such aids may tend to prolong the life of industries and activities which may no longer be wholly justified in economic terms. . . . What is needed, we believe, is a bold, comprehensive and co-ordinated approach to the underlying problems of the region.[8]

Although the Gordon Report may not have been well received in Atlantic Canada, its message has been the goal of individual governments since 1957. Unfortunately, the "co-ordinated approach" to economic development has been slow to materialize.[9]

ACOA, conceived in 1987, may be the most productive of any development plans because, instead of promoting megaprojects and inducing industry from outside to locate in the region, it is geared to assist local entrepreneurs and to work with businesses of all sizes located within the Atlantic provinces as well as those wishing to locate in the region. Still, its successes are unclear—in 1989, Nova Scotia and ACOA could not even agree on how much money had been spent in that province or how many jobs ACOA had created—and there are many problems associated with the agency.

As originally conceived, ACOA was to be as non-partisan and non-political as possible. Unfortunately, ACOA quickly became little more than a continuation of previously existing patronage agencies. A report made public in late 1993 states that "federal election time is a good time for entrepreneurs in Atlantic Canada."[10] Indeed, a major proportion of the five-year budget of ACOA was distributed prior to the November 1988 federal election. The report goes on to discuss political interference in the operation of ACOA, particularly in Nova Scotia, pointing out that 60.1 percent of ACOA grants from the agency's inception to 1989 were approved in the final two quarters of 1988. Similar patterns existed in the other three provinces. Following the Tories' victory in the 1988 election, the newly appointed board of directors was composed almost entirely of Conservative Party supporters. If ACOA is to be successful and respected by the citizenry, it will have to conform to its original concept and be non-partisan and more sensitive to local needs. ACOA, if handled properly, has the potential to be the facilitator recommended in the Gordon Report.

Every provincial government, no matter what its political philosophy, has endeavoured to end the twin problems of unemployment and poverty by providing jobs and economic development programs. The electorate constantly demands jobs from its politicians, not only at the provincial level but also at the federal and even municipal levels. The four provincial governments have been active participants in promoting development and "modernization." Each has constructed a process for economic planning. Some of these, like Nova Scotia's Voluntary Economic Planning Council, are a mixture of business and government personnel. All in all, provincial attempts to promote industry are more noted for their failures (Bricklin Automobiles, Sydney Steel, Sprung Greenhouses, heavy water, oil refineries, shipyards, and Clairtone) than for their successes (Michelin, McCain's, IMP, and Volvo).

In the relentless quest for jobs, environmental considerations often take a back seat. Many politicians are of the view that almost any industry, no matter what its social or environmental impact, is worth the investment because of the employment it creates. The only exception to this statement is Prince Edward Island, which refused to give Litton Industries all the financial assistance they desired and also refused to purchase electricity generated by nuclear fission in New Brunswick.[11]

No examination of Atlantic Canada would be complete without a section on the fishery, the backbone of the rural Atlantic economy, particularly in Newfoundland. Fishers are an independent lot who do not always appreciate government regulations. The fishery is not only a regulated industry but is also a victim of the constitutional division of powers, and often the two levels of government are at odds over fisheries policy. Constitutionally, fish do not become a ward of the province until they are landed for processing.

There may be co-operation among the Atlantic provinces on many issues, but one area where there has been no co-operation is the fishery. This is particularly true of Newfoundland and Nova Scotia. Fish, unlike politicians, do not respect provincial boundaries and, in any case, provincial boundaries do not extend to Canada's two-hundred-mile offshore limits. Thus, fishers from Nova Scotia, for example, fish in the waters off Newfoundland, and their catch is processed in Nova Scotia. Such actions annoy the Newfoundland fishers who feel that these are their waters and that residents of the other provinces should stay out of them. Naturally, the Newfoundland government sides with its citizens and squabbles develop between the two provinces. Because of these interprovincial conflicts, Newfoundland's Brian Peckford had the fishery included in the ill-fated Meech Lake Accord.

Fishery issues of the past paled in comparison to the situation in 1994. Much of the fishery, particularly in Newfoundland and Labrador waters, has been closed until the stocks recover. Over 40 000 individuals were laid off indefinitely and went on various forms of federal and provincial social assistance.[12] These layoffs were the largest and most severe in Canadian industrial history.

No one can say precisely why the fish have disappeared. Some of the reasons are overfishing by Canadian and foreign fleets, the reluctance of Canada—prior to 1994—to enforce quotas on the nose and tail of the Grand Banks (technically international waters), colder water, pollution, improved methods for counting and catching fish, and a reluctance by many in the industry to invest in aquaculture.

It's unclear whether the fish, particularly bottom feeders such as cod, haddock, and halibut, will ever return, but if they do it is estimated that less than half of the laid-off workers will ever be able to return to the fishery. The magnitude of this economic disaster cannot be measured; the closest comparison is the dustbowl conditions that existed on the Prairies during the Depression of the 1930s. Fortunately, there is a more supportive social safety net in place today, but the future, even with the 1994 renewal of the federal compensation package, remains uncertain. One wonders if the pictures painted so vividly by John Steinbeck in *The Grapes of Wrath* will be repeated by those displaced by the collapse of the fishery.

The problems in the fishery reveal a massive failure in public policy outputs and a need for imaginative public policy inputs into Atlantic Canada. This is true for both the fishery and social policy more generally. The region, particularly Newfoundland, has been tied to tradition and thus has been slow to change and modernize. Newfoundland has an illiteracy rate of 44 percent, while 80 percent of those in the fishery do not have a high school education.[13] Such statistics are an indictment of past governments and their lack of planning.

Atlantic Canada's future depends upon a successful restructuring of the economy by both federal and provincial governments. Economic restructuring is a national problem, and failure to resolve it could mean that half of the two million Atlantic Canadians will be going down the road to Toronto, Calgary, Vancouver, and Boston and causing new social problems in those cities. The figures are staggering: only 74 000 of 600 000 Newfoundlanders have jobs; of those, 40 000 are in the public sector. The real unemployment rate in the province is 63 percent.[14] The prairie dustbowl of the 1930s was a national concern; so must be the plight of those displaced in the fishery in the 1990s.

The policy outputs of the four provincial governments in Atlantic Canada run the full spectrum from economic development to social welfare. Economic development may be the most notable of these, but each province has developed a network of social welfare policies. Of course, in provinces with a weak tax base and many social problems there is still much to be done, particularly in the area of rural poverty.

All four provinces, but perhaps most notably Prince Edward Island and Newfoundland, are undergoing a process of political "modernization." The growth of urban centres and the influx of new ideas as well as economic development are leading to changes in political and social attitudes. The rural society, though still important, is not as powerful as it was in the past.

MARITIME CO-OPERATION

To those who live in the rest of Canada, Maritime union is a topic for debate, but within the region there is little support for such a project, as the Maritime union study (Deutsch Report) illustrated.[15] However, the Deutsch Report stimulated a spirit of co-operation and harmony among the provincial governments in the Maritimes. The premiers meet quarterly to debate regional problems and, whenever possible, to harmonize policy outputs, particularly concerning relations with Ottawa. The report spawned several of Canada's most notable and useful forms of intergovernmental co-operation. These include a secretariat that handles the quarterly meetings of the three premiers and co-ordinates policy and research among their provinces, the Maritime Provinces Higher Education Commission, the University Grants Agency, and the Land

Registration Agency. Moves have been made to eliminate the trade barriers between the Atlantic provinces. Reform of interprovincial trade rules is being spearheaded by Frank McKenna, who, like his predecessors Richard Hatfield and Louis Robichaud, is leading the struggle for closer co-operation. There is more successful interprovincial co-operation in the Maritimes than in any other region of Canada. These attempts to integrate policy and to work together on regional issues have paid many dividends for Maritimers, for example in tourist promotion as well as in standardization of many educational texts.

For the most part, Newfoundland has gone its own way, disregarding attempts at regional co-operation. The Conservative governments that followed that of J.R. Smallwood made it quite clear that Newfoundland was not to be considered one of the Maritime provinces, and there were very few occasions when the Atlantic region presented a united front at federal–provincial first ministers conferences. Clyde Wells is reversing this trend. Wells attends many of the Maritime premiers' quarterly meetings and, in spite of his differences with his counterparts during the Meech Lake and Charlottetown constitutional discussions, he is showing a spirit of compromise and co-operation on economic and trade matters.

POLITICAL CULTURE AND PARTIES

Atlantic Canada shares a regional political culture that has been apparent for some time. Basically, the prevailing political culture of the four provinces has revolved around three elements: cynicism, traditionalism, and regionalism.

Atlantic Canadians have historically been noted for their relative lack of both political efficacy and political trust. But there are curious contradictions in the Atlantic provinces' political culture. While the people of this region have traditionally distrusted politics and politicians and felt incapable of effecting political change, they have continued to invest high amounts of physical, intellectual, and emotional energy in politics. Residents of these four provinces are more politically attuned than are other Canadians. The result is a political culture that was characterized, in the words of former New Brunswick premier Richard Hatfield, as "an unhealthy cynicism."[16]

One of the major reasons for a cynical attitude toward politics in the Atlantic region, and particularly in the Maritimes, is patronage. The tradition of candidates "treating" the voter at election time remains one of the principal forms of patronage in the region. Those who decry these practices (most of whom are either in Central Canada or in academia) are criticized for not understanding the local system and for being naive about the political process. Those who reside in the region wonder whether it is any worse to buy votes with rum and money than it is for a politician to promise new highways, bridges, school cafeterias, hockey rinks, bowling greens, and so forth at election time. One must reluctantly admit that there is a certain validity to their argument. The tradition of "treating" is slowly dying out, although perhaps not as quickly as one might have expected, as evidence from the Nova Scotia election of 1988 illustrates.[17]

Recent events in Nova Scotia, including police investigations and Brian Mulroney's appointment of former Conservative premier John Buchanan to the Senate, have brought about a public outcry for an end to patronage and for a cleaner and more open system of government. The selection of Donald Cameron, in 1992, by the Progressive Conservatives as Buchanan's successor produced a marked change in Nova Scotia politics. Cameron, a known opponent of patronage, opened up the system of government, brought in a new political disclosure law, called for an end to patronage appointments, and initiated a system of open tenders for all government projects.[18] These reforms were popular with the public but not so with some members of his party, who, instead of campaigning, sat on their hands during the last provincial election.

Though a Liberal, John Savage is the logical successor to Cameron. Not only has he continued Cameron's reforms, but he has strengthened them by refusing to replace Tory patronage appointees with Liberal ones. For his pains, Savage has been attacked by members of his own party, who, after fifteen years of Tory rule, believe that they should be entitled to the spoils of office. In early 1994, Savage was successful in beating down the opposition to his "no patronage" policy.

One of the side effects of patronage, and it may have been a factor in the 1987 New Brunswick provincial election, concerns the punishment of constituencies that elect non-government members. Few rural voters wish to be represented by a MLA on the opposition side in the legislature. Consequently, published polls indicating that a certain party is likely to win the election may cause a stampede to the leading party. If the tradition of harassing an opposition constituency continues, perhaps it provides another plank in the argument for banning the publication of pre-election public opinion polls.

Along with voter cynicism, traditionalism is a fact of political life in Atlantic Canada.[19] Evidence of this traditionalism is diverse and can be found in every province: Newfoundland kept the Union Jack as its provincial flag until 1980, and Nova Scotia still flies the Union Jack from Province House; the last two dual-member federal constituencies were in Atlantic Canada; Prince Edward Island retained alcohol prohibition until 1948; the two-party system continues to dominate the region. One might add to this list fear of the impact of the Free Trade Agreement (FTA) as expressed in the results of the 1988 federal election. True, some of the resentment to free trade was based upon the fact that the issue of what constitutes a government subsidy was left to be resolved once the FTA became operative. If the American view—that any and all government subsidies to industries and workers were contrary to the FTA—had prevailed, Atlantic Canadians would have been savagely affected. It would have meant an end to government-assisted regional development programs and relocation grants to workers. This issue appears to have been resolved in the region's favour in the 1993 GATT Agreement, although the Americans still insist that all government subsidies end by 1998. The question of whether the GATT Agreement takes precedence over the FTA or the North American Free Trade Agreement (NAFTA) may still have to be resolved between Canada and the United States.

The region's traditionalism can also be seen in its continued support of the two major political parties. Third parties—particularly the NDP and its forerunner, the Co-operative Commonwealth Federation (CCF)—have not found Atlantic Canada to be fertile soil. Only in Nova Scotia has the NDP had continual, although minuscule, support. In that province, the NDP is currently undergoing a transformation from a party based upon trade union support in Cape Breton to one that is supported by the upwardly mobile younger generation in the Halifax area. In Prince Edward Island, at least until the 1986 election, the NDP candidates in some constituencies received fewer votes than there were spoiled ballots. In Newfoundland, the NDP has done well during by-elections, but, as is so often the case with third parties, has lost the seat at subsequent general elections.

In New Brunswick, both the Parti Acadien and Social Credit have withered and died. The Confederation of Regions (COR) has made inroads among anglophones in southern New Brunswick who are opposed to official bilingualism. In the 1991 provincial election, COR won eight seats and became the official Opposition. The party's support was generally to be found among anglophone public servants and conservative Protestants. Their vote was a negative vote, which unfortunately illustrates the continued backlash against the Acadians' desire to promote their own culture and language. Premier McKenna, like Hatfield and Robichaud before him, deserves credit for taking the unpopular road and stressing New Brunswick's cultural dualism as Canada's only constitutionally recognized bilingual province.

The future of COR is uncertain. The party is divided over leadership and platforms. The official leader of the party is not recognized as the leader of the Opposition within the legislature; this role continues to be held by the former party leader, despite his ouster as head of the party. Perhaps this political comedy over leadership will lead to COR's ultimate demise.

In the federal election of 1993, the Reform Party ran a full slate in Nova Scotia, contested seven of ten ridings in New Brunswick, but fielded only two candidates in Newfoundland and one in Prince Edward Island. No Reform candidate in Atlantic Canada finished higher than third. In New Brunswick, Reform may have influenced the outcome in one seat; the same is true of Nova Scotia. However, given Reform's performance nationally, it could become a significant factor in the future and become the first successful third party in the region.[20]

Yet another example of the region's traditionalism is the overwhelming preponderance of white males in the party elites. Atlantic Canada has been particularly slow to accept the idea of women in politics. Similarly, although there have been Black and First Nations candidates, they have usually run for the New Democratic Party and thus have suffered the same fate as that party in general. But there are positive signs of change in these areas. In 1993, after a riding redistribution that recognized the significant Black minority in Nova Scotia, Wayne Adams became that province's first Black MLA and cabinet minister. This was a significant change for Nova Scotia, a province that has not in the past been known for its tolerance of its Black and Mi'kmaq minorities. In the 1993 general election in Prince Edward Island, both the Liberal and Conservative parties were led by women. Liberal leader Catherine Callbeck became the first women in Canada to be elected as a provincial premier.

Historically, religion has played a prominent role in politics in Atlantic Canada. In Prince Edward Island, as in Newfoundland, the Conservative Party received the support of the majority of Roman Catholics. In Prince Edward Island, the parties were obliged to run a Roman Catholic and a Protestant in many of the dual-member constituencies. In 1994 the Island completed the first major redistribution of seats in the House of Assembly. One of the changes accepted by the House was to abolish all of the dual-member constituencies. The House also decided to cut the number of seats from thirty-two to twenty-seven. Because of these reforms, one suspects that religion will diminish in importance in Island politics, although it will still be a factor.[21] Religion also once played an important role in Nova

Scotia politics, but now modernization seems to have taken precedence, and religion is no longer as important a determinant in the recruitment and selection of candidates as it once was. Until recently, the Nova Scotia Liberal Party continued, almost unbroken, its tradition of alternating leaders between Roman Catholics and Protestants. Religion did not appear to be a factor, however, in the 1992 leadership campaign.

Another sign that Atlantic Canada may be abandoning some of its traditional political practices was in the use of "tele-democracy" by the Nova Scotia Liberals in 1992 to elect John Savage as their leader. This was the first time any political party in the world had used modern telephone technology to select its leader.[22] Thus, to paraphrase Tennyson, "the old order changeth," even in Atlantic Canada.

With the exception of Quebec, nowhere are regional loyalties and love of region so marked in the political process as in Atlantic Canada. Dislike of Central Canada and Central Canadians, love of ancestors, and pride in the provinces characterize the region. Ironically, Atlantic Canadians, unlike Westerners, have never produced a regionally based party that would present a unified voice in Parliament. Easterners have always maintained that it was far more appropriate for them to work through the two major political parties than through any third force. Whether this has been an advantage is debatable.

There is some disagreement about whether Newfoundland and Labrador's political culture should be grouped with that of the Maritimes. There remain many differences between Newfoundland and the Maritime provinces, particularly in the area of policy development. Nonetheless, the gradual demise of the outports has eroded many of the distinctive aspects of Newfoundland political culture, while integration into the Canadian political community has simultaneously reinforced the pervasive traditionalism and cynicism of Newfoundlanders. It appears that Newfoundland's political culture is converging with that of the Maritime provinces.

Traditionally, Newfoundland has had one of the lowest political participation rates in Canada while the Maritimes have had the highest. Here, too, one can see a change: the historically high voter turnout in the Maritimes, particularly in Nova Scotia, is decreasing somewhat, while the percentage of Newfoundlanders who exercise their franchise is increasing.

Party politics in Newfoundland remains remarkably fluid as that province struggles to build a multi-party system out of a predominantly one-party configuration. One of the peculiarities of Newfoundland politics is that it does not seem to be a detriment to move from one party to another. Many prominent Newfoundland politicians, including Brian Peckford, John Crosbie, Leo Barry, Tom Rideout, and Walter Carter have crossed the floor. The outstanding example of this is Carter, who until August 1994 was the Liberal minister of fisheries: he had held the same portfolio in a Conservative administration in which he was a Conservative member of Parliament. In the Maritimes, by contrast, switching parties is virtually a political kiss of death.

INSTITUTIONAL STRUCTURE

The institutional structure of the Atlantic region is similar to that of the rest of the country. Each of the four provinces has a unicameral legislature based upon representation by population. The continued use of dual-member constituencies that distinguished Prince Edward Island from other provinces ended in 1994. The legislatures remain true to the British parliamentary system and their own historical tradition. This is not surprising: Nova Scotia was the first British colony to obtain responsible government in 1847.

Both the Liberals and Progressive Conservatives have strong bases of support in the four provinces. In this dependent hinterland, these two parties are more closely aligned with their federal counterparts than is the case in other regions of Canada. Historically, the Liberals have been the more successful of the two parties: forty years ago one might have called this a "one-party dominant" region. An inspection of more recent election results, at least prior to 1993, illustrates that the parties have become more evenly balanced.

The judicial systems in all four provinces have undergone a form of modernization and much needed reform. This is especially true of Nova Scotia, whose judicial system was subjected to close scrutiny by the royal commission investigating the case of Donald Marshall, a Mi'kmaq wrongfully convicted of murder.[23] In 1990, Nova Scotia appointed an independent prosecutor. Now all of the provinces have a judicial council, and the appointment of provincial judges is becoming less partisan.[24] These reforms are long overdue.

CONCLUSION

Many questions remain to be answered concerning the future of Atlantic Canada. Will the Free Trade Agreement and NAFTA benefit the region? How successful will ACOA be in promoting jobs? What is the future of offshore oil and gas development and the fishery?

All four provinces are saddled with enormous debts and budget deficits.[25] The new fiscal situation means that governments have little or no money to assist most sectors of the economy, including development, education, health, and unemployment. This fact will necessitate a change of attitude in the region toward government and politicians. How this transformation will develop is an open question but, as Frank McKenna has illustrated, the successful evolution of Atlantic Canada from dependency to self-sufficiency is necessary if the region is to relieve its debt load. With the exception of New Brunswick, these provinces may soon be unable to borrow abroad. Their citizens, those who have an income, are burdened with the highest tax rates in Canada. High taxes, large deficits, and federal cutbacks do not bode well for the region's future. Indeed, a dark cloud of economic uncertainty hangs over the region.

Possibly the most important question is the region's relationship with Ottawa. Atlantic Canada has a weak national voice. True, it has had some strong individual representation by people like Allan J. MacEachen and John Crosbie, but representation by population and a weak Senate have not benefitted the region. It is rather surprising that these provinces are not clamouring for Senate reform. A Senate constructed as a voice for the regions could benefit Atlantic Canada.

There is no question that the region requires financial assistance from the federal government. Without programs like equalization, defence establishments, transportation subsidies, and ACOA, Atlantic Canadians would have an even lower standard of living than that enjoyed by other Canadians. This is a dependent hinterland. Yet does this state of dependency mean that a form of clientism and federal feudalism prevails?

Political modernization is a fact of life in the Atlantic provinces. Will modernization open the door to more women, Blacks, and Aboriginal peoples in the political process? If so, will this bring the region closer to the Canadian mainstream? Will changes in society, including more women joining the labour force and the weakening of family ties as people move to urban centres, make it possible for the NDP to break through and become a meaningful participant in the political process? Will the Reform Party become an important political factor?

The fishery remains a pre-eminent concern among Atlantic Canadians. Will the waters of the Atlantic continue to cool? Will American, Canadian, and European fishers continue to rape the fishery? Will those displaced by the collapse of the fishery find new employment? Will fish farming become a viable alternative to their old way of life?

French–English relations remain unresolved. Will COR continue to make inroads in New Brunswick, and perhaps elsewhere, among anglophones opposed to bilingualism, or will the realities of Canadian dualism be accepted as part of the price Atlantic Canadians must pay to live in a federation of which they are major beneficiaries?

Finally, what about Atlantic Canadians' standard of living? Will the changes that are already apparent in the political process mean changes in the quality of life? There is no doubt that the residents of Atlantic Canada, despite their economic and geographic handicap, enjoy a remarkable lifestyle. The respect for family and community and "a sense of place" is very pronounced in these provinces. The residents may dislike Ottawa and "Upper Canadians," but they know their continued existence depends upon federal aid for the region.

There are compensations, as Dalton Camp has stated, for the handicaps experienced by Atlantic Canadians. The major public policy questions for the 1990s and beyond are: Can this lifestyle be maintained while the political economy is being modernized? Will the economic gap between the Atlantic provinces and the rest of Canada ever be closed?

At the same time, it must be stated that Atlantic Canada has become overly dependent upon government hand-outs. All four provincial governments now realize that the traditionalism that has permeated the region must be changed if there is to be any hope of revitalizing the stagnant economy and avoiding the bleak future facing many of its citizens. This is a Canadian problem. Countless federal governments have bought votes in Atlantic Canada with various forms of "pogey" and inappropriate fisheries policies. It is up to the government of Canada to bring about a change in the existing state of dependency in the region by supporting the reformist zeal of figures like Frank McKenna and Clyde Wells, who are proposing radical reforms. These reforms must not fail if the positive aspects of life in Atlantic Canada are to be preserved.

Notes

[1] Dalton Camp, "The Maritimes Revisited" in *An Eclectic Eel* (Ottawa: Deneau, 1981), 113–14.

[2] Data collected by the author from questionnaires distributed to voters in the 1992 Nova Scotia Liberal leadership selection process.

[3] *The Report on Maritime Union: Commissioned by the Three Maritime Governments* (Fredericton, 1970). The commission was chaired by John J. Deutsch.

[4] W.A. Mackintosh, *The Economic Background of Dominion–Provincial Relations*, Carleton Library Series No. 13 (Toronto: McClelland & Stewart, 1964), 153.

[5] The region did receive increased Senate representation when Newfoundland entered Confederation in 1949. Instead of redistributing the existing twenty-four seats as had been done in the West in 1905, six new seats were created. See section 51a of the Constitution Act. Based on population, the region is over-represented in the House of Commons.

[6] An aspect of this situation may be observed whenever the federal minister for regional development is from Quebec. In such circumstances, Atlantic Canadians fear that Quebec concerns will take precedence over their own.

[7] *Halifax Chronicle-Herald*, 3 Oct. 1989, B3.

[8] *Final Report: Royal Commission on Canada's Economic Prospects* (Gordon Report) (Ottawa: Queen's Printer, 1957), 104.

[9] For details on past attempts to promote regional development, see Anthony Careless, *Initiative and Response* (Montreal: McGill-Queen's University Press, 1977), and Donald Savoie, "The Continuing Struggle for Regional Development Policy" in *Canada: The State of the Federation 1985*, ed. Peter Leslie (Kingston, ON: Institute of Intergovernmental Relations, 1986).

[10] *Halifax Chronicle-Herald*, 16 Dec. 1993, 1.

[11] Litton Industries, which had been "asked" by the federal government as part of a contract award to locate in Atlantic Canada, then opened "negotiations" with the other provinces. In the end, they decided that Nova Scotia's inducements were the most attractive and settled close to Halifax.

[12] *Globe and Mail*, 4 Jan. 1994, B4.

[13] Ibid., 6 Jan. 1994, A6.

[14] Ibid., A1 and A6.

[15] *Report on Maritime Union*.

[16] For more details on Atlantic political culture and political parties, see Agar Adamson and Ian Stewart, "Party Politics in Atlantic Canada: Still the Mysterious East?" in *Party Politics in Canada*, 6th ed., ed. Hugh G. Thorburn (Scarborough, ON: Prentice-Hall, 1991).

[17] Following the September 1988 Nova Scotia provincial election, successful prosecutions for vote buying were carried out in Shelburne (rum) and Guysborough (gravel) constituencies.

[18] For a discussion of Donald Cameron's views on patronage, see Jeffrey Simpson, *Spoils of Power: The Politics of Patronage* (Toronto: Collins, 1988), ch. 8. Simpson gives a good description in chapters 6 through 9 of patronage in Atlantic Canada.

[19] Another aspect of the region's conservatism is that it has the lowest bankruptcy rate in Canada. People are unwilling to take a chance in business.

[20] Preston Manning's Parliamentary Chief of Staff, Steve Greene, was Reform's candidate in Halifax. His position should help Reform develop policies attractive to Atlantic Canadians.

[21] The redistribution in PEI was forced on the politicians by the court, which had agreed with a group of citizens that the old redistribution was in conflict with the Charter.

As the next election will not take place until 1996 or 1997, it is too early to say exactly how the new electoral map will impact on the role of religion. Some seats may, by unwritten consent, become Catholic or Protestant seats. This was the situation in Nova Scotia for a number of years following the redistribution of the late 1960s. An independent redistribution commission in Newfoundland and Labrador has also recommended that the number of districts be reduced from fifty-two to forty-five. The minister in charge says that the government supports the recommendations, but it has yet to introduce the required legislation. The argument in favour of reduction centres around deficit reduction.

[22] For details on "tele-democracy" and the 1992 Liberal convention, see Agar Adamson, Bruce Beaton, and Ian Stewart, "Pressing the Right Buttons: The Nova Scotia Liberals and Tele-Democracy" (paper presented at the Canadian Political Science Association, 1993).

[23] For details on this issue, see *Report of the Royal Commission on the Donald Marshall Jr. Prosecution* (Halifax: Province of Nova Scotia, 1989).

[24] Judicial councils are composed, in most cases, of judges and a few senior lawyers. It is the job of the councils to act as a watchdog for the public and as a complaints body on the performance of judges. The councils have the power to discipline and, in some cases, dismiss judges.

[25] The estimated provincial deficits for the four Atlantic provinces in 1994 are (in millions of dollars) Nova Scotia—$904; New Brunswick—$349; Newfoundland—$223; and Prince Edward Island— $52. *Toronto Star*, 24 Dec. 1993, B4. In 1993–94, Nova Scotia spent 21.7 cents of every dollar raised on debt charges. In New Brunswick, the rate is 14.6 cents, for Newfoundland 16 cents, while in PEI it is 15 cents. The national average is 13.7 cents. It is not surprising that New Brunswick has the best credit rating in the region. See *Halifax Chronicle-Herald*, 19 Aug. 1994, D1.

SUGGESTED READING

Adamson, Agar, and Ian Stewart. "Party Politics in Atlantic Canada: Still the Mysterious East?" In *Party Politics in Canada*. 6th ed. Ed. Hugh Thorburn. Scarborough, ON: Prentice-Hall, 1991.
A study of the political culture, political parties, and elections in the four provinces.

Adamson, Agar, Bruce Beaton, and Ian Stewart. "Pressing the Right Buttons: The Nova Scotia Liberals and Tele-Democracy." Paper presented at the Canadian Political Science Association, 1993.
This paper is a detailed study, based upon survey research, of the 1992 Liberal leadership selection process.

Bickerton, James P. *Nova Scotia, Ottawa and the Politics of Regional Development*. Toronto: University of Toronto Press, 1990.
A detailed study of regional development in Nova Scotia, unfortunately predating ACOA.

Fairley, Bryant, Colin Leys, and James Sacouman, eds. *Restructuring and Resistance: Perspectives from Atlantic Canada*. Toronto: Garamond Press, 1990.

Matthews, Ralph. *The Creation of Regional Dependency*. Toronto: University of Toronto Press, 1983.
A key work on dependency theory and regional development. This is one of the strongest critiques of the "establishment" and its approach to regional development.

Mandel, Maurice, ed. *Atlantic Canada Today*. Halifax: Formac, 1987.
Although now somewhat dated, this work describes in detail the economy of the Atlantic region.

Savoie, Donald J. *Regional Economic Development: Canada's Search for Solutions*. 2nd ed. Toronto: University of Toronto Press, 1992.
Savoie's research was the basis for ACOA. His work on regional development is without equal. Savoie is one of the most lucid writers on regional development. His approach, unlike that of Matthews, is more bureaucratic and pro-establishment.

Tomblin, Stephen G. "The Council of Maritime Premiers and the Battle for Territorial Integrity." Paper presented at Canadian Political Science Association, 1988.
This paper, which can be found in the 1988 edition of the CPSA papers, discusses the Council of Maritime Premiers and gives an analysis of the council's performance and effectiveness.

Young, R.A. "Teaching and Research in Maritime Politics: Old Stereotypes and New Directions." In *Teaching Maritime Studies*. Ed. P.A. Buckner. Fredericton: Acadiensis Press, 1986.
A sound introduction to the various aspects of modernization in Atlantic Canada. Young's argument has not diminished with age.

Guy Lachapelle

5

THE RISE OF QUEBEC DEMOCRACY

ince 1960, democratic procedures have increasingly become the pre-vailing force within Quebec and have led to noteworthy social, polit-ical, and economic changes. The achievement of political democracy has been, especially for French-speaking Quebeckers, a long and painstaking process. Quebeckers began their democratic journey two centuries ago, and they have become increasingly comfortable deciding what direction that journey should take.

In each period of their history—the colonial pre-democratic era (1761–1867); the tutelary democracy period, during which the Catholic Church kept the people under its protection (1867–1960); and the modern democratic period (1960–)—Quebeckers have faced unique challenges. During some periods, countervailing forces were successful in maintaining the values of the status quo, but the search for greater equality was at the heart of the discussion.

French-speaking Quebeckers first faced the challenge of preserving their identity and culture when their links with France were severed and the province was subjected to assimilationist policies of various British gov-ernors. Egalitarian principles were usually absent from political decisions. The House of Assembly, which was created in 1791, was the first vehicle used to fight assimilation and to struggle for responsible government. The defeat of the Patriots in the Rebellions of 1837–38 and the demise of their reformist, secular, and state-oriented nationalism allowed the church to extend its control over Quebec society.

The church was a powerful opponent of any Quebec politician who favoured state intervention in society. It represented the prevailing ideol-ogy, which argued that the freedom of the individual had to be respected and that any government intervention would restrict and impede the development of this freedom. It further maintained that any person or group for whom the state took responsibility would have fewer personal social responsibilities. The church proclaimed the risk of the welfare state turning into a dictatorship in the field of social policy and public assistance programs. Beyond this rhetoric, it is clear that the Catholic Church feared increasing government intervention because it threatened the church's hegemony in society.[1]

Quebeckers rejected the tutelary democracy established by the church and its supporting elites by electing Jean Lesage as premier in 1960. This marked the beginning of a period of great cultural effervescence and led to the formation of modern Quebec democracy, which excluded religion from the public sphere.

These phenomena encouraged a transformation of society in many areas.

1. The secularization of attitudes.
Quebec society contested the conservative ideology promoted by the Catholic Church and became receptive to new ideologies.

2. The secularization of institutions.
Institutions changed to enhance the participation of citizens in political and social life. The state replaced the church as overseer of reforms to enhance citizens' participation in the social, political, and economic sectors. The advancement of democratic rule would be attained when all groups and classes in society were represented in the policy-making process.

3. Policy change.
Reforms were initiated to enable Quebec to attain an economic level comparable to other industrialized nations and to make it possible for Quebec to compete in the global economy;

4. Cultural, education, and language reforms.
Public policies were developed to support the uniqueness of Quebec's identity in North America, enhancing the development of French culture without impeding economic growth.

5. A reassessment of collective rights versus individual rights.
This period saw a struggle to balance collective rights (which direct governmental action) and individual rights, which might be harmed by inappropriate policies. If the sovereignty of the majority is a democratic principle, it should not be at the expense of minority rights.

The years since 1960 can be broken into distinct periods characterized by different policy emphasis. The first phase emphasized Quebec's development and control of its own social policies. That led the Bourassa government to ultimately reject the constitutional agreement that had been reached at a first ministers conference in Victoria in 1971.[2] The second period stressed political and parliamentary democracy. It began with the creation of the Parti Québécois in 1968 and continued with parliamentary and electoral reforms initiated in the 1970s. The 1980s focused on developing the economic strength of francophones through increased entrepreneurship in the province. One of the key elements in this period was to rectify the marginal role played by francophones in ownership and management of the economy.

Successive Quebec governments have sought to enhance democratic opportunities in all areas of Quebec society. As in most industrialized societies, none of the democratic stages has been fully realized in Quebec. Each stage was characterized by conflict over policy issues—social (collective/individual rights, distribution of wealth), political (national priorities, foreign policy), and economic (producers/buyers, owners/ workers)—that have shaped the path of Quebec politics.

This chapter focuses on the social, political, and economic dimensions of Quebec democracy and how public policy choices have shaped Quebec society. The first section looks at the essence of the Quiet Revolution, which was the driving force behind the democratization of Quebec society. The second section asks why federalism is perceived by many Quebeckers as an inhibitor of Quebec's democratic evolution. The conclusion assesses how the constitutional instability in which we live has threatened the gains made toward full democracy.

THE QUIET REVOLUTION:
THE RISE OF MODERN DEMOCRACY

During the Quiet Revolution, many new social forces converged to determine Quebec's future.[3] Norms and values that had previously dominated Quebec culture gave way, signalling the end of a *survivance* mentality. Religion yielded its place as the intellectual and social point of reference. For all of those Quebeckers who had waited for the end of the seemingly indestructable Duplessis regime, the election of new political leaders in 1960s brought fundamental change.

The nature of this change continues to provoke discussion. For some, the Quiet Revolution was a normal step toward modernization; Quebec was simply attempting to catch up economically with Ontario and the United States. Since the province had been lagging in many sectors, the state was used as a means to generate economic development. Those who favour this perspective argue that Quebec's social, political, and economic changes have been minimal. Some argue that the secularization of Quebec institutions has never been completed and that Quebec nationalism is still tainted by religious values.[4] Others maintain that the catching-up process initiated during the Quiet Revolution was economically ineffectual: in fact, Quebec's industrialization, which had followed that of Ontario's until the beginning of the 1960s, was delayed.[5] The same critics conclude that the modernization process of the Quiet Revolution compromised ongoing industrialization, which could later have financed social progress and democracy. Other scholars argue that the Quiet Revolution did not stop Quebec's economic marginalization. Moreover, they point out that the recent movement in favour of less state intervention, characterized by the privatization process, could also inhibit Quebec's economic growth.

At the beginning of the 1970s, some Quebeckers questioned the accomplishments of the Quiet Revolution. They argued that the implementation of democratic rules had not led to any major social change[6] and that more fundamental political changes were needed. They viewed the election of Liberal Robert Bourassa in 1970 as a backward step. The election of the Parti Québécois in 1976 was to them a clear sign that Quebeckers wanted to continue to pursue the goals of the Quiet Revolution.

Hubert Guindon views Jean Lesage's Liberal government, with its emphasis on state intervention in fields such as education, health, and economic development, as the instrument of a new petite bourgeoisie to acquire greater control over Quebec society and to consolidate its dominant role within that society.[7] This interpretation has been echoed by others who, based on an analysis of the growth of state expenditures between 1945 and 1970, argue that the great reforms of the Quiet Revolution were almost decided under Mauriece Duplessis.[8] Indeed, more recently, some authors have suggested that the Duplessis regime, especially after the Second World War, was not as reactionary as is claimed by champions of the Quiet Revolution.[9] This interpretation is often followed by a hypothetical question: If Paul Sauvé, Duplessis' successor, had not died after one hundred days in power, what would have happened to the Quiet Revolution?

Other observers like Kenneth McRoberts believe that fundamental changes have occurred. As evidence, they cite Quebec's new political scene, the decline in the birth rate, the new face of Quebec nationalism, and the institutional changes that have led to educational and social reforms, nationalization of the province's hydro-electric industry, and a more affirmative role for Quebec in the international scene.

My interpretation of the Quiet Revolution is that the changes that occurred were characterized by four key elements:

1. the development of new state functions, which led to an important growth of the financial capacity of the Quebec state;
2. an intensified role for the state in the economy;
3. a redefining of state priorities in terms of policy making;
4. the stagnation or loss of momentum of initial reforms by 1965.[10]

Thus, there is no agreement on the nature, source, or extent of changes in Quebec society after 1960.[11] Nor is there agreement on which indicators most accurately reflect those changes. Yet, if the Quiet Revolution is essentially the transformation of the role of the state in all spheres of Quebec society, we should then be able to measure that transformation.

It is important to note that budgetary changes have both short- and long-term effects. Table 1 indicates the growth of the Quebec state before and after 1960. From 1945 to 1960, expenditures in constant dollars multiplied by 4.5, while from 1960 to 1980 they multiplied by 7.6. Duplessis took seven years, between 1945 and 1952, to double the size of the provincial budget; the Lesage government did it in four years. Among all the periods that have been studied, the most important growth in state expenditures was between 1961 and 1965. After this interval, the pace remained strong until 1976. It was only after 1980 that growth in expenditures was significantly limited.

The role of the state in the economy increased continuously from 1945, if we look at its contribution as part of gross domestic product. The greatest increase was during the 1960–80 period. After 1980, there was almost no change. The question is whether there was a decline in the pace of state intervention after 1965. The data in table 1 indicate that the growth of state expenditures slackened from 1965 up until 1980. Total governmental expenditures were almost twice as high from 1960 to 1980 than they were between 1945 and 1960, both in constant and real dollars.

Another indicator of economic change is the number of state enterprises that were created. While the number of public boards increased, it did so mainly after 1966. This can probably be explained by the time lag necessary to create such enterprises. In many cases, the institutional instruments—the creation of new departments and boards—that were put in place following policy decisions necessitated the implementation of complex organizations and bureaucratic structures. The creation of state-owned

TABLE 1

Quebec State Expenditures, 1945–1990 (millions of $)

	Total expenditures (real $)	Total expenditures (constant 1981 $)	Total expenditures (per capita)	% of the gross domestic product
1945	91.1	545.5	136.4	3.0
1946	110.6	639.3	159.9	3.5
1947	148.1	787.8	196.0	4.0
1948	207.3	977.8	242.6	4.9
1949	178.8	809.0	200.2	4.0
1950	210.3	930.4	229.8	4.3
1951	244.9	971.8	237.0	4.2
1952	297.3	1134.7	270.2	4.5
1953	293.5	1120.2	260.5	4.3
1954	329.2	1237.6	281.3	4.6
1955	378.8	1413.4	314.1	5.0
1956	412.6	1484.2	322.7	4.9
1957	470.5	1656.7	352.7	5.3
1958	506.0	1756.9	373.8	5.6
1959	576.8	1961.9	408.7	6.0
1960	722.9	2434.0	496.8	7.2
1961	815.9	2728.8	524.8	7.7
1962	910.6	3005.3	567.0	7.9
1963	1043.7	3377.7	625.5	8.5
1964	1367.7	4314.5	784.5	10.0
1965	1778.3	5421.6	968.1	11.9
1966	2018.9	5868.9	1011.9	12.1
1967	2381.1	6651.1	1146.7	13.2
1968	2661.3	7173.3	1215.9	13.9
1969	3057.1	7879.1	1335.5	14.5
1970	3525.5	8683.5	1447.3	15.7
1971	4377.7	10448.0	1741.3	18.0
1972	4926.3	11120.3	1853.4	18.1
1973	5545.5	11505.2	1886.1	17.9
1974	6972.0	12653.3	2074.3	19.2

TABLE 1 - (continued)

	Total expenditures (real $)	Total expenditures (constant 1981 $)	Total expenditures (per capita)	% of the gross domestic product
1975	8391.4	13847.2	2233.4	20.5
1976	9710.6	14757.8	2380.3	20.4
1977	11442.3	16369.5	2640.2	21.9
1978	12652.9	17052.4	2706.7	21.8
1979	14242.2	17453.7	2770.4	22.0
1980	16667.7	18489.7	2934.9	23.1
1981	18678.3	18678.3	2918.5	22.9
1982	20328.7	18701.7	2922.1	23.6
1983	22497.2	19717.1	3080.8	24.4
1984	23126.5	20268.7	3167.0	22.9
1985	24611.5	20223.1	3111.2	22.6
1986	25699.5	20510.4	3155.4	21.5
1987	27972.6	21385.8	3250.1	22.7
1988	28866.6	21225.4	3225.7	22.8
1989	29880.2	21131.7	3206.6	22.9
1990	31403.3	21348.3	3234.6	23.4

Source: James I. Gow, "Les dépenses du gouvernement du Québec, 1867–1970"
(Department of Political Science, Université de Montréal, Research Paper No. 5);
Gouvernement du Québec, Le Québec statistique, 1986; Budget Speech, 1987–1990;
Statistics Canada, Financial Statistics of Provincial Government, Cat. 68-207.

enterprises and the use of the Caisse de dépôt et placement du Québec are just some examples of the increasing role of the Quebec state within the economy. The Caisse was created when Quebec opted out of the Canada Pension Plan. Through its investment policies, it has contributed greatly to the consolidation of a francophone business elite.

The number of public employees increased rapidly after 1960. Before the early 1960s, qualified personnel were scarce. The nature and practices of the Duplessis government no doubt discouraged some of the most qualified university graduates. After the Civil Service Act of 1965 was passed, the Quebec bureaucracy became more efficient and better coordinated, providing public-sector employees with better training and thus the competence and confidence to face new challenges. Between 1961 and 1987, the number of public servants in Quebec grew steadily, as table 2 illustrates. There was also a continuous increase in the number of public servants per 100 000 population until 1977. Between 1978 and 1987, while there were fluctuations with a 1984 peak, there was no per capita growth.

The Quebec state thus began to intervene more and more in many sectors of the economy not only because of its increasing financial capacity but also because of its increasing bureaucratic capacity. The state extended its role in Quebec society by entering areas where the Duplessis government had refused to tread. Thus, during the Quiet Revolution, growth in government capacity and state intervention became more visible.[12] Such a transfer of authority and power from the unregulated private sector to the state is a characteristic of modern democracy.

EMANCIPATION OF SOCIAL THOUGHT AND DEVELOPMENT OF SOCIAL WELFARE POLICIES

The conservative nationalism of Premier Duplessis posed the biggest obstacle to the development of social democracy in Quebec. But by the late 1940s, the government was increasingly subject to criticism from forces within Quebec. In 1948, a group of artists led by Alfred Pellan issued the manifesto *Prisme d'Yeux*. Their goal was to express themselves without being controlled by ideology or restricted by social barriers. *Refus global*, written by painter Paul-Émile Borduas, was published the same year. It contained a sweeping history of the Quebec nation revolting against a society where the church had full control over what to say, to think, to write, and to paint. By the 1950s, progressive forces—artists, unions, intellectuals, the media (especially Montreal's *Le Devoir*), Laval University's social science faculty, and even some segments of the church—were mounting concerted attacks on the conservative forces and ills of Quebec society that the Duplessis regime had come to symbolize. During this same time, the federal government was focusing on creating laws concerning the health and welfare of Canadians. Duplessis responded strongly by rejecting the centralizing objectives of the federal government as an affront to provincial autonomy.

In 1954, Duplessis created the Tremblay Commission, the mandate of which focused on the evolution of Canadian federalism and on federal–provincial relations since the Second World War.[13] In its report, the commission recommended that the federal government acknowledge provincial jurisdiction in certain matters, including welfare, health, and

TABLE 2

The Growth of the Public Sector, 1961–1987

	Number	Per 100 000 population	Index (1961=100)
1961	60 980ª	1 160	100
1962	65 476ª	1 219	105
1963	69 870ª	1 275	110
1964	74 191ª	1 329	115
1965	78 206	1 376	119
1966	83 382	1 442	124
1967	91 484	1 560	135
1968	92 623	1 562	135
1969	98 886	1 652	142
1970	93 648	1 557	134
1971	99 279	1 647	142
1972	100 742	1 664	144
1973	107 788	1 773	153
1974	110 182	1 800	155
1975	112 383	1 819	157
1976	114 295	1 833	158
1977	126 036	2 006	173
1978	135 406	2 148	185
1979	132 800	2 095	181
1980	135 754	2 126	183
1981	129 670	2 014	174
1982	134 971	2 083	180
1983	131 153	2 011	173
1984	155 206	2 370	204
1985	153 996	2 340	202
1986	149 863	2 291	198
1987	141 468	2 146	185

ª Estimated values

Source: Simon Langlois et al., eds., La société québécoise en tendances, 1960–1990 (Quebec: Institut québécois de recherche sur la culture, 1990), 326.

education, and provide each province with the financial means to fulfil these responsibilities. The report also expressed concern that too great a centralization of power in the hands of the federal government would have an adverse effect on the Canadian political structure.[14]

The election of Jean Lesage in 1960 marked the emergence of a health-care and social security program specific to Quebec. The introduction of the Hospitalization Act in 1961 was the beginning of a series of health-care laws that culminated in the creation of a health insurance plan by the Bourassa government in 1971. The health-care initiatives of the Lesage government are far more important than one might imagine. Besides bringing major changes to the organization of medical services in Quebec, these initiatives are also recognized by some as the main impetus behind the Quiet Revolution. Certainly, Lesage's plan dealt a huge blow to the power and influence of the church in regard to Quebec's social policy. Until the 1960s, the majority of hospitals in Quebec were owned by religious institutions. Confronted with a decline in their own capacities and facing the resolve of the Quebec government to nationalize the operation of health-care services, these religious institutions agreed to partially withdraw from the area of health care in exchange for monetary compensation.

In 1961, facing an increase in social assistance costs, the Lesage government created the Boucher Commission on public assistance, with a mandate to review the social security system in Quebec. After documenting the lack of response to the needs of the Quebec population by successive Quebec governments, the Boucher Report made four suggestions concerning the renovation of Quebec's entire social policy.

1. The provision of social security and assistance should not be considered a charity, but rather a right to which all persons in need are entitled.
2. Social policies could be combined with economic policies.
3. A general philosophy of universality and equal services should guide all social programs in Quebec.
4. The report strongly recommended that the Quebec government acknowledge its responsibilities in welfare policy.

The Boucher Report marked an important step in the development of an integrated social security program by the Quebec government.

A few months after its election in 1963, the Pearson government in Ottawa proposed to the provinces the establishment of a universal pension plan that would replace all existing programs. Lesage pointed out that a universal pension plan would mean the intrusion of the federal government into a field in which the Boucher Commission had just recommended a greater role for Quebec. He thus unequivocally declared that Quebec would never accept the federal proposal, but rather that Quebec would create its own pension plan. Such a plan would require a rapid accumulation of capital and would create massive funds for investment. Taking into account the sums involved, the Quebec government created a para-governmental agency to manage the funds. Thus, the idea of the Caisse de dépôt et placement was developed. The actual purpose of pensions—to ensure greater security for retired people—quickly became secondary to the political struggle between the federal and Quebec governments both for legislative control and for control over the vast moneys associated with the pension plan.

During a federal–provincial conference from 31 March to 2 April 1965, the Quebec and federal governments were mutually antagonistic. It was only after secret discussions between federal minister Maurice Sauvé and a highly placed Quebec civil servant, Claude Morin, that an agreement was reached. On 20 April, two pension plans were introduced: one for Quebec and a federal program for the other nine provinces. The Quebec Pension Plan is managed entirely by the Quebec government while the Canada Pension Plan is administered by the federal government. The idea that this represents a victory for "co-operative federalism" is somewhat weak; it appears, rather, to constitute a firm acknowledgment of the "legislative primacy" of Quebec in social security matters.

In 1966, the newly elected Liberal premier, Daniel Johnson, appointed a task force on health and social welfare (the Castonguay Commission). In one of its reports, the commission emphasized that social security could not only be used to prevent the effects of an economic crisis, but could contribute to the social as well as economic development of a Quebec state.[15] During a federal–provincial conference held in February 1968, Premier Johnson asked for nothing less than total control over Quebec's social welfare, in particular, family allowances, unemployment insurance, and old age pensions.

Tensions within the Quebec Liberal Party increased following its electoral defeat in 1966. In light of the constitutional demands of the new Union nationale government, the Liberal Party began to review its own constitutional position. At its 1967 convention, the party split into two factions. One side, which supported the Gérin-Lajoie Report, favoured a redefinition of federal–provincial powers within the Canadian political system.[16] The other, headed by René Lévesque, who had been minister of social affairs in the Liberal government, proposed that Quebec seek political sovereignty while maintaining economic ties with Canada. Bitter debate culminated in a vote in which Lévesque's proposal was soundly trounced, and he and his followers walked out of the convention. In the fall of 1967, Lévesque and his supporters joined to create the Mouvement souveraineté-association.

The Gérin-Lajoie Report used the "distinct society" notion for the first time, and the concept began to serve as the cornerstone to increase the power of Quebec and to grant it a special status in the Canadian federation. The report also stated that it was necessary for Quebec to take more responsibility in policy fields such as language, culture, immigration, employment, and training. It suggested that collective rights be entrenched in the Canadian constitution and that Quebec should have its own internal constitution. The election of Pierre Trudeau as prime minister and the selection of Robert Bourassa as leader of the Quebec Liberal Party ended discussions over the new constitutional package offered by the Quebec Liberal Party.

During the 1968–71 period, the efforts of the federal government were directed toward reforming the Canadian constitution, and the struggle for control over social security was at the core of all political discussions between Quebec and Ottawa. In 1969, the federal government published a document completely rejecting Quebec's demand for control over social policy. It even threatened to revoke the province's control over old age pensions, which meant taking back the gains made during the 1965 negotiations on the Quebec/Canada pension plans.[17] The discussions seemed destined to fail as the Bourassa government stood firm against the federal government's attempts to manage Quebec's pension plan. Ultimately, the disagreement led to the refusal of Bourassa to join the constitutional agreement tentatively reached in 1971.

THE RISE OF POLITICAL DEMOCRACY

Under the Duplessis regime, political rights were merely formal, and they masked the compulsion and inequality that reigned in the social realm. Major strikes at Asbestos and at the CBC clearly exposed the barriers that confronted workers of the 1950s in their quest for more political and economic rights. It was understood that to have more substantial influence over rival forces workers must organize themselves and act as a collective force. The repression imposed by Duplessis incited a tendency toward violence in labour disputes, which continued even into the 1960s and 1970s.

For those Quebeckers who favoured socialist or social democratic alternatives, choices had to be made whether to seek the advancement of democratic rule through political institutions, or to confront capitalism directly to induce reforms. The disagreement between progressive and more radical forces in Quebec society was at the heart of the debate in the 1960s about the use of representative democracy as opposed to violent political action. The Front de libération du Québec (FLQ), which began its activities in the early 1960s and had disappeared by the early 1970s, was born of mingled hope and despair by a handful of young people dedicated to the realization of Quebec independence. The October Crisis of 1970 was the beginning of the end for the FLQ. The federal government declared the War Measures Act after the FLQ kidnapped James Cross, a British diplomat, and provincial minister Pierre Laporte. Under the act, over 450 people were arrested and civil liberties were suspended. The position taken by René Lévesque and Claude Ryan during the October Crisis, pitting democratic rights and civil liberties against the more rigid approach adopted by Pierre Trudeau and Marc Lalonde, also helped to mobilize the unification of democratic forces in Quebec. The declaration of Pierre Vallières, a prominant "revolutionary," proclaiming the Parti Québécois as a force capable of attaining greater liberty ended all discussions about the legitimacy of using terrorist means to achieve greater democracy.

The role of the political parties, especially of the Parti Québécois, in achieving greater democracy was an important outcome of the October Crisis. The debate led by André Larocque in the PQ in 1972, with regard to its role and nature, is also an example of how political democracy can be achieved. The debate questioned whether the objective of the Parti Québécois should be just to win the next election or to operate as a social force unifying and directing all social and political groups in Quebec toward a common social purpose. The "electoralist" group won the debate and proposed to the PQ membership that independence would be implemented only after a referendum.

Another important issue in Quebec was the need to increase the participation of women in the political process. Quebec was the last province in Canada to enfranchise women. Although women in Quebec were granted the right to vote in federal elections after 1918, they did not win this right at the provincial level until 1940. Many interest groups and prominent leaders in Quebec lobbied for the franchise for women, but such reform was impossible under Duplessis. In 1940, the Liberal Party won the election and modified the electoral act to include women. The first woman candidate in Quebec ran in a by-election in 1947. The first woman to run in a general election did so in 1952.

Political progress for women has been slow. Even today the proportion of women candidates tends to be larger in fringe parties than in mainstream

TABLE 3

Women Candidates in General Quebec Elections, 1960–1989

Election year	Number of women candidates	Total number of candidates	Women as % of total number of candidates	Total number of elected candidates	Total number of women elected	Elected women as % of total number of elected candidates
	(N)	(N)	(%)	(N)	(N)	(%)
1960	1	253	—	95	0	—
1962	3	224	1.3	95	1	1.1
1966	11	418	2.6	108	1	0.9
1970	9	466	1.9	108	1	0.9
1973	25	479	5.2	110	1	0.9
1976	47	556	8.5	110	5	4.5
1981	83	525	15.8	122	8	6.6
1985	132	666	19.8	122	18	14.8
1989	121	557	21.7	125	23	18.4

Sources: Pierre Drouilly and Jocelyne Dorion, Candidates, députées et ministres: les femmes et les élections (Quebec: Bibliothèque de l'Assemblée Nationale, 1988), 44.

Directeur général des élections du Québec, Rapport des résultats officiels du scrutin du 25 septembre 1989.

parties. As table 3 illustrates, the participation of women in the political realm has increased steadily since 1960, but the total number of women appointed as ministers remains relatively low. Only five women were appointed to the cabinet of Robert Bourassa when the Liberal Party was elected in 1989.

The women's movement in Quebec is not concerned solely with political rights. In 1978, a publication by the provincial Conseil de Statut de la Femme, *Pour les Québécoise: égalité ou indépendence*, summarized the demands of various women's groups in Quebec: in addition to political rights, they demanded access to education, economic integration, and legal equality. The economic crisis of the early 1980s brought economic issues, particularly those affecting single mothers, to the fore, and today economic equality remains a central goal of the women's movement in Quebec.

Since 1960, Quebec has moved to improve its electoral legislation. Gerrymandering is no longer possible as electoral district boundaries are defined by an independent commission. No longer are elections held year after year under the same, increasingly obsolete electoral map. Remapping of districts is done after each election to keep pace with the electorate's geographical mobility. A rule that there can be no more than a 25 percent difference in the population of electoral ridings is used to ensure equality of representation while taking into account the particular geographical and sociological traits of a region or constituency.

Problems with petty and large-scale patronage have been addressed by regulations pertaining to party and campaign spending, limitations on individual contributions, the disclosure of contributors donating $100 or more, the introduction of public financing, and the ban on contributions from corporations. Eliminating the financial dependency of political parties on private corporations was at the core of reforming party financing.

Other factors have also contributed to the making of more democratic and honest governments in Quebec. First, governments can no longer award contracts to party associates and financial backers. Government contracts exceeding $10 000 must be assigned to the lowest bidder in a public tendering process. In 1965, the Public Service Commission was created, which enabled the province to recruit well-trained and competent civil servants shielded from the pressures and interventions of elected politicians. Recruitment is based on skill and expertise as assessed by an entrance examination. Jobs are clearly defined and there are classification levels to fit one's capabilities. Promotions depend on objective criteria, and firing can no longer be at the whim of a politician. Once workers enter the public service, they fall under the aegis of the Public Service Commission, an independent body with its own set of rules. Public servants are unionized, have the right to strike if they maintain essential services, and gain job security after a probation period. Thus, an individual can pursue a career path unobstructed by patronage or other forms of political intervention. This is not to say that favouritism and corruption no longer exist in Quebec, but there is no doubt that the democratic practices of government have undergone a major change since the Duplessis era.

THE RISE OF FRANCOPHONE CONTROL
OF THE ECONOMY

In the economic field, the Quiet Revolution cannot be restricted to the short period from 1960 to 1966. Most observers would agree that there were no significant ruptures in policy after the Liberal's defeat in 1966. The various governments that came into power during the following two decades shared a common vision of Quebec's future. Irrespective of party denomination, they pursued the same course that the Liberals had initiated in the 1960s. This vision, brought about by the Quiet Revolution, sought to rectify specific economic problems.

In 1960, Quebec francophones controlled very little of their province's economy and had only limited equality of opportunity. The primary objective of the Quiet Revolution's pioneers was to promote a greater francophone presence in Quebec's economy, be it the private or public sector. State-owned enterprises were created to guarantee francophone control in the public sector.

The greatest accomplishment of the Quiet Revolution is the partial amelioration of Quebec francophones' marginal involvement in the direction of their economy, both in terms of ownership and management. According to Marc Levine, in 1985 bilingual francophones in Montreal represented 62.3 percent of the well-paid jobs in the labour force compared to only 41.0 percent in 1961 (see table 4).

In other areas—for example, the marginalization of Quebec's economy within the Canadian economy as a whole—the problems have worsened. Regional economic disparities within Canada are still enormous, while disparities within Quebec have either increased or remained steady, depending on which indicators are used. Dependency on foreign investments seems to have decreased significantly, but in international trade Quebec is more reliant than ever on the American market, which accounts for almost three-quarters of Quebec's total exports (see table 5). The sources of its imports are somewhat more diversified. Nonetheless, it is evident that the Quiet Revolution did not resolve all of Quebec's economic difficulties.

TABLE 4

Linguistic Composition of Well-Paid Montreal
Labour Force, 1961–1985

| | | % of Total Labour Force | | |
	1985	1961	1970	1980
Francophones	44.0	54.3	71.3	75.4
Unilingual	3.0	7.6	11.8	13.1
Bilingual	41.0	46.7	59.5	62.3
Anglophones	56.0	45.7	28.7	24.6
Unilingual	32.0	23.8	10.4	7.8
Bilingual	24.0	21.8	18.3	16.8

Source: Marc Levine, The Reconquest of Montreal: Language
Policy and Social Change in a Bilingual City (Philadelphia:
Temple University Press, 1990), 197.

TABLE 5

Quebec's International Exports and Imports:
The American Share, 1976–1989

Year	Exports to the U.S. in % of total exports	Imports from the U.S. in % of total imports
1976	62.8	41.2
1977	65.0	43.5
1978	65.0	45.6
1979	63.8	51.3
1980	59.9	51.5
1981	65.0	46.4
1982	64.5	47.1
1983	69.6	53.1
1984	75.1	52.7
1985	75.8	50.5
1986	77.5	49.0
1987	77.3	47.5
1988	75.3	45.3
1989	72.8	45.0

Source: Gouvernement du Québec, Bureau de la Statistique du
Québec, 1990. Commerce International du Québec.

CANADIAN FEDERALISM AND
QUEBEC DEMOCRACY

Does Canadian federalism promote or impede democratic politics in Quebec?[18] This question is central because many Quebeckers have felt that federalism limits the majority will in Quebec. Their reaction to the failure of the Meech Lake and Charlottetown accords is the most recent example of this attitude. Quebeckers themselves voted against the Charlottetown Accord. They felt that the strong opposition to the "distinct society" clause in the rest of the country, as well as the fact that the clause was left to the interpretation of the courts, was sufficient to raise suspicion about the real intent of the accord. Some critics interpreted the fact that the reference to "distinct society" was ultimately included in the Canada clause as a rejection of Quebec demands. In comparison to what the Gérin-Lajoie Report had demanded, Quebec demands in the Charlottetown Accord negotiations seemed minimal.

The multiplicity of decision centres in any federal system makes it very difficult for the federal government to reach a consensus with the various political actors to attain important political objectives such as a reduction in the social and economic inequalities between regions. The failure, from a Quebec perspective, of all constitutional discussions in the 1980s— the repatriation of the constitution in 1982, the Meech Lake Accord in 1990, and the Charlottetown Agreement in 1992—illustrates the complexity of finding a compromise between competing regional interests. In the Canadian political system, there is strong competition between the levels of government as they attempt to voice their policy preferences. As Robert L. Lineberry writes, "Too many governments, each with the power to delay, veto or undercut policies, may make policy implementation difficult"[19] and can lead to stagnation.

Has Canada reached a level of political stagnation? Many Quebeckers believe so. They feel that the federal government's use of its spending and taxation power, especially in higher education and health care, thwarts the province's public policies and affects decision making. Many consider federal transfer payments as merely a political tool used to gain support instead of achieving greater harmonization in policy fields.

The argument given by federalists who believe in a strong central government in Ottawa is that too much decentralization without some degree of government authority cannot be effective. When there are too many strong governments, public policies are either never passed or never implemented. Intergovernmental transfer payments and sources of revenues are seen, from this viewpoint, as a means of affecting policy decisions at another level of government. Consequently, the Canadian federalists claim that non-fragmented or centralized governments are the "best" political structures for preventing hyperpluralistic stagnation.[20] By arguing that centralized political systems are the more efficient type of government, Canadian federalists support the view that political stability can be achieved only in a less fragmented society. Therefore, they suggest that a federal structure is the optimum political structure for achieving harmony between the different regional interests.

But it is becoming obvious, unless one ignores political reality, that this approach, proposed by Pierre Trudeau in 1968, failed to accommodate Quebec's interests. That this is true for sovereignist leaders should surprise no one, but it is also true for Robert Bourassa, a federalist—at least to some degree—who was in power during the unsuccessful attempts of Victoria in 1971, Meech in 1990, and Charlottetown in 1992. The federal government's spending and taxation power were and remain the sources of contention between the Quebec and federal governments. Ironically, Pierre Trudeau himself wrote in 1969, "I find it . . . extraordinary that political scientists fail to see the eroding effect that the power of the purse will have on Canadian democracy if the present situation continues to prevail, and in particular what chaos will result if provincial governments borrow federal logic and begin using their own power of the purse to meddle in federal affairs."[21] Too much decentralization and the recognition of a "special status" for Quebec were anathema to Pierre Trudeau. He was right: his type of federalism had, in fact, an eroding effect on both Canadian and Quebec democracy, and the net result is that the sovereignty option has never been so popular in Quebec.

THE FAILURE OF THE "POLITICS OF ACCOMMODATION"

Arend Lijphart suggests that elite pluralism can be successful if four conditions are present: "(1) elites have the ability to accommodate the divergent interests and demands of the subcultures; (2) elites have the ability to transcend cleavages and to join in a common effort with the elites of rival cultures; (3) they have a commitment to the maintenance of the system and to the improvement of its cohesion and stability; and (4) that elites understand the perils of political fragmentation."[22] The failure of the federalist form of elite accommodation to achieve greater political stability is evident when we observe the economic and cultural differences between Quebec and other Canadian provinces.

Canada–Quebec relations have always been perceived as the process of elite accommodation. For a long period of time, public policy was perceived as a result of the influence of the different elites representing French and English Canadians. This dualism recognized that Canada is a compromise between two nations, but the failure of the Meech Lake Accord has undermined that concept. The idea of replacing it with an association among ten equal provinces left many Quebec federalists and confederalists (the Allaire group)[23] sceptical about the possibility of elite accommodation. Since the rejection of the Meech Lake Accord, many Quebeckers are not ready for commitment to the maintenance of the Canadian political system as it is. The governing elites were unable to reach a political stability without major conflicts.

CONCLUSION

The search for a greater democracy has put Quebec in competition with the federal government. It has created a need to redefine the Canadian constitution. In the 1960s, the essence of burgeoning democracy in Quebec was the transfer of authority from church to state. The Quebec state has replaced the Catholic Church in all social, educational, and welfare matters. The state has established a network of powerful enterprises that have fostered economic development. But any further development of the Quebec state now rests on transferring additional powers from the federal to the Quebec government. This transfer has been requested by all Quebec governments since 1960. Quebeckers have concluded that the federalist-pluralist approach has failed because, in recent years, it has not recognized the Canadian duality. Federalism is an outgrowth of a pluralist theory of the state and therefore has its limitations. Political equilibrium or stability can be achieved by policy makers through the process of bargaining for political and economic advantages. The role of politicians and bureaucrats is to balance the demands of the different interests of society. Through this process, greater political equilibrium or elite accommodation should be attained. But Canadian federalism has been unable in the last thirty years to respond to Quebec demands.

The pluralist image of democratic politics is very much for many Canadian federalists like the market theory of the economy; there are always mechanisms that permit the achievement of some stability within the political system just as there are always mechanisms that satisfy consumer demands. Quebeckers' demands and attempts to influence public policy through the voting system—the support given to the Canadian–U.S. Free Trade Agreement and the election of fifty-four Bloc Québécois MPs, for example—can be seen as responses to relieve the risks imposed by the political system. The result of such a process should normally be greater political stability. But in the Canadian political system, the opposite happened because of competition and the size of the Quebec population as a percentage of the Canadian total.

This chapter has briefly described the evolution of Quebec democracy since the 1960s. The political constraints that have shaped the evolution as well as the structural and institutional characteristics of Quebec's society have been indicated. The election of the Liberals under Jean Lesage in 1960 gave Quebec the chance to build a modern democracy that could stand on its own. The various social, political, and economic reforms that have been attempted testify to a deep feeling among Quebeckers that the future is in their hands. Throughout this process, politicians such as René Lévesque and Robert Bourassa were respectful of the democratic process and followed the fundamental will of their citizens. But the search for the highest democratic rule is always a difficult task. Quebec is today, by any standard, a modern democracy, and its concerns are the same as those of other nations in the world.

NOTES

[1] François-Albert Angers, "French Canada and Social Security," *Canadian Journal of Economics and Political Science* 10, 3 (1944): 355–64.

[2] In June 1971, a first ministers conference in Victoria tentatively adopted a Canadian constitutional charter, which included an entrenched bill of rights and specific French-language rights. In addition, the Victoria Charter guaranteed Quebec a miminum of three Supreme Court judges. Upon his return from Victoria, Bourassa faced vehement opposition from other political parties, major unions, nationalist activists, and even the rank and file of his own party. Critics felt that the charter did not explicitly guarantee Quebec control of culture and social policy. Bourassa was left with little choice but to withdraw his original support for the charter.

[3] Daniel Salée, "Reposer la question du Québec? Notes critiques sur l'imagination sociologique," *Revue québécoise de science politique* 18 (1990): 83–103.

[4] François-Pierre Gingras and Neil Nevitte, "La Révolution en plan et le paragigme en cause," *Canadian Journal of Political Science* 16 (1983): 691–716. See also

François-Pierre Gingras and Neil Nevitte, "The Evolution of Quebec Nationalism" in *Quebec: State and Society*, ed. Alain G. Gagnon (Toronto: Methuen, 1984), 2–14.

5 Gary Caldwell and B. Dan Czarnocki, "Un rattrapage raté: le changement social dans le Québec d'après-guerre, 1950–1974—une comparaison Québec–Ontario," *Recherche sociographiques* 18 (1977): 9–58.

6 This is the central thesis developed by Denys Arcand in his movie *Québec: Duplessis et aprè. . .* (1972). He was not the only one sceptical about the social transformation of the 1960s in which the election of the Robert Bourassa Liberals was seen as the victory of business interest over collective interests.

7 Hubert Guindon, *Quebec Society: Tradition, Modernity, and Nationhood* (Toronto: University of Toronto Press, 1988).

8 Daniel Latouche, "La vraie nature de la Révolution tranquille," *Revue canadienne de science politique* 7 (1974): 525–36.

9 Léon Dion, *Québec, 1945–2000*, tome 2, *Les intellectuels et le temps de Duplessis* (Québec: Presses de l'Université Laval, 1993). Gilles Bourque and Jules Duchastel, *Restons traditionnels et progressifs* (Montreal: Boréal, 1988).

10 Guy Lachapelle, Gérald Bernier, Daniel Salée, and Luc Bernier, *The Quebec Democracy: Structures, Processes, and Policies* (Toronto: McGraw-Hill Ryerson, 1993), ch. 4.

11 Luc Bernier and Guy Lachapelle, "The Quiet Revolution Really Happened!" (American Council for Quebec Studies, Montreal, 20 Nov. 1992).

12 Kenneth McRoberts, *Quebec: Social Change and Political Crisis*, 3rd ed. (Toronto: McClelland & Stewart, 1988), 137.

13 Thomas Tremblay, *Rapport de la Commission Royale d'enquête sur les problèmes constitutionnels* (Quebec: Gouvernement du Québec, 1956).

14 Ibid., 312.

15 Claude Castonguay, *L'Assurance-maladie: rapport de la Commission d'enquête sur la santé et le bien-être social* (Quebec: Gouvernement du Québec, 1967), 24.

16 Comité des Affaires constitutionnelles de la Commission Politique de la Fédération libérale du Québec, "Document," *Journal of Canadian Studies* 2 (1967): 43–51.

17 Christopher Leman, *The Collapse of Welfare Reform: Political Institutions, Policy, and the Poor in Canada and the United States* (Cambridge: MIT Press, 1980), 62.

18 See Stephen Brooks, *Canadian Democracy: An Introduction* (Toronto: McClelland & Stewart, 1993), 166–67.

19 Robert L. Lineberry, *Government in America: People, Politics and Policy* (Boston: Little, Brown, 1980), 101.

20 Arend Lijphart, "Consociational Democracy," *World Politics* 20, 2 (Jan. 1969): 216.

21 Pierre Trudeau, "Federal–Provincial Grants and the Spending Power of Parliament," Working Paper on the Constitution (Ottawa: Government of Canada, 1969).

22 Lijphart, "Consociational Democracy."

23 The Allaire Report—the report of the Quebec Liberal Party's Constitutional Committee—issued in March 1991, was unequivocal. It called upon the federal government to pursue in-depth reform of the political and constitutional frameworks in three areas: the political autonomy of the Quebec state, the consolidation of the Canadian economic union, and the restructuring of Canada's political institutions.

Suggested Reading

Bernier, Gérald, and Daniel Salée. *The Shaping of Quebec Politics and Society: Colonialism, Power, and the Transition to Capitalism in the 19th Century*. Washington: Crane Russak, 1992.

A study of the social, economic, and political facets of the period between the conquest of New France by the British in 1760 and the Act of Union in 1840. The central argument is that Lower Canada's dominant societal logic is characterized by a feudal or pre-capitalist frame of reference.

Coleman, William D. *The Independence Movement in Quebec, 1945–1984*. Toronto: University of Toronto Press, 1984.

Analyzes the independence coalition that united organized labour, the francophone business class, and parts of the middle class in the aftermath of the Quiet Revolution. The central point is that the changes of the early 1960s hastened the integration of Quebec into the North American capitalist structure.

Gagnon, Alain G., ed. *Quebec: State and Society*. Toronto: Methuen, 1984.

A collection of original or revised articles on the major topics in Quebec politics. Contributions are organized into six main sections: Quebec nationalism, the national question and social classes, the new middle class, the regional question, the state and groups, and language policies and educational reforms.

Lachapelle, Guy, Gérald Bernier, Daniel Salée, and Luc Bernier. *The Quebec Democracy: Structures, Processes, and Policies*. Toronto: McGraw-Hill Ryerson, 1993.

A comprehensive analysis focusing on the policy-making process in Quebec since 1960.

Levine, Marc. *The Reconquest of Montreal: Language Policy and Social Change in a Bilingual City*. Philadelphia: Temple University Press, 1990.

Traces the politicization of the language issue in the 1960s and 1970s. Levine analyzes the impact of the three controversial language laws enacted by the Quebec government between 1969 and 1977. Explains how French-speaking Quebeckers mobilized politically and used the state to redistribute group power in Montreal.

McRoberts, Kenneth. *Quebec: Social Change and Political Crisis*. 3rd ed. Toronto: McClelland & Stewart, 1988.

Traces the roots of the social, political, and economic issues that Quebec has faced since the beginning of the 1960s. Carefully researched, the book raises interesting theoretical issues about Quebec modernization and developmental process.

Robert M. Krause

┌   ┐
   6
└   ┘

ONTARIO:
CANADA WRIT SMALL

Ontario enjoys a unique status within the Canadian state. One astute observer of the Canadian political scene has suggested that it would be incorrect to label Ontario as merely one region within Canada. "Given its central location, the identification of the regional part, Ontario, with the national whole, Canada, is understandable. To illustrate the point in very simplistic terms, it is at least conceivable to imagine Quebec, Newfoundland, or the West separating from Canada. It is inconceivable to imagine Ontario separating: Ontario *is* Canada to a degree that no other region can claim."[1] Although this observation may not be shared by everyone in Canada, there can be very little doubt that Ontario is not a province or region like the others. It is really a microcosm of the nation as a whole.

Ontario's special status can be attributed to a number of factors. It is partly a product of the fact that the province mirrors not only the fundamental cleavages—ethnic, regional, economic, cultural—within the whole of Canada, but significant aspects of the national political process (party system and legislative politics) as well. The province's status is also due to its centrality within the "core"[2] region of Canada. This centrality gives the province a level of power, wealth, and influence not found in other regions. These attributes not only influence Ontario's internal politics but also, by almost a process of osmosis, the politics of the entire country. To fully appreciate this special status and its impact on the national scene, it is necessary to understand the unique economic and political setting of Ontario, its regional make-up, the nature of its party system, the dynamics of its internal legislative decision-making process, and the subsequent interrelationship of these variables and their impact upon Ontario's position in the Canadian federation.

THE SETTING OF CENTRALITY

O ntario accounts for over 40 percent of the total value of goods and services produced in Canada. Yet, unlike many of its sister provinces, its wealth is not dependent on only one or two dominant economic activities, but rather is widely dispersed and found in most economic sectors that constitute the Canadian economy. Its agricultural sector is heterogeneous and produces total cash values that often place it first in the country. Its manufacturing sector accounts for over one-half of all the manufacturing jobs in Canada. Its mineral sector also ranks first in the country (excluding petroleum products), and its forestry sector ranks third.[3]

Ontario's population includes about thirty-five out of every one hundred Canadians. Since it has the largest population base in the country, it sends more representatives to the federal Parliament than any other province. Indeed, its membership in the House of Commons is three times greater than that of the four Atlantic provinces combined and exceeds the total of all members sent to Ottawa from the four western provinces. Its political power is evident from the 1993 federal election results. In that election, Ontario sent 98 of its 99 elected representatives to the government benches, giving the province 55 percent of all government members. Further, Ontario's representatives traditionally receive the largest number of cabinet posts, and the portfolios with the largest budgets, in the national government. Its web of influence extends beyond national political power to areas such as finance and media, which shape the values and direction of other provinces and regions. This is so because the province is home to most of the dominant organizations in these fields: banking, corporate offices, and media (CBC, CTV, magazines, films, and so on).

Although these figures lead to the conclusion that Ontario is a wealthy, heavily populated province, in fact Ontario is not economically monolithic or, in socioeconomic terms, a homogeneous province. Rather, due to its vast geographic size, it displays within its boundaries a considerable degree of regionalism.

REGIONALISM

S ome regions of the province—Toronto and southwestern Ontario— are considerably more economically diverse, and subsequently wealthier, than other regions. Some areas, such as Northern Ontario, are not as fortunate and are less wealthy and more dependent on one or two economic sectors for their livelihood.

The population is not evenly distributed across the province but rather tends to be concentrated along the Windsor–Ottawa corridor. Even within this elongated corridor, the Toronto–Hamilton area (the Golden Horseshoe) stands paramount in terms of population (over one-third of the province's people).

The northern portion of Ontario covers 90 percent of the total area of the land mass, but has only 8.9 percent of the province's total population.[4] Northern Ontario itself is not monolithic and can be divided into three distinct sub-regions that vary in size of population, economic activity, and ethnic composition: the northeast, northwest, and far north. The northeast and the northwest constitute the mid-north of the province. This region

> consists of a scattering of small cities and towns, most of them heavily dependent upon the extraction of a single natural resource. The northeast is primarily dependent upon mineral extraction whereas the northwest is primarily dependent upon forest resources. Another clear distinction between the two is the much higher percentage of Franco-Ontarians in the northeast. The third sub-region is that of the far north beyond 50 degrees latitude where the population is very sparse and consists largely of a few widely scattered Indian communities heavily dependent upon welfare and the traditional economy of hunting, fishing and trapping.[5]

Ontario was and continues to be a magnet for immigrants to Canada. In 1992–93, for example, over one-half of all immigrants to Canada (55 percent) chose Ontario as their province of residence.[6] Not surprisingly, new immigrants to the province have not settled in all regions of the province in equal numbers. Rather, they have primarily chosen the larger cities. This, coupled with the growing proportion of immigrants who come not from the traditional Northern European sources, but rather from Vietnam, Hong Kong, China, the Philippines, India, and the Caribbean, has given the urban centres of Ontario a more multicultural and multiracial character.

PARTY SYSTEM

The degree of regionalism within the province has influenced the nature of its party system. Since 1943, Ontario has been the only province in Canada with a stable three-party system. Since that time, the third party has obtained between 20 and 25 percent of the popular vote cast in provincial elections and, since 1967, no third party has obtained less than sixteen seats in the legislature.[7] Yet, as in most other provinces of Canada, the party system has been characterized by extended periods of one-party dominance. Indeed, in the eighty years between 1905 and 1985, the Conservative Party was only out of office on two occasions: 1919–23 (United Farmers and Labour coalition government) and 1934–43 (Liberal government).

In spite of this picture of party stability, the actual degree of electoral competition between the parties is much greater than the aggregate electoral results would indicate. The first-past-the-post, simple plurality electoral system utilized in the province greatly distorts the relationship between seats obtained and the actual percentage of the popular vote won by the parties. With a three-party system, two can split the opposition vote against the government, with the net result that a governing party could form a majority with approximately 40 percent of the vote. In the 1990 election, the New Democratic Party became the first party in Ontario's history to form a majority government with only 37 percent of the popular vote. The vote/seat distortion in 1990 was partly a result of the further splintering of the popular vote by other parties, which received 7 percent of the total vote.

Equally noteworthy has been the tendency, not found in other provinces, for elections to produce a minority government. Since the beginning of the three-party system, there have been four minority governments in Ontario: 1943–45 (Progressive Conservative), 1975–81 (Progressive Conservative), 1985 (Progressive Conservative), and 1985–87 (Liberal). Close electoral competition between the parties can also be observed in the brief period between 1985 and 1990 when all three parties formed a government in the province: 1985 (Progressive Conservative), 1985–90 (Liberal), 1990– (New Democrat). Election results have also hidden the degree of regional support that each political party received. As Robert J. Williams observed in his study of Ontario elections during the period between 1974 and 1981, the support for parties has varied considerably by region within the province.[8] Further, he noted that the fortunes of the corresponding federal parties have not been identical with the degree of regional support they have found in provincial elections. This pattern of regional variation has had, not surprisingly, a significant effect on the nature of parties in Ontario and on their electoral style.

As the parties cannot rely on the same people to support them in both federal and provincial elections, their appeal to the voters has become more pragmatic and less ideological in nature. As Graham White so succinctly noted, "[the] Ontario economy and society are too complex to permit polarization into two clearly defined political camps"[9] The net result is that all three parties tend to be more pragmatic than ideological in matters of public policy. This phenomenon is reinforced by the electoral competition found in the province. The lack of any great ideological distance between the parties could be seen at the time of the Liberal–New Democrat accord in 1985. This agreement precipitated the formation of a Liberal government at the expense of the Progressive Conservative Party, which had found itself in a minority government position following the 1985 election. Rather than form a coalition government, the two parties negotiated a "conditional legislative alliance"[10] in a written document that specified agreement between the parties on a host of issues to be dealt with by the Liberal government. The accord was not a radical document but was limited in its policy focus and scope of change. The reforms outlined in the accord were "of a limited nature rather than those which students of ideology would regard as fundamentally restructuring the social and economic system. The introduction of the phrase 'fiscal accountability' in the . . . documents is testimony to the pragmatic nature of reform."[11]

PREMIER, CABINET, BUREAUCRACY:
THE APEX OF POWER

At the top of the governmental structure is the premier of the province. In Ontario, the individual social background of the premier has changed relatively little since 1867. Of the province's twenty-one premiers, all but one have come from Anglo-Saxon roots, all but one have been Protestant, all have been men, and almost 80 percent have been lawyers. Also, in spite of the dominance of Ontario's principal city, Toronto, none of the premiers has called Toronto home. Premiers have generally resided in the smaller towns and cities of the province.[12]

Prior to 1990, Ontario premiers were seldom called upon to provide a "public persuader"[13] role where they needed to rally the population behind a controversial decision made by the government. They tended to be managers rather than leaders. Their primary role was to look after the store or, more accurately, to ensure that the economic prosperity of Ontario was not jeopardized. As managers, their relationship with the legislature tended not to be hands-on, but rather one of watchful attention slightly removed from the actual running of the legislature. In the decades prior to 1990, "other than attending Question period, premiers spent very little time in the legislature."[14] Further, with the executive reforms initiated in the 1970s by the Committee on Government Productivity (COGP) (a particularly apt name in the Ontario context), the cabinet structure evolved into an "institutionalized cabinet."[15] This cabinet system in many instances featured structure and process concerns (e.g., cabinet committees) that tended to dilute the power of cabinet in relation to the premier. The gradual erosion of cabinet influence went hand in hand with the growth in importance of the province's bureaucracy.

While the administrative apparatus in Ontario employs over 90 000 people, it is the much smaller complement of deputy ministers and senior officials who have had the greatest impact on the initiation, formulation, and implementation of public policy. Since the COGP reforms, their position has been enhanced considerably. During the years that William Davis was premier, from 1971 to 1985, "the political leaders [cabinet] and the senior bureaucracy learned, in the main, to work together."[16] The traditional idea that administrative and political decisions should be separate was rejected. As Edward Stewart, a man who combined both administrative and political responsibilities as secretary of the cabinet for Premier Davis from 1976 to 1985, admonished, "A deputy who claims that political considerations never influenced his or her thinking, or the advice he or she is giving to the government, is either trying to deceive the public or is of limited value to the Premier and ministers he or she serves."[17] The augmented status of the higher levels of the public service was not substantially reduced with the ascendancy of David Peterson to the office of premier. In Peterson's era all but two cabinet committees had advisory committees of deputy ministers[18] and, although Peterson modified the structural components of the executive policy-making process, he "continued to build links to the Ontario mandarinate by giving it a more active role in policy development and paid special attention to its concerns."[19]

The election of the NDP government in 1990 modified to some extent the traditional role of the premier and his relationship with the cabinet and the senior bureaucracy. Initially, Premier Bob Rae had to assume more of a "public persuader" role than that of his predecessors. While there still remained the political necessity to ensure the economic prosperity of Ontario, the lack of previous governmental experience exhibited by NDP members meant that the premier had to shoulder a larger public spokesman role. Much like other premiers, Rae has tended to dominate his cabinet, but the degree of domination was greater than that of his immediate predecessors. With cabinet ministers possessing no prior governmental experience (or, in some cases, no previous elected experience), Premier Rae has had to assume a more forceful and visible political role. Finally, under the NDP the role of the public service in policy making, while still substantial, has been subject to more "partisan" political direction initiated by outside advisors brought into the new government from past NDP provincial governments.

THE ONTARIO LEGISLATURE

The other crucial component in the decision-making process in the province is, of course, the legislative assembly and its members. As with premiers, the background of the legislators was, until recently, relatively similar. A study of legislators elected to the 1987 parliament found that seven out of ten came from three professions: business, law, and education. Additionally, while the percentage of women in the assembly doubled in the period between the 1985 parliament and 1987 parliament, they still constituted only 15 percent of the membership of the latter.[20]

As a result of the 1990 New Democratic Party electoral victory (74 of 130 seats), the occupational and gender composition of the legislature was considerably modified. With 60 first-time members in the governing caucus, the legislature took on a decidedly more diversified occupational composition, primarily at the expense of those members in business and law. Fourteen of the party's new MPPs (8 percent of the total legislature) were blue-collar workers who came from auto assembly lines, chemical plants, and steel mills.[21] In addition, the election produced a further increase in the number of women in the legislature. The twenty-eight female MLAs represented 21 percent of the legislature.

Taken together, the social background of the premiers and legislators would seem to suggest that the Ontario legislature is made up of a relatively homogeneous upper-middle-class elite. While the results of the 1990 election somewhat modified the occupational composition of the assembly, its middle-class orientation remains. In socioeconomic terms, legislators are certainly not representative of the vast diversity of the population in the province. And, while the percentage of women in the legislature has increased, the assembly remains predominately male.

The legislature is inclined more toward gradual change and limited influence, as can be observed in its size and the impact of the party system on its style and operation. The legislature in Ontario has, much like its counterparts in other provinces, changed considerably since the 1960s.

One astute observer wrote that its record had improved considerably in terms of the quality of "its members, its staff and services, its procedures, its committee system and its accountability mechanisms."[22] The size of the legislature (at 130 members, the largest provincial legislature in Canada) has had an impact on its structure, operation, and effectiveness.[23] Thus, it can be proposed that the degree of executive dominance in the assembly is proportionally less than that found in smaller assemblies. In Ontario, only about 20 percent of the total membership of the legislature is in the cabinet. This gives non-executive legislators greater room for influence than would be found in assemblies where the proportion of cabinet members to the total assembly is much higher. The larger house also permits the assembly to have a more effective and comprehensive committee system, which generally gives adequate representation to all parties in the legislature. Procedures, too, are affected by such a committee system: issues can be referred to smaller, specialized committees rather than the entire legislature. The larger assembly also gives opposition members a substantial role to play in accountability through mechanisms such as the public accounts committee and question period. Finally, the partisan political behaviour in the House, where generally good interparty relations are the rule, may well be a consequence of its size.[24] Members have more opportunity for cross-party contact in settings such as committees, which tend to foster an appreciation of colleagues' ability regardless of party stripe.

The continuing three-party system has meant that the likelihood of a minority government is greater than in either a two-party system or a one-party-dominant system where there are few, if any, opposition members (Alberta, New Brunswick). This has meant that party leaders are more likely to pay attention to their members' voices in order to help ensure the party's electoral success. As there is less ideological distance between the parties than in more polarized provincial political environments (British Columbia, for example), there is greater room for moderation and accommodation between the parties in structuring the rules, procedures, and operation of the house. Party accommodation in changing the rules and procedures of the legislature has been further enhanced in minority government situations. In the 1985–87 period of the Liberal–New Democratic Party accord, legislative procedures were implemented that substantially enhanced the power of legislators at the expense of the executive.

In spite of these factors, the legislature is still less than perfect in its decision-making capacity. As a result of the province's large population, each legislator on average represents approximately 70 000 constituents.[25]

Although the large number of constituents has led to increased staff and resources for individual MPPs, it has also meant that legislators in Ontario are to a large degree preoccupied with servicing their constituents. Their focus thus tends to be highly localized and, to a considerable extent, more province-wide issues tend not to get the attention that they deserve. The legislature as a whole tends to be "preoccupied with issues of limited scope of only local impact."[26] Finally, the Ontario legislature probably attracts the lowest political interest from its electors of any assembly in the country.[27] This unhappy state of affairs is caused not so much as a result of the legislators' tendency to deal with lesser issues, but rather with the tendency of Ontarians to view the national government as more important in their daily lives. With the focus of Ontarians on the federal government, the day-to-day events at Queen's Park often tend to be overlooked, poorly reported, and perhaps misunderstood by the electors.

PUBLIC POLICY

As decision makers, the legislature, executive, and bureaucracy are responsible for the formulation and implementation of provincial public policy. The Ontario government spends the bulk of its money on the provision of social programs (health, education, welfare). In 1994–95, Ontario spent over two-thirds of its revenues (69 percent) in social policy fields—health (32 percent), education (16 percent), and social services (21 percent).

There are several reasons for the high degree of expenditures on social policy. First, provinces have the constitutional responsibility for many of the social policy fields, including health and education. Second, the federal government stimulated growth in the area by its use of both conditional and unconditional grants to the provinces. Third, extensive industrialization and urbanization within the province have made the provision of social services necessary. Finally, there has been the political will to spend money in the area of social policy.

Expenditures, of course, require revenue. The Ontario government receives the largest share of its revenues from taxation (73 percent); personal income tax collected by the federal government constitutes a significant component of those revenues. Additionally, federal transfer payments to Ontario account for about 16 percent of the province's revenue. This, coupled with the fact that over one out of ten dollars is spent to cover the provincial debt, makes budget deliberations a highly salient element in public policy making in Ontario.

Traditionally, Ontario, as the wealthiest province in Canada, was not as severely constrained in its budgetary deliberations as most other provinces. With the recession of the early 1990s, the economic fortunes of Ontario began to decline significantly, and the NDP government was eventually forced to make dramatic budgetary changes in its 1993 budget by reducing government expenditures by $2 billion, increasing taxes by $2 billion, and cutting the wage bill of Ontario public sector employees by $2 billion in order to keep its budgetary deficit somewhat under control.[28]

The growing problem of the deficit, coupled with national policy direction and consequent fiscal relationships with the federal government, has made federal–provincial relations an even more important dimension of Ontario politics in recent years.

ONTARIO IN THE CANADIAN FEDERATION

The history of Ontario–federal relations has witnessed periods of harmony and of bitter conflict between the two governments. The cyclical nature of the relationship has been readily apparent during the last four decades. In the 1950s, under Premier Leslie Frost, the relationship was relatively harmonious, but in the 1960s Premier John Robarts had serious conflicts with the national government, as has Premier Rae in the early 1990s. Throughout the 1970s and 1980s, William Davis and David Peterson were engaged in intergovernmental relations that exhibited an almost equal mix of harmony and conflict.[29]

The differences of opinion between the two jurisdictions are the result of several factors. Conflict may result from different political parties holding power in Ottawa and Toronto, a situation that in the first 120 years of Confederation was the case over 60 percent of the time. Clashes may be part of the struggle between the two largest governments in Canada over such matters as money, power, and status. Hostility may be influenced by the leadership styles of the individuals who hold office at either the provincial or national level. Disagreements may result from policy differences between the two governments, which are influenced by regional, economic, ethnic, and class variations in Ontario and in Canada as a whole. Federal and provincial leaders also can have differences in opinion on how best to deal with the United States, a nation whose influence crucially affects both Canada and Ontario.[30] For example, Premier Peterson opposed the Canada–U.S. Free Trade Agreement that the federal government promoted during the 1988 federal election, and in the 1993 election Premier

Rae was in total opposition to the federal government's policy on the North American Free Trade Agreement (NAFTA).

While all of these factors have at one time or another had some bearing on federal–Ontario relations, Rand Dyck suggests that "the most common conflicts between Ontario and the Federal government have related to the question of provincial autonomy and problems of money, power and status."[31] The question of money or division of financial resources (revenues, expenditures, transfer payments) between the two governments has been a matter of particular concern for the Rae government, which came to power during one of the worst recessions in Ontario's history. Premier Rae accused the federal government of pursuing measures that hindered Ontario's economic growth and prosperity. Such measures included direct economic policies (capping the increase in payments to Ontario under the Canada Assistance Plan to 5 percent) and indirect economic policies (reducing Unemployment Insurance benefits, which had the effect of placing individuals on the provincial welfare rolls). In particular, Rae decried the consequences of deficit shifting from the federal government to the Ontario government, which limited revenues for the province, increased its expenditures, and necessitated increased provincial taxation. As a study commissioned by the provincial government observed, "In total, federal direct, indirect, and induced deficit-shifting to Ontario and the associated financing costs will be about $9 billion in 1993/94. This is almost all of the estimated $9.5 billion Ontario deficit."[32]

While the considerations of power, status, and autonomy between the two governments may be a primary cause for disagreement, it must be recognized that such struggles do not mean that Ontario is involved in a solely self-seeking "Ontario first" strategy in intergovernmental relations. Such a position would not recognize the policy preferences of the federal government or other provinces. Ontario's traditional bargaining posture is based upon bridge-building, balancing the interests of the entire state and requiring the premier to act in a non-partisan diplomatic role.[33] This bargaining posture is a direct consequence of the province's internal political environment.

The regional diversity found within Ontario has meant that the province's premiers have been sensitized to the need for balancing Canadian regional interests. Also, because Ontario's citizens have a strong national identification, their leaders must not act in such a way that they are perceived by Ontarians as being parochial or putting the province's interests before those of the country. Ontario's position must be perceived as one that is constructive and designed to strengthen the nation. Furthermore, the party system has meant that federal and provincial leaders, even if they are from different political parties, must accommodate each other if both are to be electorally successful within the province. Finally, Ontario is aware of its dominant economic and political position in the Canadian federation. As it has the largest stake in maintaining the "Canadian common market," it has recognized that it must exercise self-restraint when dealing with the national and the other provincial governments.[34]

This self-restraint (which might well be questioned by residents of other provinces) has a special meaning for Ontario's relations with Quebec and the federal government. The traditional stance of Ontario's premiers has been one of awareness, concern, and attempting to act as an honest broker between Quebec, the federal government, and the other provinces. This relationship with Quebec is founded upon historical, economic, and cultural factors. Historically, both Ontario and Quebec were part of the original bargain that resulted in the formation of Canada. In recognition of being the first two provinces to join Confederation, the Ontario and Quebec premiers sit on either side of the prime minister at first ministers conferences. To a considerable degree, both provinces have common economic interests. In the early years of Confederation, both were active in ensuring that the revenue from natural resources that flowed from the Canadian Shield, which they both populate, would enrich their respective treasuries. In more recent times, both have shared a common interest in fostering and maintaining the secondary manufacturing sector within their provinces, and Ontario has at times been involved in an "aggressively provincialist course usually in collaboration with the government of Quebec."[35] The economic link between the two is solidified by the fact that each is the other's best customer.

Yet, Ontario's position vis-à-vis Quebec is based on more than self-centred economic interest. Because these two provinces have the largest number of "charter" citizens (French and English) within their respective provinces, Ontario in the last thirty years or so has attempted, wherever possible, to diffuse political tensions between the two groups. This has resulted in Ontario premiers promoting, even without full-fledged support within the province, linguistic policies aimed at enhancing French–English understanding.

CONCLUSION

Ontario is in a great many ways a microcosm of Canada as a whole. The province's regional nature, its racial and ethnic mosaic, and its regionally diversified economy are all features that characterize Canada.

Regional loyalties, muted ideological politics, long stretches of one-party dominance, and periodic minority governments are all elements associated with the national party system. The main features of Ontario's legislative decision-making process—a large and expert bureaucracy, upper-middle-class legislators focusing upon matters of regional and local interest, and an executive with a strong leader who is relatively free to deal with the larger issues of state—are shared by legislative politics in Ottawa. Also, much like the national government, the province has a special interest in Quebec and its position in the federation.

It is equally apparent that Ontario's wealth, population, and consequent political power add immeasurably to its special status within Canada. This ingredient in the province's special status is often misunderstood by both its own citizens and the residents of other provinces. On the one hand, people in Ontario frequently equate Ontario's interests with those of Canada as a whole, a view that often infuriates those outside the province. On the other hand, those who live beyond its boundaries frequently misperceive Ontario as merely a province or region like all others. The reality of Ontario lies somewhere between. In the final analysis, Ontario is a province like no other.

NOTES

[1] Roger Gibbins, *Conflict and Unity: An Introduction to Canadian Political Life* (Toronto: Methuen, 1985), 112.

[2] For the distinction between *core* and *periphery,* see C.F.J. Whebell, "Geography and Politics in Canada: Selected Aspects" in *Approaches to Canadian Politics*, 2nd ed., ed. John H. Redekop (Scarborough, ON: Prentice-Hall, 1983), 3–27.

[3] See "Ontario" in Rand Dyck, *Provincial Politics in Canada* (Scarborough, ON: Prentice-Hall, 1986), 264–65.

[4] See Geoffrey R. Weller, "Politics and Policy in the North" in *The Government and Politics of Ontario*, 4th ed., ed. Graham White (Scarborough, ON: Nelson Canada, 1990), 276–77.

[5] Ibid., 276.

[6] *Globe and Mail*, 5 Aug. 1994, A4.

[7] See Graham White, "Ontario: A Legislature in Adolescence" in *Provincial and Territorial Legislatures in Canada*, ed. Gary Levy and Graham White (Toronto: University of Toronto Press, 1989), 31.

[8] See Robert J. Williams, "Ontario's Party Systems: Federal and Provincial" in *Party Politics in Canada*, 5th ed., ed. Hugh G. Thorburn (Scarborough, ON: Prentice-Hall, 1985), 304.

[9] See White, "Ontario," 31.

[10] R. Krause, R.G. Price, and R.H. Wagenberg, "A New Alternative: The Legislative Alliance in Ontario," *American Review of Canadian Studies* 16, 4 (Winter 1986): 413.

[11] Ibid., 419.

[12] Graham White, "Governing from Queen's Park: The Ontario Premiership" in *Prime Ministers and Premiers: Political Leadership and Public Policy in Canada*, ed. Leslie A. Pal and David Taras (Scarborough, ON: Prentice-Hall, 1988), 159–60.

[13] Ibid., 161.

[14] Ibid., 172.

[15] Ibid., 174.

[16] Edward E. Stewart, *Cabinet Government in Ontario: A View from Inside* (Halifax: Institute for Research on Public Policy, 1989), 47.

[17] Ibid., 49.

[18] Richard Loreto and Graham White, "The Premier and the Cabinet" in *Government and Politics of Ontario*, 100.

[19] White, "Governing from Queen's Park," 170.

[20] Robert J. Fleming, ed., *Canadian Legislatures: 1987–1988* (Ottawa: Ampersand Communications Services, 1988), 74.

[21] Paul Moloney, "14 New NDP Members Have Held Public Office," *Toronto Star*, 10 Sept. 1990, A9.

[22] Graham White, *The Ontario Legislature: A Political Analysis* (Toronto: University of Toronto Press, 1989), 261.

[23] For the impact of size upon the operation of a provincial legislature, see Graham White and Gary Levy, "Introduction: The Comparative Analysis of Canadian Provincial and Territorial Legislative Assemblies" in *Provincial and Territorial Legislatures*, 4–7.

[24] Ibid., 6.

[25] Ibid., 8.

[26] White, *The Ontario Legislature*, 254.

[27] White, "Ontario," 32.

[28] For a discussion of budgetary problems, see Rachel Grasham, "Selling the 1992 Budget: Backbench MPPs and Government Communications Strategy" in *Inside the Pink Palace: Ontario Legislature Internship Essays*, ed. Graham White (Toronto: University of Toronto Press, 1993), 294–308.

[29] Rand Dyck, "The Position of Ontario in the Canadian Federation" in *Perspectives on Canadian Federalism*, ed. R.D. Olling and M.W. Westmacott (Scarborough, ON: Prentice-Hall, 1988), 326.

[30] Ibid., 326–28.

[31] These points are covered in Donald W. Stevenson, "Ontario and Confederation: A Reassessment" in *Canada: The State of the Federation, 1989*, ed. Ronald L. Watts and Douglas M. Brown (Kingston, ON: Institute of Intergovernmental Relations, 1989), 54–57. Some of the same ideas on the traditional bargaining posture of Ontario are also found in Rand Dyck, "Position of Ontario in the Canadian Federation," 339–40.

[32] See M.C. McCracken, *The Consequences of Deficit Shifting for Ontario* (paper no. 4 prepared for Ministry of Intergovernmental Affairs by Informetrica Ltd., 1 Nov. 1993), 9.

[33] These points are outlined either implicitly or explicitly in Donald W. Stevenson's penetrating analysis of Ontario's position in Ontario–federal relations. See "Ontario and Confederation," 59–61, 72.

[34] Garth Stevenson, *Unfulfilled Union*, 3rd ed. (Toronto: Gage, 1989), 80.

[35] Ibid., 85.

SUGGESTED READING

Brownsey, Keith, and Michael Howlett, eds. *The Provincial State: Politics in Canada's Provinces and Territories.* Toronto: Copp Clark Pitman, 1992. A collection of twelve essays dealing with the development of the provincial state. The articles allow for an examination of the similarities and differences between provinces. For example, the editors note that the laissez-faire, free-market approach to state intervention in Ontario can be contrasted with the rise of the corporatist Quebec state.

Dyck, Rand. *Provincial Politics in Canada.* Scarborough, ON: Prentice-Hall, 1986. A book that deals with all the provincial governments in Canada. While not explicitly comparative, the treatment of each province allows for a comparative focus around which the unique nature of Ontario politics can be assessed.

Levy, Gary, and Graham White, eds. *Provincial and Territorial Legislatures in Canada.* Toronto: University of Toronto Press, 1989. While the book deals with the legislatures of the ten provinces, the Northwest Territories, and the Yukon, its introductory comparative essay on all sub-national legislatures and the political insights it gives in each of its chapters make it an extremely valuable book for students of provincial politics.

White, Graham, ed. *The Government and Politics of Ontario.* 4th ed. Scarborough, ON: Nelson Canada, 1990. The most informative overall treatment of Ontario, dealing with the general areas of environment and political culture, government institutions, politics, and policy. An absolutely essential book for those interested in the Ontario political system.

White, Graham, ed. *Inside the Pink Palace: Ontario Legislature Internship Essays*. Toronto: University of Toronto Press, 1993.

A series of twenty original papers written by student interns in the Ontario legislature based on their own individual experiences and observations. The articles deal with the contemporary legislature (1986–93) and cover such diverse subjects as political socialization of MPPs, question period strategies, role at caucus, policy formulation, and budget development.

White, Graham. *The Ontario Legislature: A Political Analysis*. Toronto: University of Toronto Press, 1989.

A thorough discussion of the Ontario legislature, dealing with subjects such as the setting, the participants, the legislature at work (overview, routine proceedings, legislation, and finances), committees, services to members, accountability, and the process of reform.

David E. Smith

┌ **7** ┐

WESTERN CANADA

C anada is a country of pronounced geographical and cultural regions. Excluding the North (that is, the Yukon and Northwest Territories), its regions are customarily considered to include the Atlantic provinces, Quebec, Ontario, the Prairie provinces, and British Columbia. Sometimes, in defiance of the country's most prominent topographical feature, the Rocky Mountains, British Columbia and the three Prairie provinces are considered as one region—Western Canada. That is the case in this discussion. In addition to the convenience of reducing the number of chapters on regions in a book not devoted to regionalism, there are other justifications for treating the vast area west of Ontario as one unit.

The four western provinces were settled later than the rest of the country, primarily after Confederation in 1867. Although Manitoba and British Columbia entered the federation (in 1870 and 1871 respectively) before Prince Edward Island (1873), the latter's institutions and society long predated those of British Columbia and Manitoba. As well, and to a unique extent, federal government policies—on immigration, the tariff, and railways, for example—determined the development of the four western provinces. Partly because of that influence, these provinces share a tradition of suspicion of the federal government and central institutions. This suspicion is revealed in their electorates' distinctive voting record and support for parties other than the Liberals or Conservatives (witness the enormous support in Alberta and British Columbia for the Reform Party in the federal election of 1993). Although all Canadian provinces have depended in varying degrees on the exploitation of natural resources for their wealth, the four western provinces have depended more than the rest, either because they are less economically diversified than Ontario and Quebec (which have large secondary-industry sectors) or because their natural resource base is much greater than that of the Atlantic provinces.

Nonetheless, there are also significant differences between British Columbia and Alberta, Saskatchewan, and Manitoba. Again, to begin with geography, the Prairies are flat, and British Columbia is not. The southern portions of the fertile plains became the base of grain, Canada's major export in the first half of this century. In turn, the grain economy dictated the pattern of prairie immigration and settlement, the system of land tenure, the location of railways and roads, and a multitude of other responses, both public and private. British Columbia's mountainous terrain impeded settlement of the interior and largely confined population to the river valleys and coastal deltas. The forested slopes of the mountains became the base of the province's major resource industry—timber—while the long, indented coastline and the warm Pacific Ocean spawned a lucrative fishery. Contrary to the popular image of the agrarian Prairies, the northern half (or Shield portion) of this area is heavily treed, though not with valuable Douglas fir that grows in British Columbia. Nonetheless, the governments in Edmonton, Regina, and Winnipeg have worked hard, though with mixed success, to develop this resource, especially to produce pulp and paper.

Western Canada is well endowed with natural resources, both below and above ground. Some, such as coal, are found east and west of the continental divide, while others are limited to one or the other side of the mountains: metals in British Columbia, potash in Saskatchewan, natural gas and oil mainly in Alberta but also in Saskatchewan. The difference in natural resources between British Columbia and the Prairie provinces lies less in their variety or location than in the public policies that have surrounded their extraction. Of crucial importance was the decision by the government of Canada to retain control over the natural resources of the Prairie provinces as each province entered Confederation. Ownership was transferred to all three only in 1930. Neither British Columbia nor any other province shared in this discriminatory treatment. Instead, under section 109 of the Constitution Act, 1867, they retained possession of their resources when they entered Confederation.

Although more will be said about the resources question later, at this point it is useful to recall that the three Prairie provinces were the only provinces to be created by statutes of the Parliament of Canada, in each instance out of the vast territory lying between Hudson Bay and the Rockies, which was transferred by Great Britain to the federal government after 1868. By contrast, the colony of British Columbia negotiated its own terms of entry into Confederation, and its existing government and territory became part of Canada by action of the imperial government. The distinctive origin of the Prairie provinces explains the antipathy to the federal government more commonly found on the Prairies than in British Columbia, as well as one product of that antipathy—the long search by prairie residents for institutions and processes to protect themselves from further dictation by Ottawa.

Thus, whether Western Canada is one region or two depends on the context in which the question is asked. On balance, the topographical differences between British Columbia and the other three provinces are less important to understanding Western Canada than the fact that all four provinces share a sense of isolation from Central Canada. That isolation is only partly a function of distance; equally significant has been a series of federal policies—economic and cultural—over which westerners believe they have had little influence and which in western eyes neither reflect their values nor contribute to the well-being of their region. Arguably, these policies have provided the strongest stimulus toward creating a western Canadian identity, an observation borne out by a growing tendency in the West for governmental and non-governmental bodies to form a united front when dealing with their national counterparts.

SETTING

History: A Different Kind of Frontier

Major settlement did not occur on the Prairies until after the arrival of the Canadian Pacific Railway (CPR) in 1885. In British Columbia, it began a few decades earlier but was largely confined to the southern tip of Vancouver Island. Yet in the previous two centuries European and Canadian traders had regularly crossed the West in search of furs. Posts and routes were established throughout the West and North by the North West Company, based in Montreal, and the Hudson's Bay Company (HBC), based in London and given monopoly trading rights after 1670 to Rupert's Land, the area drained by rivers flowing into Hudson Bay. In 1821, the two companies united under the name Hudson's Bay Company, and in 1847 that company secured control of Vancouver Island. The Native population in the West had its first encounters with Europeans as a result of this fur trade. Long before the period of mass settlement at the end of the nineteenth century, the West was the scene of a mercantilist trade, exporting raw materials—in this instance, fur—and importing finished goods. Along with other factors, this trade, via the Hudson Bay route or around the South American horn to Britain and Europe, made the West an imperial, not a Canadian, frontier.[1] In this respect, the early history of the Canadian West was vitally different from that of its southern neighbour. The American frontier advanced across the continent from east to west, enveloping all before it and bringing with it a strong infusion of American institutions and practices. Perhaps befitting a country with already sharply defined regions, the Canadian frontier assumed a different character in different parts of the country: in the West, the predominant ethos was derived from the distant imperial power.

The West's experience of government and trade in the hands of the monopolistic HBC, whose decisions were made outside the region, proved but a prelude to later experiences, the most obvious parallel being the CPR's singular influence after 1885. Other contacts might be based more closely to home—for instance, the Roman Catholic Church and its missions, whose religious orders often represented the most sustained contact Natives had with Europeans—but most were part of an imposed institutional framework that determined the West's early development. In the colonial period, the frontier was populated not by independent-minded individuals seeking escape from the confines of civilization but by clerks, clerics, and petty bureaucrats.

Confederation, the transfer of Rupert's Land and the North-West Territories by Britain to Canada, the unrest at Red River in 1869, and the desire of Ottawa to provide for peaceful settlement throughout the West led to the creation in 1873 of the North-West Mounted Police. Thus another institutional restraint was added to western life, one that, with rare exceptions, guaranteed an orderly and organized period of settlement. The success of the mounted police depended upon the peaceable nature of the Native people and on the pervasive respect both Natives and whites held for the law. That respect was intimately linked to British traditions surrounding the courts and judiciary. A major concern in the study of politics is the means by which societies establish their legitimacy; it is no exaggeration to say that the legitimacy of the West's early institutions derived substantially from their British origins.

At least until the First World War, when a strong sense of Canadian nationalism began to develop in the West, westerners used imperial references to define their development. The empire offered a set of values for Canadians in other regions of the country too; but in those areas there was also a domestic experience on which to build. The size and sparse population of the West, whose governing institutions were external to the region and even to Canada, discouraged the development of similar internal unity. The "separation" of the West from the rhythm of national life, a feature that grew stronger even as Canada expanded westward, was established early because of the region's distinctive setting.

Economy: Benevolent Dependency

The dependency that first appeared in pre-settlement days later became an object of public policy, or so it seemed to westerners after they became part of Confederation. Its bedrock was the National Policy, proclaimed by Prime Minister John A. Macdonald in 1878. Initially, that policy was limited to a tariff to protect Canadian industries, but eventually it came to embrace a set of initiatives that included construction of a transcontinental railway and promotion of western settlement. Built with gifts of public money and public land, the CPR also received preferential treatment in the form of exemption from local taxes and a monopoly on traffic between its line and the international boundary. Prairie farmers needed the railway to haul their grain to distant ports for shipment abroad, but they paid heavily for the privilege. "It was the frontier which paid [for the railway]," wrote Chester Martin in *"Dominion Lands" Policy*. To illustrate his claim, he noted that "for more than 650 miles of Ontario mileage for the main line of the CPR, not a single acre of land subsidy came from the Province of Ontario," while Saskatchewan "contributed nearly half the acreage of the whole federal railway land grant system."[2] Under these conditions, which deprived territorial governments of valuable land and resources, no railway could be popular, and hatred of the CPR became an article of faith for western farmers.

At the end of the nineteenth century, when the CPR wanted to build another line from southern Alberta through the Crow's Nest Pass into British Columbia to tap the coal and mineral traffic of the area, farmers' hostility toward the CPR was so intense that the federal government agreed to further railroad subsidies only in exchange for a guarantee from the CPR to fix its freight rates on western goods in perpetuity. These became the famous Crow's Nest Rates, widely known as the farmers' Magna Carta. After being temporarily suspended during the First World War, they became enshrined in statute in the 1920s. Their abolition required an act of Parliament, which was passed in 1983 after acrimonious debate within the grain industry, in Parliament, and between the western provincial and federal governments.

Passion over the rates suggests another western obsession—railways. For British Columbia, where promise of a railway had been a key condition for its entry in 1871, the CPR symbolized the commitment of Confederation; on the Prairies, an efficient network of rail lines to serve the thousands of scattered grain elevators proved indispensable to the success of the wheat economy and to the widely dispersed population dependent upon it.

Compared to other areas of the country, where distances were shorter and where alternative means of transportation (water or road) played a vital economic role, the West, and especially the Prairies, looked overwhelmingly to rail. This background helps to explain the intense regional feeling that accompanied federal proposals to curtail rail services, either through rail-line abandonment, as implemented in the 1970s, or closure of parts of VIA Rail, as proposed at the end of the 1980s.

As we have already mentioned, Ottawa retained control of prairie resources, which included the most important resource of the early twentieth century—land—because it wanted to promote orderly settlement of the West and it thought this would not happen if each province determined its own settlement policy. In addition to blocks of land set aside to support schools and help finance the railway, other blocks were designated for homesteading. Through an aggressive policy, the federal authorities directed hundreds of thousands of immigrants from Europe, the British Isles, and the United States to the West and permitted some who were bound by religion and language to settle as groups. This is the origin of the Prairies' unusual collection of ethnic settlements, still evident today in the Canadian census and election returns.

By the 1920s, western settlement had ended and, with it, the reason for federal control of resources. Ironically, the transfer of resources to the Prairie provinces in 1930 coincided with the onset of a decade of severe drought and depression, which forced these provinces into near-bankruptcy and renewed dependency on Ottawa, first for relief and then for economic rehabilitation.

Would the 1930 transfer have been made had the federal government known of the rich reserves of oil and natural gas that lay under the Prairies? Fifty years later, when the price of international oil skyrocketed and Alberta and Saskatchewan stood to gain "windfall" profits, the federal government intervened through its National Energy Program to regulate the domestic price of this resource. Ottawa's argument that a moderated price increase was in the national interest sparked furious dissent in Alberta and Saskatchewan, since no other province had had the price of its natural resources curtailed for any reason.

The dependency of the West on federal policies is a more complex subject than westerners usually admit. On the one hand, unlike the Prairie provinces, British Columbia never suffered the indignity of being treated as less than an equal partner in Confederation. Political scientist Donald E. Blake asserts that, because the development of its forests, mines, and hydroelectric power always remained in its own hands, "the province has prospered independently of federal policies. . . . The historical record provides little support for basing grievances on a quasi-colonial past or on federal obstacles to provincial prosperity."[3] On the other hand, while federal policies have had a determinative influence on the Prairie provinces, it is less than conclusive that they have been detrimental to the well-being of these provinces. For instance, throughout the twentieth century, except for the decade of the 1930s when the region's grain industry was ravaged by drought and depression, the prosperity of the Prairie provinces—whether measured by per capita income, level of employment, or other common indices—surpassed that of all the provinces east of the Ottawa River.

It has become part of prairie folklore to claim that federal policies have thwarted the economic diversification of the region. Yet recent research disputes this claim, arguing that western dependence upon a resource economy is due to irreconcilable conditions, of which distance from markets and associated transportation costs are the primary discouragement to secondary manufacturing.[4] More heretical still is the view that federal policies—beginning in 1935 with the creation of the Canadian Wheat Board (CWB), which was ultimately to exercise monopoly powers over the marketing and transport of wheat, and continuing through a variety of later federal programs designed to promote regional economic security— have sustained the West and its agrarian way of life. Partial confirmation of this position is found in the fears expressed at the effect of the Free Trade Agreement with the United States on the operation of the CWB and on various subsidy and stabilization programs designed to support western agriculture.

The federal government may have been benevolent in its treatment of the West, but that has not made western dependence less demeaning. This treatment does help to account, however, for the sense of frustration that the receiver and the giver both experience, which manifests itself in a search for political remedies to an unequal relationship. A large part of the discontent arises from the region's inability to assert any significant control over its economy. That happens because regional resources are so important a component of the national economy and because most of them are components of international or interprovincial trade, both of which come under federal jurisdiction.

Demography: A Region Unlike the Others

By any demographic measure, the western provinces are unusual in Canada. In absolute numbers, as well as in proportion to their individual total populations, each has more Native people than any other province. Nonetheless, for most of this century the provincial governments ignored

Native peoples when formulating public policy. In recent years, such neglect has not been possible. Developments at different levels of politics account for the change in attitude. First, within the provinces, Aboriginal people are more visible due to their migration from reserves and remote areas into the major cities of the West. Second, and in the national context, Native land claims and treaty rights, as well as the Charlottetown Accord in 1992, with its provisions for Aboriginal self-government, have forced the provinces to consider the distinctive claims of Aboriginal people. Finally, the human rights values promoted by the United Nations and its agencies have been cited as an international standard against which governmental action on behalf of Aboriginal peoples is to be judged. As a consequence, westerners are more aware, though not necessarily more enlightened, than their fellow Canadians about Native issues. Throughout the debates on the Charlottetown Accord, there was support for Aboriginal self-government across the country, although it was least strong in the four western provinces.[5]

Outside of Quebec, the provinces with the smallest proportion of people of British descent are the Prairie provinces. According to the 1986 census, less than 25 percent of prairie respondents who named a single ethnic origin called themselves British (the figure for British Columbia was 33 percent).[6] The contrast between British Columbia and the other western provinces is even more striking in historical perspective. British Columbia began as a pre-eminently "British" province (with a miniscule Asian minority who had initially been brought to Canada to help build the CPR), while from the first flood of prairie settlement, a strong European presence qualified assertion of British domination in that region. Before and after the First World War, some prairie Anglo-Canadians resisted this non-British influence, and in Saskatchewan they went so far as to support the Ku Klux Klan's anti-foreign campaign. By the 1950s, however, the non-British component of the prairie population had become "old ethnics," and ethnic distinctions themselves had almost disappeared. In Manitoba and Saskatchewan, more recent immigration has been so slight as to leave this situation undisturbed. By way of contrast, in 1986, 16 percent of all Canadian immigrants lived in British Columbia and 9 percent in Alberta; these people constituted 22 and 16 percent of their respective provincial populations. The characteristics of these new immigrants are different from those of the earlier settlers: rather than being isolated in rural locations and engaged in agriculture, they gravitate to the large cities and work at a range of occupations. There is not the space in this chapter to explore the ramifications for regional politics and society of these dramatic changes in immigration patterns, except to note that in provinces like British Columbia and Alberta (and even more in Ontario, where in 1986 one in four residents was an immigrant) the "new ethnics" constitute a vigorous force in Canadian society. When combined with deliberate multicultural policies, this new force will predictably unleash pressures to diverge from the older western Canadian belief in pluralism tempered by common institutions and one common language. Recent polls, such as one in 1993 for the Council of Christians and Jews, found that 72 percent of Canadians want newcomers to "adapt to the way of life of the majority."

In the past, the West has never been receptive to claims made on it by any ethnically defined groups. This tradition is, in part, the source of the hostility some westerners have shown to official bilingualism, which is embodied in the federal Official Languages Act, 1969. In their eyes, French Canadians represent only another ethnic group. While French was a dominant language in the days of the fur trade and even into the early years of Confederation, the francophone population of the western provinces is now small and concentrated in a few historic communities, such as St Boniface, Manitoba, Gravelbourg, Saskatchewan, and St Albert, Alberta. The opposition to the federal government's commitment to bilingualism, evident in protests before the Royal Commission on Bilingualism and Biculturalism in the 1960s, and which accelerated in response to policies initiated by Trudeau and Mulroney in the 1970s and 1980s, reveals critical differences in political values that help to explain the strength of regionalism.

One final demographic factor of importance in understanding Western Canada relates to migration trends, for they are markedly different in different parts of the region. In the first thirty years of this century, the area of greatest expansion was Saskatchewan and Manitoba. Before the Depression and drought, when wheat was undisputed king of the prairie economy, these two provinces, with Winnipeg as the commercial and transportation hub of the Prairies, experienced rapid growth. But after the Depression, Saskatchewan slipped from the most to the least populous of the four provinces, while Manitoba and its capital stagnated. Since the Second World War, the growth provinces have been Alberta and British Columbia, the former primarily because of the expansion of the oil industry and its suppliers, the latter for a variety of reasons, some of which—like climate—are not related to a generally prosperous economy. In the period since 1961, Manitoba and Saskatchewan have consistently lost more people than they have attracted, while Alberta, which looked to oil to lessen its dependence on the unpredictable grain economy, saw its population grow dramatically due to interprovincial migration, gaining 197 000 people between 1971 and 1981 (the years of the oil boom) but then losing 27 000 people in the next five years, as the industry went into a slump. British Columbia, more diversified and therefore more protected from similar fluctuations, invariably gained population through interprovincial migration. Alberta and British Columbia also experienced higher rates of natural population increase and greater foreign immigration than the other two western provinces.

The composition of these population flows requires analysis, for the age, sex, and ethnic characteristics of new arrivals have major implications for public policy and political choices. Similarly, the decline of the two easternmost provinces of the region has meant that these provinces have an older population whose needs and concerns differ from those farther west. Such analysis cannot be pursued, however, in this chapter.

Politics: Conformity and Radicalism

The old parties of Canadian politics—the Liberals and Conservatives—evolved out of the politics of the United Canadas before 1867. After Confederation they organized elsewhere, as new provinces were admitted to the union, so that by the 1890s it was possible to speak of a national two-party system at both levels of the federation. That uniformity disappeared at the end of the First World War, when a series of "new" or "third" parties appeared. To date, the first of these—the Progressives—still holds the title as the most successful third party in a single election in Canadian history, winning sixty-five seats in the 1921 election and all but six of the Prairies' forty-three seats. That election was a watershed in national politics: thereafter the old parties were unable to reassert their absolute control. In the decades since, all but one of the third parties that have fought in national elections with some degree of success can trace their origins to the Prairies. The exception is the Bloc Québécois, which in the 1993 federal election campaigned only in Quebec. From birth, the Co-operative Commonwealth Federation (CCF) saw itself as a national party, but it always depended upon western agrarian support and organization for success, a situation not dissimilar from that facing its successor—the New Democratic Party (NDP)—in the 1988 and 1993 general elections.

One of the perennial questions of Canadian politics is why third parties took root on the Prairies, and flourished later in British Columbia, but have enjoyed so little success elsewhere in Canada (the obvious exceptions being in Quebec, and in the unexpected victory of the NDP in Ontario in 1990). Clearly, the answer is not simply economic deprivation, or Atlantic Canada, which has the most depressed economic indices in the country, should be a hotbed of dissent. Instead, it is the region most loyal to the old parties. Arguably, Western Canada's disposition to experiment politically is bound up with the factors already discussed in this chapter: physical and historical isolation, economic dependence, and demographic distinctiveness.

The old parties that grew up in Central Canada were constructed so as to accommodate the linguistic and religious duality of that area. The search for a balance—between English and French, Protestant and Roman Catholic—led to what might be termed a politics of culture. While in the West periodic clashes between these sets of interests might occur, notably in the Riel Rebellions or the conflict surrounding the Manitoba School Question (when, in 1890, that province legislated unilingualism in place of bilingualism), they never provided a sustained basis for political organization. Instead, because of the region's rapid settlement, social pluralism, and economic growth and collapse, the politics of the West revolved not around culture but around progress and development, or protest, or class, or, significantly, around a rejection of politics altogether.

If there can be such a species as the politics of administration, or bureaucracy, then it took root in a province like Alberta, where one-party dominance became the rule, and electoral and legislative competition the exception. In provincial politics, only Saskatchewan in the long term and Manitoba more recently have witnessed the alternation in power of two parties. Between 1952 and 1991, Social Credit governed British Columbia for all but three years, and since 1905 only four parties (Liberal, United Farmers of Alberta, Social Credit, and Progressive Conservative) have governed Alberta, for periods of 16, 14, 37, and 22 years, respectively.

In democratic systems, political parties are normally viewed as fundamental agents of consensus and unity. That was the role of the early Liberals and Conservatives, and it is possible to interpret Confederation itself as an achievement of partisan accommodation. It is partly because of this crucial function of parties that Canadian history and politics attribute such importance to nation builders like Sir John A. Macdonald or nation maintainers like William Lyon Mackenzie King, both of whom during their periods as prime minister met and overcame challenges to national unity. It is in the same context that former prime minister Brian Mulroney believed that the failed Meech Lake and Charlottetown accords were needed to achieve national consolidation.

The failure of the old national parties to win and hold support in the major regions of Canada is a powerful criticism directed at leaders, whether they be Liberals rejected by westerners or Progressive Conservatives rejected by Quebec voters. Canadians expect the old parties to fulfil this unifying function; yet in Western Canada in the last seventy years, they have performed this task very poorly. Following sixteen of the twenty-two general elections since 1921, a majority of Quebec's members of Parliament have sat on the government benches; this was true for Ontario and the Atlantic provinces in fifteen elections; for the West, the corresponding number is six. No other statistic so starkly underlines the West's political separation from the Canadian mainstream.

FEDERALISM AND THE WEST

The Problem of Representation

The eternal question of Canadian politics concerns English–French relations, or the question of national unity. Canadian history before 1867 and Canadian politics since then have focused more intensely on this matter than on any other; in this century, for example, the conscription crises of both world wars, battles over minority language rights, and, more recently, official bilingualism and Quebec separatist movements have preoccupied a succession of federal governments. Yet, as this chapter has shown, there is another dimension to the unity question—that of western Canada, which for the last seven decades has repeatedly demonstrated its discontent with national politics. Gradually, that discontent has come to centre on the subject of representation or, more precisely, on the perceived failure of national governmental institutions to respond to the West's desires.

The representation problem arises from the stark fact that two-thirds of Canada's population live in Quebec and Ontario. This means that of 295 seats in the House of Commons those provinces occupy 174. No political party wishing to form a government can succeed without strong support in one or another of these provinces. And no government party can remain in power unless its policies appeal to those provinces. The crux of the problem lies in Canada's system of cabinet government. This system operates on the principle of majority rule, the effectiveness of which requires stringent enforcement of party discipline. The concentration of power that results from this principle is fundamentally different from that found in the United States, for example, where the executive (the president) and the legislature (Congress) are independent of one another and where, as a result, the president and the congressional parties must engage in complex bargaining to secure the passage of legislation. Much more than in the United States, Canadian government is a question of being in or out of power, and for a long time the West has felt itself to be out of power.

It is for this reason that westerners have in the past experimented with third parties, hoping thereby to deprive either of the two leading parties of a majority and thus force a minority government to respond to regional demands. That was the strategy of the Reform Party in the 1993 election, but it is not the party's long-term objective, which is to realign Canadian parties along a left–right axis. On balance, third parties have failed as dependable instruments of regional pressure on government. A party like the CCF/NDP, with strong social welfare objectives, did achieve indirect success nationally by forcing Liberal and Conservative governments to acknowledge these concerns through their legislation (for example, the King government introduced family allowances, the Diefenbaker government national hospitalization insurance, and the Pearson government medicare).

More recently, westerners have opted for a new strategy to promote their interests. If non-conformity in the support of parties achieved less than desired results, then perhaps (they reasoned) the rules of the game, rather than the players, should be changed. That is the origin of the West's, and particularly Alberta's, enthusiasm for Senate reform. Suggestions to reform the upper chamber of Parliament are not new. What is new is the single objective of most recent proposals: to lessen the absolute power of the prime minister and cabinet over Parliament. While their details are complex, the proposals invariably seek to give the provinces a role to play in the selection of senators, thereby removing some or all of that power from the prime minister (where it has rested since Confederation). As well, they usually confer on a reformed Senate some new role in the approval of government appointments and, most importantly, they aim to achieve greater equality of provincial representation in the Senate. Currently, there are four senatorial regions—the West, Ontario, Quebec, and the Maritimes, with an additional number of Senate seats reserved for Newfoundland and the Yukon and Northwest Territories. In practice, this system means that Nova Scotia and New Brunswick, for example, have more senators than do the considerably more populous western provinces.

A reformed Senate, with greater power in the national government and greater equality of representation, appeals to an area of the country that has long complained of the exclusion of its interests from national attention. But advocates of Senate reform are wary of plans in which a more representative upper chamber is gained at the expense of distortions to the House of Commons. This was the primary complaint of the British Columbia government against the Charlottetown Accord, which would have made the provinces equal in terms of Senate representation but, in return, would have guaranteed Quebec 25 percent representation in the lower house in perpetuity.

Senate reform is most popular in Alberta. Although discussed elsewhere in the region, it is the Alberta government and provincial interest groups that have most strongly promoted the proposal. Why this is so has yet to be fully explored. Initial areas of investigation include the relative absence in the provinces of a tradition of competitive parties, accompanied by an entrenched predisposition to see government solely as an instrument of administration. It is clear that Senate reform would introduce changes to the form of disciplined party government that currently operates in the House of Commons. Thus, in the other western provinces, where party competition is more prevalent than in Alberta, such consequences of Senate reform are reasons to treat the proposal with caution.

Similarly, other proposals for institutional reform, such as the introduction of proportional representation (PR)—which would see seats in the House of Commons allocated to parties according to the proportion of popular vote won rather than, as now, on a winner-take-all basis—have received mixed support in the West, with Alberta most in favour. The advantage of PR, in light of general election results where the Liberals, for instance, have won as much as 24 percent of the Saskatchewan vote but none of its seats, is obvious if representation of voters' opinion is the sole criterion for evaluation. Of course, there are other criteria, among them the belief in the need for strong parties and strong government, which some critics believe PR would undermine.

Because the operation of Canadian federal politics has stifled the representation of western regional interests, the western provinces have long been active in what political scientists call province building. In essence, the term refers to "the multifarious activities of provincial governments" by which they seek greater autonomy to advance the interests of their economies and societies.[7] The concept encompasses such innovations in Saskatchewan as the CCF's central-planning mechanisms and its host of Crown corporations to develop that province's economy. It also applies to the Conservative government's activist involvement in the direction of Alberta's economy after 1970. Province building has much wider implications than are suggested here, extending, for example, to the growth of professional provincial bureaucracies that possess the expertise to bargain with their counterparts in other provinces and in Ottawa. Although the western provinces are neither the only nor the first provinces to engage in this activity, they have discovered in province building a route by which they can advance their unique interests, one that is doubly useful because they believe the institutions of the national government to be unresponsive to them.

CONCLUSION

The triumph of Confederation in 1867 rested in the accommodation of English- and French-Canadian interests through a common set of institutions. Out of that achievement emerged an eminently stable government and a free, peaceful, and prosperous society. But the original federal bargain adjusted uneasily to change. That was the reason why the central government sought at the outset to control the expansion and development of the West. And it was these assertions of control—of the region's resources, economy, and politics—that westerners rejected. The integration of the western provinces into national institutions—both public and private—has been fitful, as the region's distinctive history, economy, demography, and politics guaranteed it would be. The cultural basis of the original federation had no counterpart in the West; and because it had no counterpart, the West perpetually felt out of sympathy and out of touch with Central Canada, whose needs and desires Confederation was designed to fulfil.

NOTES

[1] See Barry M. Gough, "The Character of the British Columbia Frontier," *BC Studies* 32 (Winter 1976–77): 28-40, and R.O. MacFarlane, "Manitoba Politics and Parties After Confederation," *Canadian Historical Association* (1940): 46.

[2] Chester Martin, *"Dominion Lands" Policy*, ed. Lewis H. Thomas (Toronto: McClelland & Stewart, 1973), 74.

[3] Donald E. Blake, "Managing the Periphery: British Columbia and the National Political Community" in *National Politics and Community in Canada*, ed. R. Kenneth Carty and W. Peter Ward (Vancouver: University of British Columbia Press, 1986), 173.

[4] See Kenneth H. Norrie, "Some Comments on Prairie Economic Alienation," *Canadian Public Policy* 2, 2 (Spring 1976): 211–24, and "A Regional Economic Overview of the West Since 1945" in *The Making of the Modern West: Western Canada Since 1945*, ed. A.W. Rasporich (Calgary, 1984), 63–78.

[5] Richard Johnston, André Blais, Elisabeth Gidengi, and Neil Nevitte, "The People and the Charlottetown Accord" in *Canada: The State of the Federation, 1993*, ed. Ronald L. Watts and Douglas M. Brown (Kingston: Institute of Intergovernmental Relations, 1993), 24–25.

[6] Canada, Statistics Canada, *The Nation: Ethnicity, Immigration, and Citizenship*, cat. no. 93-109 (Ottawa: Ministry of Supply and Services, 1989), vii and table 1.

[7] R.A. Young, Philippe Faucher, and André Blais, "The Concept of Province-Building: A Critique," *Canadian Journal of Political Science* 17, 4 (Dec. 1984): 783–818. See also Edwin R. Black and Alan C. Cairns, "A Different Perspective on Canadian Federalism," *Canadian Public Administration* 9, 1 (March 1966): 27–44.

Suggested Reading

Blake, Donald E. "Managing the Periphery: British Columbia and the National Political Community." In *National Politics and Community in Canada*. Ed. R. Kenneth Carty and W. Peter Ward. Vancouver: University of British Columbia Press, 1986.

The analysis of British Columbia's relations with the rest of Canada is a corrective to the western literature that more often focuses on the Prairie provinces. Through his examination, Blake suggests that British Columbia is both like and unlike its fellow western provinces.

Conway, J.F. *The West: The History of a Region in Confederation*. Toronto: Lorimer, 1983.

A short, sharp, critical analysis of the West in Confederation. While there are numerous references to British Columbia, the argument focuses predominantly on the discontents of the Prairie provinces. The book's tone is reflected in the subtitle of its conclusion—"The Politics of Desperation."

Dyck, Rand. *Provincial Politics in Canada*. Scarborough, ON: Prentice-Hall, 1986.

This introductory text is divided into four parts, the last devoted to "The Western Provinces." Each chapter examines the "setting" of a province, its political culture, institutions, evolution, and recent politics. Much more detail is included, with the result that the student is presented with the most thorough summary available of the political history of each province.

Martin, Chester. *"Dominion Lands" Policy.* Ed. with intro. by Lewis H. Thomas. Toronto: McClelland & Stewart, 1973.

The bases of the Prairie West's grievances against the federal government are set out in detail, and with a literary style that makes the case memorable and, for some, irrefutable.

Joan Price Boase

8

FEDERALISM AND FEDERAL-PROVINCIAL RELATIONS

olitical systems can be organized in several different ways. Since the passage of the Constitution Act, 1867 (formerly the British North America Act), Canada has had a *federal* system of government. This means there are two levels of government that can legitimately make laws affecting the Canadian people. The federal, or national, government can legislate for all Canadians in the ten provinces and two territories; a provincial government's legislation is binding only on those living within that province's boundaries. Neither level of government has an absolute right to legislate in all areas. The Constitution Act sets out the constitutional division of powers—that is, those areas where each level of government may legislate. These enumerated powers (primarily in sections 91 and 92 of the act) are often referred to as the *jurisdictions* of the two governments.

The choice of a federal form of government was a deliberate one in 1867, but the Constitution Act that established it reflects an ambivalence, which has persisted, toward governing. The framers of the Canadian constitution simultaneously looked at the government in the United Kingdom and at the federal system established in the United States in the eighteenth century and attempted to combine what they perceived to be the best elements of the two systems. The result was a constitutional document with ambiguities that only became evident over time and whose imprecise language was open to different interpretations. The fact that the imprecise language allowed different interpretations permitted some necessary flexibility, but it also precipitated much federal–provincial wrangling. The ambiguities and the different interpretations resulted from two fundamental tensions in the original constitutional agreement. First, the language of the act, which established a federal state, reads more as though it were describing a unitary state. Second, the act attempts to reconcile a federal system with a parliamentary system of government.

UNITARY, FEDERAL, AND CONFEDERAL STATES

A *unitary state* is one where all legislative power is vested in a single level of government, which means that one legislature retains total sovereignty or supreme power over the entire state. Within a unitary state (such as the United Kingdom), there are necessarily lower levels of government that exist to manage local affairs. These governments have their legislative powers delegated to them from the central government, which always retains the right to rescind these powers. For example, in the 1920s, the British Parliament in London delegated to Northern Ireland the power to establish its own legislature in Belfast. Decades later, the British government decided that this experiment had been a failure, and it abolished the legislature in Northern Ireland. Subsequently, this region elected political representatives to the British Parliament, and retained only local governments whose power was delegated from London.

Legally, in a *federal system*, the central parliament cannot abolish the provincial or state legislatures, for their legislative power is their own, within their jurisdiction, and is guaranteed by the division of powers in the supreme law of the land, the constitution. In Canada, the relationship between the provincial governments and their local governments is like that between governments in a unitary state. Local governments may make laws binding on their constituents, but this power has been delegated to them by the provincial government and can always be withdrawn: it does not have a constitutional guarantee.

Clearly, a federal system, with its sovereignty or legislative powers divided between two levels of government, is more decentralized than a unitary system. A *confederal system* is more decentralized still. A confederal system is one where the individual states each retain full sovereignty but delegate specified powers to a central body, retaining the right to rescind these powers and opt out of the confederation. There is not a clear example of a confederation in the modern world but, with its continued integration, the European Union (EU) comes close. The various members of the EU have delegated power over certain economic affairs to a central European parliament, although each individual state has legally retained full sovereignty. However, as integration proceeds, interdependence among the states increases, exacerbating the difficulties of opting out.

It is helpful to use a continuum to better understand the relative characteristics of these political systems. Figure 8.1 allows us to measure the relative degree of, and changes over time in, centralization and decentralization in individual states. The United Kingdom is situated close to the centralized end (although it is less centralized than in the past) and the EU, while not quite integrated enough to be a true confederal system, is moving in that direction. Systems move along the continuum as they become more or less decentralized. The United States, a federal state, is somewhat more centralized than is Canada, another federal state. In fact, the evolution of Canadian federalism has seen it move sharply along the continuum from the centralized toward the decentralized end.

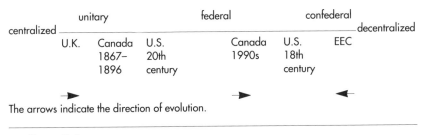

Figure 8.1

The ambivalence of the framers of the Canadian constitution is based on the fact that, while they ostensibly were designing federal structures (evident in the federal–provincial division of powers), they imbued them with many features of a unitary state (in sections that clearly intended the central government to be predominant), and then called the result a confederation!

A PARLIAMENTARY SYSTEM AND FEDERALISM

The second fundamental tension arises from the effort to superimpose a federal structure on a parliamentary system. The short preamble to the Constitution Act, 1867, states that the provinces wish to be "federally united ... with a Constitution similar in principle to that of the

United Kingdom." The subsequent sections draft a constitution in many ways more similar to that of the United States than that of the United Kingdom, which does not, in fact, have a formal, written constitution. The development of parliamentary government in Britain was a gradual evolution in governing tradition, which led to recognized and accepted constitutional conventions. These conventions (such as responsible government and parliamentary supremacy) are considered inviolate and, under the preamble to our constitution, they became fundamental (although unwritten) principles in the Canadian system of government.

The convention that is the most difficult to reconcile with a federal—and written—constitution is that of parliamentary supremacy. It has been said that the doctrine of parliamentary supremacy means that the government at Westminster can pass virtually any law unchallenged, short of "changing a man into a woman." This is because the executive and legislative power are fused in Parliament. In the United States, by contrast, there is a separation of power between the executive and legislative branches (the president and Congress). Such a doctrine of supremacy would appear to be the antithesis of a federal system whose very purpose is to divide sovereignty (or legislative powers) between two quite distinct levels of government. Nevertheless, the principle of parliamentary supremacy has persisted. Its importance to contemporary thinking on government in Canada was evident in discussions leading up to the adoption in 1982 of the Charter of Rights and Freedoms, which gives judges the power to strike down legislation, thus further restricting parliamentary supremacy.

As one might expect, the unclear language and fundamental contradictions upon which the Canadian constitutional order is based have led to some very interesting developments in the evolution of federalism and federal–provincial relations. Before we trace the different stages in this evolution, it would be helpful to examine the reasons why the framers of the constitution chose a federal system of government in 1867.

Why a Federal System?

The "fathers of federalism" wanted to establish a new political community in the northern half of the North American continent. This territory consisted of several colonies of Great Britain, including Prince Edward Island, Nova Scotia, New Brunswick, Newfoundland, British Columbia, and the United Province of Canada. To the northwest was an immense but sparsely populated tract of land that was valued primarily for its resources and as a link to British Columbia, the westernmost colony on the Pacific Ocean. It was a challenge to unite these disparate entities into a single nation, and a federal system seemed the only means of addressing their individual political, economic, and cultural needs.

In the political sense, federation served several purposes. First, it separated the troubled Province of Canada, which had been described as consisting of "two nations warring in the bosom of a single state,"[1] into the provinces of Quebec and Ontario. These two new provinces and the two well-established political systems of Nova Scotia and New Brunswick formed a federal union. It is unlikely that Nova Scotia and New Brunswick would have agreed to union if they had not been able to retain their own long-established political structures. The Constitution Act also established a central government in Ottawa and provided for the admission of other colonies and the expansion of the state west to the Pacific. In so doing, it founded a recognizable political entity north of the American border, filling a "dangerous power vacuum" in British North America and providing a legitimate resistance to aggressive American expansionism in the West.[2]

In the economic realm, the federal agreement divided the levers of control between the two levels of government. It gave what at the time were considered to be the important levers (peace, order, and good government; trade and commerce; banking; the lion's share of taxation) to the central government in section 91, and the unimportant levers (direct taxation, licences, hospitals, and "matters of a merely local or private nature in the Province") to the provincial governments in section 92. Although the original act contained a provision (section 109) that resources would remain under provincial control, the federal government retained ownership and control of the resources of Manitoba, Saskatchewan, and Alberta when they became provinces. In effect, this created a group of second-class provinces and clearly indicated the intention of developing a federal state economically dominated by the central government and central economic interests.

The Constitution Act—and the federal system itself—also addressed the more immediate concerns of the individual provinces by giving them jurisdiction over all matters that were considered to be the responsibility of local governments as well as those matters upon which the historical differences between the French- and English-speaking communities rested. Thus, provincial powers included education, health, and welfare, municipal institutions, the administration of justice in the province, and shared power (with federal paramountcy) over agriculture and immigration. It was anticipated that in matters of a "local and private nature" (section 92(16)) the provinces would be free to pursue their own priorities, and that the French-speaking majority in Quebec would have the power to ensure the continuation of its cultural and linguistic traditions.

Even in its approach to addressing the particular political, economic, and cultural needs of the provinces, the act exhibits the ambivalence of the fathers of Canadian federalism. Politically, although each province had its own legislature, the federal government retained the power to appoint the lieutenant-governor, the Queen's representative in each province. The lieutenant-governor was given the power to reserve provincial legislation subject to review by the federal cabinet, and the federal cabinet was given the power to disallow provincial legislation so reserved. This provision clearly circumscribed the doctrine of parliamentary supremacy within the provinces and legally established a relationship between Ottawa and the provincial governments similar to the colonial relationship between Ottawa and London.

Economically, the founders also sought to circumscribe the powers conferred on the provinces. While section 92(2) of the act grants the provinces "exclusive" right to make laws in relation to direct taxation, section 91(3) states that the Parliament of Canada will have "exclusive" legislative authority over "the raising of money by any mode or system of taxation." Furthermore, section 92(10)(c) contains the ominous provision that the Parliament of Canada may declare certain "works" wholly situated within a province to be to the "general advantage" of Canada.[3]

The provisions relating to the preservation of the cultural traditions of English- and French-speaking Canadians were also subject to ambiguous interpretations, perhaps because the framers were more concerned with protecting the English community within Quebec than the French community outside that province. Both languages were to be permitted in Parliament, in the legislature of Quebec, and in the courts of both their jurisdictions. In addition, federal and Quebec records and journals were to appear in both languages. None of this was required of the legislatures of the other three original provinces.

The relationship between language, religion, and education has often been a fuzzy one. Although the Constitution Act protected denominational schools wherever they existed before 1867, it is silent on the language of instruction. Given demographic differences among the provinces, this has created confusion. In nineteenth-century Quebec, Catholics were almost all francophones while Protestants were almost exclusively anglophone. Ontario, with a sizeable number of Irish immigrants, in addition to a francophone minority, had both French and English Catholic schools. In Manitoba, demographic changes, in which the relative size of the French population declined as European immigrants and settlers from Ontario flocked to the province, set the scene for the divisive Manitoba School Question. In 1890, the provincial government unconstitutionally eliminated denominational schools after declaring the province unilingual. Both acts were deliberate attempts to obstruct the expansion of French-speaking communities in the West.

It is clear that the ambivalent approach to the development of a political system in Canada began with the attempt to emulate both the British and the American systems by superimposing a federal system on a parliamentary form of government. The problems that arose from this arrangement were compounded by the ambiguous political relationships that were established and by the provisions of the 1867 act that dealt with economic and cultural concerns. The historical evolution of federal–provincial relations in Canada has been greatly affected by these ambiguities and contradictions.

THE EVOLUTION OF FEDERAL–PROVINCIAL RELATIONS

The ambiguities implicit in the foundations of Canadian federalism have been pervasive in the years of its evolution. As Canada experienced social, economic, and technological change, and as demands on governments grew—especially in the second half of the twentieth century—relations between the two levels of government were forced to change and adjust, and they have often reflected the fundamental contradictions. They have also reflected the frequently conflicting perceptions of Canadian federalism that have been held by political leaders. Not unexpectedly, then, the history of the evolution of federal–provincial relations has been a rather convoluted one, further complicated by Canada's long and often controversial relationship with Britain. Although Canada became a sovereign state under the Statute of Westminster in 1931, Britain remained involved in Canadian constitutional affairs in two ways. First, because agreement could not be reached until 1982 on a method of amending the constitution in Canada, the British Parliament retained the responsibility for amendments, although it exercised the power only on request from Canada. Second, until 1949, a committee of British justices—the Judicial Committee of the Privy Council (JCPC)—remained Canada's final court of appeal, the arbiter of the federal system. The effects of eight decades of JCPC decisions have been far-reaching in the development of federal–provincial relations in Canada.

For many years, the conventional wisdom of those who were close observers of the constitutional decisions of the JCPC was that this committee had wilfully and even capriciously tampered with the intentions of the original framers of the Canadian constitution. Its early decisions mostly reflected the unitary language of the 1867 act, and some have referred to this period as one of "quasi-federalism," as the JCPC upheld federal legislation that it perceived to be "national" in nature, but had been challenged on constitutional grounds. Many decisions of the JCPC in the 1890s and subsequently, however, reversed the centralist trend, and the federal powers of reservation and disallowance gradually fell into disuse in the twentieth century. Relationships between the federal and provincial governments were irrevocably changed as the JCPC (sometimes with quite innovative reasoning) began to uphold the broadening spheres of authority of the provincial governments, although federal government actions that were national in nature were upheld when an emergency situation (such as war) could be identified.

Much has been written about the decisions of the justices of the JCPC and their propensity for treating the British North America Act simply as a British statute (which it was) rather than as a constitutional document (which it also was). It has been suggested that the justices deliberately attempted to impose on the colony their view of "classical" federalism (that is, governments equal in power and functioning in isolation within their enumerated jurisdictions), even if it did not coincide with the original intentions of the framers of the act. A perceptive article by Alan Cairns suggests, however, that the decisions of the JCPC were not capricious but were, in fact, an essential reflection of developing political realities in Canada.[4] Another, and simpler, explanation for the contradictory decisions of the first sixty years in particular is that the judicial interpretations may also have occasionally reflected the underlying Canadian ambivalence toward the union with its unitary language, federal structures, and confederal title.

Whatever the explanation for the judicial decisions, it is undeniable that political relationships and the federal–provincial balance of power have been fundamentally altered since the agreement in 1867, and jurisdictional competition has become endemic. The original ambiguities have persisted and have emerged as opposing perceptions of Canadian federalism, which are manifest in the federal–provincial negotiations that have often dominated Canadian politics since the Second World War. We will now examine the evolution of federal–provincial relations in the second half of the twentieth century.

FEDERAL–PROVINCIAL RELATIONS SINCE THE SECOND WORLD WAR

P eriods of war (1914–18 and 1939–45) and crisis (the Depression of the 1930s) have seen widespread acceptance of the centralization of governing powers and the strengthening of the government in Ottawa—*centralizing* or *centripetal federalism*. Other periods in Canadian history, with the exception of the two decades immediately after 1867, have seen efforts by the provincial governments to strengthen their powers vis-à-vis Ottawa—*decentralizing* or *centrifugal federalism*. Quebec and Ontario have led the way toward decentralization, and the other provinces, some more enthusiastically than others, have accepted the "provincial rights" or "compact theory" argument.[5] The metaphor of a swinging pendulum has frequently been used to describe the alternations from centripetal to centrifugal federalism, and disagreement over the centralist-decentralist balance has often led to discord. Whether the federation is perceived to be too centralized or too decentralized depends on the view one holds of the purpose of the government in Ottawa.

A centralist view of Canadian federalism accepts the proposition that the federal government may identify "national" interests, even in areas of provincial jurisdiction (such as health care, postsecondary education, pensions, day care), and use its enormous spending powers to persuade the provinces to accept federal activity in these areas. The centralist view also believes that Ottawa, as the "senior" government that represents all Canadians, should take the initiative in these areas to ensure that all Canadians have an equal standard of services. The decentralist view, on the other hand, adheres to a more classical form of federalism and argues that the identification of a national interest and pursuit of a national program in a field of provincial jurisdiction has the effect of distorting provincial priorities, since provincial governments are in a better position to determine their own needs. From this perspective, the use of federal spending power to ensure national programs amounts to coercion rather than persuasion and violates the federal principle. The tensions between these incompatible perceptions have been clearly evident in federal–provincial relations since the Second World War, when the Canadian government identified various welfare programs that it considered to be in the national interest and sought to have them implemented.

Such moves by the federal government and the resistance to them, particularly by the larger provinces, have led to a great number of meetings among ministers and officials of the two levels of government. These meetings have come to be known as *co-operative, administrative,* or *executive federalism.*[6] The proliferation of federal–provincial interactions in the second half of the twentieth century is a Canadian phenomenon that has led to a unique model of federalism. In the practical sense, the result of these interactions has been the development of an interdependence between the two levels of government in virtually all areas of governmental activity. In the political sense, since the provincial governments have been called upon to administer most of the federally initiated and shared-cost programs, consultation and co-operation have become imperative. Provincial bureaucracies have expanded in both a quantitative and qualitative sense and have developed administrative expertise that rivals that of the federal government. Like large bureaucracies everywhere, they are interested in protecting and promoting their own interests, and the provinces have come to demand that Ottawa confer with them before it makes any major moves, even in areas constitutionally assigned to the federal government. The evolution of federal–provincial relations since the Second World War is perhaps best demonstrated by a brief examination of the history of shared-cost programs.

The History of Shared-Cost Programs

It has been suggested that the framers of the constitution demonstrated a lack of foresight when they gave the lion's share of taxation to the federal government and jurisdiction over social welfare to the provincial governments. In 1867, however, perceptions of the important areas of government were quite different from what they are today, and the division of powers was decided with other priorities in mind. It was not until the Depression of the 1930s that the great disparity between the provinces' responsibility and their ability to raise revenue became fully apparent. Much of the history of federal–provincial relations since 1940, with its periods of co-operation and conflict, reflects attempts to reconcile this disparity: that is, the increasing interactions between the two levels of government have most frequently been driven by the need to discuss revenue-sharing arrangements to finance the welfare state.

Despite the constitutional difficulties, Canadian governments have developed social programs with a minimum of constitutional change. A major royal commission in the 1930s, the Rowell-Sirois Commission, conducted an exhaustive study of dominion–provincial relations and the federal–provincial division of responsibilities and resources. It recommended a broad redistribution of responsibilities and revenue sources and a return to the balance of power as it was originally conceived in 1867. This was to include the transfer to Ottawa of exclusive rights to income and corporation taxes and succession duties to enable the federal government to pursue national planning of essential welfare services. Although a constitutional amendment empowering Ottawa to establish a national unemployment insurance program was obtained in 1940, provincial resistance to the thrust of the Rowell-Sirois Report essentially killed any further modification in the division of powers and responsibilities. At a dominion–provincial conference convened in 1941 to consider the report, fierce opposition to its proposals for the centralizing of financial power was expressed by the governments of Quebec, Ontario, Alberta, and British Columbia. This ensured that future developments in the area of social welfare responsibility would be a result not of centralized strategic planning but of ad hoc adjustments and endless federal–provincial discussion and bargaining.

To support the war effort, the provincial governments did agree in 1941 to give the federal government temporary control over the personal and corporate tax fields. When the war ended, Ottawa decided that it should retain these sources of revenue. When the Liberal government called a federal–provincial meeting in 1945 to discuss postwar reconstruction, it was to embark on more than a decade of paternalistic centralism. Ottawa assumed the leadership role in both economic and social welfare policy, although not without provincial resistance, and the realization of its goals required frequent federal–provincial consultation.

The years from 1945 to 1970 saw great changes in the relationships among governments in Canada. During the early years of this period, relations were relatively harmonious, as the acceptance of centralism during the war years carried over into the immediate postwar period. Ottawa achieved dominance through a series of tax-sharing agreements with the provinces, which permitted it to collect 75 percent of all Canadian tax revenue. Although Quebec and Ontario refused to agree to the tax-sharing arrangements (Ontario agreed to a modified form in 1952), the federal government was able to wield its financial authority and achieve its purposes. It did this by means of grant-in-aid or conditional grant programs that were based on the transfer of large sums of money to the provinces in return for social legislation that met enunciated federal standards. For the most part, the provinces acquiesced, although Quebec under premiers

Maurice Duplessis and Jean Lesage refused federal involvement and "opted out" of most of the federal programs, citing interference with provincial autonomy.

By means of these shared-cost conditional grant programs (which the Rowell-Sirois Commission had warned against), the federal government was able to have national standards established in hospital and medical insurance, postsecondary education, the Canada Assistance Plan, vocational education, and other areas.[7] In 1965, when the Canada Pension Plan was established under Prime Minister Lester Pearson, Quebec was permitted to opt out of the plan, create a similar provincial plan, and still receive its share of federal funding. The development of these various plans had irreversible effects on the dynamics of federal–provincial relations, as each new agreement followed intense intergovernmental conferences involving officials, cabinet ministers, as well as first ministers and their advisors.

The change in relations was gradual but, in retrospect, can be seen as inevitable. In the 1940s and 1950s, federal–provincial interactions were mostly unstructured and informal, with occasionally more formal first ministers' conferences held to discuss financial arrangements and the initiation and administration of national programs. Slowly the organized machinery grew, as the increasing meetings of liaison committees demanded more federal and provincial expertise. Federal dominance continued into the 1960s, but the balance was shifting toward the provinces, and tensions and conflicts became more frequent in federal–provincial relations. During this decade, there was a rise in Quebec nationalism, and Quebec's many successes in gaining control of a greater share of revenue encouraged the other provinces to become more aggressive in their negotiating sessions with Ottawa. There was also a growing awareness, at both levels of government, of the increasing political importance of many areas of provincial jurisdiction. The result was more conflict in federal–provincial bargaining, frequent provincial demands for revenue to match their responsibilities, a gradual dissipation of federal dominance, and increasing federal–provincial interdependence.

The provinces continued to object to the conditional grant system for both philosophical and practical reasons. They demanded more tax room to meet their growing responsibilities and more provincial control of their constitutionally guaranteed jurisdictions. The federal government was also becoming disenchanted with the shared-cost programs. The open-ended nature of the financing arrangements meant that the costs of the programs were unpredictable and uncontrollable, and made budget planning difficult. The federal government also came to the realization that it was perceived as the tax collector, while the provincial governments were receiving most of the political credit for social programs. Under the government of Pierre Trudeau in the late 1960s and early 1970s, Ottawa attempted to disentangle itself from, and place ceilings on, its transfers for some programs. Subsequently, following many intense meetings of the federal and provincial finance ministers, a new fiscal arrangement was negotiated that governed federal contributions to the established programs of hospital and medical insurance and postsecondary education. An extremely complex law, the Established Programs Financing and Fiscal Arrangements Act, was passed in 1977, allowing Ottawa to extract itself from its open-ended commitment to provincial programs by means of a more predictable cash transfer and the granting of an additional share of taxes to the provinces. With the passage of this act, provincial governments were less constrained in their identification of priorities; there was a real shift of financial power toward the provinces, and by 1983 Ottawa's share of total taxation had dropped to 47 percent from 57.3 percent in 1975–76. It is also worth noting that the discussions preceding these changes to major social programs primarily involved finance ministers, not program ministers: the financing arrangements were considered to be of more importance than discussions of the substantive aspects of these plans.

The long history of the development of shared-cost programs ensured that, by the 1970s, the machinery of federal–provincial relations was institutionalized. Under Prime Minister Trudeau in 1976, the Federal Provincial Relations Office became a central agency of government the Finance Department, Treasury Board Secretariat, and other major federal departments developed their own units of federal–provincial expertise and many full-time intergovernmental specialists were hired. The provinces established similar machinery: led by Quebec, which created the first Intergovernmental Affairs Office in 1964, the other provinces gradually developed bureaucratic structures modelled on those of Ottawa and Quebec City. Federal–provincial relations had become a major growth industry.

While a knowledge of the development of shared-cost programs is essential to an understanding of intergovernmental relations in Canada, it is also important to realize that elaborate federal–provincial machinery is active in almost all policy areas. There are constant meetings, both formal and informal, among ministers, committees of officials, various advisory bodies and councils, and individual representatives of different policy areas within the governments. The many bureaucratic federal and provincial specialists, besides having different policy priorities and institutional concerns, often have personal agendas that lead them to protect and enhance their own and their government's sphere of power.

Although almost all intergovernmental meetings are held in camera (in secret), the federal–provincial meetings with which Canadians are most familiar are the televised annual first ministers conferences. These conferences are convened by the federal government, and the first ministers and their enormous entourages of advisors discuss an agenda that has been set by Ottawa. Such conferences have given Canadians a view of relations among governments quite different from the centralist concept of the postwar years. It is a picture of assertive and well-informed premiers holding their own in discussions with the prime minister, who often appears to be just one of eleven. It is interesting to note that federal government representatives in the 1950s and 1960s were reluctant to encourage the development of such formal structures for federal–provincial interaction, fearing that they would weaken Ottawa's dominant position. The televised proceedings have shown that their fears were justified.

Whereas the first ministers conferences were primarily concerned with welfare programs and financing agreements in the 1950s and 1960s, other policy areas took on higher profiles thereafter. Constitutional issues dominated the agenda from 1968 to 1971, followed by the need to address the energy crisis, inflation, and environmental concerns. Constitutional issues were dominant again between 1978 and 1982, and these discussions culminated in the passage of the Constitution Act, 1982. Throughout these periods, the provincial premiers aggressively sought further decentralization of the federation.

The years of the last Trudeau government, between 1980 and 1984, were a brief period of renewed central dominance that occurred at great cost to relationships among governments in Canada. The federal government undertook unilateral initiatives on three crucial and divisive issues: energy pricing, constitutional change, and what it perceived to be a threat to the national medicare plan. The indignant and hostile reactions of the provincial premiers to these initiatives took the form of a struggle to determine which level of government should dominate in the federal system. Canadians appeared to be exhausted from the incessant federal–provincial wrangling, and in 1984 they gave Brian Mulroney's Progressive Conservative Party a huge majority in the House of Commons at least partly because of his promise to restore peace to intergovernmental relations.

Peace did come in the first two years of the Mulroney government. He and his ministers took a less adversarial approach in their relations with the provinces, and acceptable energy accords were reached with the Atlantic and western provinces. An early first ministers conference on the economy was successful, and for a while it appeared that a more co-operative and conciliatory federalism would result. This does not seem to be the nature of Canadian federalism, however: hostility is often just beneath the surface, easily triggered by real or apparent federal encroachment on provincial sensitivities.

The Mulroney government came to power during a period of fiscal restraint (although an expanding economy), and in its determination to address the federal deficit it severely reduced federal transfers to the provinces. Conflict arose over what was perceived to be an attempt to shift both the federal debt and the political costs onto the provinces. The Conservatives also antagonized both the West and the East with some of their high-profile policies: the awarding of a controversial aerospace contract to Montreal rather than Winnipeg, VIA Rail cutbacks, high interest rates, and the decision in 1989 to unilaterally impose a very broad goods and services tax. Most of these policies were perceived to favour Central Canada over the East and the West, and the federal–provincial truce that was declared in 1984 proved to be only a brief hiatus.

Amid the acrimonious debates and negative reactions to Conservative government economic and deficit-reducing policies, the Mulroney government came close to achieving constitutional harmony. In the spring of 1987, a rare federal–provincial unanimity on constitutional amendment was reached behind closed doors: it was presented to the country as the Meech Lake Accord. This agreement proved to be highly controversial, and when it was threatened by new governments in three provinces, federal and provincial representatives crisscrossed the country in an attempt to have the recalcitrant legislatures pass the amendment. The accord died in June 1990, after divisive secret negotiations and public recriminations. Within two years another unanimous constitutional agreement, the Charlottetown Accord, was reached but when it was presented to the country in a referendum in October 1992, a majority of Canadians voted against it.

Despite these two examples of federal–provincial harmony in the constitutional field, bitter divisions remained over economic and social policy, and these were exacerbated by the election of NDP governments in three provinces in the early 1990s. The Mulroney government continued to reduce transfer payments to the provinces, and all governments faced severe budgetary deficits.[8] The election of a Liberal government under Jean Chrétien in the fall of 1993 brought renewed hope for amicable federal–provincial relations needed to address persistent social and economic problems. The early months of Chrétien's term were quiet, as governments in Canada tried to learn from one another how best to tackle their deficits while retaining essential services. The federal and provincial governments made significant steps toward eliminating the crippling non-tariff trade barriers among the provinces, and they appeared ready to focus together on economic issues and postpone the exhausting constitutional discussions. The election in Quebec, in September 1994, of a Parti Québécois government, committed to separation, ensured that governments' attention would again be divided.

CONCLUSION

The dynamics of federalism in Canada have evolved enormously since the Constitution Act was drafted in 1867. Although much of the history of the "high" politics of first ministers conferences seems driven by conflict and competition between the two levels of government, it is important to realize that each year there are also hundreds of harmonious federal–provincial interactions occurring, at the level of "low" politics, among committees, individual bureaucrats, and ministers. While there have certainly been spectacular failures of the former, the success of the latter relationships has allowed the development of a welfare state, produced an irreversible interdependence between the two levels of government, and shown that if governments exercise the political will it is occasionally possible to transcend constitutional difficulties and even their own parochial tendencies.

NOTES

[1] Lord Durham used this phrase in his famous 1840 report on the problems of Upper and Lower Canada. His suggested solution was a union of the Canadas into Canada East and Canada West, which occurred in 1840. This did not, however, resolve the difficulties.

[2] Garth Stevenson, *Unfulfilled Union: Canadian Federalism and National Unity*, 3rd ed. (Toronto: Gage, 1989), 21.

[3] For example, shortly after World War II, the federal government used this section to assume jurisdiction over uranium, so that it could control nuclear energy policy.

[4] See Alan Cairns, "The Judicial Committee and Its Critics" in *Constitution Government and Society in Canada* (Toronto: McClelland & Stewart, 1988).

⁵ The compact theory of Confederation is based on a belief that Confederation was an agreement between two "founding nations," the French and the English. It was developed in the nineteenth century and assumes equality of status. It was expanded into a theory that outlines a conception of Confederation as a compact among all the provinces.

⁶ See Smiley's discussion of executive federalism in *The Federal Condition in Canada* (Toronto: McGraw-Hill Ryerson, 1987), ch. 4.

⁷ These shared-cost programs meant that the federal government would pay 50 cents of every dollar that the provincial governments spent in these areas, provided certain conditions were met. The Canada Assistance Plan, established in 1966 by the minority Pearson government, was an agreement that Ottawa would match provincial spending on "needy" persons, as defined by the provincial governments.

⁸ One source estimated that by the end of the 1994–95 fiscal year, the federal government would have offloaded $29.4 billion onto the provinces through unilateral changes in its contributions under the EPF system. R.A. Jenness and M.C. McCracken, "Review of the Established Programs Financing System," *Informetrica*, 19 Oct. 1993.

Suggested Reading

Cairns, Alan. "The Living Canadian Constitution" and "The Judicial Committee and Its Critics." In *Constitution Government and Society in Canada*. Toronto: McClelland & Stewart, 1988, 27–85.
These perceptive articles, originally written in 1977 and 1971 respectively, are essential reading for students of the historical evolution of Canadian federalism.

Fletcher, Martha. "Judicial Review and the Division of Powers in Canada." In *Canadian Federalism: Myth or Reality?* 3rd ed. Ed. Peter Meekison. Toronto: Methuen, 1977, 100–122.
This excellent article traces the important JCPC and Supreme Court decisions and discusses their impact on the legal framework within which the federal and provincial governments operate.

Milne, David. *Tug of War: Ottawa and the Provinces Under Trudeau and Mulroney*. Toronto: Lorimer, 1986.
As the title indicates, the focus of this study is the competitive relationship between the federal and provincial governments. Milne examines the power struggle that occurred under the Trudeau government in the early 1980s, and compares it to the brief period of reconciliation that took place under Mulroney's first mandate.

Monahan, Patrick, and Kenneth McRoberts. *The Charlottetown Accord.* Toronto: University of Toronto Press, 1993.

This collection of essays is a broad look at contemporary issues in Canadian federalism.

Smiley, Donald. *The Federal Condition in Canada.* Toronto: McGraw-Hill Ryerson, 1987.

A scholarly and reflective assessment of the forces at work in contemporary Canadian federalism and the "continuing constitutional agenda."

Stevenson, Garth, ed. *Federalism in Canada: Selected Readings.* Toronto: McClelland & Stewart, 1989.

This collection of essays by scholarly writers, past and present, is grouped into four sections: the constitutional division of powers, the social and economic background of Canadian federalism, federalism and party politics, and intergovernmental relations over the years. An excellent anthology of influential articles.

Peter Aucoin

9

THE PRIME MINISTER AND CABINET

The prime minister and cabinet are positioned at the pinnacle of power within our system of parliamentary government, both constitutionally and politically. Accordingly, one image we have of the executive is that of "an all-powerful institution, an entity able to impose its policies at will."[1] Indeed, popular accounts sometimes go so far as to claim that we have an "elected dictatorship" between elections because the prime minister is leader of a government that generally controls a majority in the House of Commons through the exercise of party discipline. Rather than elected members of Parliament controlling the government, it is argued, the reverse is actually the case. Democracy operates, it is claimed, only at general elections when voters directly elect their MPs and thereby indirectly choose which party will constitute the government.

There is also a second and competing image. As Bakvis and MacDonald succinctly put it, this is the image of the executive as "unduly responsive to a wide range of particular interests and special pleading . . . spendthrift, and . . . unable to make hard decisions."[2] This image has the prime minister and cabinet constantly pandering to numerous interests (provinces, local constituencies, various pressure groups, or lobbyists) because the two major political parties that have formed a government (the Liberal and Progressive Conservative parties) are viewed as having essentially the same approach to politics and governance. They try to accommodate as many interests as possible in order to retain or strengthen public support. They will be all things to all people to gain popular support; both are equally likely to head for whatever is considered to be the centre position of public opinion. It is hard to distinguish between parties of this sort. Elections thus have been horse races between the "ins" (the government party) and the "outs" (the opposition party), or personality contests between two party leaders (the prime minister and the leader of the Opposition). Accordingly, when in power, the prime minister and cabinet are prone to spend too much in their efforts to meet as many demands as possible. Conversely, they try to avoid making decisions that offend special interests.

To some extent, each of these images is accurate. The Canadian prime minister and cabinet have much greater control over the formulation and administration of Canadian public policy than an American president has with regard to American public policy. An American president must contend with a Congress that can and does constrain the exercise of executive powers and plays havoc with the administration's legislative agenda. It is also the case that Canadian parties and politics differ from other comparable countries that use the system of parliamentary government. In Great Britain, Australia, and New Zealand, for instance, there are only two major parties. There are sharper ideological distinctions between these parties than in Canada, reflecting a relatively greater capacity to integrate major interests within parties.

These two apparently competing images also reveal important, if somewhat misleading, perceptions of the realities of Canadian governance. The Canadian system of government does allow for a significant concentration of authority and power within the governmental system. At the same time, there exists a considerable diffusion of power and influence within the practice of governance.[3] Political parties as institutions are relatively unimportant in governance, aside from their critical role in elections and, consequently, in supporting or opposing the government. Interest groups, broadly defined to include businesses and unions as well as organized groups, on the other hand, are very important in governance.[4] Because interest groups, along with the mass media, have a major role in leading and shaping public opinion on matters of public policy, they are able to penetrate government at the level of both ministers and their bureaucracies.

This chapter on the prime minister and cabinet must be read with these considerations in mind. The chapter itself attempts to draw attention to these themes throughout, at least insofar as the design and practice of cabinet government are affected by them.

THE CONSTITUTIONAL SYSTEM

Under the Canadian system of parliamentary government, and contrary to the formulation sometimes found in Canadian textbooks, there exists a constitutional separation of executive and legislative powers. The Constitution Act, 1867, section 9, vests executive powers in the Queen (or Crown) and establishes a Privy Council for Canada "to aid and advise in the Government of Canada" (section 11). In practice, this means that the governor general, the Queen's representative, acts on the advice of the prime minister in certain matters, and on the advice of the cabinet, of which the prime minister is head, in others. The Constitution Act, 1867, section 17, then vests legislative powers in the Parliament of Canada, which consists of *"the Queen. . .* the Senate, and the House of Commons" (emphasis added).

However, because the powers of the Queen are effectively exercised by the Queen's ministers (that is, Privy Councillors), one can speak of a fusion of the executive and legislative branches of government in the exercise of legislative powers. For instance, only members of the Queen's government, or ministry, may introduce legislation to tax or spend (Constitution Act, 1867, section 54). Second, the vast majority of legislative proposals now emanate from the government and not from those MPs who are not members of the government. Finally, cabinet ministers, individually or collectively, also exercise significant delegated legislative powers: many, if not most, parliamentary statutes—that is, laws passed by Parliament—require the executive to make the detailed rules and regulations that give effect to the general intentions of statutes, and these rules and regulations have the force of law. In exercising these executive powers, as well as in providing executive leadership in the formulation and implementation of public policy and the administration of public services, the prime minister and ministers of the government remain separate from the House of Commons and Senate.[5]

Under the Canadian constitutional convention of responsible government, a convention adopted by the British North American colonies prior to Confederation, the government must command the confidence of the elected House of Commons. The government is thereby "responsible" to the House of Commons.[6] This convention is realized in practice through the system of party government: the leader of the party that can command the confidence of a majority of the members of the House of Commons heads the government. This simple majority may be constituted either by the members of the prime minister's own party, if they hold a majority of seats in the Commons (majority government), or, if this party does not have a majority of the seats, the MPs from the prime minister's party and MPs from one or more other parties who are willing to support the government (minority government). A third possibility, used only twice in Canadian government (at Confederation itself and during the First World War), would be for the prime minister to form a government jointly with the leader of one or more other parties (coalition government). In the discussion that follows, it is assumed that the government is formed on either a majority or minority basis.

Under the so-called confidence convention, a government that loses the confidence of the Commons has two options. First, it can resign, and the governor general must seek a new prime minister to form a new government. This last happened in 1925, although at that time the prime minister's resignation was actually requested by the governor general. Second, it can dissolve the House of Commons and call a general election, as the Clark government did in 1979. In this case, it remains the government until after the election. Following the election, it continues as the government if it either wins the election with a majority of seats (as the Trudeau government did in 1974), or at least carries enough seats to serve as a minority government (as the Pearson government did in 1965). However, if it finds itself in neither of these situations, it resigns (as the Clark government did in 1980) and a new government is formed.

A government can also be forced to resign following a defeat in a general election called without a loss of confidence in the previous Parliament (as the Campbell government did when it was defeated in 1993). A government also comes to an end when a prime minister resigns or dies in office. In either case, the governor general simply calls upon the new leader of the governing party to form a new government, as in 1993 when Brian Mulroney resigned. After the Progressive Conservative Party selected Kim Campbell as party leader, she became prime minister and formed a new government.

Under this system of responsible government, conducted by way of party government, a party leader is called to form a government and thus be prime minister without the governor general any longer exercising any personal discretion.[7] The governor general simply calls upon the leader of the party that, given the respective standings in the Commons, appears to be able to command majority support among the MPs. The governing party itself determines who will be its party leader and thus prime minister. The practical application of this, as well as the separate existence of the executive vis-à-vis the legislature, was amply demonstrated in 1984 when the Liberal Party chose John Turner as party leader and he was therefore called to be prime minister, even though he did not have a seat in the House of Commons (or the Senate). He was fully entitled to exercise the powers of the prime minister, and he did. His government went down to defeat later that year, and he carries the distinction of having been prime minister without at that time having a seat in Parliament.

PRIME MINISTER AS CHIEF EXECUTIVE
AND PARTY LEADER

As outlined above, a prime minister is both the leader of the government and party leader. As leader of the government, or chief executive, the prime minister assumes the principal prerogative powers of the governor general. As such, the prime minister forms the government and thereby selects who will be ministers. In Canada, this power of selecting (and dismissing) ministers is exercised personally by the prime minister. A prime minister can select ministers from either the House of Commons or Senate, or even from outside Parliament. In this last case, the convention is that the new minister will either seek to obtain a seat in the Commons as soon as possible, normally through a by-election if a general election is not pending, or be appointed to the Senate. If such a minister seeks a seat in the Commons and fails to be elected, the convention is that he or she resigns as minister. Although the government is responsible only to the House of Commons, at least one senator has always been appointed to the cabinet as government leader in the Senate. However, it is not unusual for more than one senator to be appointed to the cabinet; important cabinet portfolios were held by senators in the Clark, Trudeau, and Mulroney governments either to represent certain provinces or because the prime ministers wanted these individuals in their cabinet.

Although prime ministers normally consult with their trusted advisors in their parliamentary party caucus (the members of their party in the Commons and Senate) and in their party outside Parliament, the practice in Canadian parties is not to constrain the personal exercise of this power. This contrasts, for instance, with the Australian and New Zealand Labor parties when they form the government in their countries. In these two cases, the Labor parliamentary party caucus actually selects who will be in the cabinet, although the Labor prime minister, as in Canadian practice, still determines the assignment of ministerial portfolios (that is, responsibility for the various departments in the government).

In constructing a government and assigning portfolios, a Canadian prime minister also determines how the so-called machinery of government will be structured. This entails the organization of the cabinet and its membership, its committee system, and the formal procedures and processes for cabinet operations. In addition, the prime minister may appoint ministers who will not be members of the cabinet. Until 1993, this was done in only a couple of instances.[8] In 1993, however, Prime Minister Jean Chrétien appointed eight such ministers, called secretaries of state. These secretaries of state are junior ministers who serve under cabinet ministers in particular portfolios. As such, they are part of the ministry, or government, and they become members of the Queen's Privy Council. But they are not members of the cabinet. With this innovation, we can make a distinction between cabinet and ministry whereby the ministry encompasses both cabinet ministers and ministers not in the cabinet. The prime minister may also appoint parliamentary secretaries—MPs who assist cabinet ministers, primarily in their parliamentary duties. These parliamentary secretaries have never been considered to be part of the ministry. Unlike secretaries of state, therefore, they have not been appointed members of the Queen's Privy Council. Finally, the prime minister chairs the cabinet, determining how it operates in practice. The prime minister is clearly much more than a first-among-equals within the cabinet: the government is the prime minister's government.

In addition to these critical powers, the prime minister appoints the deputy ministers (the senior public servant in each department), who, under the direction of their minister, are responsible for advising on policy and administering the operations of their respective departments. The prime minister also selects judges of federal and superior provincial courts, senators, governor generals, and provincial lieutenant-governors, and approves (in practice if not in law) the appointment of the chairs and members of the boards of directors of various federal Crown corporations or commissions. In many if not all cases, these appointments illustrate the conjunction of the prime minister's roles as chief executive and party leader. Some of these appointments are based on patronage: they are used to reward the party faithful or the prime minister's personal supporters. In some cases, patronage is coupled with the strategic aim of having these appointees bring the governing party's political and policy objectives to bear upon whatever duties are entailed in the offices to which these persons are appointed.

As party leader, a prime minister must retain the support of cabinet ministers in particular—given that they invariably represent the leadership of the parliamentary party—as well as the larger party caucus and the party association outside Parliament. In the case of Canada's two governing parties, the Liberals and Progressive Conservatives, however, the party leader has a considerable measure of independence from both the cabinet and the parliamentary caucus. This is the result of the practice in both parties of selecting the leader through a convention of the national party association. This has meant party conventions to which delegates are selected by the local constituency associations of the party across the country, by special groups within the party (e.g., youth associations), or by virtue of occupying a position in the party association or the parliamentary caucus. As Mackenzie King, Liberal leader from 1921 to 1948, is reported to have told his caucus colleagues, "A leader not chosen by the caucus is not responsible to it."[9] This practice of the party-at-large selecting leaders, as well as dismissing them (as happened to John Diefenbaker and Joe Clark), contrasts with the practices of the major parties in Britain, Australia, and New Zealand. In these countries, party leaders, including those who are prime minister, require the confidence of their parliamentary party caucuses. This power is real. In recent years, for instance, Margaret Thatcher in Britain and Bob Hawke in Australia were each removed as party leader, and thus prime minister, by their respective parliamentary party caucuses. Finally, in Canada the power of the prime minister via-à-vis cabinet or parliamentary party colleagues has been strengthened by the degree to which the two major parties and the mass media have personalized political leadership and electoral politics.

CABINET FORMATION: REPRESENTATIONAL IMPERATIVES

The formation of a cabinet constitutes high art in Canadian politics. It does so precisely because of the conjunction of several representational imperatives.[10] First, a prime minister must form a government that reflects the collective leadership of the governing party. Although prime ministers obviously want to reward those who have most helped them gain the party leadership, they must also give careful consideration to their opponents within the parliamentary party, at least those who have a following among competing factions within the party. The limits of size, even with a large cabinet (or large ministry), invariably mean that some personal supporters are left out, while some opponents are included.

Second, the Canadian cabinet, as a scholar and later a minister himself described it, possesses a "federal character."[11] From the formation of the first cabinet in 1867, prime ministers have had to construct cabinets whose members represent the provinces of the federation. It was recognized at the outset that the cabinet, rather than the appointed Senate, would be the central mechanism for representing provincial interests in the federal government.[12] The fact that not all provinces always elect MPs from the governing party complicates the prime minister's selection of ministers. On occasion, capable MPs from certain provinces must be overlooked because their province has elected more than a sufficient number of MPs on the government side. Conversely, there have been numerous instances of less capable MPs being selected for cabinet posts simply because their province has elected few government MPs. In recent decades, both the Trudeau and Clark governments were forced to resort to the appointment of senators to cabinet, beyond the usual one senator who serves as government leader in the Senate, in order to have certain provinces represented in cabinet.

Third, prime ministers have had to pay attention to representation on the basis of socio-demographic factors, including ethnicity, religion, and gender. The first of these has expanded and been transformed over the years; the second has declined in importance to the point where it no longer is a factor; and the third has become a salient consideration in recent years.

At times, a prime minister is relatively lucky: various combinations of representativeness fortuitously present themselves in the personnel available to the prime minister. At other times, cabinet selection constitutes a real conundrum; there are bound to be major complaints from factions within the party, provinces, regions within provinces, major cities, or other under- or non-represented segments of the population. It is not surprising that, at least until Prime Minister Campbell appointed only twenty-five members to her first cabinet in June 1993, Canadian cabinets had increasingly become much larger than their counterparts in Britain or Australia. The last Mulroney cabinet numbered thirty-nine; by contrast, the British cabinet numbered twenty-two and the Australian cabinet eighteen. Ironically, what was once considered a democratic virtue (namely, a cabinet whose size was determined primarily by its representative character), by 1993 had become a political vice: cabinet size had become a symbol of government waste and extravagance.[13]

In strictly comparative terms, however, the size of the Canadian cabinet prior to 1993 was misleading. The very representational imperatives that increased the size of cabinets constrained prime ministers from excluding any ministers from the cabinet. Britain and Australia have approached this question quite differently. In both of these political systems, it has been acceptable to have ministers who are not in the cabinet. In Britain, for example, there are 88 ministers, only 22 of whom are in the cabinet. The 66 not in the cabinet serve as ministers to assist the 22 who are in the cabinet. There is, in effect, a two-tiered ministry: cabinet ministers and non-cabinet ministers. The former are senior or portfolio ministers; the latter are junior ministers. Australia has also adopted a two-tiered system, but in this case there are far fewer junior ministers. Indeed, there are fewer junior ministers than senior ministers—12 compared to 18. In the Australian case, however, parliamentary secretaries to ministers are also used to assist ministers in a greater variety of ways than has been the practice to date with parliamentary secretaries in Canada. In this respect, it is noteworthy that when she announced that her cabinet would have only 25 ministers, Prime Minister Campbell indicated that parliamentary secretaries would assume "a stronger and more visible role in support of Ministers."[14]

Equally noteworthy is the fact that, beginning in the early 1970s, a good number of Canadian cabinet ministers were appointed as ministers of state to assist; that is, they served as ministers within the portfolio of a more senior minister. For example, a minister of state for fitness and amateur sport was assigned to assist the minister of health and welfare. These ministers of state were essentially junior ministers, not unlike Chrétien's new secretaries of state. They had specific responsibilities to represent the interests of particular political constituencies within government but possessed no statutory powers in regard to the administration of government policies and programs. However, they were formally in the cabinet and thereby served on cabinet committees. In reducing the size of the cabinet, Campbell eliminated all such ministers of state. By not appointing ministers of state to assist, but rather creating a new kind of ministerial position outside of cabinet, Chrétien has sent a clear signal that these secretaries of state are to be junior ministers in every respect.

The large size of recent Canadian cabinets that resulted from successive responses to the various representational imperatives had two major, and related, consequences for the structure of cabinet. The first was the need to construct a complex cabinet committee system in order to cope with the fact that a cabinet with thirty-some members could not function as an efficient executive decision-making body. Beginning in the late 1960s, therefore, the cabinet was increasingly structured in a hierarchical fashion, with an inner cabinet consisting of the most senior ministers. The full cabinet met less and less frequently and seldom as a forum for government decision making. The second consequence was that, by virtue of this use of an elaborate cabinet committee system, it was possible to enlarge the size of the cabinet even further by appointing ministers, especially ministers of state to assist, to represent an increasing number of specific sectors of Canadian economy and society.[15] This meant a greater specialization in the design of ministerial portfolios. On the one hand, as noted, there were the several ministers of state to assist in various portfolios. On the other hand, new portfolios were created. The Mulroney government, for example, decided that it was not sufficient to have ministers from the various regions in the cabinet to represent the interests of their regions or provinces in the formulation and administration of the government's economic development policies. Rather, it concluded that there also had to be a specific minister (and department) assigned responsibility for economic development policies for particular regions. It thereby created new ministerial portfolios to head departments or agencies for Atlantic Canada (Atlantic Canada Opportunities Agency), Western Canada (Department of Western Economic Diversification), Quebec (Federal Office of Regional Development–Quebec), and Northern Ontario (Northern Ontario Development Board).

The increasing development of highly specialized portfolios was impressive, at least from the vantage point of representing a great diversity of interests in the assignment of ministerial positions. This organizational response reflected, in no small measure, the fragmentation of interests in Canadian society and the economy. It was this excess of diverse representation in the cabinet that led to concerns about the degree of cabinet attention to special interests and the inefficiency and expense that this entailed.[16]

Combined with the need to be seen to be responding to the demand for a "leaner" government, Prime Minister Campbell's streamlining of the cabinet was meant to address the problems created by cabinets designed to give priority to representation over efficient and effective government.[17] In addition to eliminating all ministers of state to assist, Campbell merged some portfolios and assigned some ministers more than one portfolio. Chrétien retained most of these mergers and continued to assign more than one portfolio to a number of ministers. For example, Chrétien appointed David Dingwall minister of public works and government services (a merger of these two portfolios had been effected by Campbell) and minister responsible for the Atlantic Canada Opportunities Agency. One could argue that, before Campbell, this actually would have been three portfolios. These options have always been available to a prime minister; the more streamlined the cabinet, the more likely that these options will be used.

MINISTERIAL PORTFOLIOS

In designing a cabinet, a prime minister must decide on two related, but distinct, organizational questions. First, how specialized should ministerial portfolios be and on what bases should they be constituted?

Second, what should be the decision-making structure and procedures of the cabinet as a governing body? No prime minister approaches these matters in a vacuum; the existing system is never entirely redesigned. Major organizational changes to the existing system are difficult; there are always elements of the old mixed with the new. Moreover, these questions are not just complicated, in the sense that a great deal depends on the technical details; they are also complex, in that no one aspect of organizational design can be considered entirely in isolation from other structural aspects. Government structure is a complex system of interrelated parts.

In approaching the question of portfolio design, a prime minister must construct a cabinet with essentially two different types of portfolios. First, some ministers must be assigned individual responsibility for the policies and programs of government that regulate various kinds of social and economic behaviour and provide public goods and services. These ministers are responsible for the *operational* departments of government. These portfolios and their departments can be organized on at least three different specialized bases or some combination thereof. They can be organized according to the primary functions they perform (the portfolios and departments of defence, environment, transport, unemployment insurance, health services, and so forth). Second, they can be organized according to particular categories of citizens (the portfolios and departments of Indian affairs, veterans affairs, youth, seniors, status of women, and the like). Without exhausting all possible alternatives or combinations, they can be organized according to various regions (the portfolios and departments/agencies for regional economic development in Atlantic Canada, Western Canada, Quebec, and Northern Ontario noted previously.)

To the extent that a prime minister uses more than one basis for organizing ministerial portfolios and departments to carry out the operations of government, the more complex the system becomes. The reason for this is not simply that there are likely to be more rather than fewer ministers and departments; by using different organizational bases, the responsibilities of ministers and their departments must inevitably overlap, even duplicate, one another to some degree. This will then require that various mechanisms and procedures be developed to provide for the necessary co-ordination of departments with interrelated policies and programs. The increasingly complex system of cabinet committees was one response to the need for such co-ordination at the level of ministers where their departments had shared interests in major areas of public policy; another was the proliferation of interdepartmental committees of public servants from these same departments.

The second type of portfolio entails the assignment of responsibilities for government-wide, or *corporate,* policies. In the development of cabinet government in the British tradition, for instance, the one pre-eminent consideration in the evolution of the position of prime minister was the idea that there had to be a co-ordinated, government-wide approach to the budget of the government. In Britain, this is symbolized by the fact that the prime minister still carries the formal title of First Lord of the Treasury, in recognition of the fact that there has to be a first minister who is responsible for co-ordinating the raising and spending of public monies by the ministry of the Crown. This reflects the fact that there is only one public purse containing the revenues that come from taxpayers.

From this initial corporate portfolio of First Lord of the Treasury, the portfolio of prime minister emerged. In addition to the prime minister, however, all cabinets now have a number of corporate portfolios. In recent Canadian experience, for example, there have been corporate portfolios for fiscal and general economic policy (minister of finance), government expenditure policy and general administrative management (president of the treasury board), foreign affairs (secretary of state for external affairs, now called minister of foreign affairs), federal–provincial relations (minister of federal–provincial relations, now called minister of intergovernmental affairs), constitutional and legal affairs (minister of justice), regulatory affairs (minister for regulatory affairs), legislative strategy (the leader of the government in the House of Commons), and public service (minister responsible for public service renewal). The corporate character of these portfolios means that these ministers have government-wide mandates. The minister responsible for foreign affairs, for instance, must ensure that all ministers and departments of government adhere to the government's foreign policy when they have dealings with other states or international institutions in their specialized areas of public policy.

The government-wide character of these corporate responsibilities is amply demonstrated by the fact that prime ministers have on occasion assumed personal responsibility for some of these portfolios. For several decades after the establishment of a department of external affairs, for instance, the prime minister of Canada also assumed the position of minister responsible for this portfolio. More recently, Prime Minister Trudeau was, at times, his own minister of federal–provincial relations. These exceptions aside, however, over time Canadian cabinets witnessed an increased specialization of the corporate portfolios of the government and thus the number of ministers assigned these tasks. This development contributed to the expansion in the size of the cabinet as well as the number of cabinet committees used in executive decision making.

CABINET STRUCTURES

It would be highly misleading to suggest that a prime minister first decides who will be in the cabinet, then decides how portfolios will be designed, and finally decides on the structures of cabinet government. As noted above, these decisions are interrelated. Moreover, decisions on these matters are determined in some large measure by a prime minister's personal philosophy of leadership, management style, and political objectives—what I have elsewhere called a prime minister's "paradigm of executive leadership."[18] A prime minister must also take into account the political forces and values extant at any given point in time. Given these several determinants of cabinet design, one, or more likely some combination, of four basic modes of cabinet government will invariably be emphasized: the collegial, conglomerate, command, or corporate mode.

The Collegial Mode of Cabinet Government

One mode of cabinet government is perhaps most often associated with the basic idea of cabinet government, namely *collegial* decision making. Given the fact that the cabinet is a collective executive, it is often assumed that this is the only legitimate mode of cabinet government: ministers bring their policy proposals to their cabinet colleagues, and ministers then collectively arrive at a decision, taking into account their different perspectives. Their different perspectives derive, of course, from the fact that each is responsible for a different facet of government policy. This approach, accordingly, promotes collective policy formulation by having all members of the cabinet or a committee participate as members of a team seeking consensus.

When the size of the full cabinet allows for this kind of ministerial deliberation and decision, the collegial mode can be chosen as the principal way in which government policy is determined, assuming of course that the prime minister wishes to proceed in this manner. In the first several decades immediately following Confederation, this mode was predominant precisely because governance was largely about the distribution of patronage, primarily in the form of government appointments and contracts for public works. The distribution of patronage demanded a political consensus among the members of cabinet who represented the different provinces. This meant that ministers could not regard their individual portfolios as personal fiefdoms to be managed as they saw fit. Rather, they had to bring both major and minor items to cabinet to obtain the approval of their cabinet colleagues, who, whatever their specific portfolio responsibilities, had an interest in the distribution of patronage as it affected their province, region, or city (or, for that matter, their own constituency).

More recently, this mode of cabinet government has been adapted to the development of the cabinet committee system, especially during the Trudeau governments. To the extent that it is used in this context, one objective is to promote a collective co-ordination of policies across broad sectors of government policy, where several ministers and their departments have overlapping or interrelated responsibilities, but without having to bring all matters of decision to the full cabinet. The most obvious and general illustration of this has been the use of cabinet committees to co-ordinate government policies in the broad sectors of social and economic development policies. Every cabinet since the introduction of standing committees for cabinet decision making in the 1960s, including the Chrétien cabinet, has had at least one committee to co-ordinate policies in each of these two broad sectors.

The use of a cabinet committee system for collegial decision making, again especially as deployed by the Trudeau governments, also can serve to check the tendency for individual ministers to be captured by their departmental officials to the point that they become primarily departmental spokespersons rather than cabinet ministers responsible for ensuring that their departments function as part of an integrated whole.[19]

The application of the collegial mode of decision making means, of course, that individual ministers are restricted in the exercise of their statutory authority as chief executives for their portfolios. The greater the extent to which the full cabinet is used as the forum for collegial decision making, the more centralized the decision-making process will be; the greater the extent to which cabinet committees are used, the more decentralized it will be. In either case, ministerial and departmental autonomy is sacrificed to a more integrated authority structure.

The Conglomerate Mode of Cabinet Government

A second mode of cabinet government conforms to what is perhaps a less common, but still acceptable, notion of how cabinet ought to operate. This second mode, what I call the *conglomerate* mode, reflects the fact that within cabinet government there obtains a division of responsibilities among ministers for particular areas of public policy. To the extent that the prime minister and cabinet assume that individual ministers should exercise their statutory authority in regard to their specific respon-sibilities (and thereby do not require or encourage them to bring mat-ters before cabinet for a collective decision, let alone collective policy formulation), the cabinet operates as a conglomerate of specialized min-isterial portfolios. The decisions of individual ministers constitute government policy no less, but authority is exercised by individual ministers.

This mode of cabinet government, it has been suggested, characterized the structure of cabinet during the emergence of the modern administrative state, beginning in the 1920s and extending to the 1950s. It has been labelled by Stefan Dupré as the "departmentalized cabinet," given that individual ministers were very much in charge of government decision making as it applied to their particular departments.[20] In some large measure, this mode was adopted because much of the patronage that had previously required the use of collegial decision making had been removed from the discretion of ministers. Public servants were now appointed and promoted by an independent civil service commission on the basis of merit, and contracts for public works and government supplies and ser-vices were increasingly subject to public tendering laws. Ministers and senior bureaucrats in the operating departments of government were now con-cerned primarily, if not exclusively, with regulating a mixed public–private economy and constructing a social welfare state. While cabinet had to provide a general sense of direction to government policy, it was used primarily as a forum to resolve major conflicts between ministers. As such, whatever co-ordination of government policies and programs was required tended to be undertaken by the relatively small group of depart-mental deputy ministers. The departmentalized cabinet, not surprisingly, was accompanied by the golden age of the bureaucratic mandarins.[21]

The modern equivalent of this mode of cabinet government finds expression in efforts since the mid-1980s to decentralize decision making from cabinet and cabinet committees (and thus the central policy and management agencies of government) to individual ministers and their operational departments.[22] There has even been a formal government initiative to this end entitled "Increased Ministerial Authority and Accountability," which was introduced in 1986.

Most recently, the gradual return to the conglomerate mode has been augmented by the consolidation of ministerial portfolios undertaken by the Campbell government in 1993, with its resulting reduction in the number of cabinet ministers and departments. Following the lead of Australia, this streamlining allows a greater degree of policy and expenditure deci-sion making to take place within individual ministerial portfolios. It has the potential, accordingly, to reduce the burden on collective cabinet decision making while increasing the effectiveness and efficiency of government decision making. It does so by reducing the need for interministerial and interdepartmental co-ordination because authority over a wider range of policies is located within single ministerial portfolios.

The Chrétien government, upon assuming office shortly after this consolidation of portfolios, maintained the basic structure put in place by the Campbell reorganization. In addition, the number of standing cabinet committees was reduced to four, and the full cabinet, consisting of the prime minister and twenty-two ministers, is "the senior forum for collective decision-making."[23] The degree to which the cabinet figures in government decision making, other than for strategic policy and plans, will thus primarily be determined by the extent to which there are conflicts between ministers over the exercise of their individual statutory authority.

The Command Mode of Cabinet Government

A third mode of cabinet government is one that finds few supporters, except perhaps among those who are at the centre of power. This is what I call the *command* mode of cabinet government. It essentially takes two forms. The first is the exercise by the prime minister of personal power, either by imposing a strategic policy agenda on the cabinet or by intervening in the domains of individual ministers with respect to specific policy items. Many commentators have characterized this approach as "prime ministerial government," or even "presidential government" (comparing the position of prime minister to the American presidency and assuming, inaccurately, that a president actually has more personal power than a Canadian prime minister). Beginning with Prime Minister Trudeau, commentators unhappy with the exercise of prime ministerial leadership have attacked him and his successors for overriding what, in their view, is the proper model of cabinet government, usually considered to be the collegial mode. This view ignores the fact that the prime minister, as head of government, possesses the constitutional authority to lead the cabinet in setting its strategic direction and, as J.R. Mallory notes, "the undoubted right to issue orders in any department without consulting the minister."[24]

The second form of this mode of cabinet government has been the use by the prime minister of a small circle of the most senior ministers to set the government's strategic policy priorities and plans and to settle major disputes among ministers, including those not party to this inner circle. Aside from the use of a small war cabinet within the larger cabinet during the Second World War, the development of an explicitly hierarchical structure to cabinet first emerged not long after the introduction of the cabinet committee system under Prime Minister Pearson. This approach was partly a response to the increased size of the cabinet. Shortly before Pearson's resignation, a priorities and planning committee was created and chaired by the prime minister. As deployed by the Trudeau government during the period 1968 to 1979, this committee stood at the apex of the cabinet committee system. The logic of this design was taken one step further by the short-lived Clark government, which turned the priorities and planning committee into a formal inner cabinet with the authority to make final decisions on various matters of strategic importance. Although the new Trudeau government that came to power in 1980 reverted to the previous title for this committee, namely priorities and planning, it retained the increased powers that Clark had given to his inner cabinet.

The Mulroney government kept this basic framework in place after its electoral success in 1984, but the membership of the priorities and planning committee increased in size. At around twenty members, it was hardly an effective strategic executive body, and problems of co-ordination at the centre of government reflected this. Accordingly, shortly before the 1988 election an informal operations committee was formed under the leadership of the deputy prime minister, who had begun to function essentially as the general manager of the Mulroney government. After the 1988 election, the role of this steering committee, which consisted of a handful of key ministers, was formalized in a cabinet system reorganization. The hierarchical character of the Mulroney cabinet was further developed with the subsequent creation of an expenditure review committee. Chaired originally by the prime minister (and later by the deputy prime minister), the membership of this committee had some significant overlap with the operations committee. The inner circle of ministers at the apex of power thus comprised those ministers who were simultaneously members of the priorities and planning, operations, and expenditure review committees. Ministerial resistance to the increasingly hierarchical character of the Mulroney government was partly responsible for the elimination of the expenditure review committee in 1991.

In 1993, in her initial design of a cabinet, Prime Minister Campbell did away with the priorities and planning committee and restored responsibility for strategic plans and priorities to the full cabinet. She did maintain the operations committee, however. Prime Minister Chrétien's cabinet did away with the last vestige of this hierarchical approach to cabinet government by eliminating even the operations committee; the full cabinet is once again "the senior forum for collective decision-making."[25]

The Corporate Mode of Cabinet Government

A fourth mode of cabinet government is both conceptually and organizationally the most complex. It entails an approach to cabinet government that places a high priority on centralized co-ordination of the government's corporate policies; hence the labelling of this as the *corporate* mode. This approach is most identified with the Trudeau government wherein there was a fascination with co-ordination.[26] As Doern and Phidd put it, "almost half of the Trudeau [government] departments exist[ed] to coordinate the other half."[27]

Although exactly what constitutes a government's corporate policies may be open to question, the essential characteristic of the corporate mode of cabinet government is the attempt to ensure that the various operational departments of government conform to the corporate policies of the government both in the design of their policies and programs and in their management practices. The burden of these corporate policies on the operational portfolios of government may be light or heavy depending on how many corporate portfolios and cabinet committees there are to impose corporate policy objectives on the rest of the governmental system.

The increasing use of the corporate mode of cabinet government, at least until very recently, can be seen in the growing numbers of corporate policies and cabinet committees as well as in the expansion in the number and scope of corporate policies for which they are responsible. Because the Canadian cabinet has always had a federal character, with its emphasis on regional representatives, from the outset there was a recognition of the need for a corporate approach to cabinet government.

This is best illustrated by the fact that since 1867 there has been a cabinet committee for expenditure and general administrative management. This committee—the Treasury Board—has seen its corporate responsibilities expand considerably, especially since the 1960s. In addition to its traditional responsibilities for the expenditure budget and financial administration generally, it now is responsible for, among other things, collective bargaining with public service unions, affirmative action and employment equity policies, various other aspects of personnel and human resource administration, program evaluation, official languages policy, and common services policy (the various services and facilities provided to operational departments by a number of "common services" departments and agencies). The policies decided upon by the Treasury Board apply government-wide to all departments and agencies.

In addition to the Treasury Board, successive governments added the following corporate policy committees to the cabinet system:

- **Federal–provincial relations committee:** responsible for ensuring that all government policies and programs adhere to the government's policies and strategies in relation to provincial governments;
- **Legislation and house planning committee:** responsible for considering all policy proposals that require legislative approval in light of the government's legislative timetable and strategy in relation to the politics of Parliament;
- **Communications committee:** responsible for making certain that all new government initiatives possess a public communications strategy that is in line with the messages the government is seeking to have the public receive (a political public relations function);
- **Regulatory affairs committee:** responsible for ensuring that the proposed regulations made by various government departments and agencies conform to the government's general approach to the use of regulations as a public policy instrument;
- **Expenditure review committee:** responsible for examining all major federal expenditures and identifying areas for cuts in spending (in addition to the work done by the Treasury Board);
- **Foreign affairs:** responsible, among other things, for examining departmental proposals that have implications for Canada's foreign policy;
- **Trade committee:** responsible, among other things, for examining departmental proposals that have implications for Canada's international trade policy.

This corporate mode of cabinet government cannot but result in a system of executive decision making in which the major policy and program proposals of individual ministers must be assessed from two different perspectives: how they relate to the operational responsibilities and objectives of other operational portfolios, and how they relate to the corporate policies of the government. Cabinet or the relevant policy sectors committee is required to examine proposals from the vantage point of the policy sector, asking, for example, whether a particular agricultural policy proposal fit within the government's broad economic development policy plans. Cabinet or a corporate policy committee is required to examine the same proposals from the vantage point of one or more corporate policy perspectives— does the agricultural policy proposal fit within the government's expenditure policy plan?

Prime Minister Campbell streamlined this system of corporate cabinet committees. Prime Minister Chrétien has gone even further. Only two such committees remain: the Treasury Board and the special committee of Council (responsible for reviewing, in particular, regulations made under delegated legislation). To the degree that corporate policies are the subject of cabinet consideration, this function will increasingly be performed by the full cabinet. On the other hand, with one or two exceptions (e.g., there is no one minister assigned responsibility for regulatory affairs in the Chrétien cabinet), most of the corporate portfolios that have been created since the 1960s remain. In addition, one major new one has been added, namely a senior minister responsible for public service renewal, and this corporate mandate has been given to the same minister, Marcel Massé, who also holds the intergovernmental affairs portfolio. The stated intention of the government is that it will pursue its objectives in relation to these two corporate policies simultaneously—that is, reorganizing the federal government at the same time that there is a reorganization of federal and provincial responsibilities in areas of duplication and overlap. However, the pursuit of these corporate objectives does not entail corporate cabinet committees to develop or coordinate policy.

CONCLUSION

Although the basic constitutional norms governing the powers and roles of the prime minister and cabinet have remained constant throughout Canadian political history, the informal dynamics have changed considerably. The reasons for this are the different approaches taken by different prime ministers to the structure and operation of cabinet government. The prime minister, as government leader and party leader, has significant discretion to shape the government as he or she sees fit. This has been amply demonstrated in the major changes that have been effected since the 1960s.

These changes began with a dramatic increase in the number of cabinet ministers and ministerial portfolios as prime ministers sought to represent an increasing number of sectors and segments of the Canadian polity in government and to enhance the corporate dimension of executive government. An elaborate committee system accompanied these developments and increasingly the structure became simultaneously fragmented and centralized, with ministers responsible for operational portfolios subject to a complex set of coordinating mechanisms in the form of policy sector committees and corporate policy committees. The ineffectiveness of this structure eventually gave way, in the 1990s, to substantial reduction in the size of cabinet, the elimination of some portfolios and the consolidation of others, and a major reduction in the number of cabinet committees.

Jean Chrétien, building on changes made by Kim Campbell, has reversed the priority given to the various representational imperatives, even to the point where he has a cabinet without a representative from one province (Prince Edward Island). In terms of what Bruce Doern calls the "efficiency–democracy bargain," Chrétien has emphasized the former over the latter.[28] By creating a distinction between cabinet ministers and non-cabinet ministers (secretaries of state), he has opted to structure and manage his government according to the conglomerate mode of cabinet government.

Under this approach, cabinet constitutes the principal forum for collective decision making, but such decision making is reserved primarily for resolving major disagreements or conflicts among cabinet ministers. Cabinet ministers are thus expected to manage their portfolios using their individual statutory authority. They must adhere to the strategic priorities and plans as well as to the corporate policies of the government, but they are to refrain from constantly bringing matters to their cabinet colleagues for collective decisions. This approach thereby gives relatively greater priority to individual portfolio management as the norm for government decision making and has been facilitated by the consolidation of portfolios.[29] This approach brings Canada further into line with international trends in public management, with an emphasis on delegating authority from corporate structures to the operational structures of government.[30] Combined with the Liberal government's strategy for "getting government right,"[31] less formal, but no less significant, changes in the management of cabinet government can be expected. Whether these will be sufficient, given the exigencies of the contemporary malaise in politics and governance remains to be seen.

NOTES

[1] Herman Bakvis and David MacDonald, "The Canadian Cabinet: Organization, Decision-Rules and Policy Impact" in *Governing Canada: Institutions and Public Policy*, ed. Michael Atkinson (Toronto: Harcourt Brace Jovanovich, 1993), 48.

2 Ibid, 48.

3 See M.M. Atkinson and W.D. Coleman, eds. *The State, Business and Industrial Change in Canada* (Toronto: University of Toronto Press, 1989).

4 See Paul A. Pross, *Group Politics and Public Policy* (Toronto: Oxford University Press, 1992), and W.D. Coleman and G. Skogstad, eds., *Policy Communities and Public Policy in Canada* (Toronto: Copp Clark Pitman, 1990).

5 See W.A. Matheson, *The Prime Minister and Cabinet* (Toronto: Methuen, 1976).

6 See Peter W. Hogg, "Responsible Government" in *The Canadian Political Tradition*, 2nd ed., ed. R.S. Blair and J.T. McLeod (Scarborough, ON: Nelson Canada, 1993), 2–44, and S.L. Sutherland, "Responsible Government and Ministerial Responsibility: Every Reform Has Its Own Problems," *Canadian Journal of Political Science* 24, 1 (March 1991): 91–120.

7 See Andrew Heard, *Canadian Constitutional Conventions* (Toronto: University of Toronto Press, 1991).

8 Matheson, *Prime Minister and Cabinet*, 66.

9 R.K. Carty, "Three Canadian Party Systems" in *Canadian Political Party Systems*, ed. R.K. Carty (Peterborough, ON: Broadview Press, 1993), 547.

10 Colin Campbell, "Cabinet Committees in Canada: Pressures and Dysfunctions Stemming from the Representational Imperative" in *Unlocking the Cabinet: Cabinet Structures in Comparative Perspective*, ed. Thomas T. Mackie and Brian W. Hogwood (London: Sage, 1985), 61–65.

11 Norman Rogers, "The Evolution and Reform of the Canadian Cabinet," *Canadian Bar Review* 11, 4 (April 1933): 101–21.

12 Herman Bakvis, *Regional Ministers: Power and Influence in the Canadian Cabinet* (Toronto: University of Toronto Press, 1991), 16.

13 See Peter Aucoin and Herman Bakvis, *The Centralization–Decentralization Conundrum: Organization and Management in the Canadian Government* (Halifax: Institute for Research on Public Policy, 1988).

14 Canada, Office of the Prime Minister, *Release*, 25 June 1993, 3.

15 Peter Aucoin, "Cabinet Government in Canada: Corporate Management of a Confederal Executive" in *Executive Leadership in Anglo-American Systems*, ed. Colin Campbell and Margaret Wyszomirski (Pittsburgh: University of Pittsburgh Press, 1991), 139–60.

16 Bakvis and MacDonald, "The Canadian Cabinet," 48.

17 Canada, Office of the Prime Minister, *Release,* 25 June 1993, 3.

18 Peter Aucoin, "Organizational Change in the Machinery of Canadian Government: From Rational Management to Brokerage Politics," *Canadian Journal of Political Science* 19, 1 (March 1986): 3–27.

19 See Richard D. French, *How Ottawa Decides* (Toronto: Lorimer, 1984).

20 Stefan J. Dupré, "The Workability of Executive Federalism in Canada" in *Federalism and the Rule of the State*, ed. Herman Bakvis and William Chandler (Toronto: University of Toronto Press, 1987), 236–58.

[21] See J.L. Granatstein, *The Ottawa Men: The Civil Service Mandarins, 1935–1957* (Toronto: Oxford University Press, 1982).

[22] See Aucoin and Bakvis, *Centralization–Decentralization Conundrum*.

[23] Canada, Office of the Prime Minister, *Release*, 4 Nov. 1993, 2.

[24] J.R. Mallory, *The Structure of Canadian Government*, rev. ed. (Toronto: Gage, 1984), 93.

[25] Canada, Office of the Prime Minister, *Release*, 4 Nov. 1993, 2.

[26] Colin Campbell, *Governments Under Stress* (Toronto: University of Toronto Press, 1983).

[27] G. Bruce Doern and Richard Phidd, *Canadian Public Policy: Ideas, Structure and Process*, 2nd ed. (Scarborough, ON: Nelson Canada, 1991), 155.

[28] G. Bruce Doern, "Efficiency–Democracy Bargains in the Reinvention of Federal Government Organization" in *How Ottawa Spends: A More Democratic Canada? 1993–1994*, ed. Susan Philips (Ottawa: Carleton University Press, 1993), 203–29.

[29] Peter Aucoin and Herman Bakvis, "Consolidating Cabinet Portfolios: Australian Lessons for Canada," *Canadian Public Administration* 36, 3 (Fall 1993).

[30] Peter Aucoin, "Administrative Reform in Public Management: Paradigms, Principles, Paradoxes and Pendulums," *Governance* 3, 2 (1990): 115–17.

[31] Marcel Massé, "Getting Government Right" (address to the Public Service Alliance of Canada, Regional Quebec Conference, Longueuil, 12 Sept. 1993).

Suggested Reading

Aucoin, Peter, and Herman Bakvis. "Consolidating Cabinet Portfolios: Australian Lessons for Canada." *Canadian Public Administration* 36, 3 (Fall 1993): 392–420.

An account of the major downsizing of the Canadian cabinet, in 1993 under Prime Minister Kim Campbell, viewed from the perspective of the 1987 changes to the Australian cabinet and the subsequent experiences in that political system.

Bakvis, Herman. *Regional Ministers: Power and Influence in the Canadian Cabinet.* Toronto: University of Toronto Press, 1991.

A superb examination and analysis of one of the fundamental features in the informal dynamics of the Canadian cabinet system, namely the role of regional ministers and the forces that give regional ministers significant clout in government decision making.

Mancuso, Maureen, Richard G. Price, and Ronald Wagenberg, eds. *Leaders and Leadership in Canada*. Toronto: Oxford University Press, 1994.

An edited volume with several chapters dealing, from different perspectives, with prime ministers and cabinet ministers.

Savoie, Donald J. *The Politics of Public Spending in Canada*. Toronto: University of Toronto Press, 1990.

An award-winning book on one of the most critical functions of governance and the dynamics of cabinet government in the management of the public purse.

Savoie, Donald J. *Thatcher, Reagan, Mulroney: In Search of a New Bureaucracy*. Toronto: University of Toronto Press, 1994.

An excellent account of Prime Minister Brian Mulroney's efforts to reshape the Canadian government and public policy as compared to the experiences in Britain under Prime Minister Margaret Thatcher and the United States under President Ronald Reagan.

Stan Drabek

THE FEDERAL PUBLIC SERVICE: ORGANIZATIONAL STRUCTURE AND PERSONNEL ADMINISTRATION

Once Parliament debates and ultimately passes legislation, what then happens? How is policy implemented and administered on an on-going basis? What structures, processes, and people are involved in this implementation? This chapter will try to answer these and other questions, concentrating for the most part on the operations of the federal government.

The public service[1] is probably one of the most talked about but least understood components of the total Canadian governmental structure. We can define the *public service* as an organized group capable of implementing programs and policies as well as providing advice on the development of policy to its political masters in the cabinet. Public servants operate in a framework that is non-partisan and anonymous.

The constitutional division of powers largely determines whether the federal or provincial public service administers a particular policy. For example, the federal government determines and administers defence policy, while provincial governments deal with educational issues. In some cases, such as agriculture, both federal and provincial governments and their public services are involved.

Canada's bilingual nature and geographic size have an impact on the federal public service. Critics of official bilingualism question the necessity of providing services to both francophones and anglophones, and criticize the hiring practices that result from such a policy. Others question whether regional differences are sufficiently taken into account when the federal public service in Ottawa implements and administers national policies for distant areas.

Finally, the growth of government is another important theme in our study. For a long while people demanded that governments play an increased role in society. They called for consumer protection, expanded educational and social service policies, and the protection of the environment. Government involvement in these areas has meant an expanded role for public servants.

ORGANIZATIONAL STRUCTURES

Since government is involved in myriad activities, the most efficient organizational principle is to create specialized organizations entrusted with the task of achieving the objectives of government. Specialization means the allocation of responsibilities, the division of work, and the arrangement of personnel in different types of structures. There is no single organizational structure for the federal public service; rather, various organizational structures exist for different purposes. Differences among the types of organizations stem from internal structuring, the question of accountability (to Parliament and to cabinet ministers), and the freedom of action or autonomy given to the organization. In general, the operational structures of the Canadian federal government can be categorized under the following headings:

- departments (i.e., Environment, National Revenue);
- statutory regulatory agencies (National Transportation Agency, Canadian Radio-television and Telecommunications Commission); and
- Crown corporations (Canadian National Railways, Canada Post Corporation).

Departments

Political scientists find it difficult to describe exactly what a government department is. Perhaps J.E. Hodgetts provides the best definition when he describes it as "an administrative unit comprising one or more organizational components over which a minister has direct management and control."[2] Departments are structured as pyramids with operational staff at different hierarchical levels performing different functions. The pyramid usually peaks in the position of deputy minister, who is administrative head of the department. The deputy minister is responsible to the minister who has the political responsibility for the department's actions.

Government departments are established by statute and have an intended function to perform and a program or set of programs to administer. Departments are a means to achieve a goal: for example, the newly formed Department of Human Resources Development provides social service programs. Over the years, as programs and government involvement expand, the number of departments has grown. Depending upon the exact definition, there are at least twenty-three departments within the federal government.

As programs expand and the administrative goals of an organization broaden, departments tend to undergo a series of reorganizations. Political considerations play a definitive role in administrative reorganization. The historical development of the former Department of Trade and Commerce is illustrative. It was originally established to assist Canadian business at home and abroad. To fulfil an election promise, the Liberal government under Lester Pearson created a separate Department of Industry from various units of the old Trade and Commerce Department. Later these two departments merged to become the Department of Industry, Trade and Commerce. By the 1970s, political policy emphasized the development of the Canadian economy in regional terms; hence the creation of the Department of Regional Economic Expansion. For efficiency purposes, the former foreign component of Trade and Commerce was ultimately shifted to the Department of External Affairs. The most recent manifestation of these various reorganizations is a revitalized Department of Industry with a re-emphasis on the original domestic programs and economic goals of the old Department of Trade and Commerce.

Some political scientists categorize government departments according to their functions, referring to vertical departments and horizontal departments. *Vertical departments* (also called line departments), such as Agriculture, are directly involved in administering programs that respond to the needs and expectations of the public or of a particular segment of the public. *Horizontal departments* fall into two separate categories: administrative co-ordinative departments and policy co-ordinative departments.[3] Administrative co-ordinative departments, such as the Department of

Public Works and Government Services, provide assistance to other government departments. Policy co-ordinative departments, such as the Treasury Board Secretariat or the Privy Council, co-ordinate government policy activities. These latter departments are also referred to as central agencies because they are regarded as the elite parts of the federal bureaucracy and are the centres of power and decision making.

The regional variations of Canada, its distances and its linguistic differences, mean an administrative decentralization of activities. Some government programs involve direct contact with the public and "on the spot" administration rather than the provision of services from one office located in Ottawa. For example, there are employment centres located in many Canadian cities and immigration offices located at border points. These are referred to as field offices, while the headquarters of a department is usually located in Ottawa.

The other two operational structures mentioned above—statutory regulatory agencies and Crown corporations—constitute a category called Crown agencies, or what Hodgetts has referred to as "structural heretics." Each of these categories has specialized structures that differentiate the agency from ordinary government departments.

Statutory Regulatory Agencies

Statutory regulatory agencies perform the function of regulation, which the Economic Council of Canada has defined as "the imposition of constraints, backed by government authority, that are intended to modify the behaviour of individuals in the private sector significantly."[4] Agencies practise both direct and social regulation. *Direct regulation* is mostly economic in nature and is concerned with such things as return on investment and regulations concerning the participation of firms in specific areas, such as the natural resources sector (a function of the National Energy Board). *Social regulations* aim at attaining broad social objectives in a wide variety of areas, ranging from transportation safety (National Transportation Agency) to Canadian content regulations in the media (Canadian Radio-television and Telecommunications Commission). In a way, social regulation can also be considered direct in nature since it does regulate the private sector.

To accomplish its task, a regulatory agency performs adjudicative (quasi-judicial), legislative, and administrative roles. For example, under the authority of the Broadcasting Act, the Canadian Radio-television and Telecommunications Commission (CRTC) regulates federally incorporated telecommunications carriers as well as radio, television, and pay-TV systems. The CRTC also develops broadcasting policies with corresponding rules and guidelines. The roles performed by a regulatory agency demand a unique organization structure: the structure of an ordinary government department is not appropriate. One might say that regulatory agencies are created to take a contentious or technical issue out of the realm of politics through the process of an impartial hearing. Such agencies must therefore be specialized, impartial, and independent of direct political control.

Structurally speaking, regulatory agencies do not necessarily follow the hierarchical model of government departments. Many agencies, such as the National Energy Board, have a board consisting of appointed members including a chair. Terms of appointment usually range from three to ten years. The board represents the ultimate decision-making level in the organization and is roughly parallel in nature to the departmental deputy minister. Rather than a minister directly responsible for the regulatory agency, there is a "designated" minister in Parliament who fields and passes on to the agency questions that arise in the House of Commons about the operations of the organization. For example, the Minister of Natural Resources takes on this role with respect to the operations of the National Energy Board.

Because of its regulatory and semi-autonomous nature and its lack of direct ministerial control, a regulatory agency is not subject to the same amount of parliamentary supervision as is a regular government department. Regulatory agencies tend to be more flexible than departments in their operations and in their implementation of government policy.

In recent years, governments have made some moves toward *deregulation*. This refers to decreasing the number of rules and regulations administered by regulatory agencies, especially in transportation and telecommunications, and reducing the size of some of these agencies. For example, the National Transportation Agency proposed change to "modernize and streamline" the rules and regulations applying to international charter services.[5] The rationale for deregulation is to let the market shape the nature of the particular sector. Fewer rules, decreased governmental demands for information, and increased competition will, according to proponents of deregulation, mean cheaper costs and allow new businesses to compete in sectors previously protected by rules and regulations. Critics of deregulation claim that increased competition will result in a situation where small companies suffer as they are squeezed by larger corporations. To its critics, deregulation means that large companies are unlikely to provide all necessary services, only those that are profitable, and that public safety will suffer as a result.

Opinion remains divided on whether deregulation has accomplished what its proponents said it would. Some people supported the idea of "re-regulation"—that is, the reimposition of some of the old rules and regulations—to maintain fair competition and prevent the development of restrictive competitive practices by dominant business forces.

Crown Corporations

Crown corporations, such as the Canadian National Railways (CNR), the Canadian Broadcasting Corporation (CBC), and, until its recent change of ownership, Air Canada, have been an important factor in the historical development of Canadian government. Like regulatory agencies, Crown corporations are complex and specialized organizations structured to meet particular objectives. They are also difficult to define. In fact, a precise definition is so elusive that estimates of the number of Crown corporations in Canada in the early 1980s have varied from 336 to 454, depending on the criteria.[6]

Historically, the reasons for the establishment of Crown corporations have varied widely. They include rescuing a series of bankrupt railways (the creation of the CNR); preserving Canada's cultural independence (the CBC); providing a window on the natural resources sector (Petro-Canada); and maintaining railway passenger services (VIA Rail).

Many (but not all) Crown corporations resemble private businesses in terms of structure and personnel administration.[7] The main difference is in ownership. Individual investors own shares in a private business organization such as Bell Canada. It is the federal government, in the name of the people of Canada, that owns the shares of a Crown corporation.[8]

As is the case with other governmental organizations, Crown corporations are subject to classification. The "official" classification is found in the Financial Administration Act as amended in 1984. This act establishes a regimen of accountability to Parliament for three categories—Schedule II, III(1), and III(2). In general, the greater the financial need of the corporation, the more rigorous the accountability requirement. Schedule II corporations are involved in basic administrative research of information functions (National Research Council, Atomic Energy Control Board). They rely heavily on government funding and are, therefore, subject to the most accountability and control. Schedule III(1) corporations are those that compete with private enterprise but rely on government funding to make up operating deficits (Canada Mortgage and Housing Corporation,

VIA Rail). They are also subject to demands of accountability and control, but less so than Schedule II corporations. Schedule III(2) corporations are the least subject to governmental control. They compete directly with private corporations (CNR with the privately owned Canadian Pacific, for example), but they are financially viable and much less dependent on government financial assistance. They have, in effect, managerial autonomy.

Crown corporations are governmental institutions and are held accountable through different methods of political control. One important method is financial in nature. Schedule III(2) corporations must submit their capital budgets for approval. Schedule II and III(1) corporations must submit both capital and operating budgets to the respective minister and to Treasury Board for approval. A second method of control is the power of the government to issue a directive to the Crown corporation. This directive could impose a political consideration that may affect the stated economic interests and mandate of the corporation. A third method of control is the requirement that all Crown corporations submit to the responsible minister an annual corporate plan that includes their objectives and expected performance. At the same time, the corporations must also submit to the minister year-end annual reports of their operation. A fourth important method of control is the ability of government to appoint the boards of directors of Crown corporations. The boards play an important role in that they serve as a liaison between ministers and the administrative management of the corporations.

Students of Crown corporations pay a great deal of attention to appointments made by governments to the board of directors of these companies. What criteria are used? Usually, appointments to the boards of Crown corporations are made for periods of up to three years. Appointees are part-time directors who usually work with a full-time chief executive officer and other members of management. The appointment of the chief executive of a Crown corporation rests with the government of the day. When filling vacancies on the board of directors of Crown corporations, governments tend to appoint the party faithful as a reward for service to the party. For example, when Air Canada was still a Crown corporation, the Mulroney government appointed to its board loyal Conservatives, including Frank Moores, a former Conservative premier of Newfoundland, and David Angus, a former chair of the fund-raising arm of the federal Conservative Party. Liberal governments in the past have done the same thing. (It will be interesting, given its pre-election rhetoric on ethics in government, to see whether Jean Chrétien's Liberal government will avoid the excesses of the past.) This pattern of appointment is referred to as *patronage*. However, given the calibre of most of these appointments, perhaps the term "political appointments" would be more accurate. One could also argue that, given the old boys' network, private corporations are equally prone to make patronage appointments to their boards of directors.

Board appointments tend to reflect the geographic divisions of the country. As the national public broadcaster, the CBC is regarded as an essential instrument of Canadian cultural development, with a mandate to reflect for both national and regional audiences Canada and its regions. According to the 1992–93 Annual Report, the CBC board of directors has six members from Ontario, four from Quebec, and one each from Alberta, British Columbia, Manitoba, Nova Scotia, and Newfoundland. Of the Ontario representatives, two are officers of the company—the chair and the chief executive officer.

Although there is regional representation of sorts, board presentation still reflects the population and political importance of Central Canada. The new Chrétien Liberal government has instituted a policy of downsizing Crown corporation board membership. It will be interesting to see how this will affect regional representation and the composition of a Crown corporation board such as the CBC.

Over the years, the major issue concerning Crown corporations has been whether they should have managerial autonomy or whether they are simply instruments of public policy. *Managerial autonomy* refers to an arm's length relationship between the government and the corporation and usually applies to Schedule III(2) or similar corporations. These corporations are most similar to the private firms they compete with and, consequently, the argument is that they be allowed to pursue their own paths. This includes the right to make a profit. Several Crown corporations, including the CNR and, more recently, the Canada Post Corporation, have shown profits and have paid dividends to the government.

Arm's length also means little or no government interference in the organization's business decisions. This has been achieved in the case of the CNR, in part through its abandonment of underused branch lines. Even though they may have political repercussions, these decisions are meant to make operations more profitable. From a business perspective, managerial autonomy is also justified by the fact that the publication of detailed information about budgets might undermine the competitive position of the corporation in its sector.

By contrast, the *instruments of policy* approach stresses the fact of government ownership. In this view, the Crown corporation should be used as another method of implementing the government's social and economic policies. Government directives, not arm's length relationships, are the standard procedure. Such an approach would allow for the provision of services at cost or even at a loss where there was a political demand, as is the case with VIA Rail.

A specific use of the instrument of policy approach was the Trudeau government's establishment of Petro-Canada in the American-dominated oil and gas industry so that Canada might have some control over its resources and prices. From a policy perspective, Petro-Canada was also a way of tapping offshore resources that might not have been developed by the private sector. The Conservative government of Brian Mulroney moved Petro-Canada from the instrument of policy approach to an arm's length approach. The corporation has a mandate to make a profit, thus becoming a candidate for privatization.

In recent years, the issue of privatization of Crown corporations has come to the fore as neoconservative philosophy and marketplace economics have influenced the policies of many governments in the world, including Canada. *Privatization* refers to the sale of a Crown corporation to the private sector. This can be done in one transaction, as was the case with Northern Transportation Agency, or in stages, as with the privatization of Air Canada. Underlying the trend to privatization is the belief that government should not manage corporations that the private sector could run profitably. The government, according to this view, should not use corporations to implement policy. Profitability of a Crown corporation clearly indicates to the supporters of privatization that private enterprise could provide that service. Profitable Crown corporations are prime targets for privatization and are the easiest to sell to the private sector.

Decisions on privatization are based on political factors. Governments such as the one that was led by Brian Mulroney, oriented to the marketplace economy, tended to accelerate the process of privatization. A future government may veer back to the instrument of policy approach. There are indications, however, that the process of privatization will not be completely undone. The Chrétien government seems to be taking an ambivalent approach on this issue so far. On the one hand, one of the first moves of the government was to void the sale of Pearson International Airport to the private sector. On the other hand, the government later announced a proposed policy of "commercialization" (privatization) of certain aspects of air transportation policy, including the sale of smaller airports and radar traffic control at airports.

PERSONNEL RELATIONS AND HUMAN ADMINISTRATION

The staffing of government organizations—the human element—is an important matter, especially given the demographic and geographic differences within Canadian society and the development of specialized departments and agencies that administer government policies and provide advice on these matters. Who are these public servants?

In this section, we will highlight some of the more important aspects of federal personnel administration. Space precludes discussion of related topics, such as the specific role of the Public Service Commission in the hiring and placement of public servants and the guardianship of the merit principle, or the role of the Treasury Board Secretariat in the classification of public servants and the collective bargaining process. The first section will concentrate on the historical development of the patronage/merit approaches to personnel administration in the federal public service. We then examine representative bureaucracy (especially francophone, women's, and minority representation); the question of political rights for public servants and its effect on the idea of a neutral public service; and, finally, recent events following the creation of Public Service 2000.

Patronage/Merit Appointment Systems

No analysis of the public service is complete without reference to the patronage/merit issue. For a number of years after Confederation, the personnel administration system was characterized by patronage. Given the uncomplicated and generally clerical nature of government activities at the time, few disputed this system: it was accepted that changes in government usually meant changes in public service personnel.

The growth and increasingly specialized nature of government activities created a demand for a highly skilled and more politically neutral public service that would be able to work with any government, regardless of its political orientation—hence the development of a merit system of personnel administration.

Merit (generally understood as "what you know" as opposed to "who you know") is somewhat difficult to define in operational terms. Some claim that merit should have a flexible meaning that changes with fluctuating demands and circumstances. Nevertheless, an accepted statement of the merit principle is that Canadian citizens should have a reasonable opportunity to be considered for employment in the public service, and selections must be based exclusively on merit or fitness for the job.[9] The first step in this direction was taken with the passage of the 1908 Civil Service Act, which established a Civil Service Commission dedicated to the implementation of the merit system of appointment. However, the act applied only to the "inside" (Ottawa) part of the bureaucracy, which was the smaller part of the federal civil service in terms of numbers. Only the 1918 Civil Service Act pointed the federal service firmly in the direction of political neutrality, efficiency, and the merit system.

During the decades after the passage of the 1918 act, merit really meant the elimination of patronage and the establishment of a politically neutral public service. Only with the increase in government activities, the demand for specialization due to technological development, and the influence of the scientific management school of administration did the meaning of merit expand to include efficiency and, later, representativeness. At the same time, there were complaints that the application of the merit system had resulted in too many cumbersome controls to protect the public service.

Efficiency received a strong boost from the studies of the Royal Commission on Government Organization (Glassco Commission) in 1962–63. The commission stressed the need for economy in the provision of public services, and its motto was "let the managers manage." The Glassco Commission then added flesh to the bones of the definition of the merit principle. Efficiency and capability finally overtook political neutrality as the guiding factors of the merit principle. Recently, other factors have added more depth to the meaning of merit, particularly in terms of a representative bureaucracy.

Representative Bureaucracy

The question of which Canadians "should have a reasonable opportunity" to be considered for employment is part of the merit principle as well as the broader question of representative bureaucracy. In general, a *representative bureaucracy* reflects the various components of a society. The aim is to represent groups of people in relation to their proportion of the population. Ultimately, this would make the public service more responsive to all elements of society.

The first move in this direction occurred during the 1960s with the impact of the Quiet Revolution in Quebec and the report of the Royal Commission on Bilingualism and Biculturalism. Both events stressed francophone grievances about their inadequate level of participation in the federal public service, especially in the higher policy-making positions such as deputy minister.

The Liberal government of the day, under Lester Pearson, accepted the thrust of the royal commission's argument that more francophones should be hired for public service positions and appointed to policy-making positions. The government promised to proceed with plans to ensure that the federal public service would reflect in numbers and accountability those Canadians whose first language was French. Further impetus for this effort came from the Official Languages Act of 1969, which declared English and French to be the official languages of the public service. Attempts were also made to make the public service more bilingual, especially in Ottawa and within policy-making positions.

The notion of "progress" in terms of representative bureaucracy is a matter of interpretation. Some people argue that the public service should be numerically more reflective of a country's population so that it can be more responsive to the groups that make up society. Administrative and policy decisions must take into account the fact that at least 25 percent of the Canadian population is French speaking, particularly since the values and attitudes held by the two linguistic groups can differ. Another viewpoint claims that the push for a bilingual public service jeopardizes the idea of a bureaucracy based on the merit principle because merit is sacrificed for representativeness, although some would agree that bilingualism itself could not be considered a factor in the overall definition of merit.

A more recent consideration in the debate over representative bureaucracy is that of gender parity. Like francophones, women have been underrepresented in the federal public service, especially at the policy-making levels. Because of the historical importance accorded to francophone–anglophone linguistic relations in Canada, the barriers to francophone representation were overcome earlier than were those facing women. Feminist groups and public opinion have led the government to quicken the pace of accommodating more women in the public service. In the late 1980s, for example, an increasing number of women were promoted to the influential policy-making positions of assistant deputy minister and deputy minister, a development that would have been unthinkable even ten years earlier. In February 1994, Jocelyne Bourgon was the first woman to be appointed Clerk of the Privy Council, the top job in the public service.

To ensure continued opportunity for women and other groups such as Aboriginal people and people with disabilities, the government implemented an employment equity program in 1985. The declared aim of this program was to eliminate hiring practices that excluded these groups from employment as well as to correct any procedures that placed them at a disadvantage in other personnel administration matters such as classification, promotion, or pay. Employment equity, or affirmative action, stresses the concept of equal outcome. Affirmative action has been sanctioned by the Canadian Charter of Rights and Freedoms, especially section 15, which guarantees "equal protection and equal benefit of the law without discrimination." Applied to the public service program of employment equity, this section means that "preferential treatment for groups which have historically suffered from discrimination does not constitute reverse discrimination."[10]

Supporters of strong employment equity programs indicate that only a quota system will achieve the aim that a group's representation in the public service should approximate its percentage of the population. Critics of this approach maintain that it undermines the merit system and prevents people outside a defined minority from being appointed or promoted. This is the stuff of strong debate.[11] Nevertheless, in the federal public service there is no quota system in place for women, Aboriginals, visible minorities, and the physically disadvantaged. Rather, the Treasury Board Secretariat has set in place a series of targets that public sector managers should be working toward in order to ensure a more representative bureaucracy. This indicates that the merit principle is ever-changing, and its implementation is enhanced by expanding access to public service employment and equity programs.

One might ask whether the fine words on representative bureaucracy have been translated into practice. According to statistics provided by the Public Service Commission, francophone participation in the federal public service (as defined by the commission) has increased slightly from 27.2 percent in 1977 to 28.6 percent in 1992. At the same time, francophones constituted only 23 percent of the executive category, which includes the top executive levels of the bureaucratic structure.[12] Statistics concerning women's representation in the public service also indicate an upward trend, no doubt influenced by employment equity programs. Women's participation in the public service has increased dramatically from 27.3 percent in 1967 to 45.9 percent in 1992. Figures for the executive category indicate a steady increase, although the proportion of women in this class was only 17.1 percent in 1992.[13]

These statistics indicate that progress toward a more representative bureaucracy is slow. While it is true that the percentage of francophones, women, and other minorities in the public service is increasing, their representation in the top decision- and policy-making levels has a long way to go. It is here that improvements must be concentrated.

Political Rights of Public Servants

This section deals with the political rights of public servants, an offshoot of the political neutrality discussed in the section on merit. Political neutrality traditionally meant that federal public servants had to be above suspicion of partisanship, which in turn meant that they were not allowed to participate in political activities. Given the desire for a politically neutral public service, the Civil Service Act of 1918 prohibited public servants from engaging in partisan political activity of any kind, with the exception of voting. Violation of this prohibition meant dismissal. These restrictions were not changed until the Public Service Employment Act of 1967. This act allowed public servants (with the exception of deputy ministers) to run for political office if the Public Service Commission felt that their employment would not be compromised. If elected, the individual had to resign from the public service. Over the years, a small number of public servants have taken advantage of this provision and have been allowed to run for office. The 1967 act also permitted employees to contribute to the political party of their choice and attend political meetings, but they could not campaign for or against any candidate or party.

The Supreme Court settled the issue of the political rights of the public service in the 1991 decision *Osburne v. Canada* (Treasury Board). The court struck down a section of the Public Service Employment Act prohibiting some political activities on the part of public servants as a violation of the freedom of expression clause in the Charter of Rights and Freedoms. The prohibition was deemed to be beyond what was necessary. However, the court also stated that top bureaucrats—those involved in mapping government policy—must remain politically neutral. The decision appears to be an even-handed and logical approach to the matter.[14]

A "New and Improved Public Service": Public Service 2000

The decade of the 1980s brought demands for a change—termed a "renewal"—of the federal public service in adapting to a complex new environment. Critics called for a more efficient and responsive public service. One of the first initiatives in this direction was the implementation of increased ministerial authority and accountability, which gave deputy ministers more managerial autonomy and flexibility.

At the same time, the Conservative government began to focus on its free market approach to government. Deficits became an overriding issue, and the results were fiscal restraint, hiring freezes, and pay freezes for public servants. These and other measures, such as across-the-board spending cuts and contracting-out, had a demoralizing effect on the public service.

As part of their overall policy thrust to change the role of government, the Conservatives seized the opportunity to initiate a thorough revitalization of the public service. In December 1989, they announced the creation of Public Service 2000, a series of task forces whose ultimate goal was the more efficient provision of government services. Service, innovation, people, and accountability became the catchwords of the task force that, in 1990–91, researched and issued reports on such diverse topics as classification, training and development, and staff relations.

Some public service unions were wary of a government agenda. They questioned the lack of a real consultative process and regarded Public Service 2000 as having been created by managers for managers. They also suspected that efficiency really meant "doing better with less."

The utilization and renewal process of Public Service 2000 has been slow. Securing the consensus of such diverse actors as the Public Service Commission, the Treasury Board Secretariat, the Clerk of the Privy Council, deputy ministers, and public servants has been challenging. The only hard evidence of progress is the Public Service Reform Act, which, among other things, simplified the classification system, allowed a redeployment scheme within categories, and established a definition of merit based on minimum qualifications for a position.

At the time of writing, the Liberal government has not made any specific announcements about Public Service 2000. However, Prime Minister Chrétien did appoint Marcel Massé, a former public servant and Clerk of the Privy Council, as minister responsible for the public service. Obviously, the last of Public Service 2000 has not been heard.

CONCLUSION

The federal public service is in a constant state of flux. Departmental structures come and go. New functions such as environmental protection policy mean the establishment of new departmental organizations. Governments create, enlarge, and then downsize regulatory agencies. Crown corporations are being sold off to the private sector.

Personnel administration has changed from an emphasis on political neutrality and the application of the merit principle on the basis of efficiency to a wider application of the merit principle—one that includes representation, responsiveness, equal access, and equity. This means that more people are given the opportunity to become public servants. A wider meaning of merit gives a different complexion to the nature and workings of the public service.

What does the future hold for the federal public service? One issue comes to mind immediately: size. How large government should be is a philosophical discussion between those who believe that the best government is one that governs least and others who insist that government must be involved in the economy and society to protect citizens from exploitation.

Privatization, deregulation, and the recent hesitancy of governments to undertake new activities all indicate that the growth of the public sector in the immediate future will be slow at best. No doubt government will undertake new activities, but the wholesale expansion of the past few decades has been braked by public attitudes and the problem of finances. Any future expansion of the public sector will have to rely on the force of public opinion and its reflection in the priorities of political parties.

The future federal public service will be leaner in overall numbers, more representative of the Canadian population as a whole, and more responsive. As in the past, departments, regulatory agencies, and Crown corporations will continue to exist and the implementation and administration will continue at a high level of professionalism.

NOTES

[1] The term *civil service* also appears in the literature but currently most writers use the term *public service*. Another term used to describe the entire public service is *bureaucracy*.

[2] J.E. Hodgetts, *The Canadian Public Service: A Physiology of Government, 1867–1970* (Toronto: University of Toronto Press, 1973), 89.

[3] These categories are developed further in G. Bruce Doern, "Horizontal and Vertical Portfolios in Government" in *Issues in Canadian Public Policy,* ed. G. Bruce Doern and V. Seymour Wilson (Toronto: Macmillan, 1974), and K. Kernaghan and D. Siegel, *Public Administration in Canada: A Text,* 2nd ed. (Scarborough, ON: Nelson Canada, 1991), 164–65.

[4] Canada, Economic Council of Canada, *Responsible Regulation*, An Interim Report by the Economic Council of Canada, November 1979 (Ottawa: Minister of Supply and Services, 1979), xi.

[5] Canada, Office of Privatization and Regulatory Affairs, *Federal Regulatory Plan 1990* (Ottawa: Minister of Supply and Services, 1989), 336.

[6] Treasury Board of Canada Secretariat, *Crown Corporations and Other Canadian Corporate Interests* (Ottawa: Minister of Supply and Services, 1984), 3; John W. Langford and Kenneth J. Hutman, "The Unchartered Universe of Federal Public Corporations" in *Crown Corporations in Canada: The Calculus of Instrument Choice*, ed. Robert Pritchard (Toronto: Butterworths, 1983), 233–73.

[7] Advisory Crown corporations, such as the recently dismantled Economic Council of Canada, have different organizational structures than the commercially oriented ones such as CNR.

[8] There is another type of organization, called a mixed corporation, in which government and private enterprise or individuals are the shareholders. Petro-Canada now falls into the category since 30 percent of its total shares are now held by the public. *Annual Report, 1992*. The process of privatizing Petro-Canada began in 1991.

[9] R.H. Dowdell, "Public Personnel Administration" in *Public Administration in Canada: Selected Readings*, 4th ed., ed. K. Kernaghan (Toronto: Methuen, 1982), 196.

[10] K. Kernaghan and D. Siegel, *Public Administration in Canada: A Text* (Toronto: Methuen, 1987), 489.

[11] For a discussion of this question, see Prem P. Benimadhu and Ruth Wright, *Implementing Employment Equity* (Ottawa: Conference Board of Canada, 1992); Harish Jain and Rick D. Hackett, "Measuring Effectiveness of Employment Equity Programs in Canada: Public Policy and a Survey," *Canadian Public Policy* 15, 2 (1989): 189–204; Alan Redway, *A Matter of Fairness: Report of the Special Committee on the Review of the Employment Equity Act* (Ottawa: Queen's Printer, 1992).

[12] Figures from Canada, Public Service Commission, *Annual Report 1987* (Ottawa: Minister of Supply and Services, 1988), 15; Canada, Public Service Commission, *Annual Report 1992* (Ottawa: Minister of Supply and Services, 1993), 10, 28. Prior to 1 January 1992, the executive category was known as the management category.

[13] Public Service Commission, *Annual Report 1992*, 10, 28.

[14] *Globe and Mail*, 7 June 1991.

SUGGESTED READING

Adie, R.F., and Paul G. Thomas. *Canadian Public Administration: Problematic Perspectives*. 2nd ed. Scarborough, ON: Prentice-Hall, 1987. Another standard Canadian text that uses the approach of presenting opposing viewpoints on different issues in public administration.

Hodgetts, J.E. *The Canadian Public Service: A Physiology of Government.* Toronto: University of Toronto Press, 1973.

Still influential and applicable in spite of its age. The book concentrates on the interaction between the environment and structural contexts of the public service and the resultant decision making.

Kernaghan, Kenneth, ed. *Public Administration in Canada: Selected Readings.* 5th ed. Toronto: Methuen, 1985, 205–57.

A historical synopsis of personnel administration up to the mid-1980s.

Kernaghan, Kenneth, and David Siegel. *Public Administration in Canada: A Text.* 2nd ed. Scarborough, ON: Nelson Canada, 1991.

A classic public administration textbook. Comprehensive in its coverage of public administration topics and issues. Provides Canadian examples.

Langford, John W., ed. *Fear and Ferment: Public Sector Management Today.* Toronto: Institute of Public Administration of Canada, 1987.

A collection of essays on the changing work environment of the public service and such resulting problems and issues as employment equity, conflict of interest, and coping with restraint.

Tupper, Alan, and G. Bruce Doern, eds. *Privatization, Public Policy and Public Corporations in Canada.* Halifax: Institute for Research on Public Policy, 1988.

A collection of essays exploring the role of public enterprise in Canadian political life. Provides good historical overviews of specific corporations, the problems and issues involved, and the effect of government privatization plans in the 1980s.

A one-stop reference to the issue of human resource administration is hard to come by. Perhaps the best approach for the student would be to consult Canada, Treasury Board, Public Service 2000, *PS2000: Reports and Summaries of the Task Forces* (Ottawa, 1990) for a recent general review of the area and proposals for change.

Richard G. Price
Maureen Mancuso

11

TIES THAT BIND: MEMBERS AND THEIR CONSTITUENCIES

Since 1867 there have been several noteworthy changes in Canadian politics involving the relationship between elected representatives and those they represent. These changes include the rise of disciplined parliamentary parties, extension of the franchise to women and non-property holders, selection of political party leaders by provincial and national party convention, simultaneous constituency elections, and the prominence of the mass media as participants in the electoral and governing processes. Yet one thing has not changed: MPs and MLAs continue to represent territorial units called ridings or constituencies, and do so with considerable vitality and enthusiasm.

In a study conducted for the journal *Parliamentary Government*, MPs agreed that constituency work forms a major part of their responsibilities: those contacted estimated that they spent from 50 to 80 percent of their time on constituency issues.[1] Clearly, being able to respond to the needs and wishes of the constituency is a pivotal facet of a legislator's job. Members of Canada's legislatures typically respond to their constituencies and constituents in four ways:

1. Symbolic responsiveness.
Parliamentarians communicate with individuals and groups via newsletters or quarterly reports, and demonstrate their commitment to the constituency by congratulating individuals for personal achievements. Messages to students, community volunteers, couples celebrating anniversaries, and so on represent a member's search for personal support.

2. Policy responsiveness.

On a number of political issues that crowd the public agenda, legislators endeavour to represent the views and opinions of their constituents. What is optimal is congruence between the expressed preferences of constituents and the positions favoured by the representative.

3. Service responsiveness.

The growth of government in the post-Depression period has resulted in MPs and MLAs becoming ombudsmen or rectification agents who are called upon to intercede with bureaucracies to rectify a wrong.

4. Allocative responsiveness.

In order to promote the economic and cultural interests of their constituents, representatives serve as project boosters. They assist municipalities in obtaining funds for important capital projects (community centres, arenas, government offices) and help businesses qualify for government grants, projects, or contracts.[2]

The responsiveness of MPs and MLAs to their constituencies results from characteristics inherent in two separate but overlapping milieus: the *recruitment environment*—the sphere of selection, election, and re-election—and the *legislative work environment*—the sphere of debate, question period, and committee deliberation (see figure 1). Experiences in these environments serve to strengthen members' responsiveness by encouraging effort spent on the constituency or by discouraging efforts spent elsewhere. We will illustrate how career forces and parameters interact to keep the attention and activities of Canadian parliamentarians focused on their ridings.

THE RECRUITMENT ENVIRONMENT

The recruitment environment includes three reinforcing institutions: a political culture that emphasizes the virtue of local representation, a selection process in which federal and provincial candidates are nominated by local constituency parties, and an electoral system in which one candidate represents each riding and victory requires only a plurality of votes.

Public Expectations: A Culture of Local Representation

Observers have long argued that federal and provincial politics in Canada are conducted in a maze of political cultures. For Pammett and Whittington, "political culture is viewed as being composed of attitudes, orientations,

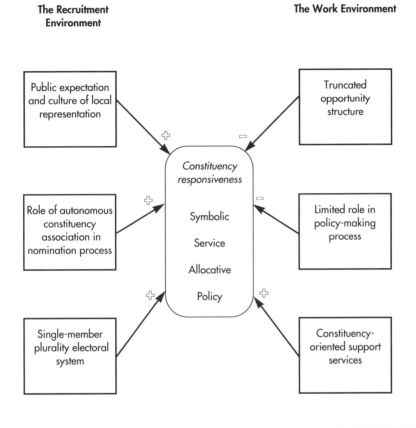

The Recruitment Environment

The Work Environment

Figure 1: Legislative Environments and Constituency Representation

values, beliefs, emotions, images and in functional terms it is viewed as a determinant of political action or behaviour."[3] These orientations focus on four objects: the political community (province, federation, territory, or nation), the regime (the government and constitution of Canada), the authorities (the people and positions who make up the government), and, especially, individuals' views of themselves as political participants. Local political culture is a cultural-representational linkage of immediate interests, involving citizens' expectations of elected members and elected member perceptions of citizen expectations.

According to repeated studies conducted by the Canadian Institute of Public Opinion, there is little question about what Canadians expect from their elected leaders. Average citizens expect members to vote according to the view of constituents and believe that Canada would be better off if leaders were more responsive to the views of ordinary Canadians (see table 1). The results of a *Maclean's* public opinion poll in January 1993 buttress these findings. Of all persons contacted, 71 percent said MPs should vote according to the majority view in their riding, while 21 percent said MPs should decide according to their own conscience and beliefs. Only 7 percent thought MPs should vote as their political party required.[4] An earlier study discovered that, when asked what members of Parliament should consider their first duty, 62 percent said it should be looking after the needs of constituents; 18 percent said serving as a watchdog with respect to government activities and spending; 7 percent said passing laws; and 6.5 percent said party loyalty.[5] The Canadian people clearly believe that a member's first responsibility is to his or her constituents. They expect MPs (and, by extension, MLAs) to emphasize those aspects of their job that involve service and allocative responsiveness.

TABLE 1

Public's Perception of MPs and Leaders' Responsibility to Represent the Public

Panel A: Members of Parliament should vote according to:

	Own view %	Constituents %	Undecided %
1981	29	61	10
1976	34	58	8
1972	29	63	8

Panel B: If the nation's leaders followed the views of the public, Canada would be:

	Better off %	Worse off %	Other %
1991	74	8	11
1986	59	15	26
1976	60	13	27

Members' perceptions of their duties similarly emphasize constituency responsibilities. A panel study of new members of the House of Commons (1974–78) asked MPs to reflect upon and describe their own view of the job of a member prior to receiving their party's nomination. Over two-thirds defined this job in terms of constituency work—being an ombudsman and communicating with and representing constituents. This emphasis on service and allocative responsiveness overshadowed such activities as attending House debates and engaging in committee work, as well as responsiveness to caucus. Asked how they perceived their responsibilities, various respondents replied:

> I'm an ombudsman. It involves representing constituents to government and the government to your constituency.

> To take the concerns or problems of my constituents and direct them to the proper departments for solution.

> To solicit cabinet ministers for projects in my riding, represent the riding generally, and legislate.

> Getting answers back to people. There is a lot of satisfaction in helping people with their problems.[6]

What is especially interesting about these results is that they reflect constituency-oriented attitudes of new members before they have discovered, as will be discussed, that their opportunities in the legislature itself are rather limited. From the beginnings of their legislative careers, members appear to be focused on their constituencies.

There are reports of similar perceptions of constituency expectations among MLAs.[7] In Prince Edward Island, constituency demands on members' attention are high:

> Islanders expect to have direct personal access to their MLAs; despite their part-time status, legislators are always "on call.". . . Islanders just take for granted that if they walk into the office that you're there.

In Ontario, much of a member's resources are devoted to servicing the constituency:

> MPPs' personal staff spend most of their time on constituency business, as opposed to more broadly based policy concerns. Similarly, though resources certainly are available to assist members in their

roles as legislators, far more services cater to the needs of the members as local representatives, as ombudsmen, as constituency case workers, and ultimately as incumbent politicians seeking re-election.

In Newfoundland, the bond between representative and represented is strong and clearly acknowledged:

[The] role as intermediary between citizens and government officials (both elected and appointed) is one in which many members find satisfaction. In the province of Newfoundland it has historically been the most commonly noted function of an MLA. Members devote a substantial portion of their time and effort to dealing with the problems and request of their constituents; for the most part these demands emanate from individuals rather than from groups.

Federal and provincial representatives agree with their constituents that elected members should primarily serve the interests of constituents. Although members cannot always vote as their constituency would prefer, they "take care of the folks back home" through careful deployment of personal and staff resources. This shared commitment to local representation is the first tie that binds parliamentarians and constituents.

Local Constituency Associations and the Nomination Process

Nominees for federal and provincial legislatures are currently selected from a field of politically active local aspirants by autonomous constituency parties that are responsible for scheduling and supervising nomination meetings and, between elections, for trying to maintain a schedule of partisan activities attractive to members.[8] These two features—community involvement of candidates and the significant role of the local party—constitute the second tie binding members to constituents.

An exhaustive study of all 3083 individuals serving in Parliament (the House of Commons and Senate) between 1967 and 1984 reports that slightly less than one-half of all parliamentarians (48 percent) were sent to the House of Commons with no prior elected political experience.[9] Less than one-quarter (22 percent) went directly from municipal politics to the House of Commons. Thus, between 1967 and 1984, 70 percent of all MPs entered the House of Commons with minimal elected political experience.

This rather notable absence of pre-parliamentary office holding (especially provincial incumbency) does not imply a lack of local or community involvement. Indeed, exactly the opposite is the case. A case study of members of the 28th Parliament reported that most MPs were very much products of their own constituencies. The average MP had lived in the constituency for thirty-four years and had become active in political party work at the age of twenty-nine. Almost two-thirds (62 percent) had held one or more party offices at the constituency, provincial, or federal level, and four-fifths (83 percent) had been active party workers when first nominated for public office. The level of party organization cited as most important in securing nomination was the constituency party (46 percent).[10]

Provincial members have reported similar backgrounds. A survey of all MLAs reported that 82 percent resided in their riding at the time of election, 79 percent had worked for a political party previous to election, one-half had held local office (municipal office or school board), and one-quarter had been both active party workers and local office holders. MPs and MLAs appear to be firmly rooted in the life of local party organizations and the community as a whole when they seek elected office. This pre-parliamentary integration of members into the community and partisan fabric of their constituencies influences their responsiveness to constituents.

This integration is encouraged and enhanced by the centrality of the local constituency organization in the nomination process. Constituency associations developed slowly after Confederation but, by 1930—at least at the federal level—both the "Liberal and Conservative parties officially had constituency associations in every constituency across Canada in order to field virtually complete slates of candidates in each general election."[11] Similarly, MLAs are typically nominated by independent constituency parties. The process of nomination and renomination brings candidates into contact with two groups of constituents upon whom MPs and MLAs can rely for current information about local issues and problems: core partisans and local party activists.

John McMenemy argues that core partisans serve as local party ambassadors who communicate party stereotypes to friends, neighbours, and business associates. Core partisans are defined as

> those Canadians who express either a "very strong" or "fairly strong" intensity in their party identification, who voted for that party in at least two recent, consecutive federal elections four years apart (1980 and 1984) and who have publicly manifested their political personality by engaging "sometimes" or "often" in one of several standard gladiatorial activities (trying to convince friends to vote as they do; attending a political meeting or rally; contacting public

officials or politicians; spending time working for a political party or candidate). Thus, in 1984 the core partisans of the three parties constituted 16 percent of the electorate.[12]

These core partisans also perform an important representational function: they provide MPs and MLAs with advice about constituency needs and opinions. This relationship between members and constituents occurs because nomination campaigns are intense competitive experiments in personal organization and have only a single victor. Winning a party nomination thus involves mobilizing core partisans. Once nominated and elected, MPs and MLAs cannot always poll constituents when circumstances require. Accordingly, it is quite natural that they turn to core partisans for guidance, opinions, and judgments about current constituency sentiment.

Nestled within this pool of core partisans are local party activists, a considerably smaller group of men and women who maintain ongoing contact with their representative. William Irvine has confirmed that "in Canada, as in Britain, MPs are in much closer contact with the politically active segment of their constituencies than they are with 'everyone.'"[13] Activists differ from their "inactive" neighbours in several respects. They are, for example, more likely to contact their MP and believe that their MP has actually helped them. They perceive the MP as available and helpful to the riding as well as effective at explaining government activities, getting projects for the riding, and working in Parliament. Not surprisingly, their predictions of the future work of their members are more favourable than those of average voters.[14]

Because representatives have often emerged from the ranks of party activists or core partisans, it is not surprising that they tend to share with these individuals constituency-oriented beliefs and perceptions about their job as legislators. Roots in the community and prior involvement in the party constituency association produce legislators who focus on constituency concerns. Continuing contact with local party activists only serves to sharpen that focus.

THE SINGLE-MEMBER PLURALITY ELECTORAL SYSTEM

Countries vary widely in the type of electoral systems used to recruit legislators. These differences range from Israel, where the entire country is a single constituency, to Canada where each representative has his or her own riding. Canada's single-member plurality system constitutes the third recruitment tie linking members and constituents. No two constituencies in Canada, either at the provincial or federal level, are the same, or even very much alike. Because each constituency is represented by only one member in the legislature, it comes to expect that its representative should respond to its unique needs, problems, opportunities, and interests.

Because Canada's electoral formulae (federal and provincial) do not require constituencies to contain an equal number of voters, members from different ridings find themselves called upon to represent areas with widely varying populations. House of Commons constituency populations range from a low of less than 23 000 to a high of 233 300; even within each province, the size of federal constituencies varies considerably (see table 2). At the provincial level as well, the average number of voters per member varies dramatically, from a low of less than 1500 in Newfoundland to a high of almost 79 000 in Ontario (see table 3). The effect of population size on representational relationships between members and constituents is worth emphasizing. To people living in Prince Edward Island, service responsiveness means that MLAs are expected to personally satisfy constituent requests, complaints, and problems. In Ontario, the public is satisfied if someone in the constituency or Queen's Park office, or the member, rectifies a constituent problem. Size of constituency begets size of staff: in larger provincial jurisdictions, legislators confronted by massive service and allocative demands have increased office, staff, and constituency resources to address those demands.

Federal and provincial constituencies vary in their social, economic, and cultural attributes. Federal constituencies differ from each other in many respects, including proportion of residents who are francophone or anglophone, immigrants, small-business people, employed in agriculture, unemployed, and home owners or apartment dwellers. Total family income also varies enormously.[15] That Canadian legislators are sensitive to their own constituency context is demonstrated by the following constituency descriptions offered by MPs:

> The Western Arctic Riding stretches from the Mackenzie River Valley to the Barren lands in the East. Large & small communities make up the riding including Yellowknife, the Capital. Population includes Dene, Metis, Inuvialuit and Europeans. Some 12 languages are spoken here. Industries vary from High Tech, Oil and Gas and Mining to traditional ones like Hunting and Trapping. Much Tourism which is important to the Economy. (Honourable Ethel Blondin-Andrew, Western Arctic)

TABLE 2

Population Differences in House of Commons Constituencies, 1991

	Number of MPs	Average population of constituency	Range in population of constituency
British Columbia	32	102 564	70 562 – 142 797
Alberta	26	97 906	69 717 – 128 566
Saskatchewan	14	70 638	60 732 – 85 358
Manitoba	14	77 996	64 555 – 93 794
Ontario	99	101 867	57 057 – 233 302
Quebec	75	91 946	50 295 – 152 721
New Brunswick	10	72 390	54 510 – 91 759
Nova Scotia	11	81 812	61 525 – 113 013
Newfoundland*	6	99 809	79 263 – 109 064
Prince Edward Island	4	32 441	30 058 – 34 266
Yukon and the NWT	3	28 482	22 943 – 34 706

* Excludes Labrador.
Source: 1991 census, Statistics Canada.

TABLE 3

Differences in the Size of Constituencies for Provincial Legislatures

	Number of MLAs	Mean Number of Voters in the constituency	Range in sizes of constituencies
British Columbia	69	25 652	3 174 – 42 160
Alberta	83	18 685	8 105 – 31 536
Saskatchewan	64	10 464	6 309 – 20 741
Manitoba	57	12 778	6 653 – 22 705
Ontario	130	46 672	19 165 – 78 899
Quebec	125	37 366	10 354 – 50 526
New Brunswick	58	8 649	3 968 – 17 863
Nova Scotia	52	11 992	5 034 – 20 086
Prince Edward Islandl	16	5 576	2 042 – 11 964
Newfoundland	52	6 960	1 468 – 9 626

Urban. Contains large Business Sector, Port of Vancouver, and densely populated Downtown residential neighbourhoods of varied income levels. Ethnic mix of residents include Greek, Chinese, Japanese, French, Spanish, German, Ukrainian and Italian. (Honourable Kim Campbell, Vancouver Centre)

Mostly rural, small towns, predominantly agriculture. Some forestry. Heavy oil projects; Petrochemical industries. 7 Native Reservations and three Metis Settlements. Significant Francophone population. Low to middle income levels. Some tourist attractions—Lac La Biche and Cold Lake. (Deborah Grey, Beaver River)[16]

The potential for legislative responsiveness (symbolic, service, policy, and allocative) is thus a consequence of population size, the complexity of local constituencies, and the sheer number of government programs capable of generating demands for personal assistance. The responsiveness of MPs and MLAs to demands for help is influenced by two interrelated considerations: the desire to be re-elected and the perception that constituency responsiveness (and constituency service work in particular) is associated with being re-elected.

While elections like the federal in 1984 and 1993 and the provincial in Ontario and New Brunswick in 1987 are dramatic and capture the attention of the media, they are not typical results. The prevailing pattern is for governments to be re-elected and hence for incumbents to be returned to office. For example, there were 117 provincial elections between 1945 and 1986, but only 28 changes in government, a turnover rate of only 24 percent. During the same period, the average percentage of provincial legislative seats changing hands was approximately 19 percent.[17] In short, in Canadian politics the message seems clear: incumbents tend to be retained and government parties tend to be re-elected.[18] While incumbents are vulnerable to national swings, like they were in 1993 when 205 members of the House of Commons were defeated, most members do seek re-election.[19] Yet, there is evidence that this trend may be reversing somewhat. Michael Atkinson and David Docherty, in their work on the careers of members of Parliament, found that in the seven elections between 1968 and 1988 approximately 56 percent of all turnover was caused by electoral defeat; the remaining 44 percent was caused by voluntary retirement.[20] As in the United States, more and more legislators—either due to career frustration, stagnation, or simply exhaustion—are choosing to exit politics of their own volition.

As professional politicians, MPs and MLAs recognize the enormous electoral importance of party, leader image, and issues. In order to protect themselves from modest swings in public opinion, legislators try to establish a "personal vote" or electoral following by engaging in and advertising their constituency activities. This personal following, in the minds of members, is associated with constituency work. For example, 90 percent of all MLAs surveyed in 1972 agreed that "the services a provincial legislator performs for constituents are important in getting re-elected."[21] The anticipated electoral benefit of constituency work is perhaps best summarized by Drummond and Fletcher:

> In parliamentary systems such as those currently operative at the federal and provincial levels in Canada, where backbench legislators must take a largely reactive posture in the policy-making process, the importance of individual members resides primarily in two roles: service to constituents and the personal attraction of electoral support. There is considerable evidence that legislators see these roles as interdependent. . . . Doing constituency service work may not guarantee re-election, but the failure to do so will ensure defeat.[22]

The single-member plurality electoral system emphasizes the accountability of MPs to their constituents. Since the tradition of party discipline deprives members of an opportunity to vote in accord with constituency opinions and sentiments, incumbent members seek to create a personal constituency following by providing symbolic, service, and allocative favours for their riding. The electoral system, then, constitutes the third recruitment tie binding representatives and their constituencies.

THE WORK ENVIRONMENT

The second set of ties that bind Canadian representatives to their constituencies arises as a direct result of the structure of the legislative work environment. Several institutional factors serve to reinforce links with constituents and the constituency. These include the limited possibilities for career advancement within the legislature itself, the peripheral role accorded MPs and MLAs in the policy process, and the network of constituency-oriented support services provided to legislators. The first two factors, by restricting legislators' opportunities in the national or provincial arena, help to focus their attention on their constituencies, which remain their exclusive domains. The third factor enhances this trend by encouraging legislators to spend more time and effort on their constituency.

The principle of party discipline is the main organizational feature of the legislative work environment.[23] Institutional arrangements within the Canadian parliamentary system elevate parties over individual politicians. Legislators are conditioned to accept party voting as an essential feature of the parliamentary system and to believe that the media and the public will be harsh judges of those who defy their party leadership.[24] Legislators owe their election to their respective political parties as much as to their own personal efforts and, in today's media age, electoral success hinges to a great extent upon the image and popularity of the party leader. When Canadians choose an MP or MLA, they also choose a government. This fusion of the choice of executive and legislative candidates fosters a team mentality rather than the individualistic mentality nurtured in most systems that have a formal separation of executive and legislature.[25] Virtually every aspect of a member's interactions within the legislative work environment is mediated by partisan considerations. It is this primacy of party that inhibits an MP's or MLA's pursuit of policy responsiveness.

Career Structure and Opportunities

In order to encourage active and constructive contributions to the attainment of party goals, a party leader must provide incentives, both material and psychological, to individual legislators.[26] One of the main incentives available is the prospect of advancement. Party leaders have at their disposal a number of positions that carry additional remuneration and perquisites. There are far more of these positions available to the prime minister and the premiers than to the leaders of the opposition parties.

On the government side, the most obvious such positions are cabinet portfolios, which carry with them not only additional compensation but heightened public exposure and influence in the policy-making process. The number of ministerial positions to be handed out is a prerogative of the prime minister and premiers. The 1994 Chrétien cabinet stands at twenty-two and the size of provincial cabinets varies from eleven in Prince Edward Island to thirty in Ontario.

Only a fraction of the government backbenchers will ever find themselves elevated to cabinet. The remainder still have open to them a number of positions on the parliamentary career ladder. These include speaker and deputy speaker, house leader, whip, parliamentary secretary, and committee chair. Most of these positions—with the notable exception of committee chairs in the House of Commons—offer additional pay allowances (see table 4). In the federal legislature, some seventy government MPs can expect to raise themselves above the level of ordinary back-bencher during a parliament.[27] At the provincial level, the number of such positions available will vary from province to province, and from premier to premier.

On the opposition side, fewer prestigious and remunerative positions are available to legislators. The only formally recognized positions (other than party leader) that carry with them an additional stipend are whip and opposition house leader. A few senior opposition MPs can expect to chair legislative committees in the House of Commons, and one opposition member will ordinarily be named chair of the Public Accounts Committee in the House as well as all of the provincial assemblies. Appointment to the shadow cabinet provides an informal distinction, and is seen by many as an indication of eventual ministerial appointment should their party assume power, although in reality no party leader makes such a guarantee. Thus, opposition members experience even more restricted career mobility than do government members, especially since Canada's electoral history is marked by long periods of one-party dominance.

The small number of elevated positions available in Canadian legislatures, combined with the large number of potential aspirants to those positions, might be expected to cause fierce competition among legislators for such appointments. In many cases, however, individuals realize or are made to realize fairly quickly that they are not cabinet material: they may be too old, too young, from an over-represented region, too ethnic or not ethnic enough, lacking in education or political instincts, or otherwise deficient in one of the many attributes that must be balanced in appointing cabinet ministers and filling other highly visible and easily criticized legislative posts. But even the most peripheral backbencher is central to his or her con-stituency's political life. Those who may never make it big in the legisla-tive work environment can become very big indeed in the world of the riding.

Role of Legislators in the Policy Process

Canadian legislators suffer from restrictions on the extent to which they are able to play an active and meaningful role in setting and implementing the legislative agenda. The legislative autonomy of MPs and MLAs is increasingly being displaced as a source of communication and information

TABLE 4

Allowances for Canadian Legislators

Additional Allowances	Commons	Senate	Nfld.	PEI	NS	NB	Quebec	Ont.	Man.	Sask.	Alta.	BC	Yukon	NWT
Prime Minister (Premier)	$73 600		$54 923	$48 200	$52 012	$48 936	$63 129	$45 420	$26 600	$52 300	$59 858	$45 000	$30 496	$74 715
Cabinet Minister	$49 100		39 834	37 000	37 055	32 625	45 092	31 749	20 600	36 610	47 053	39 000	22 260	67 275
Speaker	$49 100	31 000	39 384	15 700ᵃ	37 055	24 469	45 092	24 139	12 000	21 778	47 053	39 000	7 420	67 275
Deputy Speaker	$25 700		19 917	7 900ᵇ	18 533	15 000	21 043	10 102	3 500	8,167	23 526	19 500	5 565	3 000
Leader of the Opposition	$49 100	23 800	39 384	37 000	37 055	32 625	45 092	32 701	20 600	36 610	47 053	39 000	22 260	
Third Party Leader	$29 500				18 533	12 000	21 043	23 280	15 600	19 056	20 914		4 452	
Chief Government Whip	$13 200	7 500	6 000	3 000	2 380	1 500	21 043	12 491	2 500	8 167	8 000	6 000		
Chief Opposition Whip	$13 200	4 800	6 000	3 000	1 785	1 500	18 037	9 576	2 500	8 167	6 000	6 000		
Chief Third Party Whip	$7 500				170	1 500	9 018	8 618		4 084	5 000			
Parliamentary Secretaries	$10 500		18 673				12 025	9 808		8 167		6 000		
Deputy Chair, Cmte of Whole	$10 500		9 983					10 012	2 500	4 084	11 763	3 000		3 500
Ass't Deputy Chair, Cmte of Whole	$10 500							7 017						
Opposition House Leader	$23 800		19 917	3 500			21 043	12 491	2 500	8 167	10 000	6 000		
Third Party House Leader	$10 100							10 655			8 000			
Deputy Government Whip	$7 500						9 018	8 560		4 084	6 000	3 000		
Deputy Opposition Whip	$7 500						9 018	6 175		4 084	5 000			
Standing Committee Chair			8 000ᶜ				15 031	9 092		4 084	4 200	225/dayᵈ		3 000

ᵃ Includes expense allowance (tax free).
ᵇ Includes expense allowance (tax free).
ᶜ Public accounts committee only.
ᵈ Paid only when House is not sitting and business has been referred.
Source: Robert J. Fleming, Canadian Legislatures 1992 (Toronto: Global Press, 1992).

for the executive by interest groups, which possess specialized information vital to the operation of the machinery of government, and by the media, which are able to focus public discussion more effectively than individual legislators. In an age of electronic communication, cabinet need not depend upon backbenchers to relay information to and from the electorate—a short televised address or telephone opinion poll is far more efficient.

Constitutional provisions ensure that only ministers may introduce legislation involving revenue raising or expenditure. Thus, backbench members are prohibited from initiating bills of any significance. Although any member can introduce a private member's bill, the opportunity to do so is limited and, despite the reforms of the McGrath Committee—which established that at least six private member's bills must be debated and voted upon each session—the success rate for these bills remains low.

The committee system holds out the most attractive prospect for individual legislators who wish to make a meaningful contribution to the policy process. In the House of Commons, the recent introduction of a legislative committee structure has provided backbenchers with more to do, but the committees' effectiveness is still hampered by the fact that bills go to committee only after they have been approved in principle in second reading. The Chrétien government has proposed that bills be sent to committee immediately after they have been introduced. This would give members the opportunity to rethink the basic principles of the bill before it is voted upon in the House. Some committees have succeeded in forcing the government to alter provisions of major legislation, but such rare instances do little to comfort members who remain frustrated with the limited impact they have on the shaping of policy. In an attempt to increase their effect on the policy-making process, federal committees have in recent years been granted permanent staff, increased support services, and the right to travel to collect information essential to their investigations. Nonetheless, they continue to be plagued by instability caused by high membership turnover and absenteeism.

Provincial legislatures experience the same difficulties, but the smaller size of many assemblies adds logistical constraints that further hamper the effectiveness of a committee system. The provinces have often suffered a severe shortage of private members on the opposition side of the House—the backbone of a viable committee structure—especially in a minority government situation or when one party has an overwhelming majority. Smaller legislatures also find that resolving issues in committee of the whole negates the need for an active committee system. Thus, even in the one arena in which backbenchers are theoretically freed from constitutional and partisan restrictions on their ability to affect policy decisions, problems of structure and efficiency further limit the degree of influence they can bring to bear.

The other avenue in which members might seek to influence the direction of party policy is caucus. These closed-door meetings of party members normally occur once a week, and it is in these sessions that members are released from the fetters of party solidarity and can voice their opinions and views candidly, without fear of recrimination. Once the door is opened, the expectation is that even those who disagree with the party position will be supportive in public. As the case of Progressive Conservative MPs David Kilgour and Alex Kindy (who voted against the Mulroney government's Goods and Services Tax) demonstrates, boat-rockers are discouraged or even expelled. Dissent within the ranks leaves the leader vulnerable to attacks from the other side and from the media. Within opposition parties tolerance for disagreement is somewhat greater than in the government, as there is no fear that dissent could bring the government down.

Members of the government caucus are ordinarily accorded the privilege of hearing legislative proposals before they are introduced into the House. While this preview does not routinely produce changes in legislation, it does serve as a means of drumming up support within the caucus and provides a forum in which government members can discuss proposals and policy initiatives with cabinet ministers.[28] Government backbenchers can use this forum to make suggestions and voice concerns over proposed legislation. But, in practice, not all ministers regularly seek the advice of their backbenchers, and some treat caucus more as a warm-up than a policy-making tool. Opposition members are, of course, denied this channel of potential influence altogether.

Very few legislative decisions are made by individual private members. Party discipline and the requirements of cabinet government combine to restrict policy-making influence to a small cadre of members, and even the mechanisms that purport to spread such influence more widely are not always effective. No such limitations affect MPs and MLAs in their constituency offices. Riding association executives may have an important say in choosing who is to be nominated but, in terms of prestige and influence, the representative is the local kingpin. Legislators who become frustrated with a party or government that limits their input can find they have a great deal of effect in the constituency arena. Some MPs may never have their views heard in the legislature to their satisfaction, but they are almost assured of front-page coverage back home, no matter what issue they address, and a single letter on MLA stationery may be enough to extricate a constituent from a bureaucratic tangle. MPs and MLAs in their constituencies play to a receptive and favourable audience rather than a legislature that can seem largely indifferent to their contributions.

Support Services

Legislators are provided with allowances that permit and encourage them to spend time servicing their constituencies. In addition to their salaries, members of all Canadian legislatures receive an expense allowance, which is intended to defray the costs of representative functions, both in Ottawa and the constituency. Costs that arise from the responsibilities of their elected position include a second home, apartment, or hotel room; meals while in transit; hospitality in Ottawa for visiting constituents; and an increased clothing budget.

All legislatures provide some funds to help cover the expense of travel between constituency and legislature. Without this allowance, many members would be able to return regularly to their constituencies only at great personal expense. These travel allowances normally detail specific provisions for travel by air, bus, boat, or train. In addition, all jurisdictions except Prince Edward Island, Newfoundland, New Brunswick, and the Yukon provide for a car allowance. The House of Commons covers travel through a point system: each member receives sixty-four points per year; one round trip between Ottawa and a member's constituency, via any mode of transportation, uses up one point. The most generous travel plan is found in Alberta, where legislators are afforded the luxury of unlimited air and bus travel within the province. Ontario ensures unlimited travel for members by bus or train, as well as an unlimited mileage allowance for driving within the constituency or between the constituency and Queen's Park. In the House of Commons and the legislatures of Quebec, Ontario, and British Columbia, members are permitted to transfer some of these travel perks to their spouse or other family members.[29]

Members of most legislatures are furnished with funds to set up and staff an office in the constituency. These offices have proven to be vital in the performance of a representative's duties and as a communication link with the electorate. A constituency allowance ensures that members are able to rent office space, pay utilities, purchase office supplies and equipment, and hire support staff. Only the legislatures of Prince Edward

Island, New Brunswick, and the Yukon do not provide such a constituency allowance. Elsewhere the allowances vary in terms of generosity and restrictions. The House of Commons is the most supportive of its members in their constituencies: a significant portion of an MP's global operating budget must be spent on the operation and staffing of a constituency office. At the beginning of each parliament, new MPs receive $5000 ($3000 for re-elected MPs) for the purchase of furniture and equipment. MPs also enjoy free mail and telephone privileges and have access to electronic mail networks. The provinces are not as generous: there are no free mail or telephone privileges in Nova Scotia, and many other legislatures will pay for these services only upon submission of receipts. Despite these variations, most of the provincial legislatures encourage and support the efforts of their members in the constituency.[30]

The variation in the degree to which legislatures are willing to help defray constituency expenses is almost certainly related to differences in the size of ridings. An Ontario MPP represents on average about 70 000 constituents, and members of the Quebec National Assembly have constituencies of approximately 52 000. In the Atlantic provinces, and in Manitoba and Saskatchewan, the average is only about 18 000 constituents, and in Prince Edward Island only 3200.[31] Legislators from Ontario and Quebec thus face more frequent demands for services in the constituency. The same is true for the House of Commons, where the average constituency size is around 85 000. The House has also formally recognized the problems caused by spatially large or densely populated constituencies. For several years, these types of constituencies have been accorded special status: members representing them have been granted additional allowances to help them in their constituency work and have been permitted to exceed established limits on election expenses.[32] In combination, these geographic and electors' supplements currently provide additional allowances to more than one-half of the members of the House.

CONCLUSION

Factors in both the recruitment and legislative work environments help to encourage Canadian legislators to concentrate their efforts on their constituencies. In the recruitment environment, three factors serve to attract and retain the attention of legislators to their constituencies. Members and their constituents share cultural expectations of strong responsiveness to local community concerns. Party riding associations and members' involvement with them constantly renew the link between legislator and local activist. Finally, an electoral system that specifies a one-to-one mapping between constituencies and representatives, and allows significant variation in constituency size, population, and composition, forces legislators to remain cognizant of the unique characteristics and interests of their particular riding.

In the legislative work environment, circumstances conspire to deflect legislators' efforts from full-time parliamentary policy work. By default, such circumstances reinforce the commitment to constituency service. The slim possibility of advancement within the parliamentary ranks suggests to many legislators that their discretionary time and effort is better spent in an arena where they are almost guaranteed to be appreciated. The limited opportunity for backbenchers to affect the policy process in the legislature sharply contrasts with their power to perform "bureaucratic miracles" at home. A system of allowances that facilitates and supports constituency work and expenditures helps to make local community work attractive.

This matrix of forces seems to be in a state of flux. Increasingly, constituencies have issued demands for more responsive legislative behaviour from their representatives. It remains to be seen whether this heightened interest will lead to an eventual relaxation of the strict party discipline that continues to overshadow most activity in the legislative work environment. In 1993, the federal Liberal Party, then in opposition, issued an eighteen-point plan entitled *Reviving Parliamentary Democracy*. One of the central tenets of this program was that the insistence on party discipline would be decreased and that the *no-confidence doctrine* would be relaxed. Now in government, the Liberals have yet to make substantive changes in this direction. They may be prodded into taking action by the fallout from the referendum over the Charlottetown Accord and the dramatic results of the 1993 federal election.

Along with such policy initiatives as the Goods and Services Tax, the Charlottetown Accord provides an example of the absence of policy responsiveness between government members and the public. Prior to discussions about the second round of constitutional reform, six in ten Canadians were against the Meech Lake Accord. The first two surveys about the Charlottetown reform package revealed that more than half of Canadians surveyed had no opinion about the reforms. Public opinion changed dramatically by 7 October 1992, when opinion about the accord was evenly divided between supporters and opponents. Less than two weeks later, opposition to the accord climbed to 50 percent while support remained constant at 40 percent. On voting day, the public defeated the accord, 54.4 to 45.6 percent (see table 5). The views of Canada's parliamentary leadership, all of whom supported the accord, were sharply at odds with public opinion.

Canada's style of representation, characterized by a mixture of responsive choices and strict party discipline in the House of Commons, probably ended with the 1993 federal election. Although the Liberal Party formed a majority government and the Progressive Conservative Party was reduced to two seats, it would be incorrect to interpret this result as a case of one old party replacing the other. More than one hundred of the sitting MPs belong to the Reform Party and the Bloc Québécois, and

TABLE 5

Perceptions of Meech Lake and Charlottetown Accords

Panel A: Public Attitudes Toward Passing or Opposing the Meech Lake Accord

	In favour of %	Opposed %	Don't know %
June 1991	20	59	22
Jan. 1991	24	52	25

Panel B: Views of the Charlottetown Constitutional Reform Package

	In favour of %	Opposed %	Don't know %
Jan. 1992	13	25	62
Oct. 1991	15	28	57

Panel C: Believe that the Constitution of Canada should be Renewed on the Basis of the Agreement Reached on 28 August 1992

	Yes %	No %	Undecided %
16 Sept. 1992	42	29	29
7 Oct. 1992	41	41	18
21 Oct. 1992	40	50	10
Results of Referendum Vote	45.6%	54.4%	

both challenge conventional thought about representation. Reform presents the greatest challenge to individual parliamentarians and the House as an institution because of its emphasis on direct democracy. Its focus on the constituency and placing more power in the hands of voters is illustrated by its advocacy of a revised oath of office for MPs and use of referendum, initiative, and recall. Members of Parliament would swear allegiance to the constituents as well as the Queen and would thus be beholden not to party leaders but to their constituents.[33] Acting upon the policy wishes of constituents would require a relaxation of party discipline and changes in the rules of the House of Commons.

Changes to the constitution and important public policy would require approval in a national referendum, which would be binding on the government. Approval, as advocated by Reform, would require a "yes" vote by a simple majority of all voters as well as a majority vote in two-thirds of the provinces. The concept of initiative means that 3 percent of the eligible voters could force the government to hold a referendum on a particular bill. The referendum question would appear on the ballot in the following federal election. Finally, voters could remove MPs—for undefined reasons—through the instrument of the recall.

The success of Reform in the 1993 federal election is due, in part at least, to public demand for policy responsiveness, unhappiness with the yoke of party discipline in the Commons, and the frailty of symbolic, service, and allocative responsiveness. The lesson of the GST, Charlottetown, and the 1993 federal election is that future members—if they desire re-election—need to pay closer attention to the policy wishes of their constituents. Ironically, such a development might weaken responsiveness: members who find themselves freer to vote against party dictates and pursue meaningful policy initiatives may no longer need to turn to the constituency out of frustration with their limited role in policy making. Nevertheless, barring significant electoral reform, the ties that bind members to their constituents, especially in the recruitment environment, can be expected to remain strong and lasting.

Notes

[1] Bob Miller, "On the Front Lines," *Parliamentary Government* 6, 2 (1986): 3.
[2] Malcolm E. Jewell, "Legislator–Constituency Relations and the Representative Process," *Legislative Studies Quarterly* 8 (Aug. 1983): 303–4.

[3] Jon H. Pammett and Michael S. Whittington, "Introduction: Political Culture and Political Socialization" in *Foundations of Political Culture*, ed. Jon H. Pammett and Michael Whittington (Toronto: Macmillan, 1976), 2.

[4] Anthony Wilson-Smith, "Time to Listen," CTV Poll, *Maclean's*, 4 Jan. 1993, 18–22.

[5] *Globe and Mail*, 10 Sept. 1982, 1–2.

[6] Richard G. Price, Harold D. Clarke, and Robert M. Krause, "The Socialization of Freshman Legislators: The Case of Canadian MPs" in *Foundations of Political Culture*, 211–38.

[7] Gary Levy and Graham White, eds., *Provincial and Territorial Legislatures in Canada* (Toronto: University of Toronto Press, 1989). See chapters on Prince Edward Island, Ontario, and Newfoundland.

[8] This discussion does not extend to the territorial legislature of the Northwest Territories, which features no political parties.

[9] Doreen Barrie and Roger Gibbins, "Parliamentary Careers in the Canadian Federal State," *Canadian Journal of Political Science* 22 (March 1989): 137–45.

[10] Allan Kornberg and William Mishler, *Influence in Parliament: Canada* (Durham, NC: Duke University Press, 1976). See ch. 2, "The MPs: An Overview," 58–101.

[11] Roman R. March, *The Myth of Parliament* (Scarborough, ON: Prentice-Hall, 1974), 51.

[12] John McMenemy, "Getting to Know the Parties by the Company We Keep: Local Sources of Party Imagery" in *Canadian Parties in Transition*, ed. Alain G. Gagnon and A. Brian Tanguay (Scarborough, ON: Nelson Canada, 1989), 312.

[13] William P. Irvine, "Does the Candidate Make a Difference? The Macro-Politics and Micro-Politics of Getting Elected," *Canadian Journal of Political Science* 15 (Dec. 1982): 767.

[14] Ibid., 768–69.

[15] Munroe Eagles, "Local Effects on the Political Behaviour of Canadians" in *Canadian Politics: An Introduction to the Discipline*, ed. Alain G. Gagnon and James P. Bickerton (Peterborough, ON: Broadview Press, 1990), 285–307.

[16] John Bejermi, *Canadian Parliamentary Handbook* (Ottawa: Borealis Press, 1993), 142, 162, 264.

[17] Peter McCormick, "Provincial Political Party Systems, 1945–1986" in *Canadian Parties in Transition*, 152–85.

[18] For analyses of the effects of incumbency, see three articles by Michael Krashinsky and William J. Milne: "Some Evidence of the Effect of Incumbency in Ontario Provincial Elections," *Canadian Journal of Political Science* 16 (Sept. 1983): 489–500; "Additional Evidence on the Effect of Incumbency in Canadian Elections," *Canadian Journal of Political Science* 18 (March 1985): 155–659; and "The Effect of Incumbency in the 1984 Federal and 1985 Ontario Elections," *Canadian Journal of Political Science* 19 (June 1986): 337–43.

[19] David Docherty, "Should I Stay or Should I Go? Career Decisions of Members of Parliament" in *Leaders and Leadership in Canada*, ed. Maureen Mancuso, Richard G. Price, and Ronald Wagenberg (Toronto: Oxford University Press, 1994), 245–65.

[20] Michael Atkinson and David Docherty, "Moving Right Along: The Roots of Amateurism in the Canadian House of Commons," *Canadian Journal of Political Science* 25, 2 (June 1992): 295–318.

[21] Harold D. Clarke, Richard G. Price, and Robert Krause, "Constituency Service Among Canadian Provincial Legislators: Basic Findings and a Test of Three Hypotheses," *Canadian Journal of Political Science* 8 (Dec. 1975): 520–42.

[22] Robert J. Drummond and Frederick J. Fletcher, "Political Communication and Orientation to Legislators Among Ontario Voters" in *Parliament, Policy and Representation*, ed. Harold D. Clarke et al. (Toronto: Methuen, 1980), 104.

[23] Once again, with the exception of the "partyless" Northwest Territories.

[24] Paul Thomas, "Parliamentary Reform through Political Parties," in *The Canadian House of Commons: Essays in Honour of Norman Ward*, ed. John C. Courtney (Calgary: University of Calgary Press, 1985), 46.

[25] Bruce Cain, John Ferejohn, and Morris Fiorina, *The Personal Vote: Constituency Service and Electoral Independence* (Cambridge: Harvard University Press, 1987), 214.

[26] Thomas, "Parliamentary Reform through Political Parties," 45.

[27] C.E.S. Franks, *The Parliament of Canada* (Toronto: University of Toronto Press, 1987), 45. This figure is, of course, dependent upon the size of cabinet, the frequency of cabinet shuffles, and the turnover of parliamentary secretaryships.

[28] Franks, *Parliament of Canada*, 45.

[29] The details of the various travel allowance schemes in operation in the provinces and the House of Commons can be found in Robert J. Fleming, ed., *Canadian Legislatures 1992* (Toronto: Global Press, 1992), 104–11.

[30] Ibid., 123–27.

[31] Levy and White, *Provincial and Territorial Legislatures*, 8.

[32] For a complete discussion of the specifics of these additional allowances, see John C. Courtney, "Parliament and Representation: The Unfinished Agenda of Electoral Redistributions," *Canadian Journal of Political Science* 21, 4 (Dec. 1988): 682–84. For an update of the figures, see Fleming, *Canadian Legislatures 1992*, 124.

[33] Sydney Sharpe and Don Braid, *Storming Babylon: Preston Manning and the Rise of the Reform Party* (Toronto: Key Porter, 1992), 169–87.

Suggested Reading

Atkinson, Michael M., and Paul Thomas. "Studying the Canadian Parliament," *Legislative Studies Quarterly* 18 (Aug. 1993): 423–47. A comprehensive review of the literature on Parliament. A very useful introduction to the approaches and methodologies associated with studying Parliament and parliamentarians.

Ferejohn, John, and Brian Gaines. "The Personal Vote in Canada." In *Representation, Integration and Political Parties in Canada*. Ed. Herman Bakvis. Toronto: Dundurn Press, 1991, 275–302.

Papers of the Royal Commission on Electoral Reform and Campaign Finance. This is the only analysis of the relationships between a member's constituency activities and the member's local share of the vote.

Franks, C.E.S. *The Parliament of Canada*. Toronto: University of Toronto Press, 1987.

Required reading for students interested in Parliament. Most of this text, quite properly, deals with the House of Commons and focuses upon different models of parliamentary government, parliamentary parties, members' backgrounds, committee work, workload, and institutional reform.

Mancuso, Maureen, Richard G. Price, and Ronald Wagenberg. *Leaders and Leadership in Canada*. Toronto: Oxford University Press, 1994.

For a new account of the complex relationships between representation and leadership, see Herman Bakvis, "Cabinet Ministers: Leaders of Followers?"; Ian Stewart, "Scaling the Matterhorn: Parliamentary Leadership in Canada"; and David Docherty, "Should I Stay or Should I Go? Career Decision of Members of Parliament."

White, Graham. *The Ontario Legislature: A Political Analysis*. Toronto: University of Toronto Press, 1989.

A Comprehensive analysis of legislative politics at Queen's Park, Canada's largest legislature outside Ottawa. Topics include a thorough discussion of the members, the legislature at work, committees, services to members, and the process of reform.

Stephen Brooks

12

PUBLIC POLICY AND POLICY MAKING IN CANADA

> Almost every aspect of policy-making in Canada
> remains shrouded in ignorance if not mystery.
>
> *Richard Simeon*

In the two decades since the above pronouncement was made, the study of public policy has emerged as one of the more fashionable areas of Canadian political science. More courses are offered in it, more students take them, and more political scientists direct their research energies toward public policy than was the case when Richard Simeon lamented the ignorance in which policy making in Canada was shrouded. Along with the field of public administration, it has probably been the fastest-growing sector in the discipline. Whether this flurry of interest and activity has helped to pull back the shroud, revealing the lineaments of the subject that lies underneath, is another question. Before we consider what is known about Canadian policy making, we need to answer some basic questions about our subject. What is public policy? Why do some matters become policy issues, attracting the attention of governments, the media, and societal groups, while others do not?

One of the most frequently cited definitions of *public policy* is that of American political scientist Thomas Dye. According to Dye, public policy is "whatever governments choose to do or not to do."[1] Policy involves conscious choice that leads to deliberate action, such as the passage of a law, the spending of money, an official speech or gesture, or some other observable act. But it may also involve inaction. No one would disagree that a concrete act like the passage of a law counts as policy. But how can inaction reasonably be described as policy? The answer depends on whether or not the failure to act takes place in the context of political controversy.

Government inaction sometimes results from ignorance that a "problem" exists. For decades, carcinogenic PCBs (polychlorinated biphenyls) were used, stored, and disposed of without much thought. There was no public policy on the handling of these deadly chemicals before it was realized that there was reason for concern. When the public was alerted to the compound's cancer-causing properties, the use, transportation, and disposal of PCBs became policy issues. Government inaction before that time obviously had health consequences for those who were exposed to PCBs and certainly allowed the accumulation of stockpiles of what today is one of the most widely feared toxic chemicals. But this was not deliberate inaction. There was no public policy on PCBs, just as there was no policy on the production and handling of many other industrial chemicals, because there was no significant level of awareness that a problem existed. It makes no sense to speak of policy where an issue has not yet been formulated in problematic terms. Once it has, inaction by policy makers becomes a deliberate policy choice.

An example of inaction as government policy can be seen in the case of Aboriginal land claims. The land claims issue erupted onto the public scene in the 1970s as a result of enormous investment projects, like Quebec's James Bay hydro-electric development and Ottawa's proposal to build an Arctic gas pipeline, that clearly threatened the traditional lifestyles of northern Aboriginal communities. The number of land claims escalated rapidly during the 1970s and 1980s, but progress toward their settlement was excruciatingly slow. A bare handful of claims had been settled by the 1990s. Although Ottawa and several of the provinces appeared to concede the legitimacy of Aboriginal land claims by establishing mechanisms to study them and negotiating with the groups involved, the fact that so little was accomplished over a relatively long period of time suggests that the real policy was not to settle claims but to avoid having to act.

The land claims case raises another question. Is policy necessarily what policy makers say it is? In other words, if we want to determine what public policy is on some issue, should we direct our attention to official government pronouncements or to the actual record of what has and has not been achieved? Of course, no one takes all official pronouncements at face value, just as it would be foolish to assume that an individual's motives and intentions are always what he or she claims them to be. Vagueness and ambiguity are often deliberate and are always part of the recipe for political longevity in democratic political systems. The bottom line on determining what actually constitutes public policy comes down to this: both official claims and concrete actions should be looked at carefully, and one should be prepared to find that actions often speak louder than words.

The determination of policy is even more complicated than this. It often happens that a government's most sincere efforts misfire, failing to achieve the expected goals and perhaps even aggravating the situation they were intended to improve. Consider a policy of government-controlled rents. Critics of rent controls have long argued that such a policy in fact hurts the lower-income groups it is intended to benefit, by discouraging developers and investors from building new rental accommodation for the low end of the market. As the supply dwindles, prices inevitably are pushed up. If and when this happens are we justified in saying that government housing policy favours the less affluent? In fact, a program, law, or regulation hardly ever "solves" a problem in the sense of eliminating the conditions that inspired controversy and demands for action in the first place. When problems do disappear, this is more likely to be the result of changing societal conditions than a direct consequence of government policy.

Cynicism is a normal enough response when the official pronouncements of government do not coincide with its actions or when policies fail to produce the expected results. When this happens, and it frequently does, we should not jump to the conclusion that policy is just "sound and fury, signifying nothing." Gestures, symbols, and words are important components of the political process. They are often valued in their own right, and their capacity to reconcile and to divide should not be under-estimated. The "distinct society" clauses of the Meech Lake and Charlottetown constitutional accords, which recognized Quebec as a distinct and pre-dominantly francophone society within Canada, turned out to be the most contentious features of these defeated proposals outside of Quebec. It was not so much that non-Quebeckers perceived that the constitutional recognition of Quebec as a distinct society would have material consequences. Instead, it was the symbol of special status for Quebec that was objected to by many and that led opponents of Meech Lake and Charlottetown to label the accords as sell-outs to Quebec. Governments influence the allocation of symbolic values—what Raymond Breton calls the "symbolic order"—in society. And, as in the case of material benefits and burdens, satisfying one group's symbolic aspirations may mean denying those of another group.

THE AGENDA AND DISCOURSE
OF POLICY MAKING

There is another, more general sense in which the symbols, gestures, and words manipulated by policy makers are important. They constitute the *political agenda*, defining what is relevant in public life, how issues are defined, whose views should be taken seriously, and what sort of "solutions" are tenable. A law, a statement by a political leader, media coverage of a group's policy demands or of some situation or event all provide an affirmation of the relevance of a problem and the values and conflicts associated with it. If I may be excused a bit of jargon here, political issues and policy problems are constructed out of the conflicting values and terminologies that different groups put forward when they compete for something that cannot be shared so as to satisfy all of them. These issues and problems do not exist apart from the words and symbols used to describe them. They are constructed, in the sense that political issues and policy problems do not possess an inevitable character that is inherent in them. Whether we even recognize them as political issues and policy problems and how we respond when they are brought to our attention both depend on the particular forces that shape the political agenda in a given society. These forces change over time, and so, therefore, does the political agenda. As American political scientist Murray Edelman observes, "conditions accepted as inevitable or unproblematic may come to be seen as problems; and damaging conditions may not be defined as political issues at all."[2]

Once we accept that the political agenda is not an inevitable product of social and economic conditions, we are confronted with the question of why some of these conditions become formulated as problems and others do not. This leads to a consideration of the various agents of cultural learning—family, schools, mass media, the workplace, the state—that together generate the ideological parameters of society. To understand the practical importance of cultural learning, consider the following examples.

Until a couple of decades ago, the extensive and profound differences in the career opportunities, incomes, and social roles of men and women were not generally seen to be a problem. As cultural attitudes have changed, these unequal social conditions have become a prominent item on the political agendas of virtually all industrialized democracies. Gender politics and the policy debates that surround such issues as abortion, pay equity, affirmative action, sexual harassment, pornography, and publicly subsidized day care are constructed out of the arguments, claims, and demands for action put forward by women's organizations and their spokespersons, and the counter-arguments, claims, and demands of others who feel compelled to respond to their definition of the problem. The same can be said of any policy issue. What emerges from such exchanges is a *policy discourse*—an unfolding tapestry of words and symbols that structures thinking and action—that is constructed out of the multiple definitions (or denial) of the problem.

The capacity to influence this discourse is more than half the battle. Every group, organization, and individual with the least bit of political acumen knows this, so the first line of attack is often through the media. Governments have a distinct advantage in the struggle to shape the contours of policy discourse. They have virtually guaranteed access to the public through media coverage of official statements, press conferences, and other orchestrated efforts to communicate a particular message (and influence public opinion). Moreover, they are able to tell their story through paid advertisements—the federal government has for years been the largest single advertiser in Canada—and through government information services directed at households and organizations. The messages governments communicate, particularly when they touch on controversial issues, are often greeted with cynicism by the media and the public. But even then they receive a hearing. One reason for this is the official authority of the source. Even if the government's messages are not considered to be credible, its capacity to influence the outcome of an issue means that the information it disseminates is not likely to be ignored. Cynicism, vocal opposition, and an unsympathetic media are not enough to close off the channels through which government can influence policy discourse.

Despite the formidable information and financial resources at their disposal, governments are a long way from being able to control either the policy agenda or the policy discourse that develops around an issue. This was evident in the campaign leading up to the national referendum on the Charlottetown Accord, held on 26 October 1992. Going into the campaign, public opinion polls suggested that a solid majority of Canadians supported the accord. But like snow before a chinook, this soft support melted away, notwithstanding the fact that all three official parties in the House of Commons, all ten provincial governments, and most of the heavyweights of the business and labour establishments backed the accord. When one considers the enormous amount of information that Ottawa distributed in the period before the campaign formally began, there can be no doubt that the pro-accord forces vastly outspent their opponents. Superior resources were not enough to control the debate that took place, and ultimately the accord's detractors triumphed.

The Charlottetown episode is not so unusual. Indeed, much of the time governments are on the defensive, reacting to the claims, demands, and interpretations put forward by opposition political parties, societal groups, and the media. The social power of the interests advancing them largely determine whose "problems" reach the political agenda and whose arguments, interpretations, and proposals are taken seriously in the policy-making process. In fact, the capacity to influence policy discourse would seem to be one barometer by which the power of different interests could be measured.

But this is too simple. Politics in capitalist democracies is open-ended enough that ideas and reforms that very clearly are not favoured by the powerful are often woven into the fabric of policy discourse and are institutionalized through public policies. One would be hard pressed to explain the policy successes of the women's movement, and the arguments associated with gender-based differences in such matters as employment and pay, from the standpoint of dominant class interests. Or consider the entry of Aboriginals, visible minorities, and the disabled into modern political discourse. These are groups that lie far from the epicentre of social and economic power in Canadian society. Despite this, they have been able to influence the agenda of politics and the actions of governments in this country. Moreover, there are some policy areas that neither engage the public's attention nor mobilize powerful social and economic interests. Where this is the case, the ideas and preferences of bureaucrats and experts may carry greater weight than usual. We should not assume, therefore, an automatic correspondence between the ideas that get onto the political agenda and the pecking order of social and economic interests in society.

This is not to say that policy discourse is a wide open mêlée in which every voice has an equal opportunity to be heard. It has become popular to speak of *systemic bias*, a term intended to capture the selectiveness of the policy system. Some points of view, it is claimed, never get articulated, and some policy outcomes are virtually precluded by the biases inherent in the cultural and institutional warp and woof of society. At one level this is obviously true. For demographic, historical, and political reasons, language has a prominence in Canadian politics that it does not have in the United States. Conversely, individual rights and freedoms occupy a more significant place in American political discourse than they do in Canada and most other capitalist democracies. In saying, then, that any society and political system have particular biases, we have not said much, or at least not much that is very interesting. The more interesting question is what these biases reveal about the sources and distribution of power and about the capacity of different social and economic interests to influence the actions of government. Let us turn now to the relationship between power and public policy in Canada.

POWER AND PUBLIC POLICY

In *How Canadians Govern Themselves*, a booklet published by the Canadian government, Senator Eugene Forsey observes that "government is our creature. We make it, [and] we are ultimately responsible for it."[3] Electors ultimately determine what governments do, what policies they pursue and with what means. We may call this the *democratic ideal*. It starts from the simple and irrefutable premise that governments are elected by the people in periodic elections. Legislators cannot afford to be complacent and unresponsive because voters can replace them with the candidates of some other party. The power to determine public policy—at least its broad contours and direction—lies with the people by whose consent governments act. While formally accurate, this description of the Canadian system of democratic government is completely unreliable as a guide to where the real power to shape policy lies. But if power does not lie with the "people," where does it lie?

There is no single answer to this question. Instead, there are several versions of policy making that offer different answers to the questions of who influences policy, when, and how. They may be grouped under the following four labels: *pluralism*, *public choice*, *class analysis*, and *statism*. Each theory views political power as being concentrated in many fewer hands than is suggested by the ideal of democratic government. Together they constitute the main theoretical explanations of how power and public policy are related in Canada. We will look at each of them in turn.

Pluralism

Groups and their efforts to influence government action are at the heart of pluralist explanations. The major players are likely to be organizations representing—or at least claiming to represent—the interests of groups that perceive themselves as having a stake in how government deals with a given issue. Policy, then, is the outcome of a competition between organized groups. Governments are not neutral bystanders in this process. They have their own interests to promote and defend: bureaucrats' interests in the size of their budgets, in the preservation and perhaps expansion of their program and responsibilities; politicians' interests in re-election, in their own career advancement, and in whatever personal ideals they may want to promote. Nevertheless, the pluralist explanation of power and public policy is fundamentally a society-centred approach to understanding policy making. It locates the principal forces shaping state action in the societal milieu. Its focus is on the role played by interest groups, culture, and the media, as well as on environmental factors like the structure of the economy and a society's demographic characteristics.

Any serious effort to come to grips with policy formation must explain why it is that some interests are more successful than others in shaping the political agenda and government action. Pluralists do not suggest that the competition between groups is an equal one. Business interests are especially likely to be singled out as dominant players. As the American political scientist E.E. Schattschneider observes, "The flaw in the pluralist heaven is that the heavenly chorus sings with a strong upper-class accent. . . . The system is skewed, loaded and unbalanced in favor of a fraction of a minority."[4] Theodore Lowi argues that policy making "is biased not so much in favor of the rich as in favor of the established and organized."[5] (As it happens, business interests with superior resources and access to policy makers are always among the best organized in capitalist societies.) Charles Lindblom speaks of the "privileged position of business," which he attributes to a combination of superior financial resources and lobbying organization, greater access to governmental officials, and, most importantly, propagandistic activities that—directly through political advertising and indirectly through commercial advertising—reinforce the ideological dominance of business values in capitalist democracies.[6] Lindblom stresses the importance of the market economy as a "prison" that limits government's room for manoeuvre. Governments are necessarily concerned with how their actions will affect "business confidence" because a sharp or prolonged fall in capital investment will have a negative impact on both the economy and their popular support (to the extent that they are held responsible for the fortunes of the economy).[7]

Even though many contemporary versions of pluralism maintain that economic interests dominate in the political marketplace, politics and policy making are never reduced to strictly economic or class terms. Other lines of political conflict, including ethnicity, language, religion, gender, region, and ideology, are viewed as having a significance that is not necessarily less than class, depending upon what is at stake and which interests are mobilized to act. Pluralist theory does not view these non-economic divisions as merely class conflicts dressed up in ways that make them difficult to recognize.

The cutting edge of pluralist work on policy making in Canada has used the concept of *policy communities*[8] or, in the case of industrial policy, *sectoral policy networks*,[9] to analyze the process of policy formation. The focus of these studies is the specific constellations of state—bureaucratic and political—and societal interests that mobilize around a particular issue. Paul Pross uses the term *sub-governments* to convey the fact that within any policy community only a part of the state system is likely to be involved in the determination of policy. These concepts—policy communities, sectoral policy networks, sub-governments—are intellectual descendants of a longer pluralist tradition that recognizes the intricate and mutually dependent relations that develop between state and societal actors in determining public policy.

Public Choice

Public choice theory represents the colonization of traditional political science concerns by economics. Those working within this approach attempt to explain political behaviour, including the policy decisions of governments, in terms of a theory of individual choice according to which people operate on the basis of rational self-interest, seeking to maximize satisfaction at the least cost within the limits imposed by the information at their disposal. What keeps competition in the political marketplace from degenerating into a no-holds-barred mêlée is the existence of rules— the constitution, laws—that constitute a web of incentives and constraints influencing an individual's choices. As in the economic marketplace, the "wrong" rules will distort the behaviour of individuals, resulting in outcomes that are inefficient from the standpoint of society as a whole.

The appeal of the public choice model for students of policy making lies in its purported theoretical rigour. It provides a set of sharp analytical tools for understanding how policy is determined. Foremost among these tools is public choice theory's strict insistence on the individual as the basic unit of analysis. The state is viewed in terms of the individual politicians and bureaucrats who occupy particular positions within it, and whose coalitions and conflicts are determined by rational calculations of individual self-interest. Politicians seek to be elected and, once elected, to maintain themselves in power (their motivations for wanting to hold office are beside the point). Bureaucrats seek promotion and more control over the environment in which their organization is situated. Expansion, increased budgets, new policy tasks, and capturing chief responsibility for a policy field are all strategies that may be used to achieve these bureaucratic goals.

It is important to keep in mind that the state does not act in a single-minded way. The bureaucracy, for example, is divided into "spender" organizations, for whom financial restraint means placing limits on the goals that individual bureaucrats pursue, and "savers" who operate under a very different system of incentives for behaviour. The incentive system of individual bureaucrats also varies according to the societal interests that consume the services they provide, bureaucrats' regional focus, and their function. These divisions lead to competition and bargaining within the bureaucracy. This is also true of the elected government. Behind the facade of unity that typically characterizes single-party governments in Canada (coalition governments introduce another level of complexity), the fact that the re-election prospects of individual members of the government are tied to different constituencies (regional, special interest, and ideological), and to the various parts of the state bureaucracy they oversee, ensures that they, too, are involved in this process of bargaining within the state.

The behaviour of those within the state—the choices open to them and the strategies they pursue—is influenced by the actual and anticipated actions of special interest groups, the media, and various segments of the electorate. Public choice theory explains the actions of collective agents like political parties, the media, and pressure groups in terms of the self-interested motives of those who make up these groups. For example, one of the major Canadian contributions to public choice theory describes political parties as "loose coalitions of individuals who are prepared to work together for the election of a slate of candidates. Presumably the members believe that if the party they support were to form the government their personal interests would be better served than if some other coalition were in office."[10] Special-interest groups are successful in influencing public policy to the extent that their individual members perceive that the costs of investing in collective action are exceeded by the individual benefits they receive from group membership—what we might call the *group cohesion condition*. Equally important is the extent to which the relevant policy makers perceive that their own capacity to pursue what is important to them would be advanced by meeting the group's demands or hindered by resisting the group's pressure activities—the *credible threat condition*.

Like pluralism, public choice explanations view policy making as a highly competitive process. They share such terms as *bargaining, accommodation,* and *exchange.* Moreover, their portrayal of the state as being a mediator of competing claims, as well as having its own internal divisions to work out, is broadly similar. Though methodologically different, pluralist and public choice theories view the political world through much the same lens. It is a world in which political competition is unequal, but also in which real competition does exist and the distributional outcomes that public policy determines or reinforces are fairly open. This stands in marked contrast to the explanation provided by class analysis.

Class Analysis

Class analysis is characterized by four main beliefs.

1. Society is divided into classes, an individual's class position being determined by his or her relationship to the means of production.
2. Class is the pre-eminent basis for political and economic conflict.
3. Classes are unequal, with society divided into dominant and subordinate classes.
4. The state is biased in favour of the dominant class(es), which in a capitalist society will be those that control capital.

Together these four elements do not constitute a rigid theoretical code. Indeed, there are wide variations in the importance that those working within this framework attach to such non-economic factors as culture, technology, and the role of individuals. Class analysis does not reduce all politics to a question of economic class, but it does make the material conditions of society—"the processes by which material requirements are satisfied"[11]—the touchstone for its analysis of politics and policy making. In the words of sociologist Wallace Clement, "While the economic provides the context, it is the political and the cultural/ideological that write the text of history, the particularities of each nation, and the possibilities for the future. The script is one in which human actors have significant freedom of action."[12]

The self-declared openness and eclecticism of contemporary class analysis have not changed the fact that it views class and class divisions as social, economic, and political realities of the first order, and not mere intellectual categories. Applied to policy making, this means that the state is viewed as an agent for reproducing the class inequalities that exist in society, as well as being contested terrain where class conflicts between dominant and subordinate classes, and between different segments of the dominant class, are played out. The state's sympathies are not, according to class analysis, neutral, and the overall thrust of public policy supports the general interests of capital. The reason for this is that policy makers usually believe such policies to be in the public interest; also, failure to maintain some minimum level of business confidence leads to economic downturn, the consequences of which are reduced popular support for the government and losses in the state's ability to finance its activities. This second factor is an important structural constraint on policy makers in capitalist societies.

Some features of this model need to be stressed. First of all, for the state to serve the general interests of capital it is not necessary that policy makers be drawn from the dominant class. In fact, some argue that the fewer the personal ties between the state and the dominant class, the more effective the state will be in maintaining the interests of this class. This is because the reality of capitalist domination will to some extent be hidden by the appearance of government that is not in the hands of the members of any one class. Second, policy makers are receptive to the demands of subordinate classes. Their readiness to implement reforms that may in fact be opposed by powerful business interests does not result from any special vision on their part as to what concessions must be made to save the capitalist system from the shortsightedness of individual capitalists or sectors of the business community. Instead, it is due to the prosaic reality of governments being subject to popular pressures through elections, and also to the fact that divisions within the business community give policy makers a margin in which to manoeuvre. Governments, therefore, are willing and able to act in ways that offend parts of that community. This does not mean that policy makers are more astute about what needs to be done to maintain the capitalist system than are the capitalists themselves. It does mean that their concern for the overall level of economic activity frees policy makers from the narrower interests of particular parts of the business community.

It would be a mistake to think that policy makers ask themselves, "What do we need to do to preserve the capitalist system?" They do not need to consciously pose this question because their conception of the "national interest" coincides with the general interest of capital. As Ralph Miliband explains, "If the state acts in ways which are congruent with the interests and purposes of capital, it is not because it is driven out of dire compulsion to do so, but because it wants to do so."[13] Ideology reinforces the structural mechanisms described earlier, to ensure that the interests of the business community are not treated like those of a mere special-interest group.

Statism

Statism is a rather awkward-sounding label for those explanations of policy making that stress the independence of policy makers. By *independence* we mean the ability and inclination of elected officials and bureaucrats to act as they see fit, irrespective of the pressures and demands coming from societal groups. The role of permanent bureaucratic officials is believed to be particularly important, and indeed this approach to policy making is sometimes referred to as bureaucratic politics. As Leslie Pal observes,

> Modern public policy is increasingly, it appears, a bureaucratic affair, conceived and developed within the state, proposed as part of departmental agendas, and implemented by state authorities. Recent work has therefore focused on the influence of bureaucracy on public policy. This influence may be understood more broadly as the effect of autonomous state forces on public policy formation and implementation. While different models emphasize different forces, their common ground is a belief in the independence of state and political institutions—from bureaucracy to political parties— from other social forces.[14]

The sources of bureaucrats' influence on policy include the following:

- technical expertise;
- control over information;
- links to those groups who depend on the program the bureaucrats administer;
- permanence and stability, compared to the transience of governments and cabinet ministers; and
- claims to be apolitical, detached from the narrow preoccupations of special interests and the ideological blinders of party politics.

These are formidable resources, but they do not tell us why bureaucrats would want to impose their particular stamp on policy, influencing what gets done and not simply how it is done.

The question of bureaucratic motivation has been explored most thoroughly by public choice theorists, starting with Anthony Downs's *Inside Bureaucracy*.[15] Bureaucrats are portrayed as budget-maximizers, because a bureaucrat's pursuit of individual goals is tied closely to the resources and prestige of the bureau and the program that it administers. Bureaucratic politics, then, results from the fact that permanent officials are motivated to pursue their own organizational goals, and they have the resources that enable them to translate these bureaucratic preferences into policy.

So why do we label this approach "statism" instead of simply "bureaucratic politics"? The answer is that the goals, ambitions, and ideas of elected officials—none of which are merely responses to the demands made on them by societal groups—also influence state actions. State officials, both elected and bureaucratic, are capable of developing and putting into effect their own conception of the "public interest." Even more fundamentally, perhaps, public officials have a powerful influence on what problems are recognized as worthy of the state's attention and on how the policy response to a problem is framed.

The influence of the state on society, and not the other way around, has been the subject of a small mountain of theoretical and empirical studies since the late 1970s. In Canada, the statist framework was given a major boost by Alan Cairns's 1977 article, "The Governments and Societies of Canadian Federalism."[16] Cairns argues that "Canadian federalism is about governments, governments that are possessed of massive human and financial resources, that are driven by purposes fashioned by elites, and that accord high priority to their own long-term institutional self-interest. . . . It is abundantly clear that the massive impact of government on society at the output stage does not require a prior massive impact of society on government at the input stage."[17] Just how autonomous the state is from society, and in what circumstances, are the questions posed by this state-oriented approach to policy making.

More recently, Cairns has suggested a way of viewing politics and policy making that fuses the pluralist and statist perspectives. He uses the concept of the *embedded state* to capture the modern reality of government that has been "invaded" by society. Cairns argues that "the overall tendency is for the state to pick up and recognize more and more [societal] identities and cleavages that are reinforced by their association with the state." Whether the original impetus for state intervention is found in the demands made by particular social interests or in state officials' own attempts to achieve political or administrative goals is less important than the fact that once a state–society linkage is embodied in policies and structures, the affected societal interests have become "embedded" in the state. The divisions and identities that vie for recognition are imported into the state system. Cairns argues that policy making in Canada and in other liberal capitalist societies has become more difficult because state expansion both contributes to and is influenced by the increasing fragmentation of society.

THE PATTERN OF PUBLIC POLICY

The preceding section surveyed four general approaches to answering the question of why governments behave the way they do. For students of politics this is certainly a vital question. It also happens to be a highly contentious one, as the diversity of theoretical explanations demonstrates.[18] Only somewhat less contentious are the questions of what government does, how it does it, and with what consequences. These questions address what are more formally labelled the scope, means, and distributional dimensions of public policy. Together, they provide the basis for comparing the pattern of public policy and the role of the state in different societies, and for understanding the course of historical change within a society.

The Scope of Public Policy

We know that governments do more today than they did in the past. They pass more laws and regulations on a wider range of subjects than before; they spend a larger share of national income; they tax in more ways and at higher levels; and they employ more people to operate the machinery of government. The scope of their activities ranges from municipal by-laws requiring dog owners to "stoop and scoop" to laws affecting the most vital aspects of our lives.

Recently, the growth of government has been stalled, and even reversed, in some political systems. The welfare state, symbol of the expanded scope of government's functions, has for years had a tarnished image. Asked whether they think the current size of government is excessive, most Canadians answer in the affirmative. "Big government" has for decades ranked as the number one threat to Canada's future in the eyes of Canadians, with "big labour" a distant second and "big business" an even more distant third. Bureaucracy bashing is a popular sport among conservative and populist politicians whose ideologies and policies strike a sympathetic chord among those who believe that society is "overgoverned."

The appropriate scope of government activities is largely a matter of personal preference. Take something as mundane as the random stopping of automobiles by police to check for drunk drivers. Some people object to this practice on the grounds that it violates the individual's freedom—not the freedom to drive while intoxicated, but the freedom from arbitrary detention by the state. Others—probably most Canadians—are willing to tolerate the possibility that innocent people may be pulled over and questioned by the police, and even asked to take a breathalyzer test, as a reasonable infringement on individual freedom in the interests of public safety.

Should the state be in the business of redistributing wealth between groups and between regions and, if so, can we determine what is an appropriate distribution of wealth? Is the expenditure of public money on the promotion of bilingualism an appropriate use of taxpayers' dollars? Is there any way of determining whether a law that restricts the freedom to advertise in languages other than French, as exists in Quebec, is a justified intervention by the state in society?

The easy answer to all of these questions would be "no." If the political process results in a particular policy then this choice is by definition an appropriate one. The reason is that policy choices are political matters, so that the only sensible standard for deciding whether a policy is appropriate or not is whether it has been arrived at according to the generally accepted rules of the political system. In fact, things are not so simple. What if the rules of the political game are skewed in such a way as to encourage and promote certain outcomes and discourage, or even preclude, others?

Trying to determine whether the scope of what government does is appropriate inevitably forces us to confront our own political values. The extreme relativist position asks only whether a policy is determined in accordance with the constitution and the other rules that govern political life in a society. Such a position would lead us to accept as legitimate any policy and any level of state intervention that have been arrived at in conformity with these rules. But is a legitimate policy necessarily a good one?

As a practical matter we do, and most people would agree that we should, judge the "goodness" of the state's activities and the proper limits of its reach into the economy and society. In doing so we apply various criteria: ideological, moral, and pragmatic. A declaration that government is too big may be based on one or some combination of these criteria. Whatever benchmarks we use to judge the scope of government's activities, our assessment will ultimately reflect our fundamental expectations about politics and the relationship between citizens and the state. For example, most Canadians might view the fact that their welfare state is almost twice as generous as that in the United States[19] as confirmation of our moral superiority. Most Americans, however, might see in this comparison evidence of greater government profligacy, waste, and exploitation of working taxpayers to the north. Judgments about such matters can never be freed entirely from the grip of national culture. One can be explicit only about the criteria on which such judgments are based.

The Choice of Policy Instrument

Ends and means are inseparable. To choose a particular goal requires that a plan of action be developed and put into effect. The successful attainment of chosen goals, including the policy objectives of governments, depends on the choice of instruments for achieving them. This all sounds very rational and calculated. In the real world of policy making, as in other realms of life, the process by which these instruments are chosen is much messier. The selection of means is influenced by how things have been done in the past; by vested bureaucratic, political, and societal interests; by chance, including the individuals involved in a decision; and by ideas and beliefs that may or may not be well founded. In addition, it appears that means sometimes precede and determine policy goals. The statist and public choice theories are especially likely to locate the sources of decisions about what to do in existing structures of government and the motives of the political and bureaucratic officials who operate within them.

The instruments of public policy have changed dramatically over time. Public ownership was relatively rare in Canada's early history. The vast majority of publicly owned corporations have been created since 1960 (about 60 percent of federal Crown corporations and 75 percent of provincial ones). The extent and types of taxation have also undergone major changes. As the scope of public policy expanded, governments resorted to an increasing variety of taxes. Direct taxes on income, consumer purchases, and payroll, none of which existed at Confederation, have become major sources of government revenue. The tax system has become one of the chief instruments for the pursuit of governments' economic, social, and cultural policy objectives. Direct regulation, usually under an independent regulatory agency, has also increased dramatically. Over 40 percent of all federal and provincial regulatory laws have been enacted since 1950.

In recent years, controversy has surrounded all of the most common tools of public policy. Sometimes the issue has been whether the goals associated with a particular policy instrument—Canadian culture and the CBC, Canadianization of the petroleum industry and Petro-Canada, regional economic assistance and the Department of Regional and Industrial Expansion—are worth pursuing. More often, debate has centred on whether there is a better, generally meaning less costly, way of achieving given policy objectives. This debate has been fueled by the arguments of economists, political journalists, and business organizations about the alleged inefficiencies of publicly owned businesses and the economic distortions produced by regulation. Taxation, subsidies, and spending programs have also come under heavy criticism on the grounds that they do not accomplish the goals they ostensibly are supposed to promote. Even governments have gotten into the act. One of the first actions of the Conservative government that was elected in 1984 was to establish the Task Force on Program Review to "produce an inventory of government programs with special concern for identifying duplication, waste and inefficiencies."[20] Canada's auditor general acts as a sort of permanent critic on the instruments of policy, annually commenting on whether federal departments, agencies, and Crown corporations are providing "value for money" in their performance. The Liberal government in Quebec produced its own broadside against inefficiency in 1986, establishing task forces on deregulation, privatization, and government functions and structures.

The evaluation of how well a particular policy instrument achieves what is expected of it is not a simple task. To begin with, the government's goals may not be terribly clear, and may even be confused and contradictory. Even assuming that we can identify these goals with some precision, the only readily available standard for measuring how well they are being achieved is an economic one. It is fine to talk about "justice," "equity," "national identity," "quality of life," and other such non-economic values. But the fact that these values do not carry price tags—indeed, governments often involve themselves in the promotion of these things because the unregulated marketplace does not produce them at politically acceptable levels—creates a problem in assessing their worth. Measuring the "output" of policy is a necessary part of an evaluation of the instrument used to achieve it.

Measuring success in accomplishing goals, and doing so in an efficient manner, is no simple task, but it is easier in the private sector than in the public sector. The bottom lines that typically define organizational success in the private sector—profits, market share, share value, credit rating, and the like—are much more elusive in the public sector. Nevertheless, one thing is clear: when public and private organizations perform similar tasks, private ones generally perform them more efficiently. There is an enormous amount of empirical research in support of this generalization. Why does this difference exist? James Wilson[21] identifies three main reasons.

1. Situational ambiguity.

Public officials are less able than their private counterparts to define an efficient course of action because they are often expected to achieve multiple goals with little or no guidance—or worse, in an environment of conflicting signals—about how to manage the trade-offs between these goals. For example, what is the goal of Canada Post? If you answered "Delivering the mail as promptly and efficiently as possible," you were only partly right. Canada Post is also expected to operate in Canada's two official languages, serve customers in sparsely populated rural areas, carry out door-to-door delivery in residential districts built before the early 1980s, and implement employment equity policies. These are goals that do not burden Purolator or Federal Express.

2. Incentives.
Public officials tend to be less motivated to identify an efficient course of action. This is not because they are lazier or less intelligent than their private-sector counterparts. Rather, private-sector managers will often profit personally from improving the efficiency of their organization, whereas these sorts of payoffs are much less common and less considerable in the public sector.

3. Authority.
Even if a public-sector agency is staffed by efficiency zealots whose greatest fulfilment comes from finding ways to do more with less, they will often lack the authority to carry out their schemes for improving efficiency. Their ability to hire and fire and determine compensation levels for employees is far less than that of their private-sector counterparts. Government agencies usually depend entirely on the budget allocated to them by the legislature and do not have the freedom to impose user fees for their service or to raise money in ways not authorized by elected politicians. Measures like redesigning program delivery, closing or relocating regional offices, or altering the internal structure of the agency cannot be undertaken without the approval of other parts of government. Even when this approval is granted, the whole process is likely to take longer than in the private sector.

Who Benefits and Who Pays?

Entire books are written on this subject without there being any consensus on the distributional impact of public policy. The very term *welfare state* implies that wealth is to some degree transferred by the state from those who can afford to pay to those in need. There is no doubt that the various taxation and spending policies of governments affect the distribution of wealth. How much and to whose advantage are disputed issues. The majority opinion, however, sides with the conclusion of economist Irwin Gillespie: "In Canada, at least, a larger state has not led to a more egalitarian state."[22]

By itself, the tax system does not redistribute income from Canadian society's more affluent classes to its most impoverished ones. This is because some important taxes, notably sales, excise, and property taxes, are regressive. They take a larger share out of the incomes of the poor than they do from those of the wealthy. The fact that the personal income tax is progressive—the rate at which one is taxed increases with one's income—and that governments typically rebate part of the personal cost of regressive levies like the sales and property taxes to lower-income earners does not eliminate the regressive impact of total taxation. On the other hand, it is clear that the total effect of the transfers received under income security programs and of public spending on education, housing, health care, transportation, and a host of other programs favours the poor. The bottom fifth of income earners in Canada account for 1 percent of earned income, but just over 6 percent when all sources of income are taken into account.[23] This difference reflects the redistributive impact of government social policies.

Governments in Canada also act in ways intended to affect the distribution of wealth between regions. These regional subsidies take three main forms:

1. equalization payments from Ottawa to the less affluent provinces, intended to ensure "that provincial governments have sufficient revenues to provide reasonably comparable levels of public service at reasonably comparable levels of taxation";[24]
2. income transfers from Ottawa to individuals, like Unemployment Insurance, which are a major source of income in communities where employment opportunities tend to be seasonal or fewer than the national average; and
3. federal and provincial industrial assistance programs that subsidize businesses in economically depressed regions.

As in the case of policies geared toward redistributing income among individuals, there is no agreement on the impact of these regionally focused policies. The approximately $8.5 billion a year (1992–93) that Ottawa transfers to the economically weaker provinces in the form of equalization payments certainly enables them to finance a level of services that would otherwise be beyond their fiscal means. And the fact that certain regions benefit more than others from the UI system involves regional redistribution. Some have argued that these transfers impose a burden on the national economy without solving the problems that underlie the weak economies of the provinces that benefit from them. Regional industrial assistance programs have come in for the same criticism. In fairness, any judgment on regional development policies should also take into account the economic consequences of the billions of dollars worth of other subsidies, in forms ranging from tariffs to government contracts, that have bestowed their greatest benefits on the economies of Ontario and Quebec, often at the expense of other regions.

Government's impact on the distribution of economic well-being does not stop at individuals and regions. In all industrial societies, Canada included, the state is in the business of protecting a vast range of producer and occupational groups from the unregulated workings of the market. Canadian economist Thomas Courchene calls this the "protected society."[25] It is a society in which any group with political clout is able to persuade the state to protect its special interests, at the public's expense. Courchene's concept of the protected society recognizes that both society's privileged and its disadvantaged elements may be "welfare recipients." Indeed, the Mulroney government's own Task Force on Program Review described Canadian businesses as "program junkies"[26] addicted to the billions of dollars worth of subsidies that governments of all stripes have been willing to dole out to them.

All of the distributive effects of policy discussed to this point have involved material benefits and burdens. But as Raymond Breton observes, "Public institutions and their authorities are involved in the distribution of symbolic as well as material resources."[27] Nowhere is this more evident than in debates over constitutional reform. The acrimony and passion that led up to the defeat of the Charlottetown Accord in the 1992 referendum were inspired by differences over the vision of Canada that the accord was perceived to embody.

Canadians were asked to accept dozens of changes to the Constitution, including several highly controversial ones like distinct society status and guaranteed representation for Quebec, recognition of the right to Native self-government, and a "Canada clause" that enumerated the "fundamental" characteristics of Canadian society. It seems likely that many citizens felt confused and threatened by what appeared to be a vast and complicated reform agenda. It is more certain that English Canadians found objectionable some of the values they perceived to be embedded in the accord. No aspect of the agreement stirred more vitriol in English Canada than the guarantee of Quebec's share of representation in the House of Commons, a proposal that ran counter to the idea of majoritarian democracy subscribed to by most English Canadians. While many of the Charlottetown Accord's supporters explained their defeat with reference to the deep unpopularity of Prime Minister Mulroney and widespread mistrust of politicians and the major parties, this explanation unfairly trivialized the extent to which the accord's rejection was also a rejection of some of the ideas it was believed to contain.

CONCLUSION

There is little doubt that we know more about policy making in Canada today than when Richard Simeon lamented the "ignorance if not mystery" that surrounded this subject. The gaps that Simeon complained about have been filled by an enormous number of empirical studies, many of them sponsored by government commissions, and by a small explosion of theoretical work ranging from public choice to feminist analysis. This represents progress of a sort. Nevertheless, we are no closer to agreement on the fundamental causes and implications of policy. Indeed, the most basic disagreements among contemporary students of politics and policy are about what questions we should be asking.

Consensus and progress are not, however, the same thing (at least not when it comes to intellectual inquiry). But the fact that so much ground is being tilled by students of public policy, using a variety of methodological and theoretical implements, should alone be reason for modest optimism. One thing is certain: as the twentieth century draws to a close, the challenges facing policy makers and citizens are enormous. A national debt crisis, coping with global economic change, and the uncertain future of Quebec (and thus the rest of Canada) ensure that we are fated to live in interesting if unstable times. It all represents grist for the policy analyst's mill.

NOTES

[1] Thomas R. Dye, *Understanding Public Policy*, 3rd ed. (Englewood Cliffs, NJ: Prentice-Hall, 1978), 3.

[2] Murray Edelman, *Constructing the Political Spectacle* (Chicago: University of Chicago Press, 1988), 12.

[3] Eugene Forsey, *How Canadians Govern Themselves* (Ottawa: Supply and Services Canada, 1982), 2.

[4] E.E. Schattschneider, *The Semi-Sovereign People* (New York: Holt, Rinehart and Winston, 1960), 35.

[5] Theodore Lowi, *The End of Liberalism* (New York: W.W. Norton, 1979), 280.

[6] Charles Lindblom, *Politics and Markets* (New York: Basic Books, 1977), especially chs. 13–16.

[7] Charles Lindblom, "The Market as Prison" in *The Political Economy*, ed. Thomas Ferguson and Joel Rogers (Armonk, NY: M.E. Sharpe, 1984), 3–1.

[8] Paul Pross, *Group Politics and Public Policy* (Toronto: Oxford University Press, 1986).

[9] Michael Atkinson and William D. Coleman, *The State, Business and Industrial Change in Canada* (Toronto: University of Toronto Press, 1989).

[10] Michael Trebilcock et al., *The Choice of Governing Instrument* (Ottawa: Economic Council of Canada, 1982), 10–11.

[11] Wallace Clement and Glen Williams, eds., *The New Political Economy* (Montreal: McGill-Queen's University Press, 1989), 6.

[12] Ibid., 7.

[13] Ralph Miliband, "State Power and Capitalist Democracy" (paper read at Carleton University, Ottawa, July 1984), 6.

[14] Leslie A. Pal, *State, Class, and Bureaucracy: Canadian Unemployment Insurance and Public Policy* (Montreal: McGill-Queen's University Press, 1988), 94.

[15] Anthony Downs, *Inside Bureaucracy* (Boston: Little, Brown, 1967).

[16] Alan Cairns, "The Governments and Societies of Canadian Federalism" in *Constitution, Government, and Society in Canada* (Toronto: McClelland & Stewart, 1988). This was Cairns's 1977 presidential address to the Canadian Political Science Association.

[17] Ibid., 153–54.

[18] We have not even brushed the surface of the internal debates within these perspectives. For a brief discussion of these, see Stephen Brooks and Andrew Stritch, *Business and Government in Canada* (Scarborough, ON: Prentice-Hall, 1990), ch. 3.

[19] This is based on 1990 figures of government-paid income support for a single-parent family with two children aged nine and ten. Benefits include social assistance, family allowance, and refundable tax credits. In Canada, the level of income support is 69 percent of the average production worker's wage, compared to 37 percent in the United States. The figures are taken from *The Economist*, 11 Dec. 1993, 28.

[20] Canada, Task Force on Program Review, *An Introduction to the Process of Program Review* (Ottawa: Supply and Services Canada, March 1986), i.

[21] James Q. Wilson, *Bureaucracy: What Government Agencies Do and Why They Do It* (New York: Basic Books, 1989).

[22] W. Irwin Gillespie, *The Redistribution of Income in Canada* (Ottawa: Carleton Library, 1980), 173.

[23] Statistics Canada, *Income After Tax Distributions by Size in Canada*, cat. no. 13-210 annual, 13.

[24] Canada, Constitution Act, 1982, s.36(20).

[25] Thomas J. Courchene, "Towards a Protected Society: The Politicization of Economic Life," *Canadian Journal of Economics* 13 (Nov. 1980).

[26] Task Force on Program Review, *Economic Growth: Services and Subsidies to Business* (Ottawa: Ministry of Supply and Services, 1986), 15.

[27] Raymond Breton, "Multiculturalism and Canadian Nation-Building" in *Politics of Gender, Ethnicity and Language*, ed. Alan Cairns and Cynthia Williams (Toronto: University of Toronto Press, 1986), 30.

SUGGESTED READING

Banting, Keith, ed. *State and Society: Canada in Comparative Perspective.* Toronto: University of Toronto Press, 1986.

This is a collection of essays prepared as one of the research studies for the Royal Commission on the Economic Union and Development

Prospects for Canada. It includes an outstanding and provocative chapter by Alan Cairns entitled "The Embedded State: State–Society Relations in Canada."

Brooks, Stephen. *Public Policy in Canada: An Introduction*. 2nd ed. Toronto: McClelland & Stewart, 1993.

This textbook is aimed at students who have some background in Canadian politics and government. It examines the theories, environment, and institutions of Canadian policy making, and surveys several policy fields.

Cairns, Alan C. *Constitution, Government, and Society in Canada*. Toronto: McClelland & Stewart, 1988.

This collection of essays brings together a number of seminal works that Cairns has written over the years on the Canadian constitution, federalism, the electoral system and parties, and Canadian society.

Campbell, Robert M., and Leslie A. Pal. *The Real Worlds of Canadian Politics: Cases in Process and Policy*. 3rd ed. Peterborough, ON: Broadview Press, 1994.

Through their examination of five case studies covering a broad range of policy issues, Campbell and Pal succeed in conveying the complexity and diversity of policy making. The "real worlds" examined in this book are worlds that differ in terms of the processes, actors, institutions, and political discourse that are relevant to understanding policy outcomes.

Pal, Leslie A. *Public Policy Analysis: An Introduction*. 2nd ed. Scarborough, ON: Nelson Canada, 1992.

How to analyze, understand, and evaluate public policy are the subjects of this book. Pal's objective is to "equip even the neophyte to analyze virtually any Canadian public policy at any level of government." The bibliographic guide at the end of the book is bound to be a useful research tool for students writing papers on policy and policy making.

Savoie, Donald J. *The Politics of Public Spending in Canada*. Toronto: University of Toronto Press, 1990.

Written at a level more appropriate to senior students, this is quite possibly the most valuable contribution to the analysis of Canadian policy making in recent years. Savoie does a masterful job dissecting the political and bureaucratic forces that fuel public spending. This book is mandatory (but discouraging) reading for serious students of public policy.

BECOMING FULL CITIZENS: WOMEN AND POLITICS IN CANADA

Some of the students in my Canadian government and politics class wonder why we need to study women and politics. After all, they argue, women are participating in political life in record numbers. They point to high-profile politicians, such as Deputy Prime Minister Sheila Copps and Prince Edward Island premier Catherine Callbeck. Some students assert that, since women have come a long way, there is no need to separate them from the general population when considering the nature of Canadian politics. This view is supported by commentators like journalist Danielle Crittenden, who claims that feminism has been "wildly effective" and that the women's movement has achieved most, if not all, of its goals.[1] So why study women?

If we accept Harold Lasswell's definition of politics as who gets what, where, and when, then as conscientious students of politics we must study women's status because, by any measure, women get less than men. Women working full time in the Canadian labour force earn, on average, 67 percent of what men earn.[2] Women are concentrated in low-paying, often part-time "pink collar" job ghettos and are grossly under-represented in the professions and in management positions. Women—especially single mothers, Aboriginal, elderly, and disabled women—are more likely than men to live below the poverty line. They have less freedom of movement for a variety of reasons, not the least of which is fear of sexual assault. The rising number of women in political leadership roles belies the still low numbers in elected office; it is rare, at any level of governance, for the proportion of women to exceed 25 percent. In general, women have less control over their lives, less power, less authority, and less economic independence than do men. Students of politics should determine why, and how, this is the case.

Our sceptics may assert that women's socioeconomic status has nothing to do with political institutions or public policies. According to this line of argument, women simply make different life choices: because women bear children, they choose to raise them; they choose to work part time, in female-dominated jobs; they choose to be less involved than men in formal political arenas. In other words, political values, ideas, institutions, processes, and decisions have little or no bearing on women's place in society. Nothing could be further from the truth. The purpose of this chapter is to show just how intertwined the categories of "women" and "politics" are. Political cultures, structures, and policies shape women's lives in both dramatic and subtle ways. The industry and persistence of the women's movement has inspired, or forced, profound political change, yet political decisions and public policies continue to deny women full citizenship in Canada.

What does it mean to be a "full citizen?" We generally understand the concept *citizenship* to mean official membership in a political community. I call this *nominal* or *formal citizenship* to distinguish it from full citizenship. *Full citizenship* involves the right, and realistic opportunity, to participate in the political, social, cultural, and economic life of one's community. Any adult member of the community who is socially ostracized, or economically dependent, or culturally isolated, or denied a political voice is not a citizen in the richest sense of the word. Political participation is essential to full citizenship: "Participation in the governance of one's community is participation in the governance of oneself. Those who are governed but do not govern are not citizens but subjects."[3] Political participation is difficult, if not impossible, without the benefit of basic individual rights that permit entry into public (social, political, and economic) life. As well, effective political participation requires the social and economic resources necessary to exercise individual rights.

The patriarchal society in which Canadian women live precludes them from being full citizens. *Patriarchal societies* can be defined as those in which "men have more power than women and greater access than women to what is valued in the society."[4] Given their greater power and privilege, men in patriarchal societies control many aspects of women's lives. One of the important levers of control is politics, and "few aspects of social life are more completely and universally male dominated than politics."[5] Because women are so under-represented politically, they do not have control over their private lives; they are subject to government decisions that play a significant role in the regulation of fertility, sexuality, the division of labour and property, and the definition, formulation, and dissolution of families. Yet Canadian women have inspired dramatic changes in public perceptions of gender roles and have demanded and achieved changes in public policy that allow women to claim a certain degree of power and autonomy. For example, Canadian women no longer face legal sanctions for seeking to control the number of children they bear. Sections of the Criminal Code that prevented women from having legal access to birth control were removed in 1967, and a restrictive abortion law was struck down by the Supreme Court of Canada in 1988.

How can women be simultaneously powerful and powerless? The first section of this chapter explores this puzzle by examining the roots of women's marginality and the evolution of women's status in Canadian society. I argue that women have achieved significant gains, which are all the more remarkable given the level of resistance to change and women's lack of formal political power. I also argue that, although the lives of Canadian women have changed dramatically thanks to the persistence of the women's movement, women as a group cannot yet claim full citizenship status. Moreover, the general improvement in the status of women obscures the fact that some groups of women are profoundly disadvantaged and disempowered. In particular, First Nations, visible minority, lesbian, and disabled women face many layers of systemic discrimination based on sex, race, class, sexual orientation, and ethnicity. This conclusion inspires my second argument: that only through the political representation of women, by women, will women achieve full citizenship status in Canadian society.

MARGINALITY: WOMEN AS NON-CITIZENS AND SUBJECTS

Women are marginalized when they are not allowed to claim nominal citizenship status on their own behalf and when they are treated as subjects—that is, denied the basic individual rights generally enjoyed by citizens in liberal-democratic societies. The marginality of Canadian women can be illustrated both with historical and contemporary examples. This section briefly characterizes the position of most women from

Confederation to the achievement of "person" status. It then uses the cases of immigrant and Aboriginal women to show that the acquisition of formal individual rights did not come equally and simultaneously to all women and that some women continue to be marginalized by Canadian law and policy.

The ideological and institutional framework for Canadian government and politics was developed at a time when women were legally excluded from participation in many aspects of public life. Our institutions, values, and policies are based upon a division between the *public sphere* of business and government (dominated by men) and the *private sphere* of home and family, where women perform the roles of wives, unpaid care givers, and mothers. At the time of Confederation, women were seen as marginal to public life because they were viewed as biologically inferior and naturally subject to men. Men were, according to the thinking of the time, inherently rational, objective, competitive, and intelligent; moreover, it was believed that men made decisions on the basis of merit, formal rules, and universal standards and principles. Women, on the other hand, were regarded as innately passive, emotional, sentimental, and irrational creatures whose judgments were based on personal loyalties, intimate attachments, and moralistic considerations.[6] Thus men were seen as best suited for roles in the public sphere, while women were confined to the private realm. In fact, women's characteristics and values were regarded as incompatible with participation in the public sphere. For this reason, representation in the public world of politics and economics was thought to be adequately provided by their husbands, fathers, or sons. The sharp division of public and private spheres and the confinement of women to the latter were clearly articulated by political, medical, and clerical elites. Statements like "Woman's first and only place is in the home" and "Woman exists for the sake of the womb"[7] were commonplace in late-nineteenth-century Canada.

At the time of Confederation, women were not accorded basic individual rights. Women were prevented by law from using birth control, voting, and seeking public office.[8] They were barred from many educational institutions, including most universities and law and medical schools. Men were the legal heads of households and held the exclusive right to control family finances (including their wives' wages), to own and sell property, to sign contracts, and to exercise guardianship rights over children. Women were recognized as nominal citizens only by virtue of association with male citizens, and women's nationality was determined by their fathers or husbands. The turn-of-the-century married Canadian woman was a legal non-entity who depended for her economic survival on the benevolence of her husband. Women who left marriages, or who were abandoned by their husbands, could make no financial demands and were often left destitute. In fact, estranged husbands were entitled, under British common law, to all the earnings of their wives. Constance Backhouse cites the example of Mary Whibby of Newfoundland who, after being abandoned—along with four children—by her husband in 1853, "worked slavishly" to provide for her family. At the time of her death in 1868, she had amassed savings of $1000. Despite the protests of her son, the money was awarded to her estranged husband.[9]

Despite vast legal changes, there are women in Canada today who still experience similar levels of powerlessness and marginality. Immigrant women are a case in point. The criteria used to determine "who gets in" (who gets to apply for nominal citizenship status) do not take the sexual division of labour into account, and the opportunities for women seeking entry into Canada are often different from those presented to men. Immigration law is, in part, based on the assumption that immigrant women can be effectively represented in the public sphere by their husbands, fathers, sponsors, or employers. Immigrants can gain entry into Canada under one of three classifications: independent, family class, or business class.

> Usually, in an immigrant family, only one member is granted the independent status. In most cases it is the husband who is so designated, because he is perceived to be the head of the household, and the wife is categorized as a family-class immigrant along with the children. . . . The official view of the immigrant family, according to immigration procedures, is that of one "independent" member upon whom others depend for their sponsorship, livelihood and welfare. *Thus the immigration process systematically structures sexual inequality within the family by rendering one spouse (usually the wife) legally dependent on the other.*[10] (emphasis added)

The implications of this dependent status are significant. If the woman's husband is for some reason deported, she will be deported as well. He can threaten her with deportation as a means of controlling her behaviour. She is ineligible for social assistance (family benefits, welfare, child-care subsidies), and she does not have access to most state-funded language and job-training programs. These rules help create a situation of economic dependence, isolation, and powerlessness for many immigrant women.

Equally isolated and marginalized are Aboriginal women who have been forced to choose between family and citizenship. Many Aboriginal women have been exiled from their political communities by federal law; they do not enjoy nominal citizenship in their own First Nations. Section 12(1)(b) of the Indian Act, which was implemented in 1869 and remained in place until 1985, caused an Indian woman who married a non-Indian to lose her legal status as an Indian. However, under section 11(1)(f), an Indian man who married a non-Indian retained his legal status and band membership and transmitted this status and membership to his wife and children.[11] The rationale for this law clearly reflected the patriarchal thinking of the times, as it was intended to prevent white men from set-tling on Indian lands. White women, who had no property rights, were not a threat to government control of reserve lands. The cost of keeping white men off reserves was very high for Aboriginal women, for loss of status has profound political, cultural, and economic ramifications. Disenfranchised Indian women have no political rights in their commu-nities; they are no longer band members and therefore do not have the right to vote for and hold office in the band council or the right to vote in band referenda. Culturally, loss of status means loss of the right of the Aboriginal woman to live among her people and to raise her children in their cultural community. Economically, the loss of status means she no longer has the right to own land and inherit property on the reserve; moreover, she can-not collect band annuities and treaty payments, and she is denied access to tax abatements and special government programs for reserve and off-reserve Indians.[12]

The Indian Act was changed in 1985, and the offending section removed. However, the amending statute, Bill C-31, clearly illustrates the crucial dif-ference between nominal and full citizenship. Bill C-31 allows for the reinstatement of some of the disenfranchised women and their children: they may apply to the federal government for Indian status and thereby gain access to federal government programs and tax abatements. But Bill C-31 separated Indian status from band membership. While status can be granted by the federal government, bands determine who may reside on the reserve and who may be a band member. Various bands have, as a result of Bill C-31, developed highly exclusive membership codes restrict-ing the re-entry of reinstated women and children. In addition,

If a First Nations woman is reinstated to legal status and band membership, there is no guarantee that she can assume the bene-fits of membership because these are contingent upon reserve res-idence. Residence may be denied her, her children, and her husband not only on a de jure basis by exclusionary band by-laws, but also on a de facto basis by not providing them with the services or housing needed for their resettlement on the reserve. *Without residence for her family, a reinstated woman is denied the ability to live in her cultural community and to gain access to the full range of rights for Indian women.*[13] (emphasis added)

In other words, many First Nations women have received nominal citizenship under Bill C-31, but few have been accorded the rights and privileges necessary to be welcomed as full citizens. Those who have returned to their bands are often pejoratively categorized as "C-31s" and face "diminished social status in their communities."[14]

These examples illustrate two crucial points. First, Canadian women and men have a different history with regard to claiming nominal citizenship status. Not all Canadian men have held formal citizenship rights since Confederation,[15] but women's claim on citizenship has been much more tenuous, as it was initially provided only via a male intermediary, and in some cases was denied altogether. Second, all three examples show that, although women's legal and political subordination rests on a clear distinction between public and private spheres, a significant amount of government intervention is required to maintain traditional gender roles and to exclude women from the public life of their communities. The split between public and private worlds is in many ways unnatural and imposed by government action, as public-sphere actors make laws that intrude into and regulate the private sphere.

Since the late nineteenth century, the women's movement has resisted and challenged the confinement of women to the private sphere. Women were active in party politics and group politics before they won the rights to vote and to run for office. Women's party affiliates (such as the Toronto Women's Liberal Association) and several national women's groups, including the YWCA and the National Council of Women of Canada, were formed in the pre-suffrage era. Working-class women contested the rigid division between public and private spheres out of economic necessity, and by the turn of the century large numbers of women were employed in poorly paid, sex-segregated jobs. Although their very presence in the paid labour force challenged the prevailing assumption that a woman's true calling was as a wife and mother, this same assumption "deterred the transient female work force from organizing and agitating for better wages and conditions."[16]

The first wave of the Canadian women's movement demanded that the vote be extended to women, but the movement's goals extended far beyond the quest for suffrage. Women's groups lobbied for social, economic, and political reforms because they were concerned about the labour-force exploitation of women and other ill effects of industrialization. Woman's suffrage was seen as an important mechanism for articulating these broader reform ideas and pressing for social and economic justice. The suffrage movement began in the 1870s, but the quest for women's political rights was a lengthy and fragmented process, as strategies and alliances differed from province to province.[17] Between 1880 and 1900, the majority of Canadian municipalities granted the franchise to property owners of both sexes, which of course did not include many women. Women received the provincial franchise (and the right to contest legislative office) first in Manitoba, Saskatchewan, and Alberta in 1916, and other governments followed suit: British Columbia and Ontario (1917), Nova Scotia and the government of Canada (1918), New Brunswick (which granted the vote in 1919 but withheld the right to contest office until 1934), Prince Edward Island (1922), Newfoundland (1925), and Quebec (1940). However, the quest for universal suffrage was not complete until 1960: prior to this date, Aboriginal women (and men) with government-assigned status under the Indian Act were denied the right to vote.

The acquisition of the most basic of political rights did not mean that Canadian women were regarded as persons under the law. In addition to the struggle for suffrage, Canadian women fought a long battle for the right to be recognized as eligible for admission to the legal profession and, later, to the Senate. Various "persons cases" came before the courts,[18] but the best known is the case of the women from Alberta who sought women's right to be appointed to the Senate of Canada. The federal government argued that, since in 1867 women were denied the right to hold office, the writers of Canada's constitution did not mean to include women as "persons" under section 24 of the Constitution Act, 1867. The Supreme Court of Canada agreed. However, the Supreme Court was not the highest court of appeal at that time; the Judicial Committee of the British Privy Council was. In 1929, the JCPC overturned the Supreme Court decision, declaring (most) Canadian women to be persons.

By 1930, most women enjoyed many of the political and legal rights of individuals. They could vote, hold office, inherit and own property, enter the professions, and seek custody of their children. Did these formal, legal rights mean women were welcomed into the public sphere of law, business, industry, and politics? In a word, no. There is a significant difference between the acquisition of legal citizenship rights and the ability to fully exercise and benefit from these rights.

TOLERATION

Individual rights distinguish the subject from the citizen, but they do not confer full citizenship. Extending legal rights to women does not in and of itself challenge the distinction between public and private realms. When women's participation in the public sphere is merely tolerated, and even actively discouraged by societal norms and attitudes, recognition of women's right to participate in the public sphere is a largely symbolic act. "Toleration is not an active principle, it is a passive one. It places a premium on the elimination of tangible barriers but makes no commitment to a positive value of inclusion and membership."[19] Policies of toleration (eliminating laws that bar women from public pursuits) do not change the social and economic barriers to participation. Economic barriers include financial dependency, the sexual division of labour, inadequate child care, unequal wages, and job discrimination. Social barriers are structured by the perception that a woman's place is in the home. Women who do not remain in the home are seen as unnatural and unwomanly. As well, Aboriginal, disabled, lesbian, and visible minority women face added social and cultural barriers to their participation in the public sphere.

The example of women's labour-force activity during and after the Second World War illustrates the extent to which women's public sphere participation is politically and socially constructed. Women's paid labour was tolerated, then actively encouraged, during a time of economic need, only to be rejected when the war was over. The war economy depended on the labour of women, but the federal government carefully managed the wartime labour force through its National Selective Service Agency, which was established in 1942. This agency included a Women's Division, which quickly set about the task of compiling a national registry of young women who could be recruited into war industries. While the registry contained the names of married women, initially only single women were targeted by federal government propaganda and worker relocation programs.[20] By the summer of 1943, the demand for workers was so strong that the federal government actively recruited married women into full-time employment, offered tax incentives to married women, and provided government-funded day-care services to war industry employees. As the labour shortage continued to grow, the federal government allowed women into the War Emergency Training Program and into non-traditional occupations such as welding, aircraft assembly, ship building, and electronics.

Economic need forced the Dominion government to recruit women, even married women with children, into the labour force and male-dominated jobs. But women's participation in the war economy was regarded as a purely temporary measure. "Even before peace was achieved, most Canadians expected women, especially those who were married, to rededicate themselves to work in the home."[21] After the war, governments and industries quickly advanced the idea that women should stay at home and the federal government cancelled its training programs, tax incentives, and daycare services. From 1947 until 1955, married women were not allowed to hold jobs in the federal public service. Mass persuasion was used to convince women that, although their wartime work had been essential, it was now time to go back to their "real" role as homemakers. Media portrayals of women exploited the contented wife and mother stereotype and emphasized women's role as consumers.[22]

That legal rights, while essential to women's citizenship, promote little more than toleration of women's participation, is also clearly seen in the political realm. With the exception of women who held Indian status, Canadian women attained the right to run for federal political office in 1918, but in the period between 1920 and 1970 few women exercised this right and even fewer were elected to Parliament. Only seventeen women held office in Ottawa during this period, reflecting the emphasis of traditional gender roles. Politics was considered a man's world, and women's roles and interests were assumed to reflect their private-sphere duties and responsibilities. Issues related to the private sphere (the family, women's reproductive and care-giving roles, wife battering, and sexuality) were considered private, thus non-political. Women who chose political roles were "privatized"; that is, their political participation was regarded as merely an expression of their private-sphere roles and interests.

Gertrude Robinson's study of media coverage of female politicians illustrates the extent to which early women parliamentarians were regarded as deviants, or as women first and politicians last. For instance, Flora MacDonald and Judy LaMarsh were asked by reporters, "Are you a politician or a woman?" as though the two were mutually exclusive.[23] Robinson argues that media descriptions of political women between 1920 and the late 1960s attempted to explain this apparent contradiction by privatizing female politicians and their interests. One of the strategies employed by the press was an overt focus on the MP's appearance and family relationships. Judy LaMarsh wrote that "columnists asked me about anything and everything except about my job. . . . My home, my cooking, my hobbies, my friends, my tastes, my likes and dislikes.[24] Another approach characterized women politicians as spinsters, thereby implying that single women chose political life because they were unsuccessful in traditional female roles.

Female politicians who used their positions to champion gender equality inspired considerable discomfort among political and media elites. Robinson cites the case of Thérèse Casgrain, the leader of the New Democratic Party in Quebec and an outspoken activist for the cause of women's rights, who was told by the publisher of a Trois-Rivières newspaper to return to the home: "Let her cook, sew, embroider, read, card wool, play bridge—anything rather than persist in her dangerous role of issuer of directives."[25] Decades after their formal admission into electoral politics, Canadian women continue to experience active resistance to their participation in political institutions. When Sheila Copps, now deputy prime minister, was a member of the Liberal opposition in the Ontario legislature, she was told by a government backbencher to "go back to the kitchen."[26] Copps was later called a "slut" by a Tory backbencher. Former Prime Minister Kim Campbell faced a reprise of the "spinster" approach when opponents made an issue of her marital history during the Progressive Conservative Party's leadership contest. Campbell's twice-divorced status was contrasted with her main competitor's traditional family.[27] And during the 1993 federal election, newspapers like Montreal's *La Presse* and the *Toronto Sun* asked fashion designers what Campbell should do to improve her personal style: the *Sun* suggested that the prime minister wear a red push-up bra.[28] Clearly, blatant stereotypes continue to shape media and elite attitudes toward political women.

Canadian political parties also illustrate the concept of toleration, as party structures and practices have inhibited women from achieving political power. Until the 1970s and 1980s, the Liberal and Progressive Conservative parties segregated women into auxiliaries, where they performed the important but menial tasks of party organization, such as soliciting memberships, hosting social events, and conducting much of the routine campaign work and envelope stuffing. The sexual division of labour in party politics continues. Sylvia Bashevkin has documented the "law of increasing disproportion," whereby the higher one goes in the party organization, the fewer women there are to be found. In 1992, for instance, women were 70 percent of the local riding secretaries of major Canadian parties, but only 20 percent of the candidates.[29] Moreover, most women run for political office in lost-cause ridings. Despite the fact that voters do not see sex as an electoral liability, and despite evidence showing that voter attitudes may give female candidates an electoral advantage, competitive parties continue to resist nominating women to winnable ridings.[30]

The few women who succeed in winning election are at best tolerated and sometimes encounter outright hostility. New Democrat MLA Marie Laing, who served in the Alberta legislature from 1986 to 1993, was laughed at when she discussed the issue of sexual assault in the legislature. "Other times members have talked . . . and joked around when I have spoken, as if in shutting out the information I talk about, they can deny it."[31] Several prominent female politicians have described their experiences in the corridors of political power as deeply alienating. Audrey McLaughlin put it this way: "When a woman enters the House of Commons, she enters what in significant ways is an old-fashioned men's club. There are all sorts of reminders—some subtle, some not so subtle—that this is not a woman's place."[32] Or, as Sheila Copps reflected, "from the moment you step inside [the House of Commons], you sense that this place is foreign to women, alien to our spirit of cooperation."[33]

INCLUSION/SAMENESS

Inclusion means that women are included (not simply tolerated) in the paid labour force, political institutions, organized religion, the cultural milieu, and other aspects of social and public life. Policies that promote inclusion do one of three things. First, they can allow greater freedom for women in the private sphere. For instance, the decriminalization of birth control and abortion allows women some freedom to plan their families. Second, the state can provide services that reproduce, or complement, private-sphere labour. Governments can fund support services, such as child care and care of the elderly, sick, or disabled. Third, policies of inclusion, such as pay equity and employment equity, can attempt to remove discriminatory barriers to women's integration into the public sphere. Perhaps the best-known and most powerfully symbolic policy of inclusion is the sex equality guarantee in the Canadian Charter of Rights and Freedoms. Section 15 prohibits sex-based discrimination in law and allows the creation of policies that are designed to ameliorate the conditions experienced by disadvantaged individuals or groups. Section 28 affirms that Charter rights and freedoms are guaranteed equally to men and women.

It is often assumed that inclusion is the overriding goal of the women's movement: many believe that women want simply to be treated the same as men and to be allowed access to traditionally male roles and privileges. In fact, most women's groups do not see inclusion (or sameness) as the ultimate goal of feminism. There are two problems with the idea that full citizenship will result from simply adding women to the public sphere. First, merely including women in the public realm does little to break down the artificial barriers between the public and private spheres. Simply welcoming (some) women into male-dominated jobs and professions does not challenge the perception of the public sphere as inherently more valuable and important than the private realm. Moreover, the sexual division of labour remains. Women still have fundamental responsibility for domestic roles, and those who seek public-sphere roles must choose to work a double shift (full-time paid labour combined with full-time unpaid labour in the home) or to reject or delay private-sphere roles (by remaining single or childless or by delaying childbearing). Those who choose the double shift must make alternative provisions for their "duties" in the private sphere.

Second, the principle of inclusion is often blind to class and race differences, leading many feminists to ask, "inclusion for whom?" If the sexual division of labour is not challenged, inclusion merely allows some women to buy their way out of private-sphere obligations. But the work is still performed by women: in the case of domestic labour, child care, and care of the elderly, the work is performed by working-class women, usually visible minority women, who are poorly paid and often exploited. For instance, domestic workers employed under the Foreign Domestic Worker program have been described as "bonded labourers" who exchange their work for the potential to apply for landed immigrant status.[34] Further, we cannot assume that policies of inclusion, such as employment equity, promote the inclusion of all women. The federal government's Employment Equity program, designed to improve the representation of women, Aboriginal Canadians, the disabled, and visible minorities in the federally regulated labour force, in fact has benefited white women to the largest extent: "White women without disabilities are hired most representatively, followed in descending order by female members of visible minorities, Aboriginal women, and disabled women."[35]

If the women's movement does not see inclusion as the ultimate goal, what is its purpose? One significant aim is to expose the fact that there is nothing natural or inevitable about the separation of public and private aspects of human existence. Indeed, there is considerable overlap between the spheres. Men participate in private life and women are active in public life. The spheres are not isolated, as each affects the other. Male domination of public life and public roles would not be possible without the supportive infrastructure of home and family; in fact, women's productive and reproductive labour in the private sphere provides a foundation for the capitalist economy and liberal-democratic institutions. On the other hand, as we have seen, the idea that "a woman's place is in the home" is not a natural outcome: the Canadian state has used both subtle and coercive instruments to limit women's public-sphere participation. It is indeed true, as a basic tenet of the women's movement claims, that the personal is political. However, "if everything is construed to be political, nothing is non-political or private."[36] Feminists, in practice, do recognize a realm of personal privacy (by promoting reproductive freedom, for example).

The dividing line between public and private is constantly being rethought and redrawn. Anti-feminist groups like REAL Women and the Alberta Federation of Women United for Families promote the traditional family and advocate clearly defined gender roles. REAL Women lobbies against government-funded child care, abortion, no-fault divorce, equal pay legislation, affirmative action, and legal protection of the rights of homosexuals. Groups and political parties classified as embracing the philosophy of the new right want to reduce the role of government in society and demand deficit-reduction measures such as cuts to social services and other spending policies such as multiculturalism, bilingualism, and immigration. Clearly, there is no societal consensus on the proper conceptualization of public and private realms, and it is unlikely that widespread agreement could ever be attained. But it is important to recognize that the line is constantly being shifted by political actors, with enormous social, economic, and political consequences for women. When governments declare a "zero tolerance" policy regarding wife battering, they are recognizing political responsibility for domestic violence. When governments cut funding to child-care centres, primary education, and health-care services, they are assuming that women will take up the additional burden of providing care for children, the sick, and the elderly.

Because the boundary between public and private is constantly being contested within political life, the political representation of women is a crucial goal of feminism. Given the diversity of the women's movement, and the fact that different women are differently affected by social, political, and economic factors, feminism's vision has as much to do with the *process* of politics as with the end result. The women's movement, eclectic as it may be, seeks a political process in which all groups have a voice and the interests of all groups are taken into account, despite differences of gender, race, class, or sexual orientation. "Politics as if women mattered" is possible only if women and their many and varied goals and experiences are represented.

THE POLITICAL REPRESENTATION OF WOMEN

> I am not ashamed of saying I am a feminist, that I fight for women. I make no apologies, just as a farmer would never dream of apologizing for fighting for farmers. . . . Women make up an absolute

majority in this country. Why should our interests be considered trivial? Why should we leave it to others to represent us, and to fight our battles?[37]

What do we mean by the political representation of women? There is an important difference between representing women (numerical representation) and representing women's interests (substantive representation). The numerical representation of women is symbolic but crucial because having women in visible or powerful political positions helps dispel the myth that women are apolitical or uninterested in politics. But the mere existence of women's groups or female elites does not ensure that the interests of women will be articulated and viewed as politically relevant. The political representation of women requires more than women standing for other women; it requires female representatives to act for women.

Those who are politically engaged—as activists in the women's movement, as partisans, or as legislators—can represent women in three ways. First, they can speak about women's lived experiences in a political context. For instance, women can draw attention to problems or concerns resulting from the sexual division of labour such as child care and the double day. Also, they can point out that not all women have the same experiences, as disabled, visible minority, Aboriginal, or lesbian women face many layers of discrimination. Second, female political actors can take gender into account when undertaking a political analysis of social and economic conditions and public policy. Governments often fail to explore the differential impact of policy decisions on women and men. For example, the Mulroney government changed the unemployment insurance rules in 1993 to deny benefits to those who voluntarily quit their jobs. Liberal and NDP members of Parliament were quick to point out that the policy discriminates against those women who have no option but to leave their jobs because of sexual harassment. Third, representatives can demand or implement policies designed to advance the social and economic status of women. The overall goal is to make women's interests interesting, to put gender equality on the political agenda.

The task of making women's interests interesting has fallen largely to the women's movement, as Canadian political parties and elites have been slow to respond to demands for gender equality. Because women are under-represented in conventional political structures such as political parties, legislatures, bureaucracies, and the judiciary, the women's movement has provided an important avenue for political action. The Canadian women's movement is large and extremely diverse, as groups voice the interests of francophone and anglophone women, Native women, black women, immigrant women, disabled women, and so on. Sandra Burt identifies four types of women's groups: traditional groups, service providers, shelters, and status of women groups.[38] Many of the traditional groups, such as the National Council of Women, originated during the first wave of the women's movement; according to Burt, they help women acquire good homemaking and citizenship skills, and favour equality rights for women in the workplace. Service groups provide educational support to women by offering counselling, advice on government services, and referrals to government agencies. Shelters give respite and assistance to women and children who have been victims of violence. Status of women groups lobby for women's rights by educating the public and pressuring governments. This category includes the umbrella lobby organization, the National Action Committee on the Status of Women (NAC); groups with specific policy goals, such as the Canadian Abortion Rights Action League (CARAL); and groups designed to articulate the needs and interests of particular communities of women, such as the Congress of Black Women and the Native Women's Association of Canada.

Feminist scholars agree that the existence of a diverse and active women's movement is essential to the political representation of women because "women's movements represent values and demands that cannot be accommodated quickly or entirely through the official politics of liberal-democratic societies."[39] NAC, for example, has provided Canadian women with an unofficial but powerful "parliament of women":

> Through the construction and institutionalization of an embryonic parliament of women, NAC has created an alternative centre of public-policy proposals, legitimized as representing the views of progressive women on both "women's issues" and general issues of public policy. Indeed, apart from fielding candidates, NAC came increasingly to resemble an omnibus political party in Canada.[40]

The women's movement provides crucial, but incomplete, representation of women in Canadian political life. As we have seen, political structures and public policies can have a dramatic effect on the lives of women; therefore, mainstream political institutions cannot be ignored. Sylvia Bashevkin's analysis of the history of the women's movement suggests that both mainstream and autonomous mechanisms for political representation are essential, for "women's political . . . history continues to be enmeshed in a complex and uneasy tension between non-partisanship and independent feminism, on the one hand, and the demands of a party-structured parliamentary system on the other."[41] Women need to be represented both within and alongside the formal arenas of political power because political parties and political executives dominate agenda setting and decision making in this country.

In the 1980s, women's groups and parties began to take steps to improve the representation of women in party structures and in legislatures. There are now a variety of women's groups that devote themselves to the task of getting more women elected to political office. Groups like the Committee for '94 (whose original goal was gender parity in the House of Commons by 1994), Winning Women, and FRAPPE (Femmes regroupées pour l'accès au pouvoir politique et économique) offer symposia and training sessions for women interested in electoral politics.[42] Canada's three major political parties, and some provincial parties, have established special funds to help women candidates. However, given the enormous amount of money required to run an election campaign, the amounts offered to female candidates are nominal, ranging from $500 to $1500 per candidate.

The two most significant barriers to women's political candidacy at the federal and provincial levels are the nomination contest and the financial burden of running for political office. Simply winning the nomination battle for a competitive party in a winnable urban riding may cost over $50 000.[43] Most women simply do not have the income or the social and financial connections to raise such huge sums. The financial hurdles could be addressed by measures such as the Ontario NDP's recommended spending limit of $5000 for candidates seeking nomination.

The problem of how to ensure that women are nominated in higher numbers and in winnable ridings is not easily solved. In Canada's single-member plurality system, the process of candidate selection is organized by the constituency riding association, and parties are reluctant to interfere in this decentralized nomination process. The New Democratic Party is the only party with an affirmative action program. Despite its efforts and goal of gender parity, only 38 percent of the NDP candidates for the 1993 federal election were women. As usual, the most competitive parties fielded the fewest female candidates: in 1993, 23 percent of Conservative candidates and 22 percent of Liberal candidates were women. The Liberals did not reach their goal of 25 percent despite using the party's controversial appointment process—whereby the normal party nomination process is bypassed and candidates are appointed by the party leader—to nominate six women. Thirteen percent of the Bloc Québécois candidates were women. The

Reform Party, claiming to be intrinsically gender neutral, refused to actively recruit women during the 1993 campaign, with the result that only 10 percent of Reform candidates were women.[44]

Like the promotion of female candidates, the election of women to public office in more than token numbers is a relatively recent phenomenon, occurring in the 1980s. As table 1 indicates, between 1921 and 1967, women constituted 2.4 percent of the candidates for federal office and won less than 1 percent of the seats in Parliament. The 10 percent mark was not passed until 1988, when women won thirty-nine seats (13.4 percent of the total). The 1993 federal election brought fifty-three women to the House of Commons. Table 1 indicates the exponential rise in female representation at the federal level; whereas the percentage of women slowly increased from less than 1 percent to 9.6 percent over a sixty-three-year period, the proportion of women in the House of Commons doubled between 1984 and 1993. If this trend continues, women will make up almost 40 percent of MPs within two or three federal elections.

TABLE 1

Women Candidates and MPs in Canadian General Elections, 1921–1993 (percentage of total)

Year	Candidates	MPs
1921–1967*	2.4	0.8
1968	3.5	0.4
1972	6.4	1.8
1974	9.4	3.4
1979	13.8	3.6
1980	14.4	5.0
1984	14.5	9.6
1988	19.2	13.4**
1993	28.3	17.9

*   Average for elections between 1921 and 1967.
** Reform Party MP Deborah Grey was elected in a 1989 by-election, bringing the number of female MPs to 40 (14 percent).

Source: Elections Canada and various newspaper articles on the 1993 federal election.

Provincial gains have been more dramatic. In 1986, only 8.2 percent of provincial and territorial legislators were women,[45] but by March 1994 the number had increased to 18.2 percent. As table 2 shows, the level of representation varies quite dramatically from province to province. Only 5.8 percent of the legislators in Newfoundland are women, whereas women hold more than a quarter of the positions in the British Columbia legislature. Canadian women are best represented at the city level. The proportion of women holding council seats in Canadian cities jumped from 15 percent in 1984 to 24 percent in 1993.[46] The percentage of female mayors has also increased, from 12.5 percent in 1984 to 20.5 percent in 1993. These averages obscure an important fact: city governments are the only elected legislative arena in Canada where women have obtained parity or are in the majority. Women have equal representation in four Canadian cities (Langley, Surrey, Vancouver, and Victoria, all in British Columbia).

TABLE 2

Female Representation in Provincial and Territorial Legislatures*

Province/Territory	Number of members	Number of women members	% of women	% Change since last election
British Columbia	75	19	25.3	+13.7
Prince Edward Island	32	7	21.9	+9.4
Ontario	130	28	21.0	-2.0
Manitoba	57	11	19.3	+5.3
Alberta	83	16	19.3	+4.9
Quebec	125	23	18.4	+2.6
Saskatchewan	66	12	18.2	+10.4
Yukon	17	3	17.6	-7.4
New Brunswick	58	10	17.2	+5.2
Northwest Territories	24	3	12.5	+4.2
Nova Scotia	52	5	9.6	+3.8
Newfoundland	52	3	5.8	+2.0
TOTAL	771	140	18.2	

* The numbers are for the most recent provincial and territorial elections, to March 1994.

Source: Government of Ontario, Female Representation in the Senate, House of Commons, and Provincial Legislatures (Legislative Research Service, March 1992), and newspaper reports on the most recent elections.

As well, women are in the majority in Delta, British Columbia (57 percent of the councillors are women, mayor included) and in Richmond Hill, Ontario (66 percent). Table 3 shows that the representation of women in major and capital cities is, in many cases, significantly higher than the Canadian average of 24 percent. Moreover, seven of the eighteen mayors in major and capital cities are women (39 percent).

TABLE 3

Number and Percentage of Women Serving on Municipal Councils in Major Canadian Cities and Capital Cities, 1993

City	Total number of elected representatives (including mayor)	Date of most recent election	Number and % of women councillors (including mayor)	% change from previous election
Vancouver	11	Nov. 1993	5 (45.5%)	+18.2
Victoria	9	Nov. 1993	4 (44.4%)	+11.1
*Yellowknife	7	Oct. 1991	3 (42.9%)	0.0
*Edmonton	13	Oct. 1992	5 (38.5%)	-15.3
*Saint John	11	May 1992	4 (36.4%)	+9.2
Calgary	15	Oct. 1992	5 (33.3%)	-6.7
*Toronto	25	Oct. 1991	8 (32.0%)	+4.0
Montreal	51	Nov. 1990	16 (31.4%)	+6.4
*Ottawa	16	Nov. 1991	5 (31.3%)	0.0
Whitehorse	7	Nov. 1991	2 (28.6%)	0.0
Saskatoon	11	Oct. 1991	3 (27.3%)	-9.0
*Winnipeg	16	Oct. 1992	4 (25.0%)	+5.0
Quebec City	21	Nov. 1993	5 (23.8%)	-3.4
*Halifax	13	Oct. 1991	3 (23.1%)	+7.7
St John's	11	Nov. 1993	2 (18.2%)	-11.8
Regina	11	Oct. 1991	2 (18.2%)	0.0
Charlottetown	11	Nov. 1992	2 (18.2%)	0.0
Fredericton	13	May 1992	1 (7.7%)	0.0
TOTALS	272		79 (29.0%)	

Indicates female mayor.

Source: Canadian Almanac and Directory, 1992, *and telephone correspondence with various city halls.*

Does the presence of female elected representatives make a difference for women? In other words, do female elites act for women by articulating women's experiences, taking gender into account when discussing policy, and lobbying for or implementing policy changes that will promote the status of women? Students of women and legislative politics have concluded that women must constitute a significant proportion of the elected body before they can be effective at the elite level. A critical mass of women (somewhere between 15 and 30 percent) is necessary before women can make a difference. There is little Canadian research that examines the actions and statements of women in the legislative arena, although the existing evidence supports the argument that female politicians tend to speak on behalf of women's equality goals. For example, Manon Tremblay found that many female politicians in Quebec express egalitarian and feminist ideas in their speeches before the National Assembly.[47] Do female politicians also act for women? Tremblay and Boivin's study of House of Commons debates on abortion in July 1988 found that female MPs were more likely than their male counterparts to take a pro-choice position.[48] Parliamentarians in this case were allowed to speak and vote according to conscience rather than according to the party line, but free votes are rare in Canadian legislatures, and there are few opportunities for legislators to act outside the purview of party discipline. In the Canadian parliamentary system, a critical mass of female legislators is a necessary but insufficient prerequisite for the development of a policy-making process that takes gender into account and raises the status of women.

My study of the impact of female legislators in Alberta between 1972 and 1991[49] found that, under certain circumstances, women can make a difference to both the style and content of legislative debate. The most important barrier is the party; realistically, female legislators can only speak and act for women when voicing women's concerns and experiences is congruent with their party ideology. In Alberta, the governing Conservatives have not granted gender equality goals a high priority. Thus, women's concerns, interests, and policy demands have been voiced by opposition MPs. The amount of attention given to women's issues in the legislature increased dramatically after four feminist opposition MLAs (three NDP, one Liberal) were elected in 1986. These women had a significant effect on the tone and direction of debate; they introduced feminist analysis of a wide range of issues, analysis that was adopted by their male colleagues in the opposition ranks. More surprisingly, the debates showed that women in the legislature bypassed some of the institutional constraints on effective representation of women's interests. Female MLAs from all three parties, but particularly the two opposition parties, illustrated a willingness to co-operate across party lines. Moreover, their approach to debate and question period challenged long-standing institutional norms and illustrated a less conflictual style of legislative debate. Few generalizations can be drawn from the Alberta example. Much more research on the role and impact of elected women at all levels of government is needed before any firm conclusions can be drawn.

CONCLUSION

Women will not be full citizens in Canada until they play a meaning-ful role in their own governance. While the women's movement has had a dramatic impact on societal attitudes and political discourse, women still find themselves on the outside of a policy-making process that continues to produce discriminatory outcomes and persistently implements policies that fail to take women's contexts and experiences into account. Women's policy influence is occasionally pro-active; for example, women's groups provided the model and labour for battered women's shelters at a time when governments were regarding violence in the home as a private issue. Most of the time, however, women are forced to react to policies that have already been made. Constitutional politics provide perhaps the most vivid example of women's outsider status. During the negotiations to patriate the constitution in the early 1980s, a group of women known as the Ad Hoc Committee of Canadian Women on the Constitution lobbied first ministers for strong gender equality guarantees and won an important victory—section 28 of the Charter of Rights and Freedoms.[50] However, in a last-ditch attempt to save the Charter, the prime minister and premiers agreed to insert the so-called notwithstanding clause, which allows governments to override Charter guarantees, including the equality rights enshrined in section 15. When asked whether the legislative override provision applied to section 28, the first ministers said they weren't really sure; they had forgotten about the existence of section 28. Later they agreed that section 33 should apply to the gender equality guarantee embodied in section 28, and activists were forced to lobby the federal government and the nine provincial premiers who had signed the constitutional agreement. They were eventually successful—section 28 was exempt from the notwithstanding clause—but an enormous amount of energy and time was spent because male elites had neglected to consider women's constitutional goals and aspirations.

Women also found themselves on the outside looking in while political leaders negotiated the Meech Lake Accord. Some women sat at the table during the Charlottetown round, which expanded the process of executive federalism to include the territorial leaders and leaders of Aboriginal groups. Nellie Cournoyea, government leader of the Northwest Territories, and Rosemarie Kuptana, head of the Inuit Tapirisat of Canada, helped negotiate the constitutional agreement that Canadians later defeated in a national referendum. Yet women's groups such as NAC and the Native Women's Association of Canada rejected the accord on the basis that it did not adequately protect Aboriginal women and threatened many social policies crucial to the lives of women.

A clear political voice is needed to articulate the problems and policy demands of the most marginalized women. The "multiple jeopardy" experienced by Aboriginal, visible minority, and disabled women is simply invisible, as it has not been part of mainstream political discourse. Consider the case of Aboriginal women:

> They are often single mothers without the benefit of culturally appropriate child care programs. They and their children are often the subject of sexual abuse and "unconscionable levels of domestic violence." They have a disproportionately high rate of incarceration in correctional institutions and they still have no matrimonial property rights on reserves if their marriages break down. Clearly, the need for substantive equality and formal equality persists for Indian women.[51]

Women need to be fully involved in political agenda setting and decision making because of the role politics plays in determining the boundaries between the public and private spheres. If women are unable to have a direct say in political decisions that affect their private lives, they are truly subjects regardless of any formal individual rights they may, in theory, possess.

NOTES

[1] Danielle Crittenden, "Let's Junk the Feminist Slogans: The War's Over," *Chatelaine* (Aug. 1990), 38.

[2] Pat Armstrong and Hugh Armstrong, *The Double Ghetto,* 3rd ed. (Toronto: McClelland & Stewart, 1994), 43.

[3] Virginia Sapiro, *The Political Integration of Women* (Chicago: University of Illinois Press, 1984), 7.

4 Lorraine Code, "Feminist Theory" in *Changing Patterns: Women in Canada*, 2nd ed., ed. Sandra Burt, Lorraine Code, and Lindsay Dorney. (Toronto: McClelland and Stewart, 1993), 18–19.

5 Janine Brodie, *Women and Politics in Canada* (Toronto: McGraw-Hill Ryerson, 1985), 1.

6 Sapiro, *Political Integration of Women*, 30–31.

7 Alison Prentice, Paula Bourne, Gail Cuthbert Brandt, Beth Light, Wendy Mitchinson, and Naomi Black, *Canadian Women: A History* (Toronto: Harcourt Brace Jovanovich, 1988), 143 and 146.

8 Sandra Burt, "Legislators, Women, and Public Policy" in *Changing Patterns*, 213–14.

9 See "Married Women's Property Law in Nineteenth-Century Canada" in *Canadian Family History: Selected Readings*, ed. Bettina Bradbury (Toronto: Copp Clark Pitman, 1992), 322.

10 Roxanna Ng, "Racism, Sexism, and Immigrant Women" in *Changing Patterns*, 283–84.

11 Sally Weaver, "First Nations Women and Government Policy, 1970–92: Discrimination and Conflict" in *Changing Patterns*, 93.

12 Ibid., 94.

13 Ibid., 125.

14 Ibid.

15 Women and men of Chinese, East Indian, and Japanese ancestry were denied the vote until the late 1940s. See Chantal Maillé, *Primed for Power* (Ottawa: Canadian Advisory Council on the Status of Women, 1990), 1.

16 Jane Errington, "Pioneers and Suffragists" in *Changing Patterns*, 72.

17 Prentice et al., *Canadian Women*, 184–88.

18 See Beverley Baines, "Law, Gender, Equality" in *Changing Patterns*, 246–58.

19 Sapiro, *Political Integration of Women*, 184.

20 Prentice et al., *Canadian Women*, 297–98.

21 Ibid., 303.

22 Ibid., 307–8.

23 Gertrude Robinson and Armande Saint-Jean, "Women Politicians and Their Media Coverage: A Generational Analysis" in *Women in Canadian Politics: Toward Equity in Representation*, ed. Kathy Megyery (Toronto: Dundurn Press, 1993), 136.

24 Quoted in ibid., 135.

25 Ibid., 138.

26 Sheila Copps, *Nobody's Baby* (Toronto: Deneau, 1986), 25.

27 Jean Charest, who took over the PC leadership after the party's electoral debacle in the 1993 election, has an attractive wife and young children. See Lysiane Gagnon, "Why Isn't Campbell Judged by the Same Yardstick as Male Politicians?" *Globe and Mail* (5 June 1993), D3.

28 Murray Campbell, "Media, Parties Use New Game Plan," *Globe and Mail* (10 Sept. 1993), A6; see also, on the same page of the *Globe*, "Advice Likely to Be Ignored," under "Trail Notes."

29 Sylvia Bashevkin, *Toeing the Lines: Women and Party Politics in English Canada*, 2nd ed. (Toronto: Oxford University Press, 1993), 67.

30 Brodie, "Women and the Electoral Process," 33.

31 Alberta Legislative Assembly, *Debates* (20 March 1987), 239.

[32] Audrey McLaughlin, *A Woman's Place* (Toronto: Macfarlane Walter & Ross, 1992), 26.

[33] Copps, *Nobody's Baby*, 93.

[34] See Ng, "Racism, Sexism, and Immigrant Women," 297–99, and Vivian Smith, "Rules Yield to Need for Nannies," *Globe and Mail* (4 March 1994), A1, A5.

[35] Joanne D. Leck and David M. Saunders, "Hiring Women: The Effects of Canada's Employment Equity Act," *Canadian Public Policy* 28, 2 (June 1992): 209.

[36] Jill McCalla Vickers, "Feminist Approaches to Women in Politics" in *Beyond the Vote: Canadian Women and Politics*, ed. Linda Kealey and Joan Sangster (Toronto: University of Toronto Press, 1989), 17.

[37] Copps, *Nobody's Baby*, 56.

[38] Sandra Burt, "Canadian Women's Groups in the 1980s: Organizational Development and Policy Influence," *Canadian Public Policy* 26, 1 (1990): 17–28.

[39] Jill Vickers et al., *Politics as if Women Mattered: A Political Analysis of the National Action Committee on the Status of Women* (Toronto: University of Toronto Press, 1993), 282.

[40] Ibid., 283.

[41] Bashevkin, *Toeing the Lines,* 28.

[42] For a description of the various groups and their activities, see Maillé, *Primed for Power*, 27–30.

[43] Brodie, "Women and the Electoral Process in Canada," 40–41.

[44] See "Coast-to-Coast List of Federal Candidates," *Globe and Mail* (29 Sept. 1993), A10–11, and Linda Goyette, "Woman PM is Running Canada, but Gender Equality Has Yet to Reach House," *Edmonton Journal* (21 Sept. 1993).

[45] See Maillé, *Primed for Power*, 12.

[46] Linda Trimble, "Politics Where We Live: Women and Cities" in *Canadian Metropolitics: Governing Our Cities*, ed. James Lightbody (Toronto: Copp Clark Longman, 1995).

[47] See Maillé, *Primed for Power*, 31.

[48] Manon Tremblay and G. Boivin, "Le question de l'avortement au Parlement canadien: de l'importance du genre dans l'orientation des débats," *Revue juridique la femme et le droite* 4 (1990–91): 459–76.

[49] Linda Trimble, "A Few Good Women: Female Legislators in Alberta, 1972–1991" in *Standing on New Ground: Women in Alberta*, ed. Randi Warne and Cathy Cavanaugh (Edmonton: University of Alberta Press, 1993), 87–118.

[50] Section 28 of the Charter states, "Notwithstanding anything in this Charter, the rights and freedoms referred to in it are guaranteed equally to male and female persons."

[51] Weaver, "First Nations Women," 128.

SUGGESTED READING

Armstrong, Pat, and Hugh Armstrong. *The Double Ghetto: Canadian Women and Their Segregated Work.* 3rd ed. Toronto: McClelland & Stewart, 1994.

Documents the evolution of women's work and examines three theoretical frameworks used to understand the sexual division of labour.

Brodsky, Gwen, and Shelagh Day. *Canadian Charter Equality Rights for Women.* Ottawa: Canadian Advisory Council on the Status of Women, 1989. Analyzes the first three years of equality rights litigation under the Charter.

Burt, Sandra, Lorraine Code, and Lindsay Dorney, eds. *Changing Patterns: Women in Canada.* 2nd ed. Toronto: McClelland & Stewart, 1993. An interdisciplinary volume with chapters on feminist theory, the Canadian women's movement, Aboriginal women, immigrant women, public policy, and the law.

Maillé, Chantal. *Primed for Power.* Ottawa: Canadian Advisory Council on the Status of Women, 1990. Presents data on the representation of women in Canadian political institutions, including federal and provincial legislatures, cabinets and courts, municipal councils, the federal bureaucracy, and the Senate.

Megyery, Kathy, ed. *Women in Canadian Politics: Toward Equity in Representation.* Toronto: Dundurn Press, 1993. This volume of research studies conducted for the Royal Commission on Electoral Reform and Party Financing contains invaluable information on women's role in party politics and federal elections, including media treatment of political women.

Vickers, Jill, Pauline Rankin, and Christine Appelle. *Politics as if Women Mattered: A Political Analysis of the National Action Committee on the Status of Women.* Toronto: University of Toronto Press, 1993. A history of NAC from its inception to 1988.

Kathy L. Brock

NATIVE PEOPLES ON THE ROAD TO SELF-GOVERNMENT

The victory of the Liberals in the general election on 23 October 1993 signalled the beginning of a new era in state–Aboriginal relations in Canada. During the campaign, the Liberals had outlined a series of commitments and objectives relating to Aboriginal peoples. Although the Liberal platform was consistent with the evolution of policy in the past twenty years toward more autonomy and control for Aboriginal communities, it envisioned a fundamental change in the nature of the state–Aboriginal relationship. The proposals, if carried forward, would result in the recognition and implementation of the inherent right to Native self-government. The significance of this achievement would reach beyond the Canadian borders to other nations who are in a process of redefining state–Aboriginal relations.

This chapter examines the proposed shift in relations begun with the election of the Liberal government in 1993. In particular, the chapter focuses upon the proposals to effect Aboriginal self-government within Canada. While it is too early to assess the impact of the policies of the Chrétien government, it is possible to characterize the areas of change and to point to some of the implications these changes will have for Aboriginal peoples and the Canadian public more generally. Although the Métis and Inuit are included in these policies, the focus of this chapter is more specifically on the First Nations.

To accomplish this objective, the analysis is divided into four sections. The first section provides a brief introduction to the Aboriginal populations in Canada and outlines the need for change in their social, economic, and political status. The second section presents the Liberal platform on Aboriginal issues and traces its translation into policy objectives and initiatives. Because the establishment of Aboriginal self-government and a government-to-government relationship between the Canadian and Aboriginal governments is fundamental to a new relationship, this area of policy receives special consideration. The third section focuses on three specific initiatives relating to Aboriginal self-government, including one of the most contentious and potentially most significant areas of change—the proposal to dismantle the Department of Indian Affairs (henceforth referred to simply as Indian Affairs) and recognize First Nation governments. The final section of the chapter reflects on the political significance of these changes for both the Aboriginal community specifically and the Canadian population generally.

THE PRESENT POPULATION

In Canada, the term *Aboriginal peoples* is used to refer to people of First Nation, Métis, and Inuit ancestry. This term has become the accepted means of distinguishing these citizens from citizens of European, Asian, African, or other ancestry who have emigrated to Canada. It is an artificial construct that came into common usage following the entrenchment of "Aboriginal" rights in section 35 of the Constitution Act, 1982. Section 35 recognized and affirmed the existing Aboriginal and treaty rights of the Aboriginal peoples of Canada and defined Aboriginal peoples as including the "Indian, Inuit and Métis peoples." While it is a convenient term for distinguishing between the original and immigrant groups making up the Canadian population, it obscures real differences between the three "Aboriginal" populations. The preferred practice is to refer to each community separately, and in the case of First Nations to refer to them as such or by the proper name of their nation. So, for example, specific members of First Nations would be referred to as Ojibwa, Cree, Dakota, or Mohawk, and so on. For legal purposes, members of the First Nations registered as such with the federal government are deemed "status Indians." Other members of First Nations who are not on band lists and registered as such are often referred to as non-status Indians. The usage of the term Aboriginal is further complicated by its appropriation by status-blind organizations that purport to represent Aboriginal residents regardless of their background (First Nation, Métis, Inuit) or status.

The Canadian Aboriginal population[1] is relatively small but expanding. According to the 1981 census, the Aboriginal population represented approximately 2.0 percent of the total Canadian population or 491 460 individuals. The 1991 census data reveal that Aboriginal peoples made up approximately 2.3 percent of the total population, with 625 710 individuals reporting Aboriginal identity and 1 002 675 reporting Aboriginal origins. These figures have been disputed as under-representing the actual size of the population due to faulty data collection methods. Still, even the slight increase in the enumerated community represents a stable population base and reverses the trend toward a diminishing population in the first half of the century.

The Aboriginal population is diverse and dispersed in different proportions throughout Canada. Of the total population reporting Aboriginal identity, 460 680 are First Nation (North American Indian), 135 265 are Métis, and 36 215 are Inuit. There are 633 registered bands or First Nation communities in Canada. As a percentage of the general provincial populations, the Aboriginal population varies from lows of 0.5 percent in Prince Edward Island and 0.7 percent in New Brunswick to highs of 8.9 percent in Saskatchewan and 9.2 percent in Manitoba. In the Yukon and Northwest Territories, the Aboriginal components of the population are 16.3 percent and 60.2 percent respectively. As a percentage of the total Aboriginal population, the largest numbers of Aboriginal people reside in Ontario (18.4 percent), Alberta (16.6 percent), British Columbia (16.2 percent), and Manitoba (15.9 percent). Although the Aboriginal people form significant components of the populations in the Yukon and Northwest Territories, they make up 0.7 percent and 5.5 percent respectively of the total number of Aboriginal people spread throughout Canada. The heaviest concentrations of Aboriginal peoples tend to be found (in the North) and the western provinces.

The Aboriginal population is becoming increasingly centred in urban locations. Although data on the numbers of people of Aboriginal identity living in urban settings are not reliable, some trends may be noted. Manitoba is a good indication of one trend. According to a recent report,

Existing estimates ... place the Indian population in Winnipeg at between 15,000 and 20,000 people; and the Metis population between 40,000 and 60,000, but these estimates cannot be verified. One report indicates that the Native population has grown by 70% in the past eight years. Another report suggests that by the year 2000 AD ... 25% of the labour force in Winnipeg will be comprised of Native people. If the data cannot be verified at this time, it does nevertheless indicate a major mobility trend towards the city.[2]

As the urban population grows, its needs become increasingly apparent. Youths moving to the city often find it difficult to obtain employment and frequently must rely on welfare to provide the necessities of life. The lack of employment, absence of the support structures that were available in the home community, and the unfriendly environment can lead to higher levels of drug, alcohol, and substance abuse, violence, prostitution, and family breakdown, as well as crime and involvement with the justice system.

The Aboriginal populations in Canada are distinct societies in themselves. The vitality of Aboriginal languages is indicated by their use patterns. More than 35 percent of the Aboriginal population over fifteen years of age speaks an Aboriginal language. The highest use of Aboriginal languages occurs among the Inuit (74.6 percent), followed by on-reserve members of First Nations (65.4 percent), off-reserve members of First Nations (23.1 percent), and Métis (17.5 percent). These figures decline among the under-fifteen population (21.4 percent overall), indicating a need for greater incorporation of Aboriginal language instruction into the educational curriculum if the languages are to be maintained. Similarly, more than 50 percent of the population over fifteen participates in traditional Aboriginal activities, including hunting, fishing, trapping, storytelling, traditional dancing, fiddle playing, jigging, pow-wows, arts and crafts, and so on. Again, the Inuit (74.1 percent) and on-reserve First Nation citizens (65.2 percent) are most likely to be involved in traditional activities, and the participation rate drops among children aged five to fourteen years (44.1 percent). Still, the distinctiveness and vitality of Aboriginal cultures may be assumed from the levels of language use and traditional practices. The vibrancy of the culture is also reflected in the impact on Canadian culture of Aboriginal artists such as painters Jackson Beardy and Norval Morrisseau, singers Buffy Ste Marie and Susan Aglukark, playwright Thomson Highway, actor Graham Greene, and singer/songwriter/actor Tom Jackson.

In Canada, Aboriginal peoples experience the worst social and economic conditions of any segment of society. Chronic health problems—diabetes, high blood pressure, arthritis, heart problems, bronchitis, emphysema, asthma, tuberculosis, and epilepsy—afflict 30.6 percent of the over-fifteen Aboriginal population. Census data also reveal a higher incidence of group deaths, suicides, and substance abuse among Aboriginals. These factors not only point to causes of shorter life expectancies, they also reveal a higher level of discontent and stress in Native communities.

The marginalization of the Aboriginal population in the economy is evident in a brief review of income, employment, and labour data. In

Canada, 14.4 percent of the adult general population makes under $2000 per year, 15.4 percent make in excess of $40 000, and the largest percentage make between $20 000 and $39 999. The corresponding figures for the Aboriginal population are 25.2 percent, 5.3 percent, and 17.8 percent respectively. The largest percentage of Aboriginal people make between $2000 and $9000. Levels of social assistance and unemployment tend to be higher in Aboriginal communities, and these factors in turn contribute to the higher levels of stress among Aboriginal peoples.

These data are complex and require more analysis than can be given here. However, they point to some important implications for policy. First, the Aboriginal population is diverse. Second, the communities have very different needs according to their cultural make-up, location, size, and nature. Third, the data clarify the need for a change in the conceptualization and provision of programs and services to the Aboriginal community. Clearly, past methods of policy definition and delivery have failed.

PLANNING CHANGE: THE LIBERAL AGENDA

"The priority of a Liberal government will be to assist Aboriginal communities in their efforts to address the obstacles to their development and to help them marshal the human and physical resources necessary to build and sustain vibrant communities."[3] With these words, the Liberal Party announced its intentions to change the direction of Aboriginal policy in Canada as part of its election platform. The details were outlined in the "Red Book," as it was commonly known, or *Creating Opportunity: The Liberal Plan for Canada*. The plan was expanded upon by the leader of the Liberal Party, Jean Chrétien, in both a formal speech and press release on 8 October 1993. The Liberal platform had been derived from party policy resolutions passed unanimously at the 1992 National Liberal Party Convention and from the recommendations of the 1990 report of the Aboriginal Peoples' Commission of the Liberal Party, which was created by Jean Chrétien and composed of Aboriginal representatives.

The impetus for the initiative on Aboriginal policy came from the recognition that past policies had failed Aboriginal communities. According to the news release accompanying the October 1993 policy announcement, change was needed because "the socioeconomic conditions of Aboriginal peoples are the poorest in the country. 'Aboriginal communities are tired of government foot dragging on these serious problems,' Chrétien said."[4] These observations were expanded upon in the Red Book:

> The place of Aboriginal peoples in the growth and development of Canada is a litmus test of our beliefs in fairness, justice, and equality of opportunity.
>
> For generations, Canadian society has failed this test. Many Aboriginal people face enormous problems, both in their communities and in the cities across Canada where they live: absence of meaningful employment and economic opportunities, unequal educational opportunity and results, poor housing, unsafe drinking water, and lack of health services. They suffer also from the destruction and lack of respect for Aboriginal languages, values, and culture.
>
> Past and current ways of dealing with these conditions are not working. It is time for a change. We must define and undertake together creative initiatives designed to achieve fairness, mutual respect, and recognition of rights.[5]

The Liberal response to this situation was to construct a policy plan that would enable the Aboriginal communities to ameliorate their living and working conditions and to harness their own potential.

At the core of the plan is recognition and implementation of the inherent right to self-government. The Red Book broke with past policies and embraced the acknowledgement forwarded during the Charlottetown negotiations by stating clearly that the Liberals recognized that the inherent right of self-government was an existing Aboriginal and treaty right.[6] During the election campaign, Jean Chrétien declared that achieving self-government would be "the cornerstone" of the Liberal approach."[7] This commitment was carried forward in the throne speech following the election.[8]

The commitment to recognizing self-government encompassed a variety of approaches to correspond to the different needs of the various segments of the Aboriginal population. For the First Nations, the Liberal plan involved a continuation of community-based self-government negotiations, gradual winding down of Indian Affairs, recognition of the original spirit and intent of treaties, and respect for the fiduciary obligation of the Crown to the First Nations. The Liberal plan recognized the federal government's special trust relationship with the Inuit; the importance of the land claims settlements signed with the Inuit in Nunavut and Quebec; the need to settle the outstanding land claim of the Labrador Inuit; the validity of the Inuit desire for a national process for the negotiation of regional self-government agreements; and, perhaps most significantly for the political development of Canada, the importance of supporting the creation of the new territory of Nunavut in the central and eastern Arctic by 1999 under legislation passed by Parliament in June 1993. Responding to concerns expressed during the constitutional negotiations, the Liberals noted that the federal government has not recognized legislative responsibility for the Métis. It vowed to enter trilateral negotiations with the Métis and provincial governments to define the parameters of federal responsibility. The Liberals supported the funding of an enumeration process for the Métis. In the case of urban Aboriginal peoples, the Liberals promised to promote community-controlled development institutions and the network of urban Aboriginal institutions. While some of these initiatives built upon the past Conservative agenda, the Liberal approach was intended to hasten the progress toward realizing self-government.

The Liberal agenda for Aboriginal peoples was not confined to matters directly related to the realization of self-government. The general initiatives included policies designed to promote housing and infrastructure development, education and training, health and healing, Aboriginal justice, and community development, and to secure more adequate land and resource bases for Aboriginal peoples. Progress in these areas would improve the social and economic conditions of Aboriginal peoples. Moreover, improvements in these areas complement and support the development of self-government by strengthening Native communities.

THE ROAD TO SELF-GOVERNMENT

The Liberal commitment to achieving Aboriginal self-government has translated into a series of initiatives, including the continuation of community-based self-government negotiations, discussions on the inherent right of self-government, and a major pilot project launched in Manitoba to dismantle Indian Affairs and transfer jurisdiction to First Nation governing structures. Each of these initiatives will be reviewed briefly, but the dismantling project will receive more attention here given its potentially wide-ranging implications for First Nation communities in Canada. But first, a brief explanation of self-government should be offered.

What is *Aboriginal self-government*? The term is used to describe a variety of arrangements under which Aboriginal peoples would gain the powers to exercise more control over policies, legislation, programs, services, and matters affecting them through governing structures defined by their communities. For the Inuit, the drive toward self-government is being realized through negotiations, land claims settlements, and the creation of Nunavut in the Northwest Territories. Under these arrangements, self-government refers to legislative structures and (eventually) provincial status, more autonomy for local structures, and co-management over lands and resources.

The Métis perceive themselves as progressing toward a more holistic approach to self-government with substantial legislative, administrative, and executive powers vested within their communities and governing structures. One definition of self-government offered within the Métis community states that:

> Metis, as one of the Aboriginal peoples of Canada, have the inherent right to self-government, and the inherent right to land and resources.
>
> Metis self-government includes the right to establish government structures on a land base, and self-governing institutions off a land base.
>
> The nature and scope of Metis jurisdiction and authority extend to cultural, economic and social matters, and these are to be negotiated between governments and representatives of the Metis Nation.
>
> Metis self-government includes the right of access to sufficient revenues to provide services relevant to the needs and circumstances of the Metis people, on a par with those provided by the federal and provincial governments.[9]

The First Nations' definition of self-government extends far beyond self-management or administrative arrangements. It builds on traditional and accepted governing structures and communities. As the Assembly of First Nations explains,

> Self-government requires a more secure territorial base for First Nations. Land disputes must be settled honourably, fairly and swiftly. Self-government requires administrative and political institutions for First Nations citizens to discuss their governance, build consensus, and make choices as to political direction in their areas of jurisdiction. It requires a recognition of First Nations' responsibility over specific aspects of First Nations life; these responsibilities would likely include, at a minimum, education, health, child welfare, lands and resources, and justice. The responsibilities would give First Nations the authority to enact laws in these areas and

provide a secure sphere so these laws will not simply be overridden by federal or provincial laws as is now the experience with the Indian Act. An essential element of self-government is a secure fiscal base in order to meet the needs of First Nations citizens.[10]

Their governments would be autonomous and responsible to the communities instead of to Indian Affairs and the federal government.

Thus, for the First Nations, self-government translates into the recognition of their governments and an escape from the tutelage of the federal government and its bureaucracy. For the Métis, self-government means recognition of their community, unique identity, and separate governing structures and an escape from the tutelage of the provincial and federal governments. For the Inuit, self-government entails recognition of their governing structures and an escape from the tutelage of the federal government in the territories and the provincial governments in the south. However, all of these definitions envision that the Aboriginal governments would operate within the parameters of the Canadian constitution. They propose establishing a level of government with a recognized sphere of jurisdiction and autonomy independent of the federal and provincial governments but working in co-operation with them. Constitutional entrenchment of these governments would provide the full protection and recognition desired by Aboriginal communities.

It should be stressed what self-government *is not* in order to clarify what self-government *is*. Paul Chartrand argues that self-government is not based on race or the notion that, as Canadians, Aboriginal peoples must be entitled to the same benefits and rights as other Canadians. He explains that

> future consideration of Aboriginal self-government must jettison the notion that it would constitute "special treatment" for racial minorities. In seeking self-government, Aboriginal leaders seek the power necessary to maintain cultures. The cultures they have in mind are unique ways of organizing society and promoting human values; they have little to do with the maintenance of biological "cultures," the notion suggested by the idea of "race." The cultures to be protected by self-government are distinct, historical political communities.[11]

Self-government provides a means of adapting the Canadian political system and institutions to accommodate the legitimate aspirations of these distinct political communities. Inclusion of these communities then confers legitimacy on the Canadian political system.

The Liberal government has tended to accept the Aboriginal definitions of self-government but has chosen to confer upon them political recognition rather than explicit constitutional recognition. In a "backgrounder" on the inherent right to self-government, the government offered this understanding of the concept:

> There is no single model of government that will work for all Aboriginal communities given their extremely diverse needs and circumstances from sea to sea. Diversity and flexibility will continue to be key considerations given the varying legal, historical, geographical, cultural and economic circumstances of Aboriginal peoples.
>
> Areas where Aboriginal communities may wish greater control, more suitable to their culture and values, include social and economic programming in areas such as child welfare, education, health, the administration of justice, housing and economic development.
>
> . . . Urban Aboriginal people are seeking greater control over institutions which serve them so that they can better meet their specific needs, institutions such as child care facilities, health centres and schools designed to respect their cultural and language needs, among others.[12]

Implicit in this definition is the assumption that the process must be driven by the Aboriginal communities, not by the federal government. This view pervades its choice of instruments to realize self-government.

The Liberal government extended the previous Conservative government's policy of community-based self-government negotiations in March 1994. This process had begun in the 1986–87 fiscal year as part of the government strategy to implement and define self-government during the constitutional talks on entrenchment of the inherent right to self-government. These talks were intended to provide First Nation communities with longer-term funding arrangements and more autonomy and decision-making authority over programs and policies. All the same time, they sought to limit the authority of Indian Affairs. Approximately four hundred bands entered into negotiations. By 1994, fifteen negotiations were still in progress, three communities had reached tentative agreements, and one community in Alberta had signed a self-government agreement. The process had cost over $50 million between 1986–87 and 1993–94, with $30 million transferred to Aboriginal communities to fund their involvement and the balance spent on internal operating expenses.

The community-based approach to self-government was sharply criticized in a federal audit concluded in February 1993 and released in 1994. In particular, the audit noted that the Indian Affairs negotiators often lacked the skill, expertise, and authority to conclude discussions; the process was not necessarily appropriate for each band; the funding arrangements required more structure and stricter accountability; the style of negotiations was not conducive to achieving consensus quickly; and the process neglected the provinces. All of these factors had contributed to a process that was protracted, unduly expensive, and cumbersome.

The response of the Liberal government was to admit that the community-based approach to self-government was flawed but then to continue the process with conditions attached. According to a 30 March 1994 news release, the minister of Indian Affairs conceded that the process had been expensive, with low returns, but observed that it had raised the awareness of communities and federal, provincial, and territorial governments of the need for a new partnership based on the inherent right to self-government. He concluded that "many Chiefs involved in the Community-based Self-Government negotiation process want it to continue. But this process cannot remain open-ended. We have a fiscal responsibility to all Canadians to ensure their money is used wisely. Consequently I have decided to continue limited funding of this program for six months."[13] By providing, to the end of September 1994, an additional $3.225 million to fourteen negotiating groups representing forty-four communities the minister hoped to achieve tangible and practical results consistent with the government's recognition of the inherent right to self-government. The process represents an attempt to define and implement self-government at the community or grassroots level. However, it is limited in scope and in terms of the powers being negotiated.

A more comprehensive approach is contemplated with the discussions on the inherent right to Aboriginal self-government. The inherent right to self-government became the focus of the constitutional talks on Aboriginal issues in the 1980s and early 1990s. Those talks culminated in the Charlottetown Accord, which proposed entrenching recognition of the right under section 35 of the Constitution Act, 1982. For the Aboriginal communities, the right was defined as a stand-alone, pre-existing right:[14] that is, the right is not contingent upon definition by governments; it is derived from the Creator and the original occupancy of the land by these communities.

First Nations were adamant in their declaration that "this right does not come from legislation, executive action or from the pleasure of the Crown."[15] The defeat of the Charlottetown Accord by referendum meant that the right was not entrenched. The resounding rejection of the agreement by the Aboriginal communities was intended to send a signal to the Canadian governments that more consultation was required before action could be taken in this area.[16]

In January 1994, the federal government began that process of consultation with its announcement that the minister of Indian Affairs and Northern Development and the federal interlocutor for Métis and non-status Indians would begin a series of meetings on the inherent right to self-government with national and regional Aboriginal leaders, provincial and territorial governments, and other interested parties. The meetings were scheduled from January to June 1994. In March 1994, the minister emphasized to the House of Commons Standing Committee on Aboriginal Affairs and Northern Development that the meetings were premised upon the understanding that "the inherent right is an existing Aboriginal and treaty right within section 35 of the constitution."[17] Thus, constitutional discussions were not necessary to give effect to the right and were not anticipated at the time.

One of the major national Aboriginal organizations, the Assembly of First Nations, has declined involvement in the talks at the time of writing. Grand Chief Ovide Mercredi has stated that "a political assertion that the inherent right exists is meaningless."[18] In his remarks, he stressed that recognition of the right must be constitutionally entrenched. He also objected to violating the bilateral relationship between Aboriginal peoples and the Canadian government established under the treaties by including the provinces in the inherent-right negotiations. In contrast, leaders of the Inuit Tapirisat of Canada, the Métis National Council, the Congress of Aboriginal Peoples, and the Native Women's Association committed themselves with federal and provincial ministers to negotiating practical arrangements for self-government.

The discussions initiated by the Liberal government on the inherent right are significant for three reasons. First, they formally recognize the existence of the inherent right to self-government. Second, they represent an attempt to create an overarching framework for the discussions on self-government being conducted at the community level. Third, they have the potential to create a new basis for the relationship between Aboriginal peoples and the federal and provincial governments, one that is defined through a process of mutual respect. However, if a significant actor such as the Assembly of First Nations remains outside the negotiations, then the value of the exercise will be significantly diminished.

The third important initiative of the Liberal government is its commitment to dismantle the Department of Indian Affairs. The Liberals used the Red Book to announce their intention to dismantle Indian Affairs at a pace determined by the First Nations. Reaffirmations of this intention followed the election of the Liberals. On 1 October 1993, at their annual assembly, the Manitoba chiefs responded to the Liberal platform and passed a resolution to pursue dismantling when the Liberals were elected. Discussions between the chiefs and Minister Ron Irwin began in earnest in December and were carried forward by the grand chief of the Assembly of Manitoba Chiefs (AMC) in January and February. By mid-February, the AMC executive had prepared and submitted to the minister a "Proposal Regarding the Recognition of Manitoba First Nations Government." In a statement to the House of Commons on 9 March 1994, the minister committed the government to the dismantling initiative in Manitoba. The AMC prepared a comprehensive proposal outlining the process for transferring jurisdiction from Indian Affairs and other departments to the First Nations and for defining the Manitoba First Nations' governing structures. During a special assembly hosted by the Opaskwayak First Nation, the minister and grand chief signed a memorandum of understanding on the project. This document protects treaty rights, the Crown's fiduciary obligation, and existing funding, programs, initiatives, and services. It also guarantees adequate resources for the project and ensures that the project will entail a transfer of jurisdiction and be consistent with the inherent right to self-government. After three days of debate, the chiefs passed a resolution to proceed with the initiative. Shortly thereafter, officials from the AMC and Indian Affairs reached an agreement on providing resources for the project. Community consultations began in early June.

What does dismantling entail? The comprehensive discussion paper on dismantling states:

> While attempts have been made in the past to establish practical examples of aboriginal self-government, none have been as comprehensive as this. This is not a question of a single First Nation attempting to obtain control over its own affairs but of sixty-one First Nations working in concert. This is not a question of displacing the powers of Indians Affairs alone, but of displacing all federal departments associated with First Nations. And most complex of

all, the dismantling of government structures must be accompanied by the creation of fully functioning Manitoba First Nations' Governments.[19]

More specifically, in a letter to the Premier of Manitoba, Grand Chief Phil Fontaine explained that

On the simplest level, self-government means First Nations will possess the powers to determine what our governments should be and how they will exercise power, to define our communities, and to exercise jurisdiction over our territories. . . . However, the realization and implementation of that inherent right is much more complex. . . . It is neither a continuation of the current process of devolution nor a divestiture of fiscal responsibility by the federal and provincial governments. Instead it involves negotiation and cooperation between the federal, provincial and First Nation governments to effect the jurisdictional transfer. This process will begin with the transfer of jurisdiction over fire services, education, and capital management but will extend in the medium term to areas such as child welfare and justice, and in the longer term to other areas as defined by the First Nation communities. As powers are transferred, First Nations' governing structures will be adapted to serve the needs of communities.[20]

The process would take three years under the proposed plan.

A crucial component of the initiative is support at the community level. This is not an elite-dominated process. As the comprehensive discussion paper states, "this endeavour will succeed or fail depending on the support of First Nations people themselves. Lessons from the past must be learned and the wisdom applied. The people must be involved throughout the process or it will fail. They must be informed and they must be heard."[21] An extensive process of community consultation is planned with the initiative. If there is substantial opposition or limited support for the project, dismantling will not proceed.

The dismantling initiative has received some significant criticism. In his address to the Opaskwayak Assembly, the grand chief of the Assembly of First Nations observed that pilot projects like this one in Manitoba were inconsistent with the concept of an inherent right to self-government since they entailed legislative, not constitutional, recognition of the powers of First Nations' governments. The talks endangered the bilateral relationship between the federal government and First Nations by proposing to involve the provinces at a later date. At the community level, concern was expressed over the structures that would replace Indian Affairs, the uncertainty of the initiative, and the level of resources. Some trepidation has been expressed that the transfer of powers would be limited to administrative arrangements as in the past rather than policy and program design and initiation.[22] The province has expressed concern that the federal government would use this process to off-load expenses and that the First Nations are not sufficiently prepared for jurisdictional transfers.[23] Whether these concerns will be borne out remains to be seen. What is significant is that a dialogue has begun for the achievement of First Nation government.

CONCLUSION

Since the election of the Liberal government in the fall of 1993, there has been a flurry of activity involving Aboriginal issues and policy. The politics and governing instruments are in a period of flux. Many of the proposed changes have far-reaching implications for Aboriginal peoples and the Canadian population generally. If a new relationship is forged between the federal government and the First Nations, Métis, and Inuit populations, the political and governing practices of Canada will be fundamentally altered.

Why is this change being proposed at the current time? First, political events in Canada over the past decade have created an environment conducive to change. The failed constitutional negotiations, the stand-off at Oka, the increasing awareness of the failure of past policies to ameliorate the living conditions of Aboriginal peoples, and an increasing international sensitivity to the concerns of indigenous populations have all contributed to a perception that something must be done. These events led to the Conservative government's creation of the Royal Commission on Aboriginal Peoples. In turn, the creation and activity of the royal commission has increased awareness of Aboriginal issues. Canadians recognize that change is needed now.

Second, the election of the Liberals was timely. The election of prominent Aboriginal spokespersons such as Elijah Harper and Ethel Blondin-Andrew enhanced awareness, within the party, about Aboriginal issues. This consciousness was reinforced by the personal commitment of the prime minister, and ministers like Ron Irwin and Lloyd Axworthy, to

Aboriginal issues. Third, the Liberals realized that an opportunity existed to expand their voter base. With the decline of the NDP, the Liberals saw the prospects for securing the Aboriginal and northern vote. Indeed, this foresight was evident in the election-platform declaration that the Liberals were positioning themselves to become the party of Aboriginal peoples.[24]

Third, and most significantly, the Aboriginal population is pressing for change. The constitutional negotiations witnessed a rise in activity among Aboriginal organizations at the national level. The Aboriginal leadership is effectively agitating for more autonomy and better conditions for their peoples. Higher education and political participation levels have enhanced the ability of Aboriginal people to effect change and to make themselves heard. The high degree of political mobilization among this segment of the population means that their issues are likely to receive substantial attention in the future. They can no longer be ignored or deferred by policy makers.

Will the Liberal agenda be achieved? It is too early to tell. However, one conclusion is possible. A new relationship is being forged between Aboriginal peoples and the federal government, one that respects the right of Aboriginal communities to govern themselves. The inherent-right talks provide a theoretical foundation to this relationship. The community-based self-government negotiations provide an opportunity to First Nations at the grassroots level to secure immediate changes in the delivery of programs and services. The pilot project to dismantle Indian Affairs and recognize First Nations' governments in Manitoba anticipates practical implementation of the inherent right to self-government. Each of these initiatives faces substantial obstacles and challenges. But even if these specific initiatives fail, the momentum toward change is unlikely to be lost. The road to self-government is not an easy one, but there is no turning back.

NOTES

[1] Unless otherwise specified, all statistics included in this section of the paper are drawn from the 1991 census data compiled by Statistics Canada.

[2] Aboriginal Council of Winnipeg, "Proposal for Partnership on Urban Aboriginal Self-Government," Winnipeg, 1992, 5–6. The significantly higher estimates of the total Aboriginal urban population may be due to the unwillingness of some residents to be included in the census and the omission of some urban pockets from the census count.

[3] Liberal Party of Canada, *Creating Opportunity: The Liberal Plan for Canada* (Ottawa: Liberal Party of Canada, 1993), 96.

[4] Liberal Party of Canada, News Release, 8 Oct. 1993.

[5] Liberal Party, *Creating Opportunity,* 97. The Liberal view here approximates the erroneous justification that Aboriginal peoples are entitled to self-government because they have belonged to a disadvantaged racial minority. For a discussion of the dangers in accepting this view, see Paul L.A.H. Chartrand, "Aboriginal Self-Government: The Two Sides of Legitimacy" in *How Ottawa Spends 1993–1994,* ed. Susan Phillips (Ottawa: Carleton University Press, 1993), 234.

[6] Liberal Party, *Creating Opportunity,* 98.

[7] Liberal Party of Canada, News Release, "Chrétien Calls for New Partnership with Aboriginal Peoples as He Unveils Aboriginal Platform," 8 Oct. 1994.

[8] Canada, Speech from the Throne to Open The First Session, Thirty-Fifth Parliament of Canada (Ottawa, 8 Jan. 1994). The Speech read, "The Government will forge a new partnership with Aboriginal peoples particularly in respect of the implementation of the inherent right of self-government."

[9] Provided through the Manitoba Métis Federation and endorsed by the Métis National Council, May 1994.

[10] Assembly of First Nations, "Submission to the Special Joint Committee on a Renewed Canada," Ottawa, 10 Feb. 1992.

[11] Chartrand, "Aboriginal Self-Government," 239.

[12] Indian Affairs and Northern Development, "Backgrounder: Inherent Right of Self-Government," Ottawa, 19 Jan. 1994, 1.

[13] Office of the Minister of Indian Affairs, News Release, 30 March 1994.

[14] The Métis slightly qualified this definition to accord with their heritage.

[15] Assembly of First Nations, "Submission to the Special Joint Committee," 6–7.

[16] According to Elections Canada, "Federal Referendum: Unofficial Results in Specific Aboriginal Communities" (28 Oct. 1992), the average "No" vote among aboriginal people across the nation was 62.1 percent. In Manitoba, a reported 81.6 percent of the population on reserves voted against the accord. The reaction in Manitoba was due, in large part, to an October resolution passed by the Assembly of Manitoba Chiefs urging the First Nations to boycott the referendum or, if members chose to exercise their franchise, to vote against the agreement.

[17] The Honourable Ronald A. Irwin, Minister of Indian Affairs and Northern Development, "Talking Points to the House of Commons Standing Committee on Aboriginal Affairs and Northern Development" (Ottawa: Indian and Northern Affairs Canada, 16 March 1994), 3.

[18] As quoted in Rheal Seguin, "Native Self-Rule Talks Plunged into Disarray," *Globe and Mail,* 19 May 1994, Al.

[19] *Towards Manitoba First Nations' Governments: The Dismantling of Indian Affairs, the Transfer of Jurisdictions and the Recognition of First Nations' Governments,* paper prepared for the AMC by Don Goodwin (Winnipeg: AMC, 14 March 1994), iv.

[20] Grand Chief Phil Fontaine, Letter to the Honourable Gary Filmon, Premier of Manitoba, 10 May 1994.

[21] *Towards Manitoba First Nations' Governments,* iv.

[22] These concerns were expressed by community representatives at the Opaskwayak Special Assembly and throughout the negotiations with Indian Affairs officials.

[23] Premier Filmon, CJOB radio, Winnipeg, 22 and 29 April 1994.
[24] Liberal Party, "Chrétien Calls for New Partnership."

SUGGESTED READING

Boldt, Menno. *Surviving As Indians: The Challenge of Self-Government.* Toronto: University of Toronto Press, 1993.
This book analyzes self-government from a First Nation perspective.

Brock, Kathy L. "Consensual Politics: Political Leadership in the Aboriginal Community." In *Leaders and Leadership in Canada.* Ed. Maureen Mancuso, Richard G. Price, and Ronald Wagenberg. Toronto: Oxford University Press, 1994.
A discussion of the adaptation of traditional Aboriginal decision making, based on consensus, to contemporary political constraints in the Northwest Territories legislature and the Assembly of First Nations.

Cassidy, Frank, ed. *Aboriginal Self-Determination.* Halifax: Institute for Research on Public Policy, 1991.
A collection of essays reviewing the concept and implementation of Aboriginal self-government from academic, government, and Aboriginal perspectives.

Chartrand, Paul L.A.H. "Aboriginal Self-Government: The Two Sides of Legitimacy." In *How Ottawa Spends 1993–1994: A More Democratic Canada . . . ?* Ed. Susan Phillips. Ottawa: Carleton University Press, 1993.
An excellent analysis of the central assumptions upon which legitimate and enduring Aboriginal self-government must be founded.

Fleras, Augie, and Jean Leonard Elliott. *The Nations Within: Aboriginal–State Relations in Canada, the United States, and New Zealand.* Toronto: Oxford University Press, 1992.
An examination of the rise of the commitment to Aboriginal self-determination in the three nations, with a particular focus on Canada.

Mawhiney, Anne-Marie, ed. *Rebirth: Political, Economic and Social Development in First Nations.* Toronto: Dundurn Press, 1993.
A collection of papers highlighting the ways in which First Nations are acting on self-government in the areas of political, social, and economic development.

Grace Skogstad
Joy Esberey

ORGANIZED
INTERESTS

I t's that time again! Red, blue, orange, and green posters vie with real-
tors' signs on lawns and vacant lots. Strangers are anxious to shake your
hand at bus stops and in shopping malls. An election is under way, and
democracy in Canada is alive and well—or is it? On a side street,
placard-carrying citizens walk up and down outside an abortion
clinic. Canada Post delivers another sack of petitioning letters to a
minister's office. Consultants in a public affairs company supply well-
prepared analyses of forthcoming policy proposals to clients. A professional lobbyist makes a luncheon date with a junior bureaucrat. A senior
civil servant finishes a "consultation" session with an important chief
executive officer. Which is the real world of democracy?

THE LEGITIMACY OF INTEREST-GROUP ACTIVITY

A lthough interest groups have always been a part of the Canadian political system, their proliferation in the period following the Second
World War has heightened concerns about their appropriateness. The
legitimacy of individuals or firms coming together in groups to press their
concerns and interests on governments is somewhat suspect largely because
democracy in Western industrialized countries developed in association
with a specific form of representative activity. This form includes a geographically based right to vote and a monopoly over the decision-making
process by the elected representatives of the people. Of the variety of channels that link citizens to their rulers in advanced industrial democracies,
only the electoral process has unquestioned legitimacy. Within this framework, ideologically coherent, disciplined parties were accepted because they
made the electorally based legislative process more efficient.

A number of factors and developments have served to undermine this link between democratic government, on the one hand, and political parties and territorially based representatives, on the other. First, the geographically stable, economically integrated local communities on which representative democracy has been based are no longer the norm. In today's sprawling rural ridings and commuter-based urban areas, people within the same geographical constituency no longer share an identity of interests. Territorially based loyalties are everywhere being replaced by other identifications rooted in the group characteristics of occupation, language, ethnicity, or shared commitments to particular issues. As our society has become more pluralist, elected representatives are less and less able to represent the diverse interests of their constituents, and these same constituents are more and more likely to join with like-minded Canadians to form organizational links that cross constituency boundaries.

Second, parties no longer appear to be fulfilling their role in furthering representative democracy in Canada. With the exception of occasions like leadership conventions and elections, when individuals are actively recruited and encouraged to play a role, political parties are largely peripheral to most people's lives. Party financing is not dependent upon individual membership fees; most funds come from the taxpayer via the Election Expenses Act or corporate donors. The failure of parties to distinguish themselves in terms of principle, and the associated rise of brokerage parties (the goal of which is to aggregate a variety of interests), may have reinforced the need for group activity. Further, long periods of one-party dominance may have weakened the perceived possibility of changing policy through the electoral process and encouraged the politics of pressure.

The legitimacy of organized interests can be defended on grounds other than the decline of political parties in popular esteem. First, interest-group activity can be seen to be rooted in the basic democratic rights of freedom of association and freedom of expression.[1] Second, the right of groups to advocate or petition is deeply rooted in our tradition,[2] originating in the historical British struggle for the "redress of grievance." Together these two themes are encapsulated in the Madisonian doctrine in the United States that the "autonomous expression of interests" through freely organized groups is "a hallmark of liberal democracy."[3]

Organized interests can also be defended as necessary to meet the needs of modern interventionist government. The creation of the welfare state in the postwar period and the intervention of governments in the marketplace created a need for expertise that could only partially be met by increasing the size of the public service and by creating independent advisory bodies like the Economic Council of Canada. Much of the knowledge required for modern government is not in the public realm, but with private interests that relay this technical information to governments by being drawn directly into the policy-making process.

Although widespread disillusionment with the electoral process can help to justify a role for organized interests in the political process, there remains uneasiness with the extent to which interest groups are an appropriate supplement to or substitute for political parties and elected representatives. The concerns are threefold. The first is that the substitution of the group for the elected representative diminishes the influence of the individual Canadian, replacing the MP as an intermediary on behalf of individual constituents. The reality, of course, as we have seen in chapter 11, is that individual MPs have very little influence in the political system.

The second concern is that, while MPs are expected to promote the public good and the national interest, interest groups by definition promote specialist interests, likely at the expense of the public interest or good. This concern is weakened by the very real difficulty elected representatives have in identifying just what constitutes the public interest. If it is only the sum of special interests, then it is difficult to deny groups a role in public policy formation. If the interests of the whole community are greater than the sum of particular interests, then allowing public officials to define this holistic interest smacks of elitism. This difficulty in defining the public interest is exacerbated by the distortion that our electoral system creates between the wishes of individual citizens expressed in the popular vote and the translation of these wishes into parliamentary seats.[4]

The third source of uneasiness with an enhanced role for interest groups, and thus with their legitimacy, rests on the claim that the processes that form interest groups are not characterized by the same openness and widespread access as the legislative and electoral processes. If "it is not enough that democracy exists, [but] must be seen to exist," then interest-group activity is marred by the fact that much of it is shielded from public view by the same secrecy that is characteristic of the Canadian executive process. Indeed, in sharp contrast to the public visibility of the behaviour of political parties during elections and of elected representatives in the House of Commons, interest-group influence is usually contingent upon groups accepting the confidentiality of government–group discussions and being willing and able to engage in "quiet, behind the scenes consultations."[5] In this closed environment, it is not difficult for the public to suspect that deals are being made and special interests are being substituted for the public interest.

By far the greatest controversy concerning interest-group activity centres on the question of providing equal access for all interests. Diametrically
opposite views prevail here. On the one hand, a president of the Retail
Council of Canada has argued that "almost every special interest group,
be they disabled, the poor, the native people, have formed their own pressure groups" and "legislators and civil servants pay at least as much attention to these groups as to the older established lobbies of business and
labour."[6] On the other hand, a feminist activist has argued that although
groups representing women, labour, minorities, and the unemployed
exist, they are "virtually ignored."[7]

To help settle the dispute as to whether all interests enjoy the same
opportunity to affect government policy, it is useful to note that before
interests can influence policy, they must first be organized. Some interests
face greater obstacles to organizing collectively than do others. Where
potential group members who share common concerns are divided on
other grounds—by geography, ideology, ethnicity, or language, for
example—their mobilization within one association will be more difficult.
Consumers spread out across the country find it difficult to build cohe-
sive organizations as do Nova Scotia's individualistic fishers, who are
divided by the species they catch, the waters they fish (inshore, nearshore,
offshore), and their partisan attachments.[8] By contrast, group formation
is much easier where potential members are concentrated geographically
or economically, or united by a common history, ethnicity, or language. Thus,
the communal traits and historical legacy that farmers in Quebec share have
allowed them to build a very strong farm organization that wields considerable political influence. Likewise, the significant economic concentration and vertical integration among processors of forestry products
have combined with the geographic concentration of the industry to foster very strong industry associations.[9]

Governments have sometimes actively sponsored the formation of groups
that have lacked the resources or motivation to organize themselves; groups
representing the poor, women, official language minority groups, and East
Coast fishers are all examples. These government-sponsored groups, however, do not enjoy the same degree of autonomy and security as do groups
with independent financing. Thus, the National Action Committee on the
Status of Women, a recipient of government operational grants since the implementation of the *Report of the Royal Commission on the Status of Women* in
1973, had its funding slashed by the Mulroney government in 1989, after it
had campaigned strenuously against the Progressive Conservative Party's
Free Trade Agreement with the United States.

Besides providing core funding, governments can assist group organization by legislating compulsory membership in organizations. When it incorporated the Canadian Bankers' Association (CBA) in 1900, the Canadian government required all Canadian banks to belong to the CBA and, in doing so, enabled the bankers to build one of the most effective interest groups in Canada.[10] Similarly, the Quebec government has empowered the Quebec farmers' association, the Union des producteurs agricoles, with a legal mandate to represent Quebec farmers and to require all farmers to pay membership dues to it. Such government initiatives have enabled these groups to build organizations that are much more autonomous than are those that are dependent upon governments for their core funding.

The issue of disparities in the ability of interests to organize and subsequently influence public policy is at the heart of the debates about the appropriate role of organized interests in the political system. Relevant to this debate is the distinction between groups that engage in policy advocacy or lobbying, and groups that can be said to participate in policy making in terms of either formulating or implementing public policies.[11] The two activities reflect the different roles that interest groups play in policy communities.

POLICY ADVOCACY AND POLICY PARTICIPATION

The idea of an autonomous government policy-making process and an independent interest-group system, with the latter attempting to influence the former from the outside, is not an accurate picture of the policy system in practice. A more appropriate recognition of the interconnection of the two systems is captured by the concept of a *policy community*.[12] A policy community includes "all actors or potential actors with a direct or indirect interest in the policy area or function who share a common 'policy focus' and who, with varying degrees of influence, shape policy outcomes over the long run."[13] Members of a policy community share a "concern with one area of the policy problem, interaction with each other's ideas, proposals, and research, . . . and know each other well personally."[14] Thus, policy community members are internally integrated and share certain beliefs and values to a lesser or greater degree.

A policy community subdivides into two segments: the *sub-government* and the *attentive public*.[15] The sub-government consists of the decision makers; the attentive public comprises those who follow and attempt to influence policy but do not participate in policy making on a regular basis.

Thus, the farm policy community concerned with dairy policy would include (1) the sub-government of public officials, in the federal and provincial agriculture departments and in government agencies, who, along with dairy producers and processors, have been mandated to devise and implement dairy policy; and (2) the consumer associations and other interested onlookers in the attentive public.

Government agencies or departments will virtually always be part of the sub-government that makes policy in a given policy area. Interest groups may or may not be. A major distinction can be drawn between groups that remain part of the attentive public and those that form part of the sub-government. Groups that are part of the attentive public approach public decision makers as lobbyists and policy advocates from the outside, while those that are part of the sub-government can be said to be participants inside decision-making circles. The line between advocacy and participation is not an easy one to draw, as groups are often invited to serve on advisory bodies only to have their advice go unheeded. Generally speaking, however, *policy advocacy* entails attempting to influence what will or will not be a matter of public policy, the content of the policies being made, and the manner in which policies are implemented or put into effect. By contrast, *policy participation* entails the direct participation of interest groups in the process through which policy is formulated or implemented.[16] Groups may be policy advocates at one time and on one issue, and policy participants at another time and on another issue. Although this cleavage between groups that are part of the sub-government and those that are not is the most fundamental division among groups, groups in the attentive public will also vary in terms of their degree of influence on public policy.

Whether lobbying public officials from outside government circles or sitting alongside decision makers, groups will be influential to the extent to which they are able to have input into the three stages of the policy process. These are setting the agenda—what will or will not be a matter of public policy (often a pre-parliamentary stage); determining the content of public policies (a stage at which Parliament's ratification is normally necessary); and implementing and enforcing public policies (a post-parliamentary stage). Influence at each of these three stages requires that groups possess information: policy-process information, policy-specific information, and political-impact knowledge. [17]

Policy-process information relates to knowledge of how the system works, which is important for timing (the *when*) and targeting (the *whom*).[18] From the viewpoint of interest groups, determining the agenda entails one of two things: trying to get issues onto the political agenda or, alternatively, ensuring that issues that could prejudice the group's interests are kept off the agenda. Generally speaking, the efforts of groups in the attentive public will be directed toward trying to get issues onto the political agenda; groups that are part of the sub-government will be more interested in ensuring that the status quo prevails. To that end, they are likely to spend more time trying to keep issues that could disrupt the status quo out of the public arena.

How do issues and policies get onto the political agenda? Conversely, why are some issues, including important problems, kept off the public agenda? While these questions admit no easy answer, it would appear to be more difficult to get issues into the public arena than to keep them out. In part, this is because in liberal democracies solutions to problems will be assumed to lie in the private sector. Moreover, elected politicians have a number of ways of shelving or undermining issues that do not accord with their own priorities. They can offer symbolic responses that put the issue on the back burner by sending it off into the wilderness of committees of inquiry, research studies, or consultative processes. However, it is increasingly difficult for officials to keep issues off the public agenda, as groups have become skilled at enlisting the support of the mass media, and changes to committees of the House of Commons have made Parliament a more effective forum to bring group concerns front and centre.

The obstacles to injecting items onto the public agenda highlight the advantage that accrues to groups who can find a sympathetic hearing for their proposals among elected or appointed officials. This means that groups whose own goals coincide with those of public officials are likely to be more effective. But because only a finite number of issues— certainly not more than a handful—will directly engage the attention of elected politicians, the advantage clearly lies with groups that are served by the status quo. Their antennae must be alert to any policy proposals brewing in the attentive public or sub-government that would disrupt the status quo by removing or changing beneficial policies. Probably even more so than for groups seeking to introduce policy change, such groups require process knowledge—information about all the steps and stages of the policy process, each of which provides a point where proposals can be stopped, reversed, delayed, or speeded up.

Although the Canadian policy process is more structured and hierarchical than that in the United States—where there are multiple points of access and opportunities for "decisions to be made and unmade at many different locations"[19]—it, too, places considerable strain on groups' resources. Time and energy must be spent monitoring the progress of issues through the system. The key actors vary depending upon the policy issue under consideration and upon the policy community. Andrew Roman[20] suggests that the policy initiators are found deep in the bowels of the public service; they are the "privates" and "corporals" at the lower end of the public service pay scale. William Stanbury agrees, advising interest groups "to plant the seed of [their] own ideas very early in the process" since "most new ideas begin very deep in the civil service machine."[21] On the other hand, James Gillies,[22] a former cabinet minister, suggests that on a limited number of significant issues when a minister and cabinet collectively are determined to follow a particular line of action, the influence of even the most senior departmental public servants is limited. The point is that no one policy process is necessarily like another. Although public servants, the cabinet, members of Parliament, other interest groups, the media, and the public are generally members of most policy communities, how and when they affect policy proposals will differ from issue to issue. Thus, policy-process knowledge will need to be rather sophisticated.

Alarmed in the mid-1970s with their ignorance of the government's agenda and frustrated at being surprised with issues that they believed they should have foreseen and forestalled,[23] business and professional groups have since taken a number of measures to enhance the sophistication of their process knowledge. One route has been to hire a professional lobbyist or public affairs consultant company. Such companies proliferated in the 1980s when they were used by groups to provide "an early warning system" about forthcoming government policies.[24] The costliness of such consultants—retainers of $1500 to $4000 or more a month plus expenses were the going rates in 1989 for elite consultants[25]—rules them out for all but those groups with considerable financial resources. A more frequent route taken by groups, especially business groups, to strengthen their informational needs has been to restructure their organization to create government affairs divisions staffed by individuals whose sole responsibility is to monitor governments and media sources. Smaller groups may be reduced to culling such newsheets as *The Public Sector*, the Southam newsletter on key government activity affecting business and industry.

Influencing the content of public policy requires two additional types of information: policy-specific expertise and political-impact knowledge. *Policy-specific expertise* is normally technical in nature and includes information about the likely economic, structural, and other consequences of suggested policy options. Groups must be able to present specific, highly detailed proposals in a language comprehensible to public officials. *Political-impact knowledge* relates to the political costs and benefits of various policy proposals. Elected officials are especially concerned about the votes that will be gained or lost if a group's proposal is acted upon, and they need assurance that the reaction of the wider public will be favourable.[26] Both kinds of information are critical to group input into the formulation of government policy and are equally significant at the stage of policy implementation. With the legislature delegating more and more of the details of legislation—the regulations through which it is implemented—to the bureaucracy, groups with considerable expertise can play a constructive role advising the administration of possible difficulties and resistance, and sometimes participating in the policy delivery process. That same policy expertise can allow groups to delay, divert, and obstruct programs.

THE ORGANIZATIONAL DEVELOPMENT OF GROUPS

What sorts of interest groups are best able to obtain these various kinds of information essential to successful policy advocacy and policy participation? The advantage would appear to go to those groups that are organizationally developed[27] or institutionalized.[28] Organizationally developed associations possess a permanent structure that allows them to (1) generate the policy-specific and political-impact information required by governments and employ staff to lobby government officials full time; (2) communicate effectively with members so as to build the cohesion necessary for political mobilization; (3) represent members' diverse interests by informing them of developments and getting their feedback; and (4) build favourable relations with the public. All these capacities are necessary for effective lobbying. Participation in policy making normally requires, as well, that the interest group have a representational monopoly—that is, that it be the only group recognized by potential members and government alike to speak on behalf of a particular interest. Governments will normally require the latter condition in order to avoid the allegations of bias from excluded groups and the political costs that will surely ensue if participant groups are not fully representative of the particular interest.

Organizations that represent business interests are among the best developed or most institutionalized, as the Canadian Bankers' Association (CBA) illustrates. The CBA employs about a hundred people who provide expertise on financial affairs and financial institutions, engage in public relations, maintain close contacts with government officials in Ottawa and in the provincial capitals, and interact closely with the individual bank members. It can be ready on short notice to provide the government with the political and technical information needed to devise banking policy, and it can assure government that, as the sole organization that represents Canada's banks, its proposals have the support of the Canadian banking community. The consequence is that the CBA has been drawn into the sub-government that devises and administers many policies of significance to the financial community.[29]

A sharp contrast can be drawn between the organizational development of the CBA and that of most non-business groups. Take, for example, the groups that seek to represent the interests of social welfare recipients. There are several associations that represent social welfare recipients, including the National Anti-Poverty Organization, the National Council of Welfare, the Canadian Council on Social Development, and a host of other consumer groups that are concerned with additional issues. In contrast to the financial security and autonomy that the CBA enjoys, these organizations are all dependent upon the Canadian government for their funding. Moreover, none of them has sufficient staff resources to generate the expert information necessary for significant input into government policy. Their differences hamper any efforts to mount a united campaign before government. As a result of this disunity and the groups' limited capacity to represent the poor, social welfare groups have individually and collectively been politically ineffective in the late 1980s and early 1990s in thwarting the federal government's agenda for social welfare reform.[30]

THE IMPACT OF GOVERNMENT STRUCTURE ON GROUPS

We have already noted a number of ways in which the organization of the government has an impact on groups. The dispersal of authority within the executive has rendered more difficult the task of interest groups attempting to trace the course of a proposed bill or policy through the cabinet structures and the bureaucracy. Paul Pross[31] argues that despite the monitoring costs this diffusion creates, it is not without benefits for groups. The dispersion of authority among bureaucrats places them in competition with one another, he argues, and one way in which they compete to secure approval for their policies is by forging links with client groups affected by these policies. Pross argues that officials thus seek the support of interest groups and draw them more closely into the policy community as a way of legitimizing policy initiatives to other (competitive) officials.

The dispersion of authority among officials at the national level is compounded by the federal system, which, as chapter 8 describes, divides authority between the two levels of government. Fragmented authority has varying effects for groups and governments.[32] For governments, divided jurisdiction and dispersed bureaucratic authority undermine their ability to devise co-ordinated and coherent policies. This is likely to be especially problematic when governments are faced with well-financed organizations with goals of their own. In such circumstances, fragmented authorities will be highly vulnerable to group pressure. For groups, the effects of dispersed authority are less clear. The fragmentation of authority across governments and within governments may create multiple veto points at which pressure can be placed to block policies. Conversely, groups unable to secure support for their policies at one level of government may be given a second "kick at the can" if they can bring onside the other level of government and persuade it to pursue its goals. On the other hand, federalism may make it more difficult for regionally dispersed interests to build strong national organizations, and it increases lobbying costs when both levels of government must be targeted.

In short, the influence of interest groups is significantly affected not only by characteristics of the groups themselves but, equally, by characteristics of the governments with which they interact. How authority is organized within the political system—within governments and across the levels of government—affects the ability of groups to realize their goals. This can be illustrated by examining two policy communities in action. The first example demonstrates how business interests were challenged, but ultimately prevailed, when a relatively closed policy community was opened to allow access to new actors. The second example reveals the dynamic and fluid nature of interest-group structures and policy communities in the late twentieth century, as a new government institution, the Supreme Court of Canada, has become an important target of interest-group activity.

INTEREST GROUPS IN ACTION

Finance is at the heart of policy making, and the use of the tax system as a tool for achieving important national objectives puts it at the heart of the common-good/special-interest debate. In the same way, control over finance is at the heart of democracy and the major vehicle of responsible government in our political system. A government unable to win legislative support for its budget has no option but to resign. The drama of resignation and the annual ritual surrounding budget night give a false impression of tax policy making. It is more accurately seen as an ongoing process adjusted by specific amendments that are treated calmly and with little media attention—an ideal situation for interest-group activity. The very complex and technical nature of tax policy also lends itself to being dealt with through a process of quiet negotiation with interest groups.

The tax policy community has been described as "a close knit system of individual participants who are collectively responsible for the federal government's concern in taxation."[33] At the core, in the sub-government, are politicians and public servants, in an approximate ratio of 1:5. Business groups and experts in the field (the tax professionals—lawyers, accountants, investment specialists) also wield considerable influence in this policy process. The attentive public is relatively small, especially among the media and general public, reflecting the widespread belief that tax increases are inevitable and that there is little that can be done about them. When tax issues break out of this closed policy community into the limelight, we get a brief insight into the way interest groups participate in this policy arena. At the same time, we must emphasize that the very visibility of these examples underlines their atypical nature.

In the early 1960s, elements in the business sector put pressure on the Diefenbaker government to undertake tax reforms directed at relieving the burden on business. The government responded by creating a royal commission. Such commissions have served more as a symbolic response than as a major source of policy initiatives, so it was not surprising that business groups chose not to put their case to the Carter Commission.[34] They were already well represented in the tax community, and the commission chair was a respected figure in the business world. In these circumstances, inaction seemed an appropriate response, but it ignored the fact that the royal commission introduced a new, external actor to the policy field. When the Carter Commission delivered a report calling for radical changes that would have imposed a greater tax burden on selected industries, the process took on a new complexion. The issue of tax reform was now on the public agenda, and it would be difficult to confine it to the closed world of the tax policy community.

Even in these circumstances, it was difficult for policy advocates without status in the community to effect change. The situation was further complicated by an election that brought to power the Pearson Liberal government, which found itself presented with a set of solutions "that it hadn't asked for and would have preferred to avoid altogether."[35] The

Liberals responded with their own stalling tactic—a White Paper presented by Finance Minister Edgar Benson and another round of opinion-gathering on it. The mining industry, which had already gone public in a media-based "orchestrated campaign of alarm," was very active in the parliamentary committee's public hearings on the issue.[36] It was also able to forge a close alliance with provincial premiers and members of Parliament with an interest in the issue. Although the proposed reforms would have indirectly benefited the general taxpayer, there was no strong coalition of interests to sustain the pressure for reform. In contrast, "the business and financial interests, who had a great deal at stake, were far more adept at using the political system to their own advantage . . . [and] with their vast resources, they simply dominated the debate. . . . They used every avenue available to them."[37]

A major tactic used by the mining industry to build public and government support for their renunciation of the government's tax proposals was to threaten a capital strike (a refusal to invest), and to warn of the ensuing loss of jobs. With the electorate thus onside, provincial governments were quick to follow, and eventually so was the federal government, which had, in any event, not been totally committed to reform. The case demonstrates the privileged position that business enjoys in liberal democracies. As long as governments look to business to create the employment and economic growth that are necessary for re-election, governments will be in a weak bargaining position vis-à-vis business.[38] In the foregoing case, the government was able to save face when the mining sector agreed to incremental changes at subsequent phases of tax reform. But the case also demonstrates how the federal system of Canada can be exploited by groups that can use the two-tiered system of government to form alliances with provincial governments in order to pressure the federal government.

Before we leave the tax field, we should briefly consider a case that appears to contradict the foregoing view that interest groups are most effective when they participate in the policy process as part of the sub-government within the policy community. In his May 1985 budget speech, Finance Minister Michael Wilson announced that the government was limiting increases in seniors' pensions to 3 percent below the rate of inflation. In an about-face five weeks later, the finance minister reinstated fully indexed pensions for seniors.[39] The ability of "grey power" groups, like the National Pensioners and Senior Citizens Federation, to enlist the media and parliamentary support that proved effective in achieving this change suggests their success as policy advocates. However, the outcome can as readily be explained by factors external to grey power groups. One factor important to the finance minister's reversal was Prime Minister Mulroney's sensitivity to his low credibility during his first term in office. The minister of finance's proposal directly contradicted Mulroney's statement during the 1984 election campaign that universal and fully indexed pensions were a "sacred trust."[40] This case demonstrates the importance of groups being accepted as legitimate and integrated members of the policy community, able to influence decisions as they are being made and not forced to mount rearguard actions at the eleventh hour.

ORGANIZED INTERESTS AND THE SUPREME COURT

The entrenchment of the Charter of Rights and Freedoms in the Constitution Act, 1982, provided organized interests with a new target. Since that time, the Supreme Court's decisions with respect to national defence, minority language, trade union activity, and abortion have illustrated the new policy role of the court.[41] Here, the Canadian experience would seem to replicate that in the United States and Germany, where entrenched rights and judicial review have existed for some time and where the courts have become an important arena of interest-group activity.

The decision that the Supreme Court of Canada rendered in *Morgentaler v. The Queen* in January 1988, which struck down Canada's abortion law as a violation of the Charter of Rights, had been preceded by considerable interest-group activity. Pro-choice groups had fought hard to get the case before the Supreme Court, where their interventions were countered by groups representing the anti-abortion position. The struggle over this issue prompted the formation of umbrella organizations on both sides (Canadian Abortion Rights Action League, Coalition for Reproductive Choice, Campaign Life) to co-ordinate the activity of many existing women's, civil libertarian, religious, and other groups—a move we have described earlier as one toward greater organizational development.

The *Morgentaler* case[42] allows speculation as to the differing opportunities and constraints that the legal process, as compared to the bureaucratic-legislative process, presents to group activity. In contrast to the scope for influence that the political process provides for groups that can win hearts and minds, the legal process is more rational. Court cases, even jury trials, are not popularity contests. Cases are won or lost on the legal merits of the case. Further, the capacity of the legal system to respond to group goals is essentially negative: the court strikes down an existing statute, leaving a vacuum that it cannot fill. While the absence of a law can meet the goal of a group seeking to have the law removed (as in the *Morgentaler* case), courts are less useful forums for groups seeking to fill a policy vacuum.

The legal system affords a further limitation. As long as our courts hold that groups do not have "standing," an interest group wishing to achieve policy goals through the courts must act through a complainant. The aims, strategies, tactics, and perceptions of the complainant can diverge from those of the group. The complainant can therefore be an asset or a liability; if the latter, the cause as a whole may be undermined. Moreover, the court's verdict will generally apply only to the specific case of the specific individual in the specific circumstances. The case will establish a precedent and have an indirect effect on any subsequent actions, but the decision is neither retroactive nor automatically applied to all similar cases unless the law itself is declared invalid—a much rarer event than is generally believed.

What, then, is the value of using the judicial system to pursue group aims? The major value of legal action would seem to be that of agenda setting. Judicial decisions can force politicians to act in a situation in which they prefer inaction. This would seem to be a primary objective of the interest group LEAF (Women's Legal Education and Action Fund), which has brought before the courts carefully selected cases that test the meaning of the equality sections in the Charter. However, to the extent that judicial decisions force issues back into political channels—as the *Morgentaler* decision did—groups that are successful before the courts cannot count on prevailing in the political arena. In the case of abortion, the technical expertise required for drafting legislation and regulations means that the medical and legal professions are more likely to be consulted than either the pro-choice or anti-abortion groups. Once the issue moves into the legislative forum, the victory will go to those groups best able to deploy their resources (membership cohesion and conviction, finances, organizational structure) to maximize their political clout. Once again, the vulnerability of groups like LEAF, which are highly dependent upon government funding, is exposed.

CONCLUSION

The legitimizing of interest-group activity in Canada has been an incremental process. We moved from regarding interest groups as a "hidden," if not "evil," empire to accepting their legitimacy and even desirability. The latter view is captured by the preamble to the Lobbyists Registration Act proclaimed in June 1989:

> WHEREAS free and open access to government is an important mat-
> ter of public interest;
> AND WHEREAS lobbying public office holders is legitimate activity;
> AND WHEREAS it is desirable that public office holders and the pub-
> lic be able to know who is attempting to influence . . .
> NOW THEREFORE, Her Majesty, by and with the advice and
> consent of the Senate and House of Commons of Canada enacts
> as follows: . . .

The links between the "whereas" clauses are not self-justifying. The fact
that free and open access is important is a separate issue from the wider
question of how interest groups should be integrated into the political
and policy-making process. We have mentioned earlier that the Canadian
political system is based on representative and responsible government, and
both these aspects need to be considered in the case of interest-group
activity.

The election process provides a vehicle by which we can hold our representatives in the legislature and in government responsible for their
actions or inaction. How can we hold interest groups to account for their
contributions to policy making? If we are dissatisfied with a tax reform
proposal, we can (in theory) change the political actors in the policy community, but if the other actors in the sub-government remain unchanged,
what have we achieved? A related question concerns the degree to which
interest-group spokespersons themselves protect the concerns of their own
members in the face of pressures within the community to compromise.

The situation is no less ambiguous if we restrict ourselves to the representative dimension of interest groups. With a few exceptions,[43] we
have not seriously addressed the imbalance in access that exists between
business groups and other interest groups, including public-interest
groups. Policies that affect all Canadians, such as the GST, are "sold to
us" by public relations firms and advertising agencies, while those that
affect specialized groups, such as investors, are settled after discussion
with representatives of the latter. Failing a development that allows the
affected citizenry to be consulted on tax issues, Linda McQuaig[44] suggests that we must question the appropriateness of allowing special interests to be consulted on the issues that directly affect them. The justification
for such consultation—that it concerns technical issues that must be
ironed out to ensure the effective and efficient application of laws—is
not sufficient to offset the potential conflict-of-interest position in which
groups that participate in such consultations are placed. Even on highly

technical matters, groups are unlikely to be completely value-neutral and objective; they will find it difficult to place the public interest ahead of that of their clients.

The solution seems to lie with more far-ranging reforms that move interest-group activity into the open, public arena. This would remove its clandestine feature and thus defuse much criticism. Whether these changes take the shape of corporatist arrangements that would formalize the role of interest groups as decision makers,[45] or whether the process should remain informal and consultative, is an issue that Canadians will have to decide for themselves. The point to be stressed is that the issue of interest groups in politics did not end when their existence was publicly recognized. The question of the most appropriate structure for democratic interest-group input is yet to be resolved.

NOTES

[1] Roger Scott, ed. *Interest Groups and Public Policy* (Melbourne: Macmillan, 1980), 240.

[2] See "Submission on Bill C-82, The Lobbyists Registration Act," *Canadian Bar Association*, 19 April 1988, 1–2.

[3] Rod Hague and Martin Sarrop, *Comparative Government: An Introduction* (London: Macmillan, 1982), 79.

[4] Alan C. Cairns, "The Electoral System and the Party System in Canada, 1921–1965," *Canadian Journal of Political Science* 1, 1 (1968): 55–80.

[5] Kenneth Kernaghan and David Siegel, *Public Administration in Canada* (Toronto: Methuen, 1987), 410–11.

[6] Alistar McKechan, "Lobbying and Interest Group Representation . . . A Comment" in *The Legislative Process in Canada*, ed. William A. Neilson and James MacPherson (Montreal: Institute for Research on Public Policy, 1978), 221.

[7] Johanna den Hertog, "Lobbying and Interest Group Representation: A Comment" in *The Legislative Process in Canada,* 218.

[8] A. Paul Pross and S. McCorquodale, "The State, Interests, and Policy Making in the East Coast Fishery" in *Policy Communities and Public Policy in Canada*, ed. William D. Coleman and Grace Skogstad (Toronto: Copp Clark Pitman, 1990).

[9] See William D. Coleman, *Business and Politics: A Study of Collective Action* (Montreal: McGill-Queen's University Press, 1988), 210–14; Wyn Grant, "Forestry and Forest Products" in *Policy Communities and Public Policy in Canada*.

[10] William D. Coleman, "The Banking Policy Community and Financial Change" in *Policy Communities and Public Policy in Canada*.

[11] See Coleman, *Business and Politics*, 48–50.

[12] See A. Paul Pross, *Groups, Politics and Public Policy* (Toronto: Oxford University Press, 1986); R.A.W. Rhodes, *The National World of Local Government* (London: Macmillan, 1987); and Stephen Wilks and Maurice Wright, "Conclusion: Comparing

Government–Industry Relations: States, Sectors and Networks" in *Comparative Government–Industry Relations*, ed. Stephen Wilks and Maurice Wright (Oxford: Clarendon Press, 1987), 275–313.

[13] Coleman and Skogstad, eds,. *Policy Communities and Public Policy in Canada*, 19.

[14] John Kingdon, *Agenda, Alternatives and Public Policies* (Boston: Little, Brown, 1984), 123.

[15] Pross, *Group Politics and Public Policy*, 98.

[16] Coleman, *Business and Politics*, 48.

[17] Ibid., 48–49.

[18] W.T. Stanbury, "Lobbying and Interest Group Representation in the Legislative Process" in *The Legislative Process in Canada*, 183–94.

[19] Jeffrey Berry, *The Interest Group Society*, 2nd ed. (Boston: Scott Foresman, 1989), 193.

[20] Andrew Roman, "Lobbying and Interest Group Representation . . . A Comment" in *The Legislative Process in Canada*, 214–15.

[21] Stanbury, "Lobbying and Interest Group Representation," 179.

[22] James Gillies, *Where Business Fails: Business–Government Relations at the Federal Level in Canada* (Montreal: Institute for Research on Public Policy, 1981), 49.

[23] John Sawatsky, *The Insiders: Government, Business and Lobbyists* (Toronto: McClelland & Stewart, 1989), 50–51.

[24] Gillies, *Where Business Fails*, 73.

[25] Sawatsky, *The Insiders*, 50–51.

[26] Coleman, *Business and Politics*, 48–49.

[27] Ibid., ch. 3; Coleman and Skogstad, *Policy Communities and Public Policy*, ch. 1.

[28] Paul Pross, ed., *Pressure Group Behaviour in Canadian Politics* (Toronto: McGraw-Hill Ryerson, 1975), 1–22.

[29] Coleman, "The Banking Policy Community and Financial Change."

[30] Rodney Haddow, "The Poverty Policy Community in Canada's Liberal Welfare State" in *Policy Communities and Public Policy*, ch. 9.

[31] Paul Pross, "Parliamentary Influence and the Diffusion of Power," *Canadian Journal of Political Science* 18, 2 (1985): 235–66.

[32] Hugh G. Thorburn, *Interest Groups in the Canadian Federal System* (Toronto: University of Toronto Press, 1985).

[33] David A. Good, *The Politics of Anticipation: Making Canadian Federal Tax Policy* (Ottawa: School of Public Administration, Carleton University, 1980), 3.

[34] M.W. Bucovetsky, "The Mining Industry and the Great Tax Reform" in *Pressure Group Behaviour in Canadian Politics*, 93.

[35] Linda McQuaig, *Behind Closed Doors* (Markham, ON: Penguin Books, 1987), 181.

[36] Bucovetsky, "Mining Industry and the Great Tax Reform," 94–95.

[37] McQuaig, *Behind Closed Doors*, 179.

[38] Charles Lindblom, *Politics and Markets* (New York: Basic Books, 1977).

[39] Elizabeth Riddell-Dixon and Greta Riddell-Dixon, "Seniors Advance, The Mulroney Government Retreats: Grey Power and the Reinstatement of Fully Indexed Pensions" in *Contemporary Canadian Politics*, ed. Robert J. Jackson, Doreen Jackson, and Nicolas Baxter-Moore (Scarborough, ON: Prentice-Hall, 1987), 277.

[40] Ibid, 276.

[41] F.L. Morton, "The Political Impact of the Canadian Charter of Rights and Freedoms," *Canadian Journal of Political Science* 20, 1 (1987): 31–55.

[42] Robert M. Campbell and Leslie Pal, *The Real Worlds of Canadian Politics* (Peterborough, ON: Broadview Press, 1989).

[43] William D. Coleman, "Interest Groups and Democracy in Canada," *Canadian Public Administration* 30, 4 (Winter 1987): 610–22, and *Business and Politics*.

[44] McQuaig, *Behind Closed Doors*, 112.

[45] Coleman, *Business and Politics*, 276–85.

Suggested Reading

Coleman, William D., and Grace Skogstad, eds. *Policy Communities and Public Policy in Canada*. Toronto: Copp Clark Pitman, 1990.
Examines policy communities and policy networks in such sectors as banking, agriculture in Ontario and Quebec, the forestry and environmental land use in British Columbia, the East Coast fishery, occupational health and safety in Quebec, and social welfare to illustrate the variety of relationships that exist between governments and groups in Canada.

Pross, Paul A. *Group Politics and Public Policy*. 2nd ed. Toronto: Oxford University Press, 1992.
This book argues that interest groups are essential to democratic politics. Pross explains the proliferation of interest groups and changes in their policy role and impact in response to changes in the structure and functioning of the federal government. The concept of policy community is elaborated.

Pross, Paul A., ed. *Pressure Group Behaviour in Canadian Politics*. Toronto: McGraw-Hill Ryerson, 1975.
A collection of various case studies that reflect the then-dominant "lobbyist" approach to examining interest groups and governments.

Sawatsky, John. *The Insiders: Government, Business, and the Lobbyists*. Toronto: McClelland & Stewart, 1989.
This is an outsider's view of the professional lobbyists and public affairs consultant companies whose influence has grown since the 1980s.

Thorburn, Hugh G. *Interest Groups in the Canadian Federal System*. Toronto: University of Toronto Press, 1985.

Thorburn examines how federalism affects the distribution of power among organized interests, and structures how they seek to influence governments. He argues that interest groups find it difficult to cope with executive federalism and Canadian federalism more generally. The reciprocal impact of interest-group activity on federal–provincial relations is also examined.

Walter C. Soderlund

MASS MEDIA IN CANADIAN POLITICS: BASIC ISSUES IN A CONTEMPORARY CONTEXT

I n the last decade of the twentieth century, few observers would take the position that mass media do not play an important role in Canadian politics. Although no one has argued explicitly that mass media have come to occupy a position as the "fourth branch of government,"[1] it is nevertheless obvious to anyone who attempts to understand how Canadian politics works that media constitute a factor of the first order of importance. From the time of Confederation, media, in the form of newspapers, clearly played a role in the political process,[2] but that role was essentially one of spokesperson for the government or leading politicians. Today the relationship between mass media and politicians is not only more complex, but the overall role of media as an intermediary between government and society is far more important. The nature of this multi-faceted relationship is explored in the following pages.

In explaining the functions performed by mass media in the Canadian political system, it is first necessary to discuss in a broad context the relationship among mass media systems, political systems, and the societies that they serve. The seminal work in this area is *Four Theories of the Press*,[3] which outlines the characteristics of mass media behaviour in terms of authoritarian, communist, social responsibility, and libertarian systems. While this initial typology has been revised and refined over the years,[4] the crucial point remains unaltered: there is a high degree of congruence between the mass media system found in a society and the character of its political system. In fact, we would argue that the nature of the mass media system is one of a few key indicators (others being free and fair elections, a competitive political party system, and an independent judiciary) of the level of democratic attainment in a particular society. Further, if there is a degree of non-congruence between the mass media system and the political system in a society, the trend line in mass media tends to be predictive of the direction of change in the political system.

There now appear to be six fairly distinct types of mass media systems: authoritarian, communist, revolutionary, developmental, libertarian, and social democratic.[5] It is important to understand the factors that differentiate these six types of media systems as they both clarify the functions performed by mass media in Canada and highlight the unique features of Canada's particular media system.

Even the most cursory international comparative study of mass media points to the conclusion that in most political systems around the world the press is not free, but rather is controlled by governments to perform certain functions held to be important by those governments. The key to understanding *authoritarian media systems* is that governments seek to restrict the dissemination of news that they find not to their liking. Censorship tends to be the means by which control over mass media is exercised. Mass media can function independent of government, but they must be careful not to present material that would offend the government. There is obviously some room for manoeuvre on the part of bold journalists in authoritarian systems, but the price paid for overstepping the permitted boundaries can be high: fines, imprisonment, exile, or, in some circumstances, death.

In *communist systems*, the prohibition on dissemination of offensive material is replaced by the belief that mass media have a positive role to play in the creation and maintenance of the new societal value system. Thus, in communist systems, the mass media are consciously used as organs of pro-government propaganda in a co-ordinated effort aimed at achieving social control. In short, the party line becomes the media line. Mass media practitioners are seen as functionaries of the state. Independence, beyond that specifically authorized by the government, is unthinkable.[6]

Revolutionary media systems are transitional phenomena, operating during a period of time when the established order in a society is being challenged. Often located outside the borders of the country they are intended to serve, they combine uncensored news reporting with revolutionary mobilization.

Developmental media systems are also transitional, but function over a much longer period of time. They are characteristic of ex-colonial, developing areas of the world, where problems of nation building in circumstances of post-colonial dependency have left governments supposedly too fragile to survive the stinging criticism of an unfettered press. The mass media in the developmental model are seen, therefore, as championing the cause of development, while pulling their punches in reporting government failures and corruption. Obviously, developmental systems are potentially subject to great abuse, as the line between authoritarian and developmental justifications for restrictions on press freedom can in practice be difficult to draw.

Mass media systems characteristic of developed Western countries, primarily in Europe and North America, are based on the notion of a "free press," which can be defined as "the right of the press to report, comment on, and criticize its own government without retaliation or threat of retaliation."[7] Such systems, which are subject to laws defining libel, can be classified as either libertarian or social democratic.

Libertarian systems are grounded on the principle of the "open marketplace" of ideas, wherein government regulations over who can say what about whom in the mass media should be kept to an absolute minimum. Although damage may be done by inaccurate reporting, libertarians feel that, in the long run, truth will emerge, just as long as there are competing channels of information available. The United States, which has freedom of the press enshrined in the First Amendment to its constitution, offers a prime example of a libertarian media system. Regulation, if accepted at all, is used to preserve a competitive media environment. Vigorous debate cannot take place where media are controlled by one owner or political group.

The category of *social democratic media systems* is premised on the reality that the open marketplace, if left unregulated, tends toward restricted or monopoly ownership.[8] Thus, not only is government regulation essential to maintain a free press, but government subsidies to keep marginal media organizations in operation may be necessary as well. Social democratic media systems are also characterized by regulation of media content for the social good. In Canada, such regulation is seen in the Canadian content quotas imposed on radio and television in order to promote Canadian culture and prevent the assimilation of Canadians into an American value system. It is also felt that the government has a right to curtail certain types of programming—for example, excessive and gratuitous violence on television. Given the extent of government regulation of mass media in Canada, our media system falls most clearly into the social democratic type, although strong libertarian tendencies persist.[9]

ROLES OF MASS MEDIA IN DEMOCRATIC SYSTEMS

Canada has a democratic political system that is well anchored in Anglo-American traditions. Not surprisingly, its mass media system is characterized by considerable press freedom. This observation having been made, how can we describe the functions of that mass media system in its political context?

In a key work, Bernard Cohen isolated six "role conceptions" of the press in democratic political systems:[10] the press can be an informer, an interpreter, an instrument of government (i.e., a supporter of policy), a critic of government policy, an advocate of its own alternative policy, or it can interact with government as an actual policy maker. Figure 1 illustrates these six roles.

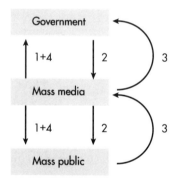

1. role of informer and interpreter of events to government and mass public
2. role of supporter, critic, and advocate of policy
3. role of informer and interpreter of mass public responses to government policy through reporting of polls, letters to the editor, coverage of demonstrations, and so on
4. role of policy maker

Figure 1: Roles of Mass Media in Democratic Systems

The informer and interpreter roles of mass media constitute the core of daily news activities. Finding news and reporting it with some degree of objectivity, accuracy, and sensitivity to their audiences is the essence of what journalists are paid to do. In democratic societies, journalists have tended to internalize norms of "fairness, accuracy, and lack of bias."[11]

Most citizens have to rely on mass media for information about events that occur outside the range of their own experience, and politicians in particular are voracious consumers of mass media information. Thus, mass media offer information and interpretation to two important constituencies in the democratic process: the citizenry and the government.

The remaining roles of the press relate to the decision-making process. In this context, mass media can either support or criticize government policy. For example, in the 1988 federal election, the *Globe and Mail* and the *Toronto Star* adopted differing editorial positions with respect to the Free Trade Agreement with the United States. The press may also adopt the advocate role and offer policy alternatives of its own. The *Globe and Mail* did this in suggesting that the Canadian government link its aid to Central America to those countries that respected human rights and complied with the Arias Peace Agreement signed in August 1987. The role of the press as policy maker entails the press interacting with government in the actual formulation of policy, as well as attempting to influence public opinion.[12]

As democratic theory assumes a responsiveness on the part of the government to the public will, it would be extremely difficult for a democracy to work without a media system that is relatively free from restrictions in moving information and opinion. Moreover, it is equally important to be able to move that information from the level of the citizenry to the government as it is to move it the other way. Although no one would argue that Canada has achieved perfection in carrying out these functions, it is unquestionable that the country ranks as one of the better functioning democracies of the world and has a mass media system that operates within the context of democratic norms. Let us examine in some detail four areas of concern in the overall interplay of the media and Canadian politics: freedom of the press, media ownership, foreign media penetration, and the quality of international reporting in the country.

FREEDOM OF THE PRESS

Freedom of the press is not an either/or proposition. There are some restrictions on press freedom in every political system. The important question to ask, therefore, is not whether there is freedom of the press, but rather how much press freedom exists and what type of restrictions are applied to press behaviour.

In democratic political systems, restrictions on the press can be viewed in the context of three types of control: governmental (legal and quasi-legal), social (attitudinal), and economic (ownership).

With respect to specific legal/constitutional restrictions on press freedom in Canada, Arthur Siegel points out that the earliest press in Canada
functioned in the classic authoritarian tradition: "The press was to be
used as an aid to governing. Journalism was tolerated rather than encouraged. The press was to be closely controlled and operated in the interests
of the governors."[13] In the evolution of Canada's media system from
authoritarian to democratic, Siegel cites the importance of the legal traditions of Anglo-American democracy, specifically the Peter Zenger case
in the colony of New York in 1734. The outcome of this case, that "truth"
was a valid defence against the charge of seditious libel, was used a century later in Nova Scotia in a case involving similar charges brought
against journalist Joseph Howe. Established in these legal precedents is the
watchdog or critic role of the press.

According to Siegel, the fact that Canada's "media system is American
in style, while our political system is British in character,"[14] leads to some
important differences that tend toward the restriction of press freedom in
Canada. He argues that the tradition of cabinet secrecy and legislation
such as the Official Secrets Act (the latter used in a 1978 prosecution of the
Toronto Sun[15]) inhibit press freedom. While "freedom of the press and
other media of communications" are listed in the Charter of Rights and
Freedoms (1982), journalists are not extended any special status beyond
that enjoyed by ordinary citizens.[16] The criminal prosecution of Canadian
journalist Doug Small over a 1989 budget leak, as an RCMP investigator
testified at Small's trial, was insisted upon by the government in order to
"teach journalists a lesson."[17] It is interesting in the case of this budget
leak that the "normal" response to such an event, namely the resignation
of the finance minister, was not only abandoned but, instead, the government broke new ground in controlling press behaviour with respect
to reportage of information deemed secret by the government. Such practice has to be seen as a disturbing development in the area of press freedom in Canada.[18]

The judicial ban on publication of details about the Karla Homolka trial,
in which she received a twelve-year sentence for her role in the deaths of
two Ontario schoolgirls, has raised the issue of press freedom to new
heights.[19] At issue are two rights: that of her husband, Paul Bernardo, to
a fair trial on the murder charges he faces for the same crime, and that of
the public to know the circumstances surrounding the highly disturbing
and publicized murders. The case is complicated by two factors. First,
contrary to most similar situations, Bernardo and his lawyers want the
details of Homolka's trial published. Second, international media in both

Britain and the United States defied the ban. This led to the situation where trial reports on newscasts originating in the United States and transmitted into Canada by cable were censored. Further, Canadians who ventured into the United States to buy American newspapers containing banned details about the trial had these newspapers confiscated at the border upon their return to Canada.[20] Canadian media organizations, while challenging the ban in the courts, have obeyed the judicial order.[21]

It is also apparent that Canadian libel laws are much stricter with respect to intent than those operative in the United States. In Canada, a lawsuit can be sustained on the grounds "that a publication is 'reasonably capable' of being defamatory—that is, the words tend to lower the person's reputation 'in the estimation of right thinking members of society.'"[22] No wonder that, when a sports columnist writing in the *Detroit Free Press* was alleged to have libelled the attorney representing hockey player Bob Probert, the attorney chose to sue the newspaper in Windsor, where the *Free Press* is widely available, rather than in Detroit. Likewise, the prime minister of the Bahamas chose to sue the American television network NBC in Toronto, where an allegedly libellous NBC news story was distributed on cable, rather than in New York where the story originated.

Subtle restrictions on press freedom could result from the fact that the Canadian Broadcasting Corporation (CBC), as a publicly owned entity, receives the bulk of its operating revenue from the government, as well as having its chair appointed politically. During the late 1970s when the Parti Québécois was moving toward its first referendum on sovereignty-association, a federal cabinet minister, André Ouellet, criticized Radio-Canada, the French arm of the CBC, for allegedly supporting separatism. Given that Radio-Canada defended itself and was defended by others, the impact of these charges is not clear. In many democratic societies where traditions of impartiality and insulation from political pressure are not as well established as they are in Canada, governments can exercise control over content. In Jamaica, for example, hiring, promotion, and firing decisions in public broadcasting have been made on the basis of political affiliation.[23]

MEDIA OWNERSHIP

As the discussion of the possible abridgement of freedom of the press arising out of government ownership of the CBC should make clear, there is a relationship between press freedom and ownership. In the Canadian case, it has *not* been government ownership that has been of primary concern.

Ownership of Canadian mass media is a mixture of private and public types. Ownership of electronic media is characterized by public (CBC) and private radio and television networks and stations co-existing in an uneasy, competitive relationship.[24] Print media, on the other hand, are privately owned, with the trend over the past three decades strongly in the direction of chain ownership. It is this phenomenon of chain ownership, which has reached near-saturation in Canada,[25] combined with "cross ownership" (control of both print and electronic outlets in the same market by the same group), that has caught the attention of those concerned with possible abuses of power latent in these conditions.

The primacy of economic forces over political decision making is a well-established tradition in Canadian scholarship. The works of John Porter and Wallace Clement explicitly framed Canadian media as a part of the interlocking corporate elite, functioning as a legitimizing voice for the continued rule of the dominant class.[26]

The evils of chain ownership per se were first given widespread attention in 1970 in the *Report of the Special Senate Committee on Mass Media*[27] (the Davey Committee Report), which recommended legislation to curb further consolidation of ownership of the country's newspapers. Approximately ten years later, the Royal Commission on Newspapers[28] (the Kent Commission) was created to examine the newspaper industry in the wake of the closing of competitive newspapers in Ottawa and Winnipeg by two of Canada's largest newspaper chains. Fundamental to both the Davey Committee and Kent Commission inquiries is the underlying assumption that chain ownership is inherently bad. Critics assume that the consolidation of power in a relatively few hands will restrict the amount of competing information available, and consequently that democracy will be ill served.

How valid are these fears? Just as in the case of government ownership of mass media, potential abuses on the part of corporate chain owners are a reality. However, in Canada, while it is arguable that particular chains may not necessarily be committed to bringing the highest-quality news to their readers, there is very little empirical evidence to suggest that the economic power of chains has been used in concentrated ways to affect media content. For example, in studies of media coverage of three federal elections, chain ownership as a variable in predicting substantive issue, party, and leader coverage was extremely weak.[29]

The reluctance of chains to flex their economic muscles to influence content appears related to two considerations. The first has to do with notions of fair play and non-bias. Journalists are principled, and their profession has norms of appropriate behaviour: they simply cannot be bought and ordered about by owners. The second consideration is that the motivation for ownership of mass media outlets is primarily economic, not political. Chain ownership is attractive economically because it spreads the costs of news acquisition, as well as many other costs, over a large number of units, thus increasing profitability.[30] To the extent that flaunting ideological positions will tend to alienate readers with opposing views, and that profitability is based on advertising revenue that is dependent on circulation, the reality is that Canadian newspapers have become progressively less politically identifiable during the second half of the twentieth century, when, paradoxically, chain ownership increased dramatically.[31] Although we certainly would not argue that concentration of ownership of the magnitude found in Canada is in any way healthy politically, there are no more than scattered instances where media output of chain-owned papers appears dictated by the will of the corporate owners.

A second way in which ownership may influence media product is through hiring, promotion, and firing decisions. In communist political systems, it is a virtual article of faith that Western media cannot be "free" precisely because they are privately owned: media owners will hire and promote those who agree with their point of view and fire those they find to be consistently out of step with their values. Although this position is obviously overstated, owner influence is an important area of concern as there are distinct value structures (corporate cultures) existing in all formal organizations. These corporate values are important in that they play a role in the recruitment and subsequent upward mobility of personnel, as well as in their dismissal. Potential employees, as well as employers, try to align individual desires with corporate expectations. As in courtship, when both feel comfortable, a relationship is struck. Once a hiring decision has been made, on-the-job socialization further solidifies the set of corporate values with which the recruit was at least in basic agreement before joining the organization.

While this set of processes no doubt does restrict the number of radical, revolutionary, or reactionary voices employed by major media operations, by and large the watchdog role of the press appears so strongly incorporated into mass media norms of operation that government or corporate misdeeds will not go unreported.

Taking press freedom and press ownership together, ownership (whether government or private) does to some degree almost necessarily infringe on freedom of the press. It also appears that the intelligent response to this situation is the recognition that any scheme of ownership is open to abuse. Such abuse, whether by private or public owners, needs to be challenged squarely and forcefully whenever it occurs.

FOREIGN MEDIA PENETRATION

B eing located next to the United States has been a mixed blessing for Canada. The two countries shared a similar colonial history until 1776 when the American Revolution divided British North America into what are now the United States and Canada. The relationship between the two countries has always reflected the asymmetry of power stemming from a 10 to 1 population ratio. Thus, in order to preserve a political entity separate from the United States, Canadian politicians have had to engage in nation-building strategies. High on the list of institutions that were used for the purposes of nation building were the mass media.[32]

Nation building in Canada has had to contend with a problem of dual-directional pull. On the one hand, there is the obvious need to protect Canada from the onslaught of American-based media; on the other hand, there is the need to combat more localized loyalties embedded in provincial identification, especially in the province of Quebec. It is the first of these problems that concerns us here.

Given that mass media are primary transmitters of culture, it was feared early on that American media institutions would simply spread American culture across the border into Canada. While this never materialized as a major problem during the era of newspaper primacy, it did become apparent once the broadcast media developed. Radio was introduced in Canada in 1922 and spread very rapidly across the country. Politicians and concerned citizens alike were both impressed and alarmed by the potential of this new medium of communication. Regulation of broadcasting began almost immediately, and the CBC was created in 1936, specifically with nation building in mind.[33] In spite of regulations written into a series of broadcasting acts and warnings issued by a host of royal commissions, Canadians have historically tuned in to American programming in large numbers, and Canadian networks and stations even feature American programming to attract audiences. Quotas for Canadian media content were finally introduced in 1959.

Despite the long-standing efforts aimed at curbing American media influence, the penetration of American culture and values into Canada in general and its impact on the political process has continued. In the Third World, the kind of cultural intrusion characteristic of the American–Canadian relationship has been termed *media imperialism*. In the case of Canada and the United States, there is no direct attempt to target Canadian audiences for American media programming. Cultural intrusion results rather from the spillover of American signals across the border. The fact that over half the Canadian population lives within one hundred miles of the

border puts them within easy range of radio and television signals originating in the United States. The development of cable and satellite distribution systems only intensifies the problem. It is virtually inevitable,
given the fact that the United States is the most prolific information-
producing society on earth, that Canadian cultural values, and consequently a separate identity, are being seriously undermined.

Of course, the reality that Canadians like to watch and listen to American
programming means that, to a large extent, we as media audiences are
as much a part of the problem as is the availability of American signals.
Thus, it is important to note that, while Canadians complain of American
influence in the area of communications, viewing and listening to American
programming is voluntary.

Although we should not be surprised that Canadian life in general
has been affected by the importation of American culture through mass
media, what is truly interesting is the degree to which mass media have
"Americanized" Canadian political processes. I use the term "interesting" because Canadian politics per se is not a subject of great importance
for American media. Studies have shown repeatedly that Canada ranks
relatively low on the scale of American news priorities, so it is not American
media *content* that is the culprit. The problem appears to be that American
television *style*—particularly "packaging" candidates for sale on
television—has crossed the border, resulting in what is little short of a
revolution in the process whereby political leaders are recruited, campaign for office, and are evaluated and elected by their constituents.

The consequent focus on leadership has significantly "presidential-
ized" the Canadian parliamentary system. Complex issues tend to be
neglected due to the difficulty in dealing with them in the TV news format, in which a long story may run three minutes. Leaders have to be
able to summarize their positions to fit a format that uses "sound bites"
in the range of five to ten seconds. In such circumstances, it is inevitable
that style and image will prevail over substance and policy.

Also of great concern is the impact of polls on the political process,
especially the media's reporting of them during electoral campaigns.[34]
Contrary to conventional wisdom on the subject, which indicates that
polling results do not affect the outcomes of elections, following the recommendations of the Royal Commission on Electoral Reform and Pary
Financing, legislation was passed banning the publication of poll results during the seventy-two hours preceeding a federal election. Such a ban was in
effect during the 1993 election campaign. Thus, while efforts have been made
to curb the worst excesses of the American system, there is little doubt
that the media advisor, the advertising executive, and the pollster have in

large measure replaced traditional political party operatives as key members of a campaign staff. Thus, paradoxically, the area of politics, which should be among the most insulated from the impact of American media, has been "Americanized" through the adoption of an American media style on the part of Canada's own media institutions.[35]

INTERNATIONAL REPORTING

The quality of international reporting in Canada is especially important because for most citizens it is extremely difficult to get access to information on developments outside the range of their own personal experience other than through the mass media. As a consequence, for most of us, what we know of the world is based on what we read in the newspaper, hear on the radio, or see on television.[36] Thus, there is an immense responsibility on the part of the Canadian media to report accurately and in a proper context on what is happening in the world.

Until recently, assessments regarding the quality of international reporting in Canada have, for the most part, not been very complimentary. Academic judgments[37] plus the reports of the Davey Committee and the Kent Commission have pointed out serious problems with respect to Canadian reporting of international news. Criticisms focus on three major areas: overall lack of interest in and coverage of international news, heavy reliance on foreign (mainly American) wire services for material, and neglect of specific Canadian foreign policy aspects of international news.

Before assessing the current status of international reporting, it is first necessary to discuss standards of evaluation more generally. Indeed, gaining consensus as to the quality of mass media in a democratic society such as Canada is not an easy task, partly because standards of evaluation tend to be subjective.

> Critics do not, and cannot possibly, agree on the essentials of Canadian society or even how it should be conceived or defined. Everyone conceptualizes truth, the role of the citizen, government, courts, business, and the role of mass communications differently. Unscrambling the particular criteria that critics use goes a long way to explaining why policy solutions to the problem of news quality in Canada are a long way off.[38]

The entire print sector and a substantial portion of the electronic media in Canada are privately owned. Although it is reasonable to expect these owners to display some measure of "social responsibility," it is probably unrealistic to expect them to produce media product geared in large measure to elite tastes (academic and other), when their audiences tend to have different tastes. Thus, there is a real question regarding how much and what type of international coverage should be considered adequate, and it appears that at least some past criticism was based on unrealistic expectations. Nevertheless, studies have shown real shortcomings in international coverage by the Canadian press. One comparative study of the Toronto *Globe and Mail* and the *New York Times* in the 1950s found that the *Globe* largely ignored stories on Latin America and the Caribbean. For example, comparative samples indicate that, for coverage of Cuba in the mid-1950s, 93 percent of stories were found in the *Times* while only 7 percent appeared in the *Globe*. Moreover, all of the *Globe* stories were American wire copy.[39] In many ways, this trend is easily understandable. First, the *Globe* had only a fraction of the resources available to the *Times*. Second, neither the economic nor the political interests of Canadians were as tied up in the region as were those of the Americans. Third, the geographical proximity of the United States to the region would likely in and of itself result in more coverage than in Canada.

More recent studies comparing Canadian and American press coverage in Central America and the Caribbean show considerable improvement in the ratio of Canadian to American reporting. For example, in press coverage of the Nicaraguan revolution from 1978 through 1980, the ratio was 64 percent of coverage in three leading American newspapers (the *New York Times*, the *Washington Post*, and the *Christian Science Monitor*) to 36 percent in three Canadian papers (the *Globe and Mail*, the *Ottawa Citizen*, and *Le Devoir*).[40]

For events occurring in Central America in the 1980s, the 2/3 to 1/3 ratio appears relatively stable. However, for events in the Caribbean, Canadian reporting fares better. In the case of the Grenadian election of 1984, Canadian and American coverage in a matched sample of six newspapers in each country was about equal.[41] What is even more interesting, the Haitian election crisis of 1987–88 elicited greater coverage in six Canadian newspapers (53 percent) than it did in six American newspapers (47 percent). Interest on the part of Canadian newspapers was greatest in the French-language press but was not restricted to these newspapers. The percentages of editorials and feature columns in Canadian newspapers compared favourably to those in American papers. It is true, however, that much material appearing in Canadian newspapers still originated from American wire services.[42]

The concern regarding the lack of coverage of specific Canadian foreign policy questions also needs to be reassessed. A major study of foreign policy coverage in six Canadian newspapers in the fall of 1982 found that there were nearly nine foreign policy items in each daily newspaper, far more than the researchers had expected.[43] Moreover, Canadian daily newspaper editors themselves believe that reporting on international events in the country is nothing to be ashamed of: 78 percent rated it in the "good," "very good," and "excellent" categories, while approximately half felt that it had improved over the past five years.

Coverage of international news on Canadian television has not been as thoroughly studied (at least not in a comparative framework), but in one study comparing American and Canadian network news it was found that the same criteria for newsworthiness were employed in both countries (armed conflict, terrorism, riots, and so on). At the time, American TV news tended to focus more heavily on the USSR and the world's hot spots, while Canadian news offered coverage of a wider range of countries and world events.[44]

A comparative study of television news coverage of the 1989–90 American invasion of Panama revealed that the three major American networks ran an average of 2.3 stories per day during the twenty-three-day study period, while CBC and CTV ran an average of 1.7 stories per day. With respect to volume of coverage, the study concluded that "it is hard to imagine any greater [Canadian] coverage for a story that did not involve Canadians directly."[45]

Our overall conclusion is that, during the 1980s, Canadian international reporting improved dramatically in every area in which it had previously received criticism. Getting a specifically Canadian viewpoint on the news remains the most problematic area. While leading newspapers have placed more foreign correspondents abroad, wire copy still tends to originate with American wire services.

CONCLUSION

Canada is a country with a large physical territory (second largest in the world), a population that is relatively small (about twenty-nine million), and strong regional and cultural/linguistic cleavages. It also happens to share a border with one of the world's most prolific media-generating societies. In short, it has its share of problems. Canada also has benefited from the successful implantation of Anglo-American democratic traditions. As well, it has developed important norms of non-violence and political compromise, along with the structures and attitudes conducive to a free press.

As this chapter makes clear, on the whole Canada's mass media systems have served the country well—in fact, much better than the assessments of many media critics would lead us to believe. This having been said, the relationship between mass media institutions and the political process they service is not without its problems. These problems, while differing as to specifics, will never be "solved" in the sense that they will disappear.

The related issues of press freedom and media ownership interact continually in ways that might prove deleterious for democratic governance, and it is important to be aware that abuses can arise in circumstances of government ownership/control as well as in the context of privately owned systems. Likewise, problems of Canadian national unity, compounded by the existence of strong cultural and regional identities and the at times painful reality of living next to the United States, are neither likely to go away nor otherwise be resolved, whatever enlightened policies may be decided upon by the Canadian government.

The best that we can hope for are mass media structures that attempt to cope with the set of problems that face Canada, while at the same time reporting on and analyzing these problems to the best of their ability. Although growing restrictions on press freedom in Canada are troubling, domestic political reporting has been done at least as well as is the case in other leading democracies such as Britain and the United States. In the area of Canadian reporting of the highly complex international news scene, the situation is not as problem free. There is room for improvement, especially for a greater commitment on the part of Canadian mass media institutions to bear the cost of getting more Canadian journalists into the field, thus lessening the current reliance on American wire services. Even in this area, however, one can conclude that the current situation is better than it was, and trends are running in the right direction.

It is a cliché to say that a society has the kind of mass media system it deserves. In the case of Canada, we have a society that deserves no less than an excellent mass media system, and, although there are problems associated with the operation of that system, by and large it is an excellent one.

NOTES

[1] Douglas Cater, *The Fourth Branch of Government* (Boston: Houghton-Mifflin, 1959).
[2] P.B. Waite, *The Life and Times of Confederation, 1864–1867: Politics, Newspapers, and the Union of British North America* (Toronto: University of Toronto Press, 1962).

3 Fred Siebert, Theodore Peterson, and Wilbur Schramm, *Four Theories of the Press* (Urbana: University of Illinois Press, 1956).

4 Robert G. Picard, *The Press and the Decline of Democracy: The Democratic Socialist Response in Public Policy* (Westport, CT: Greenwood Press, 1983), and William A. Hachten, *The World News Prism: Changing Media, Clashing Ideology* (Ames: Iowa State University Press, 1987).

5 Walter I. Romanow and Walter C. Soderlund, *Media Canada: An Introductory Analysis* (Toronto: Copp Clark Pitman, 1992), 25–41.

6 Hachten, *The World News Prism*, 24–27.

7 Ibid., 19.

8 Robert Picard developed this category out of the Siebert, Peterson, and Schramm social responsibility theory of the press. See Picard, *The Press and the Decline of Democracy*.

9 William Thorsell, "Media: Muzzled Views Are Good News for Reactionary Forces Everywhere," *Globe and Mail*, 27 Nov. 1993, D1.

10 Bernard Cohen, *The Press and Foreign Policy* (Princeton: Princeton University Press, 1963), 17–47.

11 L. John Martin and Anju Grover Chaudhary, *Comparative Mass Media Systems* (New York: Longman, 1984), 8.

12 For a fascinating study detailing the extent to which the Canadian press pursued its own policy agenda, see Patrick H. Brennan, *Reporting the Nation's Business: Press–Government Relations during the Liberal Years, 1935–1957* (Toronto: University of Toronto Press, 1994).

13 Authur Siegel, *Politics and the Mass Media in Canada* (Toronto: McGraw-Hill Ryerson, 1983), 85.

14 Ibid., 20.

15 Ibid., 67–69.

16 Robert Martin and G. Stuart Adam, *A Sourcebook of Canadian Media Law* (Ottawa: Carleton University Press, 1989), 73–74.

17 "Officer Gave Biased Testimony, Crown Says in Budget-leak Trial," *Globe and Mail*, 21 April 1990, 2.

18 Allan Hutchinson, "The Budget Leak: How Free Should the Press Be?" *Globe and Mail*, 1 June 1989, 7.

19 Rudy Paltiel, "Lawyers Argue over Homolka Ban," *Globe and Mail*, 2 Dec. 1993, A4.

20 Gay Abbate, "Arrests at Border to Confiscate Papers Criticized as Sham," *Globe and Mail*, 30 Nov. 1993, A5.

21 Without maintaining the desirability of either relationship, differences in the degree of press freedom in Canada and the United States are most dramatically seen by comparing the Bernardo case to that of O.J. Simpson.

22 Southam News, "Appeals Court Mulls Changes to Libel Laws," *Windsor Star*, 6 Dec. 1993, A4.

23 Aggrey Brown, "Jamaica" in *Mass Media and the Caribbean*, ed. S.H. Surlin and W.C. Soderlund (New York: Gordon and Breach, 1990), 16–18.

24 W.C. Soderlund, W.I. Romanow, E.D. Briggs, and R.H. Wagenberg, *Media and Elections in Canada* (Toronto: Holt, Rinehart and Winston, 1984), 99–116.

[25] Romanow and Soderlund, *Media Canada*, 268, calculated that, in 1991, 89 percent of total Canadian newspaper circulation was controlled by chains.

[26] John Porter, *The Vertical Mosaic: An Analysis of Social Class and Power in Canada* (Toronto: University of Toronto Press, 1965), 462–90, and Wallace Clement, *The Canadian Corporate Elite: An Analysis of Economic Power* (Toronto: McClelland & Stewart, 1975), 270, 324.

[27] *The Uncertain Mirror: Report of the Special Senate Committee on Mass Media* (Ottawa: Queen's Printer, 1970).

[28] *Report of the Royal Commission on Newspapers* (Ottawa: Minister of Supply and Services, 1981).

[29] Soderlund et al., *Media and Elections*, 90–91.

[30] Michael F. Charette, C. Lloyd Brown-John, W.I. Romanow, and W.C. Soderlund, "Acquisition et fermeture de journaux par des chaines de journaux: effets sur les tarifs de publicité," *Communication/Information* 6 (1984): 50–54.

[31] Frederick J. Fletcher, *The Newspaper and Public Affairs,* vol. 7, *Research Reports, Royal Commission on Newspapers* (Ottawa: Ministry of Supply and Services, 1981), 20.

[32] Thomas L. McPhail, *Electronic Colonialism: The Future of International Broadcasting*, 2nd ed. (Beverly Hills: Sage, 1987).

[33] Soderlund et al., *Media and Elections*, 106–8.

[34] Guy Lachapelle, *Polls and the Media in Canadian Elections: Taking the Pulse*, vol. 16, *Research Study of the Royal Commission on Electoral Reform and Party Financing* (Toronto: Dundurn Press, 1991).

[35] Soderlund et al., *Media and Elections*, 127–30.

[36] William L. Rivers and Wilbur Schramm, *Responsibility in Mass Communication*, rev. ed. (New York: Harper and Row, 1969), 14.

[37] See, for example, T. Joseph Scanlon, "Canada Sees the World through U.S. Eyes: One Case in Cultural Domination," *Canadian Forum* 54 (1974): 230, and Denis Stairs, "The Press and Foreign Policy in Canada," *International Journal* 31 (1976): 230.

[38] Edwin R. Black, "The Quality of News Media" (paper presented at the annual meeting of the Canadian Communication Association, Université Laval, June 1989), 2.

[39] W.C. Soderlund, "Western Press Coverage of Fidel Castro: The Early Years, 1953 and 1956" (paper presented at the conference Thirty Years of the Cuban Revolution: An Assessment, Halifax, Nov. 1989). For the same trend, see W.C. Soderlund, "The Cold War Comes to Latin America: Press Images of the Constitutional Crisis in British Guiana, 1953" (paper presented at the annual meeting of the Canadian Association of Latin American and Caribbean Studies, Ottawa, Oct. 1993).

[40] W.C. Soderlund, "The Nicaraguan Revolution in the Canadian and American Press," *Mass Comm. Review 20* (1993): 86–98.

[41] W.C. Soderlund, "Canadian and U.S. Coverage of Latin American Elections," *Newspaper Research Journal* 13 (1992): 55–57.

[42] W.C. Soderlund and R.C. Nelson, "Canadian and American Press Coverage of the Haitian Election Crisis" in *Mass Media and the Caribbean*, 373–89.

[43] T.A. Keenleyside, B.E. Burton, and W.C. Soderlund, "La presse et la politique etrangère Canadienne" *Études Internationales* 18 (1987): 520.

[44] S.H. Surlin, W.I. Romanow, and W.C. Soderlund, "TV Network News: A Canadian–American Comparison," *American Review of Canadian Studies* 18 (1988): 469–72.

[45] W.C. Soderlund, R.H. Wagenberg, and Ian Pemberton, "Cheerleader or Critic? Television News Coverage of the U.S. Invasion of Panama," *Canadian Journal of Political Science* (forthcoming).

SUGGESTED READING

Fletcher, Frederick J., ed. *Election Broadcasting in Canada*. Vol. 21. *Research Studies of the Royal Commission on Electoral Reform and Party Financing*. Toronto: Dundurn Press, 1991; *Reporting the Campaign: Election Coverage in Canada*. Vol. 22. *Research Studies of the Royal Commission on Electoral Reform and Party Financing*. Toronto: Dundurn Press, 1991.

    Compilations of research studies commissioned by the Royal Commission.

Grenier, Marc, ed. *Critical Studies of Canadian Mass Media*. Toronto: Butterworths, 1992.

    A reader emphasizing studies of Canadian mass media from the perspective of critical theory.

Helen, Holmes, and David Taras, eds. *Seeing Ourselves: Media Power and Policy in Canada*. Toronto: Harcourt Brace Jovanovich, 1992.

    A comprehensive reader containing a mix of new and reprinted material.

Kesterton, Wilfred H. *A History of Journalism in Canada*. Toronto: McClelland & Stewart, 1967.

    The standard work on the history of the press in the country.

Martin, Robert, and G. Stuart Adam. *A Sourcebook of Canadian Media Law*. Ottawa: Carleton University Press, 1989.

    In an era where Canadian politics is becoming "legalized," this is an extremely useful compilation of media laws and the cases that bear upon them.

Peers, Frank W. *The Politics of Canadian Broadcasting, 1921–1951*. Toronto: University of Toronto Press, 1969; *The Public Eye: Television and the Politics of Canadian Broadcasting*. Toronto: University of Toronto Press, 1979.

    Taken together, the definitive history of Canadian broadcasting.

Report of the Royal Commission on Newspapers. Ottawa: Ministry of Supply and Services, 1981.

The Kent Commission Report. Thorough, but controversial, investigation of the newspaper industry, highlighting issues of ownership.

Report of the Task Force on Broadcasting Policy. Ottawa: Ministry of Supply and Services, 1988.

The Caplan-Sauvageau Committee Report, a complete investigation into the status of the country's broadcasting industries, focuses on the development of new policies.

Romanow, Walter I., and Walter C. Soderlund. *Media Canada: An Introductory Analysis*. Toronto: Copp Clark Pitman, 1992.

A comprehensive text dealing with mass media in Canada.

Rutherford, Paul. *The Making of the Canadian Media*. Toronto: McGraw-Hill Ryerson, 1978.

Readable history of the country's mass media.

Siegel, Arthur. *Politics and the Media in Canada*. Toronto: McGraw-Hill Ryerson, 1983.

The only text focusing on all aspects of the relationship between politics and media.

Soderlund, Walter C., Walter I. Romanow, E. Donald Briggs, and Ronald H. Wagenberg. *Media and Elections in Canada*. Toronto: Holt, Rinehart and Winston, 1984.

Treats mass media coverage of Canadian elections, focusing on 1979 and 1980.

Taras, David. *The Newsmakers: The Media's Influence on Canadian Politics*. Scarborough, ON: Nelson Canada, 1990.

An excellent, up-to-date text focusing on the question of who determines media content.

The Uncertain Mirror: Report of the Special Senate Committee on Mass Media. Vol. 1. Ottawa: Queen's Printer, 1970.

The Davey Committee Report is a benchmark from which to assess the current status of Canada's mass media.

Peter Woolstencroft

LIBERAL DEMOCRACIES AND POLITICAL PARTIES: THE CANADIAN CASE

What would political life be without parties? For most of us it is hard to imagine because parties are so prominently a part of politics: for many people parties mean politics and vice versa. But the readily acknowledged centrality of parties may mean that the many things they do are insufficiently appreciated. As social institutions, parties change, sometimes leading society in new directions, sometimes responding to changes in society. Thus, we need to think about the functions and the changing character of political parties. We must ask what parties do and whether they are becoming less or more important in contemporary society.

This chapter focuses on the role of political parties in liberal-democratic political systems, with emphasis on the Canadian case. It considers the argument that parties are a declining force in modern democratic political life, even at a time when, internally, they are undergoing broadening and intensification of democratic processes. Parties, it is argued, will always be with us in some form, but in the future they will be less important politically than was the case for a good part of the twentieth century. It is ironic, then, that as the parties undergo a democratic transformation, they have a less central role in the play of democratic politics.

THE CONCEPT OF A POLITICAL PARTY

Across human societies many different forms of political parties exist. Some political parties have many members; some do not. Some have definite ideas about what ought to be done; some seem to make no precise claims. Some are broad in their support base, drawing widely from the various parts of society; others appear to be almost specialized in their support base, having members and voters drawn only from a particular part of society, perhaps a religious, economic, or linguistic group. Some speak in heated terms, using rhetoric and arguments that sharply separate them from others; other parties speak soothingly, using the language of integration, cohesion, and consensus. Some show few signs of internal party division; others are marked by public disagreement and discord. How do we make sense of the myriad forms that political parties can take?

The fundamental point about political parties is that they are organizations seeking to control the state; in liberal democracies, the way they do so is by winning elections. Political scientists employ two themes in the understanding of political parties as organizations seeking to win office. The first emphasizes ideas, programs, and policies: parties are said to be entities committed to certain policy propositions. The second stresses the winning of elections: parties are said to be organizations first and foremost dedicated to contesting elections. Each theme is useful, but to delve more deeply we must examine what parties do. We will do that by first contemplating political life without parties by suspending our sense of reality—we will put aside what we believe and think in hypothetical terms. Then we will examine what are said to be the functions of political parties in liberal-democratic political systems.

LIFE WITHOUT POLITICAL PARTIES

Consider what confronts an individual—whom we will call Citizen X—living in a large and complex society spread over a wide territory.[1] Since voting and elections are integral elements of the political process in this society, Citizen X is called upon periodically to choose a representative. In this particular election, a number of people seek office, which translates into a big problem for Citizen X. One vote is to be cast, but how does a voter choose between the many candidates and their attractive, even compelling, pleas for support? Candidate A says, "Vote for me because I have an outstanding record of community service." Candidate B counters, "Vote to re-elect me because I have been a hardworking member of the legislature." Yet another—Candidate C—calls out, "Vote for me because it is imperative that our society act to forcefully address the problem of providing jobs for young people, and I have a plan."

Citizen X clearly has a difficult decision. How to choose? For whom should the vote be cast? So many worthy candidates have offered themselves, and so many good reasons exist upon which to base a decision. For example, the incumbent—Candidate B—is known for being a hard worker, but how effective has her work been? The candidate with the excellent record of community service—Candidate A—is a strong possibility, but Citizen X is worried about his platform: while there is much that warrants support, nothing is said about changing the welfare system, and Citizen X believes that reform is urgently needed.

In the end, our good citizen decides to vote for Candidate C because she has a lot of apparently well-considered ideas about welfare reform, the issue most important to Citizen X. To Citizen X's surprise (because, he ruefully reflects, he usually supports a candidate who loses), Candidate C wins the election.

Candidate C, now Legislator C, goes off to the legislature, determined to fulfil the mandate given by her constituents. The legislature, composed of one hundred legislators, has a number of fundamental questions before it. Do they need a leader? If, so, who will be the leader? How is the leader chosen? What is the basis of leadership? What is the role of the leader? What is the relationship between the leader and the other legislators?

Legislator C also has a problem, one that parallels that which confronted Citizen X. Surprisingly, although she won office on the specific promise to bring great changes in the way that money is spent on welfare, few other legislators express interest in the issue, and they are reluctant to go in the same direction as Legislator C.

Back home, Legislator C's constituents are looking for action on the welfare issue. Eventually, because not much is happening, citizens begin to wonder about Legislator C's effectiveness in the legislature. Everybody recognizes that Legislator C has not been asleep. After all, she has made speech after speech after speech. Press reports indicate that Legislator C has been very busy in one-on-one conversations with other legislators, trying to persuade them that something has to be done about welfare. She has been eagerly talking with various groups concerned about the issue. All of these efforts, however, have had no apparent effect, very much to Legislator C's chagrin, especially as the escalating demands for action by her constituents make her anxious about her prospects in the next election. As Legislator C reflects on the situation and what might be done, it becomes apparent that there is only one way for her to be able to make progress on the welfare issue: she vows to make sure that in the next election there are candidates running in the other constituencies who are prepared to address the welfare issue in the way that Legislator C thinks makes sense. Legislator C begins to identify people who will be prepared to stand for election on the welfare reform issue. In doing so, she is thinking in terms of what most people consider to be a political party.

Switching back to the real world, where things are much less consciously determined, our imaginary Citizen X's and Legislator C's experiences point to the development of parties in liberal-democratic political systems. Both Citizen X and Legislator C were handicapped as political actors because they acted as individuals in processes that called for collective decisions and some shared knowledge about what was happening. That is, since decisions were made on the basis of how votes were cast, individuals in the system needed to know something about alternatives and what others might do. In brief, voters and legislators require organizing mechanisms to bring structure to the chaos that follows when voters and legislators act simply as individuals and not as part of a group. Legislatures developed parties because of the need for leadership and cohesion. And parties, as they evolved into competitive entities vying for votes, provided important links between politicians and voters. Politicians, of course, wanted to maximize their vote-getting abilities, and voters benefited from the parties providing choice between alternatives. Parties, then, served to organize political relationships.

LIFE WITH POLITICAL PARTIES

Because of the need for organization, the institutionalization of the party occurred quickly. For example, those seeking office in Canada in 1867 were loosely and unreliably tied to the concept of party; the notion of the leader was faint; the idea of a platform on which the party and its candidates would campaign was unknown. Victorious candidates could rightly attribute their good fortune to their personal strengths and popular appeal.[2]

In the Canada of the 1990s, parties and elections are built on the parties' leaders and their platforms; local candidates, with odd exceptions, play marginal roles, both in terms of the direction of the party and the result in the constituency. The emphasis is on cohesion and unity; any public disagreements with the leader or the election platform are quickly squelched. The well-secured rooting of the party as a fundamental institution in Canadian politics occurred within a generation after Confederation. André Siegfried, writing in 1907, observed that in Canada "the party is almost a sacred institution, to be forsaken only at the cost of one's reputation and career. It is held in esteem almost like one's religion, and its praises are sung in dithyrambs that are often a trifle absurd. Its members owe it absolute loyalty even in the smallest matters, and individual vagaries of opinion are severely condemned."[3]

LIBERAL DEMOCRACIES AND POLITICAL PARTIES

Although many parties, such as the Conservative Party in the United Kingdom, can trace their roots to pre-democratic times, it is the spread of democratic ideas and practices that explains the nature and operation of political parties. Indeed, the development and expansion of liberal democracy and the development of political parties went hand in hand. One central component of liberal democracy is the idea that elections provide the foundation for the selection of politicians. As that idea took hold, the subsequent democratization of political life meant that ordinary people—rather than the elite of society—had the right to choose political leaders. As the right to vote extended throughout society, there was a parallel development of the political party, which resulted from the realization by contenders for office that their success depended on their ability to marshall resources—money, people, ideas, policies—that enhanced their appeal to the mass of voters. We have, then, the core of the idea of the political party in a democratic system: organization of those who seek votes in order to hold office.

Any society that is large (i.e., is composed of a substantial number of people), complex (i.e., has many interests), and spread out over a wide territory needs something that is called a political party. In the large Canadian cities—Montreal, Toronto, Vancouver, and Winnipeg— parties (not necessarily of the same name as national and provincial parties) have established some roots.[4] Once we leave the municipal level of the Canadian political system to enter the domain of national and provincial politics, almost invariably we find political parties.[5] This pattern of political parties being a commonplace feature of political life suggests that they fulfil some important functions for citizens. Even though voices of anti-party sentiment are intermittently heard, the fact is that once parties are established as institutions they generally continue. As a rule, the pattern of competition between political parties is much more stable than unstable. And yet, as Canadians approach the end of the twentieth century, the stability that once was taken for granted is no longer assured.

The connection between the evolution of liberal democracy and the development of political parties points to the fundamental theme of this chapter: the appraisal of the nature and operation of parties within the framework of democratic political life. This exploration requires the examination of a number of functions that are often said to be performed by political parties in liberal-democratic political systems; then, in light of these functions, the intent is to appraise the contemporary role of parties.

FUNCTIONS OF POLITICAL PARTIES

The understanding of political parties is based on the examination of six critical functions commonly attributed to them.[6] The six functions are:

1. structuring the vote;
2. aggregation of interests;
3. recruitment of political leaders;
4. organization of government;
5. formation of public policy; and
6. integration and mobilization of the mass public.

Structuring the vote refers to the activities of parties related to the presentation of different views about what ought to be done on issues of the day. In our hypothetical example, voters had a tremendous problem because the decision in one constituency was not related to what was happening in other constituencies. Citizen X might benefit from knowing who had won in the past and who was close. Parties provide voters with information that helps them to make their voting decisions. Further, in the real world, many voters approach the voting decision with some degree of identification with a particular party. If you generally think of yourself as a Liberal, then there is high probability in a particular election that you will respond positively to the Liberal Party and its candidates and negatively toward other parties. For some voters, party identification and vote reflects the weight of tradition, extending perhaps over many generations. The vote decision, then, reflects an individual's socialization process: growing up in a family with a strong and visible commitment to, say, the Progressive Conservative Party is likely to result in that individual having positive identification with that party.

Parties also provide cues to voters that help them decide for whom they should vote. One cue is history: what the party has done in the past predicts, although not with certainty, the future. Another cue emphasizes ties with particular social and economic interests. Left-wing parties will talk about such things as the interests of the working class and the role of trade unions, while right-wing parties will talk about the importance of business and the marketplace. Voters thinking in such terms will align themselves with parties that best reflect their interests and values.

"Vote structuring is related to opinion-structuring."[7] Election platforms and policy statements are the heartbeat of this function; party names and symbols are manifestations of the attempt to create a certain image. In an age when hardly anybody wants to say anything negative about "democracy," consider how many parties have the word "democratic" in their name. In Quebec the word "Québécois" is used to denote the idea of protecting the interests of Quebeckers. In other Canadian provinces, parties develop logos that accentuate their commitment to defending their province's interests. Other politically attractive words are "progressive" and "reform," which, when incorporated into party names, convey a certain image or message.

Closely related to the vote-structuring function is the idea of the *aggregation of interests*, which refers to the phenomenon of parties finding points of commonality or agreement in a society otherwise marked by great differences in perceived interests from one individual to the next, and from one group to the next. If each citizen in Canada were asked to identify, say, the two or three demands or expectations that are most politically important to him or her, it is easy to imagine that a long list of demands would be produced. But each and every citizen would not produce a unique list. Rather, there would be some degree of overlap among the various lists of demands. Although citizens are not in fact asked to compose lists, political parties act as if they did. The job of parties is to meld what otherwise would be an unmanageable mass of demands in such a way that citizens can find some satisfaction in the platform of at least one party. A concomitant part of this process is the activities of interest groups, which perform the function of "interest articulation," in which they develop and express the political interests, preferences, and demands of their members to both the broader society and the decision makers. Parties, then, respond to various articulated demands by developing policies and election platforms that cross over what various groups call for.

Parties as *recruiters of political leaders* address the need of society to have some process that regularly brings a flow of people into positions of responsibility. Reflecting on our hypothetical discussion, the problem of leadership was evident in a number of different ways. Without parties, each constituency might not have a candidate. Some person has to speak with authority about the direction the party will take. For example, if the leader denies the importance of welfare reform, then those thinking of voting for Candidate C because of her commitment to welfare reform have to factor that information into their decision process. And in the legislature there has to be some process to identify the leaders of the parties.

The *organization of government* refers to the necessity of having some entity provide the impetus for directing the affairs of governments and co-ordinating the various offices of government. Party provides the funnel for making appointments, establishing new policy directions, and making decisions about how existing policies will be administered and implemented.

Setting public policy, at first glance, seems so obvious as to be trite; yet, without the introduction of the party's perception of its mandate and its policy objectives into decision-making processes, bureaucrats and non-party social institutions—interest groups, for instance—would structure the course of policy development. To attribute the function of setting public policy to political parties suggests that they are the conduit between the wider public and the inner circles of the state.

Integration and mobilization refer to the easing of tensions that arise from political differences, often referred to as "cleavages," and the bringing of otherwise inactive citizens into political activity. Social cleavages have the potential to be divisive, perhaps resulting in violence and civil war. By bringing varied social groups into the political process and by accommodating differences among them, political parties lower social tensions and reduce the likelihood of political fragmentation and disintegration. Parties, by being attuned to the emergence of new political forces, incorporate demands for change in their platforms and language. In Canada, for example, many parties eagerly present themselves as being on the forefront of the women's movement, environmentalism, and multiculturalism in a way that would have startled members and supporters of those parties from even ten years ago.

In sum, the six functions of political parties point to what is known as the *competitive theory of democracy*, in which one critical element is the role of political parties in strengthening democratic political processes. We need a clear understanding of what is meant by the competitive theory of democracy to appreciate the role of parties in liberal-democratic political systems.

THE COMPETITIVE THEORY OF DEMOCRACY

The competitive theory of democracy addresses the question of what happens in political systems. Every system has political processes, value patterns, and institutions that provide the framework for "who gets what, when, and how."[8] The starting point of the competitive theory of democracy is that in every system there is a political hierarchy characterized by the presence of elites, who play central roles in politics, and the mass of people, whose political roles tend to be minimal. In the absence of elections and the "competitive struggle for the people's vote,"[9] ordinary people would possess little or no influence over who gets what, when, and how in the political system. Elites would monopolize political life. Simply put, political elites, not having to pay attention to the mass of citizens, would direct the benefits of the state's actions toward themselves; their interests and perceptions about what ought to be done would override whatever the mass of society might imagine it needs. There might be a concession to democracy in the sense that political leaders would represent themselves as acting in the interests of the entire society; but nondemocratic systems, whether they be autocratic or totalitarian, are based on the denial of the right of common members of society to choose leaders through parties competing for the people's votes.

In liberal democracies, on the other hand, leaders are chosen on the basis of elections, freely contested, and votes, freely cast and fairly counted. According to the competitive theory of democracy, the fact of elections means that political parties vie with each other for the votes of citizens. Such elections result in the interests of ordinary citizens being taken into account by political elites.[10] In any election, a winning party will represent some large fraction—but necessarily only one part—of society. Its electoral coalition will bring certain interests to bear upon decision-making processes. Other coalitions of interests will be aligned with opposition parties. Sooner or later, the electorally dominant coalition will be challenged by another party that is able to build up support either by persuading voters that the dominant coalition's failures are significant or by mobilizing new interests behind the challenger. The challenger's victory, then, brings into the state a new coalition of interests that, at some future election, will be turfed from office by the successful building of yet another winning electoral coalition. The theory of democratic competition, therefore, suggests that over time the varied significant interests of society are brought into the affairs of state because politicians, needing votes from the mass of citizens, develop appeals, platforms, and policies that will be broadly popular. This is not to say that social, economic, and political elites are without influence; rather, they compete with the mass of society for influence, and the logic of democratic competition attenuates what otherwise would be the hegemonic role of elites. By developing competing coalitions of citizens, parties bring the varied concerns and interests of ordinary citizens into decision-making processes. By criticizing the governing party for being complacent or reluctant to move in a particular direction, opposition parties arouse voters to move in new directions. As parties alternate in office, various perceptions of the public interest have access to the state.

Three analytical concerns flow out of the theory of democratic competition. First, how is this democratic competition structured? Second, what is the nature of party organization? Third, what changes can be identified in the character of competition over time?

The structure of democratic competition involves two dimensions; the first is the number of parties that, because of the level of the electoral support they are able to command, are in a position either to win an election or, at least, play a significant role in the overall result. The second element pertains to the manner in which parties campaign for votes— that is, how do they present themselves to voters?

PARTY SYSTEMS

One of the ways in which political scientists differentiate party systems is on the basis of the number of parties that are significant contenders. A simple distinction is that between a *two-party system* and a *multi-party system*. The American system is often taken to be a leading example of the former because the Democratic and Republican parties are, with some minor exceptions, the only parties electing people to political office, whether it be at the local, state, or national level. In any election, the two parties command very high proportions of the votes cast. Multi-party systems, often associated with European states such as France and Italy, have a number of parties that are serious contenders to form a government. In many instances, because of the number of parties securing support in the election, no one party forms a majority in the legislature and a coalition government must be struck. Numerous factors influence whether a state has a two-party or multi-party system, but one clearly important determinant is the electoral system, which refers to the manner in which votes are counted.

One important distinction in electoral systems is whether the winner is determined simply by counting votes cast (in which case the candidate achieving more votes than any other candidate is declared the winner) or whether some other calculations occur. In the former case, commonly known as the *first-past-the-post* or *plurality system*, if there are more than two candidates, it is probable that the winning candidate will have less than 50 percent of the vote. In the latter case, one alternative is to assign parties seats in the legislature according to their *proportion of votes* won in the election. Since parties, rather than individual candidates, win seats, parties establish a list of candidates equal to the number of seats available in an area. Clearly, party leaders, who determine who is at the head of the list and who is at the bottom, are in a strong position to control the party. An alternative method for counting votes is commonly known as the *sin-*

gle transferable vote, in which voters indicate their rank-order choice of candidates. The object of this system is to produce a representative who has the support of a majority of the voters. If, on the first count, no candidate has a majority, then the candidate with the lowest number of votes is dropped, with her or his voters' second preferences distributed to the remaining candidates. This procedure continues until one candidate has over 50 percent of the votes cast.

Canada, as in so many things, seems to be a halfway house between the American case and the political development of many European states. In one sense, Canada has a two-party system because only two parties—the Liberals and Progressive Conservatives—have formed federal governments. Generally, those governments have been constituted on the basis of a majority of seats in the House of Commons. But there have been periods, most notably in the 1960s and 1970s, in which there have been minority governments, reflecting the emergence of regionally oriented parties and the failure of the two major parties to be competitive in all regions of the country. The 1993 election muddies the description because three parties hold a large number of seats in the House of Commons, but two additional parties had significant shares of the vote.

Another complexity of the Canadian political system is that in the provinces there are generally two competitive parties, but these are often quite different competitors from the national ones. This is most evident in the case of Quebec, which does not have a provincial Conservative Party. In some of the other provinces, the provincial equivalents of the major national parties have had very low levels of support, and at various times in the twentieth century there have been governments formed by "third parties."[11]

The second dimension of the structure of democratic competition consists of how political parties campaign. Some parties adhere closely to a set of well-defined philosophical principles and policies. Their finely tuned appeals and specialized positions suggest that they are akin to boutiques and, like most boutiques, they are likely to be small rather than large, specialized in their appeal rather than middle-of-the market. Communist parties are good examples of such parties; so are some social democratic parties, such as the Canadian Commonwealth Co-operative Federation (CCF)—the predecessor of today's New Democratic Party—environmental parties, and libertarian parties. These parties are often described as "movements" because they appear to be more interested in expressing their commitment to ideological principles than in winning votes and elections.[12]

In comparison to parties that parallel boutiques are parties that resemble department stores. They offer the electorate a broad range of policies covering a number of philosophical and policy positions. Just as department stores appeal to the middle of the market, these parties avoid political extremes, seeking the political middle. Consistency is not easily found in these parties' electoral pronouncements, either at one time or over time, because they are noted for their flexibility in how they present themselves to the electorate. For instance, in Canada the present-day Liberal and Progressive Conservative parties have reversed their traditional positions on the issue of free trade with the United States.

This style of electioneering is known as *brokerage politics*. Brokers serve as intermediaries between buyers and sellers. Brokerage parties locate themselves between society's various groups (which, by their separate existence, presumably are based on different perceived or real interests) by offering policies that attract broadly rather than narrowly. Classic examples include policies that appeal to both business-oriented and labour-aligned voters or to a number of different regions or ethnic groups. The process of presenting programs with wide rather than narrow appeals for support is seen by many political scientists as contributing to the integration of society. For example, by appealing to all classes rather than a single class, or by trying to represent many regions or ethnic groups instead of a select one or few, brokerage political parties ease the tensions between groups and thereby strengthen social cohesiveness. Leading examples of brokerage parties are the Republican and Democratic parties in the United States and the Liberal and Progressive Conservative parties in Canada. It is important to note that the concept of brokerage politics does not suggest that parties are necessarily identical in what they say and do, but generally the differences between the parties are few. Indeed, at times the parties may appear to have exchanged positions on the ideological continuum. Such parties are often seen as having "conservative" and "liberal" elements, and the particular face of the party in a given election will reflect which wing is dominant at that time.[13]

PARTY ORGANIZATION

One of the most important aspects of party organization is the relationship between the leaders and rank-and-file members of the party. A well-established distinction was offered many years ago by the French political scientist Maurice Duverger in his classic *Political Parties*.[14] One type, labelled as *cadre*, is dominated by the party's parliamentary caucus;

the choice of leaders comes from the deliberations of the party's elite, with other members of the party having minimal roles to play. *Mass parties*, on the other hand, are more complex entities. Although there are three types of mass party, the overall stress is on the importance of rank-and-file party members playing leading roles in the life of the party: leaders are chosen by members; philosophical principles and policies are debated and decided by party members; and party leaders are accountable to party members for their actions.

In Canada, the Liberal and Progressive Conservative parties historically have been of the cadre type, but in the twentieth century they have adopted some of the practices of mass parties, most notably the use of conventions for the selection of party leaders and policy conferences for the development of policy programs. The New Democratic Party (and its predecessor, the Co-operative Commonwealth Federation) and the Parti Québécois have tended to be parties of the mass type.

The third issue emanating from the theory of democratic competition is changes in the nature of party competition over time. The Canadian case is very instructive in this regard. A very useful analysis of this question has been developed by Ken Carty, and this section will outline his interpretation.[15]

THE DEVELOPMENT OF THE CANADIAN PARTY SYSTEM

Carty's model of the Canadian party system has three stages: 1867 to 1917, 1921 to 1957, and 1963 to the present day. His thesis is that, as Canada has evolved from a rural society to an urban and industrialized one, parties have taken on very different forms and roles.

The first period is seen as a time of party dominance. Parties were at the centre of Canada's origins and evolution. Despite the emphasis on "national development," the parties were not well-developed national institutions. The heart of the party was the parliamentary caucus, with very little thought given to matters of internal party democracy. The party caucus chose the leader, and the leader determined the policy direction the party would take. What party leaders had to do, however, was command the loyalty of partisans and voters in the country's various (and expanding) constituencies. The most effective device toward this end was patronage, the distribution of projects and jobs to political friends. The Conservative and Liberal parties dominated the system and competed on fairly equal terms across the country. But the system was underdeveloped because the parties had "no national organization or party membership to which the politicians might answer."[16]

The second period is characterized by great changes in the nature and operation of Canadian parties. The processes of urbanization and industrialization created new societal demands in the latter part of the period. In the early part, up into the 1930s, rapid settlement of the West and the hurried expansion of its agriculture challenged the dominance of the Liberals and the Conservatives. New parties emerged at both the federal and provincial levels of the system to represent various agrarian and rural interests that felt that the traditional parties were too tied to commercial and business interests in Ontario and Quebec. National politics was no longer played out at the constituency level but rather at the regional tier. Political parties played the game of brokerage politics by trying to present election platforms that balanced the newly developing regional interests. The most successful practitioners of this subtle art were Prime Minister William Lyon Mackenzie King and the Liberal Party. Having been evicted from Quebec in 1896, the Conservatives, for their part, were able to pose only limited threats to the Liberals' ascendancy, which began in that election. In the period after the Second World War, the CCF, having formed the government in Saskatchewan in 1944, interjected into the national political debate issues of the welfare state, the state's role in the economy, and, at least in its early years, the promise of the development of a socialist society.

The second period lasted until 1957, to be succeeded by yet another great change in the nature and operation of the party system, which has lasted to the present. The fundamental focus of the parties is the nation. In the words of Carty, "Parties direct their appeal to individual citizens and seek to engage their support for particular definitions of the political agenda and appropriate patterns of public policy. The national parties compete for individual support with one another and with their provincial counterparts."[17]

Two important and divergent organizational changes mark the third period and underlie the new party system. The first is reflected in the enhanced role of the party leader, whose influence and control over the important activities of the party have become increasingly dominant. For example, party appointments reflect the leader's prerogatives. In the election campaign the focus of attention, especially by the media, is on the day-to-day activities and pronouncements of the leader. Other candidates, including senior cabinet ministers, are almost invisible, save for blunders and controversies. The almost ritualistic televised debate between party leaders has nearly eliminated the role of other party spokepersons in spreading the party's message.

The second change is in the expanded role of the extra-parliamentary party, which is called upon to elect leaders, debate policies, ponder election strategy, and consider whether the leader should be replaced. One of the important consequences of democratizing the process of selecting leaders is that the party leader owes his or her legitimacy to the decision of the extra-parliamentary party rather than to the party's parliamentary caucus. Joe Clark, for example, became leader of the Conservative Party in 1976 despite having little initial support from his colleagues in the caucus. His victory at the leadership convention contained an uncertainty because the group he had to work with on a daily basis had, in the main, not supported him, but the caucus felt pressure to accept and work with the choice of the party. In the evolution of the Canadian party system, the concept of party has expanded enormously, from the few in a caucus to the thousands of party workers participating in the process of selecting a leader.

Accompanying these changes has been the increased use of television as a means of communicating directly with voters. The elections of the 1960s saw a decline in lengthy speeches given by the party leader and the rise of the photo opportunity and the television news clip. Expensive advertisements are the principal medium for disseminating the parties' messages: "hard" and "soft," "negative" and "positive" commercials are prepared and run depending on the flow of the campaign and whether the party is falling or rising. In the 1988 and 1993 federal general elections, television commercials became central battlegrounds, continuing the domination of advertising requirements and agendas over the articulation of substantive ideas and alternatives.[18]

No longer do party strategists rely upon well-informed politicos to provide information about what is happening in the constituencies. Parties spend enormous sums conducting voter research by public opinion surveys and focus groups in order to develop finely honed strategies for appealing to voters.[19] The professionalization and "electronicization" of politics have resulted in the local constituency association having very little real decision-making impact. Indeed, the party as an institution in the new party system has little to do, outside the nomination of the local candidate, but cheer the leader and raise funds.

THE DECLINING ROLE OF PARTY

Ironically, the democratization of party life has been parallelled by doubts about the continuing centrality of parties in politics.[20] The starting point for the discussion is the six functions of political parties outlined earlier.

In terms of *vote structuring*, over time the proportion of voters who regard themselves as having a moderate or strong identification with a political party has declined. Larger and larger proportions of voters make their electoral decision on the basis of their perceptions of party leaders, their opinions on short-term issues, and their evaluations of campaign events. Canadians have experienced a number of elections marked by rapid movements in levels of party support over the few weeks of an election campaign. Two leading examples are the NDP victory in the Ontario election of 1990 and the collapse of the Progressive Conservative Party in 1993.[21] Because politics in the era of television coverage and electronic campaigning is much less based on the strength of local candidates and parties, constituency issues, and traditional patterns of support, movements toward one party and away from others are amplified. Consider the province of Ontario in the 1993 federal election, which saw all but one of the province's ninety-nine seats go to the Liberals, an electoral domination heretofore unknown in the province's history. Historically, each of the parties has had strongholds that stayed true despite the overall ebb and flow of electoral fortunes. In the 1993 election, voters, regardless of where they lived in the province, responded to similar images provided by television and moved in similar ways as they made their voting decisions. Traditional bases of support weakened in the process. Party-based cues, then, are much weaker than was formerly the case, having been replaced by the episodic stimuli provided by the events of electronic-based campaigns. Party ties led to stable patterns of support; electronic appeals lead to volatility.

The central role of parties in the process of *interest aggregation* has been eroded by the spreading practice of interest groups who work outside of parties and the party system to achieve their objectives. Anthony King, in his discussion of this issue, makes two central points. First, throughout the Western democracies one can find many instances in which processes of interest aggregation did not involve parties. Second, parties have a much reduced role in the process of converting interest groups' policy demands into their (party) policies. Rather, government policies reflect the impact of leaders, cabinets, bureaucracies, and individuals acting outside of the parties. King observes, "The most that parties seem generally able to do is to present electorates with highly generalized platforms and with alternative candidates committed to general policy standpoints. Probably on major issues, most parties in the West could do little else. But they thereby leave the function of interest aggregation to others."[22]

While King's comments capture the essence of the situation, what he says must be interpreted contextually to determine the degree to which the statement reflects reality. The 1993 election provides the basis for this test. The Liberal Party responded to demands from the Canadian Federation of Mayors and Municipalities and stressed the importance of municipal infrastructure redevelopment in its campaign. Under Jean Chrétien (unlike his predecessor, John Turner), the Liberal Party also carefully considered its policy options at a thinkers' conference.[23] But the general tendency is for parties not to engage extensively in interest aggregation—at least in the sense that the concept was first developed. American parties, which have traditionally gone through an elaborate process to develop their platforms in presidential election years by inviting interest groups to make representations to a broadly based platform committee, exemplified the idea of aggregating interests. This practice never took hold in Canada. Parties do organize policy conferences, but they do not necessarily have an impact on what a party says in an election or does when in office. Leadership conventions provide opportunities for candidates to discuss a great number of policy issues, but the connection between the leadership campaign and the subsequent election platform may be tenuous. For example, the Progressive Conservative Party, despite a highly publicized policy conference in 1991 and the 1993 leadership convention that saw Kim Campbell succeed Brian Mulroney, entered the federal election campaign with a bare glimmering of policy ideas.[24]

The two functions of the *organization of government* and the *formation of public policy* can be discussed simultaneously. In both instances, administrative actors very much structure the activities and decisions of the government. Consider this reflection on the "Great Society" of American president Lyndon Johnson in the 1960s:

> In the fields of health, housing, urban renewal, transportation, welfare, education, forestry, and energy, it has been in very great measure people in government service, or closely associated with it, acting on the basis of their specialized and technical knowledge, who first perceived the problem, conceived the program, initially urged it on president and Congress, went on to lobby it through to enactment, and then saw to its administration.[25]

It would be easy to think that the American case reflects that system's peculiar pattern of institutional fragmentation and a decentralized party system. John Meisel, writing about the Canadian case, in which the executive-dominated parliamentary system and leader-oriented parties operate, observes that:

[an] important shift has occurred in the focus of power of liberal democracies, from elected politicians to appointed civil servants, whose links to political parties are indirect and increasingly tenuous. This means that parties, supposedly in control of the political process and responsible to the public for its performance, are often little more than impotent observers of processes they cannot control and the results of which they can only rubber stamp.[26]

King completes his discussion of party function by concluding that party "is likely to remain one important factor in political *integration and mobilization* . . . [but] it has never been the only one and it seems possible that its importance is declining" (emphasis added).[27] Canadians contemplating the continuing question of Quebec's separation from Canada will wonder about the efficacy of parties as social integrators. The 1993 election, which produced calamitous results for the Conservative and New Democratic parties, saw the emergence of two regionally oriented parties—Reform, based primarily in the West, and the Bloc Québécois, oriented exclusively to Quebec—that together won 106 of 295 House of Commons seats. On the other hand, the Liberal Party's handsome majority was fashioned by winning seats in every province. It held a substantial number of seats in every region, with Quebec, in a historic irony, marking its poorest showing.

More prosaically, parties seem to be declining as institutions in terms of membership. To be sure, membership rolls seem to swell in times of great interest, such as a leadership race or contested nomination meetings, but quickly fall off once the event has passed. Parties, then, seem to have lost their capacity to engage sufficient numbers of people to be members on a continuing basis. This decline in party membership is not unique to Canada. It seems to be widespread in the Western democracies, with citizens seeking out non-party-based routes to political participation.

Parties continue the *recruitment* of candidates, and very few people are elected who are not affiliated with parties. In that sense, parties can be said to be performing the function of recruitment of leaders. But an important change to the process of electing party leaders has occurred, one best exemplified by what has happened in Canada. Leadership conventions have become widely accepted since World War I as the means for parties to choose their leaders; instead of the few members of the party's parliamentary caucus selecting their leader, thousands of delegates make the choice. But many of these delegates have only a recent record of involvement in the party, and many attend only one convention.

One of the consequences of the democratization of the process of leadership selection is that the party's top position is now open to those who have little or no political experience or who have left political life and want to return. Consider the Canadian examples since the 1970s. Joe Clark became Tory leader in 1976 after only four years in Parliament; one of his opponents (Claude Wagner) had been a Quebec Liberal cabinet minister; another (Paul Hellyer) had been a federal Liberal cabinet minister; still another (Brian Mulroney) had never held elected office. In 1983, Mulroney, still without elected experience, defeated Clark for the Tory leadership. Kim Campbell became the Progressive Conservative leader in 1993 after only five years in Parliament. John Turner became Liberal leader in 1984 after being in the political wilderness since 1978; his main opponent, Jean Chrétien, left politics in 1986 and then, in 1990, won the Liberal leadership. Audrey McLaughlin won the New Democratic Party mantle having served only one year as a member of Parliament.

It seems reasonable to conclude that leadership conventions have created opportunities for outsiders and representatives of politically marginal groups to contest the parties' highest positions. It is quite possible that this tendency will continue as parties move toward the universal franchise method of selecting leaders in which each member of the party participates in the election.

This next step in the democratization of party life raises important questions that point to the decline in the saliency of the party as an institution. The Progressive Conservative Party of Alberta illustrates the issue. In December 1992 the party held a leadership election on the basis of "one member, one vote." Since no candidate received a majority of votes on the first ballot, a second ballot was held a week later. It was possible to walk into a polling place, buy a membership in the party, and vote that very day. What does "party membership" mean? What does "party" mean? Clearly very little, both for those who hold a "membership" and those who seek their votes. It is hard to see much that is substantial—other than for the obvious fact that a leader was chosen—or that strengthens the party as an institution.[28] Once the leader is chosen, he or she is free to act and only in the most unusual of circumstances would feel the constraint of party. Until the party meets next in convention, the leader need not fear a serious challenge. Democratization has opened up the party but in the process weakened the institution.

CONCLUSION

It seems impossible for a large and complex society to exist without political parties. The many functions associated with parties point to the fundamental contribution to the nature and operation of a society's political system. But, as we have seen, parties have changed considerably in relatively short periods. Will parties have a weaker or stronger role?

Elites and masses always exist. The question is, what is the political relationship between the top and bottom of society? Political competition, which is built into the electoral processes of liberal democracy, means that elites and masses share in the direction of society and the structure of rewards and benefits. The competitive theory of democracy requires the existence of spirited and well-established political parties, whether they be located in a two-party or multi-party system. Competition gives disaffected citizens the possibility of an outlet for their grievances. If you are dissatisfied with the status quo, then you and others like you have an alternative route for achieving your ends.

Such a model presupposes that the alternatives are real and not based on matters of personality, on who happens to be the leader at any particular time. Competition serves only limited ends if it merely results in one leader being replaced by another leader. Parties, then, have to be more than machines that allow the ambitious to reach high political office; they must be institutions that, within the context of electoral competition, offer citizens something much more substantial by way of choice.

The argument has been made that modern liberal democracies, Canada included, are undergoing transformations of their party systems. These changes in general point to a weakening of parties as institutions, to a diminution of their effectiveness as a force in government capable of offering significant and tangible differences to voters.

One can undoubtedly argue about the validity of the competitive theory of democracy. Critics of liberal-democratic political processes, especially the role of political parties, for example, rightly point to the often close connections between well-established and large economic interests and political parties. They would argue that changes in government do not really matter, certainly in terms of providing access to marginalized social groups, because parties are too intimately tied to corporate interests. Brokerage politics, which is at the heart of the competitive theory of politics, obscures the class nature of Canadian politics: business interests have no trouble entering the political process, while working-class interests are on the margins, with even the New Democratic Party playing the "middle of the road" game.[29]

The issue, however, is not whether the critics are right or wrong about brokerage politics and class interests, but rather what, if anything, can be done to strengthen parties so that they can be more effective political institutions. The answer is not at all obvious. For many, the intuitively right thing to do is open up parties, make them more democratic and participatory, continue the movement from the cadre to the mass form. "Let the people choose" is hard to argue against. Yet, as Canadian parties have gone through various modes of democratization, so that ordinary members of the party have significant roles to play in the selection and removal of leaders, there has been a concomitant weakening of the parties as institutions.

At the beginning of the century, André Siegfried observed that Canadian parties were strongly oriented to their leaders; but, at the same time, he pointed to the strength of party as an institution. Leaders in the first Canadian party system had to deal with local notables; in the second system, regional party leaders played significant roles. At the close of the century, our democratic evolution has accentuated the role of the leader without a parallel strengthening of the party. Parties exist because they provide citizens with outlets for the expression of their political beliefs and interests. Since this need will not disappear, parties in some form will be at the centre of political life. The absence of strong parties may mean that there is little connection between what the state does and what citizens want or expect. Citizens can change only who holds office. In an age when political competition is highly personalistic in character, the failures of government policies are easily seen as the personal failings of the leaders, which may contribute to the widespread and apparently deepening cynicism about government and politics that has marked Canadian politics since the middle of the 1960s.[30]

NOTES

[1] *Large* refers to number of people; *complex* refers to number of interests.

[2] See Escott M. Reid, "The Rise of National Parties in Canada," *Papers and Proceedings of the Canadian Political Science Association* 4 (1932). Reprinted in various editions of *Party Politics in Canada* (see note 20).

[3] André Siegfried, *The Race Question in Canada* (Toronto: McClelland & Stewart, 1966; originally published 1907).

[4] While in some cities, parties have long been established, many non-party candidates continue to be elected.

[5] The Canadian exception is the Northwest Territories. For a discussion of a non-party system, see Graham White, "Westminster in the Arctic: The Adaptation of British Parliamentarism in the Northwest Territories," *Canadian Journal of Political Science* 24, 3 (Sept. 1991): 499–523.

[6] Anthony King, "Political Parties in Western Democracies," *Polity* 2, 2 (Winter 1969): 111–41.

[7] Ibid., 122.

[8] See Harold Lasswell, *Politics: Who Gets What, When, and How* (New York: Meridian Books, 1958).

[9] An influential interpretation of liberal-democratic political processes from the perspective of competitive democratic theory is represented by the following: "The democratic method is that institutional arrangement for arriving at political decisions in which individuals acquire the power to decide by a competitive struggle for the people's vote." See Joseph A. Schumpeter, *Capitalism, Socialism, and Democracy,* 3rd ed. (New York: Harper & Row, 1950), 269.

[10] In his classic interpretation of the competitive theory of democracy, R.A. Dahl writes that "conflicts will probably occur from time to time between leaders' overt policies, which are designed to win support from constituents, and their covert policies, which are shaped to win the support of subleaders or other leaders. The keener the political competition, the more likely it is that leaders will resolve these conflicts in favor of their overt commitments." R.A. Dahl, *Who Governs? Democracy and Power in an American City* (New Haven: Yale University Press, 1961), 102.

[11] In every province from Quebec west to British Columbia, parties other than the Liberals and Conservatives have formed governments.

[12] For a classic statement of this argument, see Walter D. Young, *The Anatomy of a Party* (Toronto: University of Toronto Press, 1969).

[13] Many political science interpretations are contested; in this instance, for a strong statement of an alternate view see William Christian and Colin Campbell, *Political Parties and Ideologies in Canada* (Toronto: McGraw-Hill Ryerson, 1983).

[14] Maurice Duverger, *Political Parties* (London: Methuen, 1964).

[15] R.K. Carty, "Three Canadian Party Systems: An Interpretation of the Development of National Politics" in *Party Democracy in Canada*, ed. G.C. Perlin (Scarborough: ON, Prentice-Hall, 1988), 15–32.

[16] Ibid., 19.

[17] Ibid., 24.

[18] For an interpretation of the impact of electronic campaigning, see A. Brian Tanguay,"Canadian Political Ideologies in the Electronic Age" in *Canadian Politics*, ed. A. Gagnon and J. Bickerton (Peterborough, ON: Broadview Press, 1990), 129–57.

[19] The parties' preoccupation with polls is parallelled by the media's obsession with who is winning; see R. Jeremy Wilson, "Horserace Journalism and Canadian Electronic Campaigns," *Journal of Canadian Studies* 15, 4 (1980–81).

[20] Two essays provide a guideline for this discussion. See King, "Political Parties in Western Democracies" and John Meisel, "Decline of Party in Canada" in *Party Politics in Canada*, 6th ed., ed. Hugh G. Thorburn (Scarborough, ON: Prentice-Hall, 1991), 178–201.

[21] On the latter election, see Peter Woolstencroft, "Doing Politics Differently: The Party and the Campaign of 1993" in *The Canadian General Election of 1993*, ed. Alan Frizzell, Jon H. Pammett, and Anthony Westell (Ottawa: Carleton University Press, 1994), 9–26.

[22] King, "Political Parties in Western Democracies," 140.

[23] See Stephen Clarkson, "Yesterday's Man and His Blue Grits: Backward into the Future," in *Canadian General Election of 1993*, 29–30.

[24] Woolstencroft, "Doing Politics Differently," 13.

[25] S.H. Beer, "Federalism, Nationalism, and Democracy in America," *American Political Science Review* 72 (March 1978): 40.

[26] Meisel, "Decline of Party in Canada," 181.

[27] King, "Political Parties in Western Democracies," 128.

[28] Newspaper reports in August 1994 that Nancy Betkowski (who ran second to Ralph Klein), considered running for the leadership of the Alberta Liberal Party graphically illustrate the point.

[29] Harold D. Clarke, Jane Jenson, Lawrence LeDuc, and Jon H. Pammett, *Absent Mandate: The Politics of Discontent in Canada* (Toronto: Gage, 1984). For a thoughtful analysis of this argument, see H. Donald Forbes, "Absent Mandate '88? Parties and Voters in Canada," *Journal of Canadian Studies* 25, 2 (Summer 1990).

[30] See Harold D. Clarke and Allan Kornberg, "Evaluations and Evolution: Public Attitudes Toward Canada's Federal Political Parties, 1965–1991," *Canadian Journal of Political Science* 26, 2 (June 1993): 287–311.

SUGGESTED READING

Campbell, W., and C. Christian. *Political Parties and Ideologies in Canada*. 3rd ed. Toronto: McGraw-Hill Ryerson, 1990.

An excellent examination of the philosophical bases of Canadian political parties.

Carty, R.K., ed. *Canadian Political Party Systems: A Reader*. Peterborough, ON: Broadview Press, 1992.

This reader contains a number of very useful interpretations of Canadian parties.

Clarke, Harold D., Jane Jenson, Lawrence LeDuc, and Jon H. Pammett. *Absent Mandate: Interpreting Change in Canadian Elections*. 2nd ed. Toronto: Gage, 1991.

Four prominent analysts of Canadian voting behaviour provide an excellent discussion of the topic. Their earlier *Political Choice in Canada* (1979) gives a well-grounded account.

Frizzell, Alan, Jon H. Pammett, and Anthony Westell, eds. *The Canadian General Election of 1993*. Ottawa: Carleton University Press, 1994.

Essays discuss the parties' election campaigns, the role of the media, and the impact of television, polls, and leaders' debates.

Johnston, Richard, André Blais, Henry Brady, and Jean Crête, *Letting the People Decide*. Montreal: McGill-Queen's University Press, 1992.
A sophisticated and important study of the 1988 federal election.

Royal Commission on Electoral Reform and Party Financing. *Reforming Electoral Democracy*. Ottawa: Ministry of Supply and Services, 1992.
The four volumes published under the auspices of the royal commission provide students with a wide range of invaluable essays.

Thorburn, Hugh G., ed. *Party Politics in Canada*. 6th ed. Scarborough, ON: Prentice-Hall, 1991.
The seventh edition of this well-established collection of readings will be published in 1995.

Wearing, Joseph. *Strained Relations: Canadian Parties and Voters*. Toronto: McClelland & Stewart, 1988.
Provides a good introduction to the topic.

Wolinetz, Steven B., ed. *Parties and Party Systems in Liberal Democracies*. London: Routledge, 1988.
Although somewhat dated, this book contains a number of essays that analyze the major party systems in liberal democracies.

THE CANADIAN VOTER

E

ven by the volatile standards of modern Canadian politics, the federal election of 25 October 1993, which swept the Liberal Party under Jean Chrétien into power, installed the Bloc Québécois as the official Opposition, handed the Reform Party fifty-two seats, and annihilated the governing Progressive Conservatives, was a dramatic event. Coming just a year after Canadian voters had soundly rejected the Charlottetown Accord in a national referendum, there is little doubt that the aftershocks of these two major political upheavals will continue to be felt for some time. Yet, while there was much that was new and unprecedented in the 1993 federal election, there were also substantial links to the volatility and uncertainty of the recent past. It had been only nine years since Canadians threw out a Liberal government in a dramatic political turnaround. Volatility and change are hardly new to Canadian electoral politics. National surveys of the Canadian electorate, conducted regularly with each election beginning in 1965, portray an electorate that has changed relatively little in its fundamental characteristics and outlook, yet is easily susceptible to sudden and often dramatic swings in voting choice.[1]

Before Brian Mulroney did so in 1988, no Canadian federal government since 1953 had succeeded in winning a second consecutive parliamentary majority in an election. Of the dozen federal elections that have taken place since John Diefenbaker ended the long period of Liberal dominance of Canadian federal politics in 1957, five have been won by the Progressive Conservatives (1958, 1962, 1979, 1984, and 1988) and seven by the Liberals (1963, 1965, 1968, 1972, 1974, 1980, and 1993). In every one of these elections except 1958, "third" parties polled at least 20 percent of the total vote, often gaining enough parliamentary seats to deny a majority to the winner. Indeed, five of these twelve elections resulted in minority governments (1962, 1963, 1965, 1972, 1979). For over thirty years, elections in Canada have been anything but orderly, predictable affairs.

Canada has not been an easy country to govern, and its rulers have been rewarded with political defeat nearly as often as with victory. In the dozen elections that roughly constitute the modern Canadian political era, five federal governments went down to electoral defeat (Diefenbaker in 1963, Trudeau in 1979, Clark in 1980, Turner in 1984, Campbell in 1993), and one more came precariously close (Trudeau in 1972). Although the Liberals were the governing party for more than half of the period since 1957, their hold on power was never very secure. Even those governments that enjoyed considerable political success often found their standing with the mass public to be at risk. The two most popular federal political leaders of the modern era—Diefenbaker and Trudeau—both faded quickly in public esteem during their early years in office, turning majority governments into minorities within four years of overwhelming election victories. Virtually every federal government in the past two decades has found itself behind in the public opinion polls after less than two years in office.[2] In spite of his record majority achieved in the 1984 election, Brian Mulroney fared even worse in the affection of the public than did his predecessors. At the beginning of 1988, the Conservatives stood third in the Gallup poll, preferred by only 28 percent of a national sample. The Liberals, led by the same John Turner who had brought his party to such a crushing defeat in the 1984 election, enjoyed a comfortable lead in the polls during much of Mulroney's first term in office, even though few people felt that Turner would have made a better prime minister. Within but a few months of his dramatic 1988 election victory, Mulroney's Conservatives again found themselves trailing their adversaries in many polls.[3] By the end of 1992, as the fallout from the referendum defeat gradually settled, it became clear that the Conservatives under Mulroney had virtually no chance of re-election. The party stood at a dismal 19 percent in the Gallup poll reported in January 1993. But the Liberals led by Jean Chrétien, dubbed "yesterday's man" by many of his detractors, did not represent an attractive alternative in the minds of many voters. And with two new parties preparing to contest the approaching federal election, the levels of uncertainty in Canadian federal politics had never been greater.

VOLATILITY AND DISCONTENT

The reasons for continued volatility in Canadian politics are partly found in Canadians' attitudes toward government and in the nature of the Canadian party system. Studies of the Canadian public have long disclosed a highly negative view of the political world and extensive discontent with government, parties, and politicians.[4] Many Canadians further believe that they have little say in the affairs of government and that their representatives begin to "lose touch" with the people soon after being elected to office. These tendencies, already high in the mid-1980s, rose significantly in 1988 and again in 1993 (see figure 1). Poor economic performance, the free trade debate, the enactment of the GST, and the long constitutional struggle culminating in the 1992 referendum undoubtedly added to these general public feelings of frustration and discontent. There has been a clear tendency to place much of the blame for the problems of the country firmly on the shoulders of those in power. Canadians, of course, are not in any sense unique among citizens of Western democracies in expressing discontent with government. But while such prolonged discontent can sometimes lead to withdrawal from the political process or to the formation of protest movements, in Canada it has more often been manifested in a willingness to "throw the rascals out" when the opportunity arises.

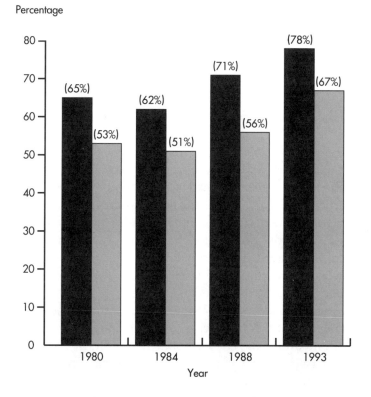

Figure 1: Canadians' Attitudes Toward Government, 1980–1993

Source: 1980, 1984 Canadian National Election Studies; 1988, 1993 Political
Support Studies.

The Canadian party system to a considerable degree has magnified and encouraged this tendency toward volatility in elections. While most Canadians express some degree of allegiance toward a political party at one time or another, relatively few are strongly partisan. In the 1984 national election study, for example, only 23 percent of those surveyed were found to be "very strong" supporters of any political party, about the same proportion as had been found in a 1965 study. Many Canadians hold different party attachments at the federal and provincial levels of government, a tendency that also explains some of the volatility in federal elections.[5] In the 1984 study, fully 35 percent of the national sample identified themselves with different parties at the federal and provincial levels. Even at the federal level alone, substantial numbers of Canadians are found to have changed their party identification, sometimes over fairly short periods of time. Between 1974 and 1980, for example, a national panel study estimated that 41 percent of the electorate had either changed or abandoned identification with a political party over the six-year period.[6] With the rise of new parties in federal politics such as the Reform Party and the Bloc Québécois, the opportunities for movement away from established party alignments have become even more pronounced.

These patterns suggest the precariousness of the base of public support on which the parties depend. We estimate that in 1984 only about a third of the Canadian electorate could be thought of as "durable" partisans—reasonably dependable, fairly strong supporters of a particular party—while two-thirds were "flexible" partisans, a voting group whose political allegiances were more susceptible to change.[7] These estimates were only slightly higher than had been found in a comparable study ten years earlier (see figure 2). Flexible partisans are more likely to change their vote from one election to another and more likely to be influenced by short-term factors associated with particular issues, leaders, or events. The flexible partisans are a continuing potential source of sudden and unpredictable change in Canadian elections, evidence of which is clearly seen in each of the last three federal elections.

Although the fundamental characteristics of the Canadian electorate have changed relatively little over the past decade and a half, its partisan political composition has changed quite markedly. In 1980, the Liberal Party held a clear advantage over its rivals in the self-identification of voters, even though many of these potential Liberal voters were also flexible partisans. By 1988, this advantage had disappeared, and the electorate showed signs of becoming more favourably disposed toward the Conservatives in terms of its fundamental composition. But such trends in Canadian

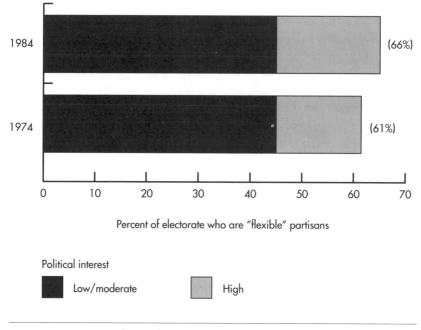

Figure 2: Partisanship and Political Interest in the Canadian Electorate, 1974 and 1984

Source: National Election Studies.

politics are often fleeting ones. Whatever advantages the Conservatives may have enjoyed among Canadian voters a few years ago are now gone, and the party finds itself in a struggle for its very survival.

PARTIES AND THEIR IMAGES

In contrast to some European democracies, it has not been possible to explain very much of the dynamics of Canadian party politics by examining long-term forces such as social class, religion, or group alignments. Ideology has likewise been notably weak as a factor in Canadian partisanship, and the Canadian party system has long defied a simple left–right characterization. A few long-term patterns, some of which may be fragments of past political alignments, did persist into the 1970s and 1980s. Catholics, for example, have often been somewhat less likely to vote Conservative in federal elections, a fact that has sometimes puzzled researchers seeking to explain the bases of Canadian parties.[8] Linguistic and regional patterns have also frequently been strong in Canadian federal politics, even though such patterns have become less reliable in recent years. But factors such as language, region, ethnicity, religion, or social class, even when taken together, have generally been able to explain only about 10 percent of the variation in voting behaviour in federal elections in Canada.[9] In part because of the inroads made by the Conservatives in Quebec in the 1984 and 1988 elections, those patterns that do exist have changed quite markedly in recent years. With the strength of the Reform Party in 1993, particularly in the West, such alignments are likely to change even further. In spite of the persistence of a few older patterns, and the continuing rise of new ones, it is nevertheless an exercise in futility to attempt to predict with any degree of reliability the behaviour of Canadian voters on the basis of socio-demographic characteristics alone.

Canadian political parties cannot call upon legions of loyal supporters whose attitudes are reinforced by strong group or ideological commitments. Rather, as we saw in chapter 17, they tend to act as "brokers" between competing interests and attempt to harness a variety of rather unpredictable short-term forces in order to achieve their goals. Questions used in a number of the national election studies help to shed light on the way in which Canadians see political parties. Data from two of these studies in each of the past two decades are shown in figure 3. The largest component of the images that people hold of the various parties tends to have to do with issues and public policy, followed closely by a category identified as "style" or "performance." The parties are most commonly viewed in terms of the dominant policies or issues of the day, and/or in terms of their performance, particularly when in government.

Each of the last five federal elections in Canada has seen an abrupt and dramatic shift in the particular issues that provided the main focus of the campaign and that contributed toward shaping the images that people held of the parties at the time. Not infrequently, parties have been able to manipulate issues for strategic purposes, as the Conservatives did with unemployment in the 1984 election campaign or the Liberals tried to do with free trade in 1988. Sometimes, however, certain issues force themselves onto the agenda whether parties wish to emphasize them or not, as the concern with budget deficits did in 1993. Parties seize upon the issues of the day and shape their own political strategies around them. But to a large extent, the policies and the performance of the party in power will act as the driving force in shaping the images of parties held by the voting public at any given time.

The party image data shown in figure 3 also disclose that, in contrast to some European party systems, Canadians do not tend to think of the

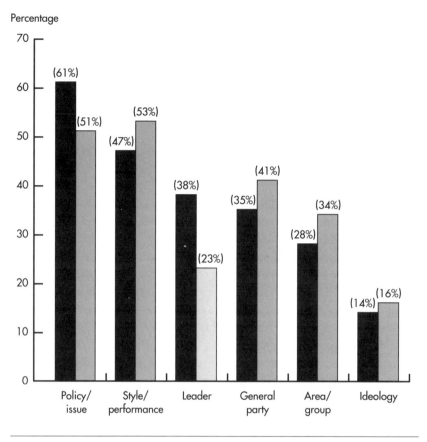

Figure 3: Voters' Images of Political Parties, 1974 and 1984

Source: National Election Studies.

parties in ideological terms. Neither are area or group images especially important, even though this might seem probable in a country (such as Canada) with strong regional and linguistic identities. For the most part, the images that the public holds of political parties tend to be highly responsive to change over time. Images of parties connected with longer-term social, historical, or ideological patterns are much less in evidence.

Party leaders have also figured prominently in Canadians' perceptions of political parties. Trudeau in the late 1960s and 1970s and Mulroney in the 1980s were dominant factors in shaping the images of their respective parties, and to a considerable extent the fortunes of their parties tended to rise and fall with those of the leader.[10] This is not a new phenomenon in Canadian politics, as the same might easily have been said of other strong personalities in the past such as John Diefenbaker, Tommy Douglas, or Réal Caouette. The pervasiveness of television and the use of televised debates between leaders in election campaigns has further enhanced this tendency. One of the quickest and surest ways for a Canadian political party to give itself a new image is to choose a new leader. Thus, as we shall see, the attempt of the Conservatives to fashion a new image for the party around Kim Campbell was, in spite of its ultimate failure, entirely consistent with the role that leaders have traditionally played in shaping Canadians' images of political parties.

THE VOTER DECIDES

The picture of the Canadian electorate portrayed here is one with relatively weak long-term attachments to parties, low ideological commitment, and high responsiveness to short-term factors such as leaders, issues, or political events. Elections themselves are major political events, and many of the attitudes of the voters toward parties and other political actors are shaped by elements that are associated specifically with particular elections. Johnston et al. argue that the campaign itself should receive greater emphasis in understanding both the strategies pursued by parties and leaders and the perceptions of voters.[11] Because its frame of reference is primarily short term, the public reacts to events as they unfold rather than to ideological or other longer-term stimuli. Only a quarter to a third of Canadian voters (primarily the durable partisans) may be said to have their minds made up with respect to voting choice well in advance of an election. A proportion of about equal size will make its decision at the time that the election is called, depending in part on the factors that precipitated the election call. Movement will also occur in response to the issues and events of the campaign and in reaction to the activities of the parties and their leaders or the effects of key campaign events such as televised leaders' debates.[12] As many as half of all voters may make their voting decisions during the course of the campaign itself, with nearly a quarter postponing their final decision until the last week (see figure 4). The 1988 campaign witnessed substantial movement in the public opinion polls during the period leading up to the call of the election, and even more dramatic swings in the polls following the leaders' debates, which took place at the mid-point of the campaign. In both 1984 and 1993, party leadership conventions held only a short time before the elections were called precipitated substantial pre-campaign movement. The collapse of Conservative support during the course of the 1993 campaign to some extent told the story of that election.

The events leading up to the 1993 election can be used to illustrate a number of the characteristics of the Canadian electorate. Following their

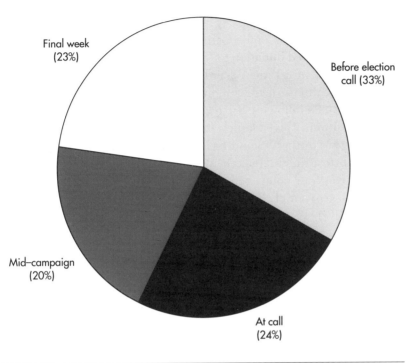

Figure 4: Reported Time of Vote Decision

Source: 1988 Carleton panel study.

victory in the 1984 election, the Conservatives quickly slipped in the public opinion polls, falling behind the Liberals within a few months after
the election. Like other federal governments of recent years, the Mulroney
government provoked largely negative public sentiment. The Conservatives
stood below 20 percent in the polls just before Mulroney's resignation
was announced in February 1993 (see figure 5). To be sure, the personal
unpopularity of the leader was only one of the factors accounting for the
Conservatives' low standing at the beginning of their ninth year in office.
Presiding over a deep and prolonged economic recession, the party in
power garnered much of the blame for continuing high unemployment
and persistent budget deficits. Its identification with unpopular policies,
such as the Goods and Services Tax and the Canada–U.S. Free Trade
Agreement, further damaged the re-election prospects of the party under
Mulroney. On 25 June, Mulroney handed over the job of prime minister
to Kim Campbell, who had been chosen over Jean Charest as the new
Conservative leader in a closely fought party leadership convention.
Although she had served in the Mulroney cabinet as minister of justice and

briefly as minister of national defence, Campbell represented the fresh new face that many felt the party needed. As a woman, a westerner, and a relative political newcomer, Campbell seemed to have the potential to deliver on her stated intention to "change the way politics is done in this country." The Conservatives' standing in the polls recovered sharply following her election as leader, in much the same way as the Liberals had recovered briefly following Turner's election as leader in 1984. Over the course of a summer given largely to pre-election campaigning, there was little change in the party standings. The monthly Gallup poll in August, taken just before the election call, placed the Liberals at 40 percent and the Conservatives four points behind at 36 percent. While there was still a long way to go, Campbell had seemingly restored her party to a position of competitiveness. Many felt that the election would be won or lost in the forty-seven-day campaign to follow.

The Conservatives' re-election prospects were further diminished by the emergence of two new political parties, which threatened to cut deeply into their traditional support. The Reform Party represented a clear threat to Conservative strength in the West and in rural Ontario. The party had established itself as a force to be reckoned with by successfully campaigning for the "No" side in the October 1992 referendum. In 1993, running candidates in all provinces except Quebec, Reform had positioned itself

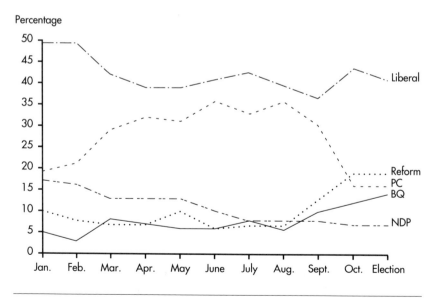

Figure 5: Party Standings in the Gallup Poll, 1993

Source: Gallup monthly reports.

to attempt a major political breakthrough. The Conservatives hoped that their choice of a leader from the West could blunt this effort, but Reform appealed both to ideological conservatives and to those disillusioned with the old line parties. At the same time, the Conservatives faced a threat from the Bloc Québécois for the support that Mulroney had successfully cultivated in Quebec in the 1984 and 1988 campaigns. While a separatist political party was hardly a new force in Quebec politics, this represented the first time that such a party had openly contested federal seats. With the Parti Québécois working actively for its success and BQ leader Lucien Bouchard enjoying considerable personal popularity in Quebec, the Bloc represented a formidable obstacle to Campbell's hopes of holding on to Mulroney's Quebec base.

The tensions in the Conservative campaign were evident from the beginning. Many senior Conservatives, having entered politics during the Clark or Mulroney years, chose not to seek re-election. Campbell, with only limited experience in federal politics, necessarily became the main focus of the Conservative campaign. Emphasizing her plan to reduce the budget deficit to zero over five years, Campbell found herself on the defensive from the beginning. She stumbled badly early in the campaign by conceding that unemployment would remain at high levels until the year 2000, and again a short time later with an off-the-cuff remark that an election campaign was not the time for a debate on social programs. Anxious to avoid too close an identification with the Mulroney years, the Conservative campaign lacked any clear policy focus. Again and again, Campbell returned to the theme of deficit reduction, an unconvincing issue for a party that had been in power for nine years.

By contrast, the Liberal campaign was a model of efficiency. A week after the election call, the Liberals released their 112-page Red Book, the product of the party's two-year policy review. It quickly became the centrepiece of the Liberal campaign, giving Chrétien a convenient reference point for his continuing emphasis on jobs and the economy and exposing the Conservatives' policy weakness. By the time of the televised leaders' debates, which took place at the mid-point of the campaign (3–4 October), the Conservatives had already slipped more than ten points in the opinion polls from their August high. The Reform Party was making significant gains, largely at the expense of the Conservatives, while the Bloc Québécois maintained a solid lead over all other parties in Quebec. The NDP, an important factor in previous elections, floundered badly from the beginning of the campaign, shackled by the unpopularity of provincial NDP governments in Ontario and British Columbia and by the wider than normal choice of alternative "third" parties.

The leaders' debates, which were perhaps the Conservatives' last best hope to revive their faltering campaign, proved to be a relatively insignificant event. Although Campbell performed well in both the French and English debates, they did not provide the decisive breakthrough that she needed to re-ignite her campaign. Unlike the debates of 1984 or 1988, which had featured dramatic exchanges that did have an effect on the campaign, the 1993 debates were quickly forgotten. The election was effectively over. In the final two weeks of the campaign, speculation centred on whether the Liberals would be able to form a majority government and on whether Reform or the Bloc would be able to form the official Opposition. Although estimates of probable Conservative seats were continually revised downward in the final days of the campaign, few foresaw the magnitude of the debacle that was to befall the party on election day.

As is often the case in single-member-district electoral systems, the Liberals won a much larger majority of seats in the 1993 election than might have seemed warranted by their modest 41 percent of the popular vote. In part because of the fragmentation of votes among four other major parties, the Liberals won representation in every part of the country, including Quebec, where traditional Liberal strength in anglophone and ethnic Montreal constituencies held up well, and the western provinces, where Liberal candidates had fared poorly since 1974. The Reform Party, although running second to the Liberals in popular vote at 19 percent, lost out to the Bloc Québécois in forming the official Opposition, as the concentration of Bloc votes in Quebec yielded fifty-four Bloc seats compared to fifty-two for Reform, all but one of which were in the West. Ontario and the Atlantic provinces went overwhelmingly Liberal. The Conservatives, with only 16 percent of the popular vote spread across the country, were reduced to a mere two seats. Campbell herself failed to win her riding, although her rival for the party leadership, Jean Charest, retained his seat in Quebec. Two months after the election, Campbell submitted her resignation as party leader, and the Conservatives embarked on the long and uncertain process of rebuilding the party.

AN UNCERTAIN FUTURE

The decimation of the Conservatives, together with the sudden rise of the Bloc and Reform, made the results of the 1993 election seem particularly dramatic. But in virtually every Canadian federal election of the past thirty years, it can be shown that there was quite substantial movement among individual voters, regardless of the outcome of that election. Nevertheless, the extent of switching by voters in 1993 was considerably greater than that found in previous elections (see figure 6), due in part to the strong swing against the Conservatives and NDP as well as the rise of the two new parties. The unprecedented levels of switching, combined with the effects of new voters and previous non-voters, show that only about a third of the 1993 Canadian electorate made the same voting choice as in 1988, a substantially smaller percentage than that estimated in previous studies.

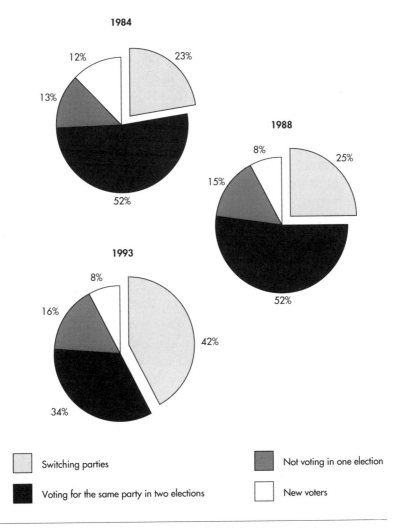

Figure 6: Stability and Change in Three Elections*

* Excludes new voters not voting and non-voters in two consecutive elections.
Source: 1984 and 1988 National Election Studies; 1993 Insight Canada Study.

The effects of new voters and of previous non-voters are not trivial, but they are relative constants in the equation of electoral change. New voters enter the electorate in every election, varying only slightly in total numbers depending upon the interval between elections and long-term population trends. Likewise, voting turnout in Canada fluctuates only modestly from one election to another, declining about 5 percent in the 1993 election. It has not thus far exhibited any longer-term downward trend similar to that found in some other countries, notably the United States. In every election, there are a number of previous non-voters who return to the electorate and a number of previous voters who leave it, as well as new voters who participate for the first time. The Canadian electorate is indeed a changing and changeable entity. Still, it seems evident that an already volatile electorate has become even more so.

The future course of the federal party system in Canada has perhaps never been more unclear than in the aftermath of the dramatic 1993 election. Modern Canadian political history demonstrates that large majorities, like that obtained by the Liberals, can readily crumble. The Conservatives, although determined to rebuild the party, face a sustained new challenge on the right from the Reform Party. Reform finds its parliamentary strength concentrated mainly in the West, and its ambition to become a national force has temporarily stalled. The Bloc Québécois, despite forming the official Opposition, appears destined to be only a transient player on the federal political stage, its political future determined more by the success or failure of a second sovereignty referendum in Quebec.

The partisan composition of the Canadian electorate in the aftermath of the 1993 election reflects some of these changes in the party system, but it is also indicative of the persistence of what is sometimes called "dealignment" in the electorate. Although the Liberals have regained some of the advantage that they once held in terms of the total number of identifiers with the party, fewer than a third of those Canadians who consider themselves Liberals identify "strongly" with the party (see figure 7). Despite the misfortunes of the Conservatives, about one-fifth of voters continue to think of themselves as Conservative, an adequate if not powerful base on which to rebuild. The new parties, while gaining some adherents, have yet to establish many "strong" identifiers. The NDP, while reduced in numbers, still retains the allegiance of a significant segment of the electorate.

It should be emphasized that such data provide only a glimpse of what the future may hold for the Canadian party system. Many Canadians continue to shun identification with any party, and the loyalty of most of those who do align themselves with parties, new or old, remains weak. In

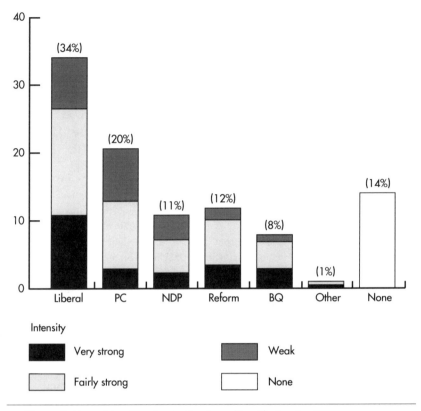

Figure 7: Party Identification in the Canadian Electorate, 1993

Source: 1993 Political Support Study.

the past, party identification in Canada has tended to display nearly as much volatility over time as the vote itself, and there is no reason to expect that this tendency will diminish in the near future.[13] In spite of the dramatic changes wrought by the 1993 election, it is likely that the Canadian party system of the immediate future will continue to reflect the trends of the recent past and to be subject to influences from new problems, policies, or leaders—both federal and provincial. The proportion of flexible partisans in the electorate continues to be high in virtually every age cohort, every region of the country, and every significant voting group. The Canadian electorate to the end of this decade and beyond will almost certainly continue to be one in which responsiveness to short-term factors such as issues, party performance and style, the personalities of leaders, or the intrusion of new political events far outweighs factors such as ideology, group loyalty, or other longer-term forces.

NOTES

[1] The discussion and analyses in this chapter are based on surveys of the Canadian public that have been conducted following every national election since 1965, with the exception of 1972. The major studies were funded by the Social Sciences and Humanities Research Council of Canada (SSHRC). Analyses based on studies up to 1979 may be found in Harold Clarke, Jane Jenson, Lawrence LeDuc, and Jon H. Pammett, *Political Choice in Canada* (Toronto: McGraw-Hill Ryerson, 1979, 1980), and in some of the more recent studies in Harold Clarke, Jane Jenson, Lawrence LeDuc, and Jon H. Pammett, *Absent Mandate: Interpreting Change in Canadian Elections*, 2nd ed. (Toronto: Gage, 1991). More detailed analyses of the 1988 National Election Study may be found in Richard Johnston, André Blais, Henry Brady, and Jean Crête, *Letting the People Decide* (Montreal: McGill-Queen's University Press, 1992). Some of the data analyzed here are from the Political Support in Canada series of studies conducted by Harold Clarke and Allan Kornberg and funded by the National Science Foundation (NSF) in the United States. Further analyses of these data may be found in Clarke and Kornberg, "Evaluations and Evolution: Public Attitudes Towards Canada's Federal Political Parties," *Canadian Journal of Political Science* 20 (1993): 287–312. Also utilized in this chapter is a survey conducted immediately following the 1993 election by Insight Canada Research Ltd. Some further analyses of this study may be found in Allan Frizzell, Jon H. Pammett, and Anthony Westell, eds., *The Canadian General Election of 1993* (Ottawa: Carleton University Press, 1994). The principal investigators of these studies, the funding agencies, and the survey units are not responsible for the analyses or interpretations of data presented here.

[2] *The Gallup Report,* monthly surveys. For the period 1988–93, see Frizzell et al., *The Canadian General Election of 1993*. A summary of monthly Gallup surveys for earlier periods may be found in Clarke et al., *Absent Mandate*, 159–61.

[3] For more detailed consideration of the 1988 election, see Johnston et al., *Letting the People Decide*, and Allan Frizzell, Jon H. Pammett, and Anthony Westell, eds., *The Canadian General Election of 1988* (Ottawa: Carleton University Press, 1989). See also Clarke et al., *Absent Mandate*, esp. 78–80 and 145–49. An account of this election by a prominent journalist is Graham Fraser, *Playing for Keeps* (Toronto: McClelland & Stewart, 1989).

[4] Clarke et al., *Absent Mandate*, ch. 2.

[5] Clarke et al., *Political Choice in Canada*, chs. 5, 16. See also Clarke et al., *Absent Mandate*, ch. 3.

[6] Lawrence LeDuc, Harold Clarke, Jane Jenson, and Jon Pammett, "Partisan Instability in Canada: Evidence from a New Panel Study," *American Political Science Review* 78 (1984): 471–83. Also reprinted in Joseph Wearing, ed., *The Ballot and Its Message* (Toronto: Copp Clark Pitman, 1991), 9–28.

[7] Clarke et al., *Political Choice in Canada*, ch. 5, and *Absent Mandate*, ch. 3.

[8] William Irvine, "Explaining the Religious Basis of Canadian Partisan Identity," *Canadian Journal of Political Science* 37 (1974): 506–633. Also reprinted in Wearing, *The Ballot and Its Message*, 80–91.

[9] Clarke et al., *Political Choice in Canada*, ch. 4. See also articles on religion, ideology, and social class by Stevenson, Johnston, Irvine, Pammett, and Lambert et al. reprinted in Wearing, *The Ballot and Its Message*, 53–193.

[10] Clarke et al., *Absent Mandate*, ch. 5. See also Lawrence LeDuc, "Leaders and Voters: The Public Images of Canadian Political Leaders" in *Leaders and Leadership in Canadian Politics*, ed. Maureen Mancuso, Richard C. Price, and Ronald Wagenberg (Toronto: Oxford University Press, forthcoming).

[11] Johnston et al., *Letting the People Decide*, 3–15 and 252–55. See also chs. 1, 4, and 8.

[12] Lawrence LeDuc, "Party Strategies and the Use of Televised Campaign Debates," *European Journal of Political Research* 18 (1996): 121–41. On the 1993 debates, see LeDuc, "The Leader Debates: Critical Event or Non-Event?" in Frizzell et al., *The Canadian General Election of 1993*.

[13] LeDuc et al., "Partisan Instability in Canada." The instability of partisanship in Canada in comparison to other countries is further examined in LeDuc, "The Dynamic Properties of Party Identification: A Four Nation Comparison," *European Journal of Political Research* 9 (1981). Also reprinted in Richard Niemi and Herbert Weisberg, *Controversies in Voting Behavior*, 2nd ed. (Washington: CQ Press, 1985).

SUGGESTED READING

Clarke, Harold D., Jane Jenson, Lawrence LeDuc, and Jon H. Pammett. *Political Choice in Canada*. Toronto: McGraw-Hill Ryerson, 1979, 1980.
    A study of the attitudes and behaviour of the Canadian electorate, investigating such topics as regional identity, political efficacy and participation, partisanship and voting.

Clarke, Harold D., Jane Jenson, Lawrence LeDuc, and Jon H. Pammett. *Absent Mandate: Interpreting Change in Canadian Elections*. 2nd ed. Toronto: Gage, 1991.
    Examines the forces of stability and change in Canadian politics during the 1974–88 period and considers the relationship of elections to public policy.

Dalton, Russell. *Citizen Politics in Western Democracies*. Chatham, NJ: Chatham House, 1988.
    Analyzes the changes that have taken place in public attitudes, values, and beliefs in Western democracies, and considers the implications of such changes in political behaviour.

Dalton, Russell, Scott Flanagan, and Paul Allen Beck. *Electoral Change in Advanced Industrial Democracies*. Princeton: Princeton University Press, 1984.

Analyzes changing patterns of electoral politics in twelve countries (including Canada) and the potential for realignment or dealignment of established party systems.

Frizzell, Allan, Jon H. Pammett, and Anthony Westell. *The Canadian General Election of 1993*. Ottawa: Carleton University Press, 1994.

An examination of the 1993 federal election campaign, including chapters on the five parties, the media, public opinion polls, and an analysis of the vote. Similar volumes are available for the 1984 and 1988 elections.

Harrop, Martin, and William L. Miller. *Elections and Voters*. London: Macmillan, 1987.

A comparative introduction to the study of elections and voting behaviour, drawing on a wide variety of studies in North America and Western Europe.

Johnston, Richard, André Blais, Henry Brady, and Jean Crête. *Letting the People Decide*. Montreal: McGill-Queen's University Press, 1992.

Analyses of data from the 1988 Canadian National Election Study, emphasizing the dynamics of the campaign and the agenda-setting and priming functions of the media and the parties.

Wearing, Joseph, ed. *The Ballot and Its Message*. Toronto: Copp Clark Pitman, 1991.

An anthology of published articles on Canadian voting and elections, compiled primarily from the *Canadian Journal of Political Science*.

Ian Greene

THE ADMINISTRATION OF JUSTICE

When I was in graduate school and trying to choose a thesis topic, I asked Professor Peter Russell for advice. Russell—undoubtedly the father of the study of law and politics in Canada—suggested the administration of justice. My heart sank, because it struck me as one of the driest topics imaginable. (No doubt some readers—except, of course, for the budding lawyers—had the same reaction when encountering the title of this chapter.) After an initial investigation of the topic, however, I changed my mind. I was surprised to learn that reality in the justice system is rather different from my original expectations. This is because the system has taken on a life somewhat independent from its original goal, which was to provide a state-sponsored means for settling disputes so that social order could be maintained. My primary objective in this chapter is to impart to the readers some of my fascination with the justice system.

The judicial process is only one means of dispute resolution, the other peaceful means being negotiation, mediation, and arbitration. The chapter will begin by considering the unique features of the judicial process. The spotlight will then shift to the court structure, judges (selection and role), and the judicial decision-making process. In the concluding section, I will challenge readers to consider whether the justice system is functioning as well as it could in the context of the Canadian version of liberal-democratic government.[1]

ADJUDICATION

The process of decision making in a court is known as *adjudication*. Adjudication is a process by which the two parties in a dispute (the litigants) put their case before a neutral third party (the judge). The judge makes a decision based on an objective set of standards (the law). The judge's decision can be enforced by the coercive powers of the state. Usually one party wins, and the other loses. Unlike mediation or even arbitration, decisions that result in compromises are rare. The judge must decide by determining the facts of the case, and then applying the law to the facts.

Most countries in the world have created courts to adjudicate disputes as a way of preserving social order and promoting fairness, factors that are essential to facilitate both business activities and interpersonal relations. There are two kinds of disputes that may be adjudicated: *public law* disputes (disputes in which the government is a party, such as criminal law, administrative law, and constitutional law cases) and *private law* disputes (disputes between two private persons, which can involve real estate transactions, contracts, family law, and suits for negligence).

As noted above, adjudication is just one of many methods of dispute resolution that are alternatives to combat. In *negotiation*, two parties attempt to resolve their dispute without the aid of a neutral third party. They do not necessarily look to objective standards, and there is often no enforcement mechanism. In *mediation*, the parties turn to a third party for help, but that person simply assists the two parties to negotiate. In *arbitration*, the neutral third party may impose a settlement, but the arbitrator is not usually bound by the same strict set of objective standards—the whole body of law—as a judge.

In private law cases, adjudication is ideally the dispute resolution method of last resort, to be used only when negotiation, mediation, or arbitration are impossible or have failed. The adjudicative service is provided by the state so that a method of last resort will be available, and private disputes can be settled without the disruption of public order.

In public law cases involving disputes between the state and private citizens, countries adhering to the principle of the rule of law submit these disputes to adjudication to promote the perception that the government is fair. The rule of law means that government officials may act only as authorized by legitimate laws—which means laws enacted by elected legislatures in democracies like Canada—and that the law must be applied equally to everyone. The use of adjudication to resolve disputes between the law enforcement authorities and the persons they accuse of crimes is intended to ensure adherence to the rule of law.

Two great adjudicative systems have developed in the world: the *common law system* and the *civil law system*.

The Common Law System

The common law system is based on the judicial system of England and Wales, the origins of which can be traced to the time of King Henry II in the twelfth century. Henry inherited a justice system based primarily on local, traditional courts, and the rules of commerce and the criminal law varied from one locality to another. Such a system not only discouraged interregional trade in England, but it also promoted disunity. Henry and his advisory council created legislation to standardize some of the criminal and trade laws across England, and the council itself heard disputes arising out of these laws.

The new legal system became a victim of its own success. Before long, more disputes were brought to the council than it could handle, and the King's council experienced a "caseload crisis" not unlike backlog problems in today's courts. Travelling justices were appointed to relieve the pressure on the council and to provide a more convenient dispute resolution service to the King's subjects. As caseload pressures continued, central courts separate from the King's council were created. The travelling judges, together with the judges of the central courts, had jurisdiction to settle certain disputes even in the absence of decrees from the King's council. Records were kept of their decisions, and judges began to refer to these records of old cases when deciding new cases. As much as possible, the precedents set by the old cases were followed in the new cases according to the principle of *stare decisis*. This judge-made law became known as the common law, because it applied to everyone.

According to the rules of *stare decisis*, as they have developed over the centuries, every court must follow the precedents established by a higher court in the same court system, and the precedents of the highest court supersede those of any lower courts. In the absence of conflicting precedents established by a higher court, a court usually follows its own precedents. The precedents of higher or equal-status courts in another common law jurisdiction are influential, but not binding. (Therefore, American Bill of Rights precedents are often cited in Canadian Charter of Rights cases, but they are only sometimes followed.) Precedents must be followed only when the facts in the current case and the precedent case are substantially the same. If a judge considers the facts in a current case to be significantly different, the judge may "distinguish" the precedent and decide the case differently.

All courts in Canada must follow precedents established by the Supreme Court. The Supreme Court itself almost always follows its own precedents.

In the mid-1970s, the court announced that it might occasionally overrule its own precedents (or those established by the Judicial Committee of the Privy Council in England, which was Canada's highest court of appeal until 1949) if it considered those precedents to be clearly wrong or inappropriate. Since that time, the Supreme Court has overruled fewer than ten precedents.[2] Such overruling will not occur frequently because it would destroy the predictability of the adjudicative system. However, because judges can distinguish appropriate precedents, *stare decisis* is not quite as rigid as it might first appear.

In addition to *stare decisis*, a second essential characteristic of the common law world is the adversary system. According to the adversarial approach, it is the responsibility of the litigants to present judges with all the facts and theory that they need to make a decision. Judges may not carry out independent investigations of the facts. Although they may research legal theory and precedents on their own, they are not usually provided with many resources to do this, and they are expected to rely primarily on the information presented by counsel representing the litigants.

It has been only in recent years that Supreme Court of Canada judges and provincial appeal court judges have been assigned law clerks to assist with legal research. Lower court judges rarely have such assistance. As a result, judicial decisions about the constitution often seem to take into account only a limited range of possibilities. This is usually because the lawyers presenting the case have narrowed the possibilities in advance, often through a lack of familiarity with the policy issues associated with constitutional questions.

In the American Supreme Court, law clerks often play a major role in formulating judicial decisions. Some Supreme Court justices do little more than proofread the decisions written by their fresh-out-of-college clerks.[3] Law clerks do not play as influential a role in appeal court decision making in Canada, but their influence is increasing as rising caseloads limit the judges' time for research and writing.

A third characteristic of the common law system is that judges do not receive specialized training in judging, but are appointed from the ranks of lawyers. This tradition dates from thirteenth-century England. Earlier in that century, the quality of the King's judges began to deteriorate, perhaps because the monarch was too busy with crusades and disputes with nobles to give the courts the attention they needed. Judges and court officials were poorly paid and, even though all judges were clergymen, they almost inevitably resorted to accepting bribes. At the end of the thirteenth century, there was a public outcry about corruption in the judicial system. In response, in 1289 King Edward I appointed a royal commission to investigate, thus setting a precedent to be followed for centuries thereafter by governments confronted with public dissatisfaction with the administration of justice. The commission found that about half of the judges in the common law courts were corrupt, and Edward removed them. He decided to look outside the clergy for replacement judges. Since the time of Henry II, there had been developing a group of legal specialists who specialized in advising litigants about how to proceed in the increasingly complex judicial system. Edward appointed some of these "lawyers" to fill the vacancies in the judiciary. Edward's solution to the crisis soon became a tradition. By the early fourteenth century, lawyers had completely displaced clerics as judges in all but one of the royal courts.

The Civil Law System

The common law world includes most commonwealth countries and the United States; the rest of the world has adopted the civil law system. The civil law system developed in continental Europe over the past few centuries. University scholars had become fascinated with Roman law, and they urged governments to adopt uniform codes of law based on the old Roman codes. For example, Napoleon I supervised the codification of French private and criminal law into a unified French Civil Code. The civil codes are organized in a logical sequence, from general principles to specific rules of law.

Judges in civil law countries generally receive specialized training; it is not assumed that the training and experience of a lawyer is adequate for judicial duties. In France, those who want to become judges attend basic law school; then they may attend the National School for Jurists if they score high enough on an admissions exam. After a year at the school and a year and a half as an apprentice, they compete for appointments as judges in the lower courts. Senior judges control promotions.

A characteristic of civil law systems is that judges place much less emphasis on precedent than do common law judges. According to the civil law approach, whenever the Civil Code is unclear, judges seeking guidance should look to the general principles in the code, the reports of the framers of the code, and scholarly writings before they research precedents. Another difference between the two systems is that civilian judges may often conduct their own investigations of the facts of a case; this is known as the inquisitorial approach. They need not rely entirely on evidence presented by counsel for the opposing sides.

Canada's legal system incorporates elements of both the common law and civil law approaches, although the former definitely overshadows the latter. After conquering Quebec in 1759, the British authorities attempted to obtain the support of Quebeckers by allowing the colony to maintain its civil legal system in the private law field. Today, Quebec's legal system still adheres to the civil law approach for private law matters, although the inquisitorial style of adjudication is not nearly as evident as it is in other civil law countries, and precedent plays a larger role because of the influence of the common law approach. With regard to public law, Quebec is a common law jurisdiction. The other provinces and the federal government are all common law jurisdictions. The Supreme Court of Canada, which is required by law to have three judges from Quebec, acts as a civil law court when it hears private law appeals from Quebec and as a common law court the rest of the time.

THE CANADIAN COURT STRUCTURE

The architects of the Canadian federation faced a dilemma when it came to designing the court system. They could have established one system of courts for disputes arising out of federal laws and another for those arising from provincial laws. The United States provides an example of such a dual court system. The dual system seems to cater to the logic of federalism, but establishing two court systems creates additional expenses and is confusing to litigants who may end up taking their disputes to the wrong court. The Fathers of Confederation rejected the dual court model in favour of what Peter Russell calls an *integrated court structure*.[4] The goal of the integrated approach is to allow for most cases arising out of both federal and provincial laws to be heard in the same court system, a system for which both the federal and provincial governments have some responsibilities (see figure 1).

The Constitution Act, 1867, granted the federal Parliament the power to establish a Supreme Court of Canada (which it did in 1875), as well as other courts, to hear non-criminal cases arising out of federal laws. Besides the Supreme Court with its nine judges, there are two other courts established by Parliament—the Federal Court (with thirty-four judges) and the Tax Court (with twenty-five judges). Most Federal Court cases deal with federal administrative law issues. Ottawa is responsible for providing the administrative support services for the Supreme Court of Canada, the Federal Court, and the Tax Court, as well as for appointing and paying all the judges to these courts. The Supreme Court sits only in Ottawa, while the Federal and Tax courts travel between Ottawa and the provincial capitals. As of 1 April 1994, Supreme Court of Canada judges earned $185 200 per year, and Federal Court and Tax Court judges earned $155 800.

All of the other courts in Canada are established by provincial or territorial legislatures, and their administrative support is provided by these governments. These provincial and territorial courts, which employ nearly 1900 judges, conduct all trials for cases arising out of federal, provincial, or territorial laws (except for the relatively few cases that are heard by

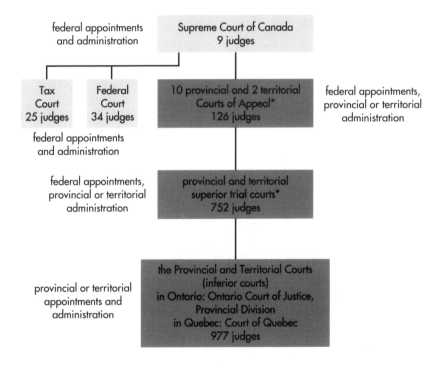

federal courts established under s. 101 of the Constitution Act, 1867.

provincial courts established under s. 92(14) of the Constitution Act, 1867.

Figure 1: Canada's Court Structure

* The provincial courts have federally appointed judges under s. 96 of the Constitution Act, 1867.

the Federal Court or the Tax Court). There are two basic types of courts that the provincial and territorial legislatures have created: *superior courts* and *inferior courts*. The *superior courts* have jurisdiction over the most serious criminal cases, including jury trials, civil or private law cases except for small claims cases (which are cases involving from $500 to $15 000, depending on the province or territory), and appeals from the inferior courts. Superior court judges are distinguished by their titles. They are usually referred to as "Madame Justice" or "Mr Justice," rather than "Judge," and are personally addressed as "My Lady" or "My Lord" instead of "Your Honour," a title used for inferior court judges. (Superior court judges are not bona fide "lords" as are British superior court judges, but most persons address them, as in the British example, out of deference to tradition.)

Even though the superior courts are established and administered by provincial and territorial authorities, their judges are appointed and paid by the federal government. This federal involvement in the provincial court system was Canada's way of avoiding the creation of a dual-court system while providing both the federal and provincial authorities with roles in the administration of justice. (This model has been copied, with modifications, in Australia and India.) The superior courts have trial and appeal divisions. The trial divisions are known by such names as "Queen's Bench," "Supreme Court," or "High Court." The appeal divisions are usually known as the "Court of Appeal" of the province or territory.

Because Canada's courts are modelled on those of England and Wales, we inherited a system in which some judges travel on circuit. Many superior court judges in England and Wales were travelling judges who held "assizes," or hearings, in the major county centres at least twice a year. If litigants did not wish to wait for an assize, they could travel to London where the superior courts sat more frequently. Prior to Confederation, the colonial governments in what were to become Canada's provinces established superior courts based on the English model, with travelling judges holding assizes in county towns twice a year. Because travel to provincial capitals was difficult in the early years, citizens demanded that judges be appointed permanently to sit in major centres outside the capitals. In 1794, Lieutenant-Governor John Graves Simcoe established a number of district courts in the major centres in Upper Canada. The judges in these courts had an inferior status, but were empowered to hear many of the kinds of cases that superior court judges would otherwise hear. Litigants could often choose between having a case settled before a district court judge, or waiting for a superior court judge's assize.

At one time, all provinces except Quebec had district courts (sometimes known as county courts). Since 1975, all of these provinces have merged their county and district courts with their superior courts. County and district court judges were appointed by the federal government. There are approximately 750 provincial superior trial court judges in Canada. They earn $155 800 per year.

The *inferior court* in a province or territory is somewhat confusingly referred to as the "Provincial Court" or "Territorial Court." The provinces have created both inferior and superior courts. The fact that most provinces have chosen to name the inferior court "*the* Provincial Court" is confusing to many. The Provincial Courts—with capital letters—in fact constitute the lower tier, or inferior division, of the provincial courts. The Provincial and Territorial Courts are by far the busiest in the country, hearing over 90 percent of all cases. The Ontario and Quebec legislatures have recently renamed their Provincial Courts the Ontario Court of Justice, Provincial Division, and the Court of Quebec. Most of the cases heard in these inferior courts are minor to moderately serious violations of the federal Criminal Code, as well as provincial offences such as highway traffic violations. The Provincial Court judges are appointed and paid by the provincial governments. There are nearly one thousand Provincial and Territorial Court judges in Canada, and they earn between $75 000 and $125 000 per year, depending on the province in which they preside.

Federally appointed judges must be selected from among lawyers who have been qualified to practise law by a provincial or territorial law society for at least ten years. They must retire by age seventy-five. Prior to the 1960s, the provincial legislatures did not require magistrates to be lawyers. Since the transformation of magistrates' courts into Provincial Courts, all provincial legislatures except in Alberta and Newfoundland require that Provincial Court judges be selected from among the bar. Even in these two provinces, very few non-lawyers are appointed.[5] The usual retirement age of Provincial Court judges is seventy.

Reform-minded political scientists and judges have criticized the provincial court systems for being too hierarchical, too difficult for the average citizen to understand, and too fragmented to allow efficient operation.[6] Former Ontario attorney general Ian Scott is the only provincial attorney general in this century who has attempted a major restructuring of the provincial court system. In 1989, following the recommendations of the 1987 Zuber Commission Report, Scott announced some sweeping reforms. The first phase of the reform created an Ontario Court of Justice, which includes all judges other than those in the Court of Appeal. This court has two divisions: General and Provincial. The General Division includes all superior court judges, except those on the Court of Appeal. The Provincial Division is formed from the old Provincial Court.

Besides the change in name, this reform has two major aspects that may impact on court reform in the other provinces. First, the administrative services for all the courts have been merged and reorganized on a regional basis rather than a "level of court" basis. Although this may sound like a fairly innocuous change, it actually has far-reaching implications. Prior to this reform, each level of court in each Ontario city had its own separate staff, leading to inefficiency and unnecessary expense. (This separation of court services is still the norm in most other parts of Canada.) The merger of court administrative services was resisted in the past by many judges, lawyers, and court staff because of a reluctance to disturb the traditional pecking order. Second, it was Scott's hope to eventually merge the General and Provincial Divisions into one court. The co-operation of the federal government will be required to bring about this unified court because Provincial Division judges will need federal appointments in order to attain the same status and jurisdiction as the General Division judges. If federal co-operation is attained, Ontario will be left with just two courts: the Ontario Court of Justice, which will handle all civil and criminal trials, and the Court of Appeal.

This proposal is controversial because some members of the legal community consider the superior court judges to be "better" judges, so that the quality of justice will be "watered down" by a merger of courts. Others, most notably Peter Russell, point out that the lower courts hear the great majority of cases that involve ordinary Canadians. From this perspective, merger is likely to improve the chances that the quality of justice services provided will be equally high for all Canadians.[7] Scott's reforms can be considered as a testing ground for court reform in Canada. It will be worth following the successes and failures of the Ontario reforms as they unfold.

JUDGES

Appointments

The Canadian constitution gives the provincial governments the power to appoint inferior court judges, and the governor general the power to appoint provincial superior and district court judges, as well as the judges of the federal courts (Supreme Court of Canada, Federal Court, and Tax Court). In practice, the governor general's appointing power is carried out by the federal cabinet, with the minister of justice and prime minister playing the leading roles. Decisions about the chief justice positions in provincial superior courts and the federal courts, however, are by tradition the prerogative of the prime minister.

Until recently, political patronage was the major factor in almost all federal and provincial judicial appointments. For example, 54 percent of the Quebec Court of Appeal judges between 1867 and 1972 had previously been cabinet ministers or elected legislators,[8] and a third of all judges appointed by the federal government in Ontario, Quebec, and Manitoba between 1905 and 1970 had previously run for elected office—most for the party that made the judicial appointment.[9] Patronage is a somewhat less important factor than it was two decades ago, but in 1985 the Canadian Bar Association reported that patronage remained an important consideration in judicial appointments by provincial governments in the three Maritime provinces as well as in Ontario, Manitoba, and Saskatchewan. Only in British Columbia, Quebec, and the Supreme Court of Canada was patronage not a "significant factor" in federal judicial appointments.[10] Research has shown that the patronage factor was as strong in the first Mulroney government as it had been during the Trudeau years.[11] The fact that patronage has remained the basis for judicial appointments for so many years indicates that it did not necessarily produce bad judges. It was just that the pool of potential judges was limited to lawyers who had paid their dues by working for the party in power.

The first crack in the patronage system appeared in 1967, when Justice Minister Pierre Trudeau began to consult the Canadian Bar Association about the suitability of persons being considered for judgeships. A committee of the Bar Association would rate the persons on the list provided by Trudeau as "well qualified," "qualified," or "not qualified." The government would then use this advice as it saw fit. This consultative approach remained in effect until 1988, and there is only one report of someone rated as "not qualified" being appointed during that time. Even with this approach, patronage remained the prime determinant of judicial appointments because the minister of justice decided which names to submit to the Canadian Bar Association for review. Nevertheless, the reformed system did ensure that ability would play a greater role in federal judicial appointments than had previously been the case.

Patronage in federal judicial appointments became a key factor in the outcome of the 1984 federal election. During the televised debate between

John Turner and Brian Mulroney, Mulroney criticized Turner for appointing five Liberal MPs to the bench not long after Turner became prime minister. Turner said that he had no choice. Former prime minister Pierre Trudeau was planning to make the appointments before leaving office, but this would have left Turner, the new prime minister, without a majority of seats in the House of Commons. To save the Liberal majority, Trudeau agreed not to make the appointments if Turner would appoint the judges after the election was called. Mulroney accused Turner of failing to do the "right thing," and promised that, if he were elected, he would base judicial appointments on merit rather than patronage.

This promise led to the establishment of consultative committees on judicial appointments in each of the provinces in 1988. The five-person committees (composed of representatives of the provincial or territorial law society, the Canadian Bar Association, the federal judiciary, the provincial or territorial attorney general, and the federal minister of justice) replaced consultation with the Canadian Bar Association. The consultative committees were not empowered to search for good judicial candidates, but only to investigate the credentials of those persons who had filed an application for a judgeship with the Commissioner of Federal Judicial Affairs. During the first year of operation of the new system, the government did not publicly advertise the new appointment procedure. As a result, most of the applicants considered by the consultative committees were those who were already on file with the minister of justice under the old system. The consequence was that patronage remained a major ingredient in federal judicial appointments. This situation is not likely to change unless the consultative committees are given the power not only to screen candidates presented by the federal executive, but also to actively recruit good candidates to apply for judicial positions. The Chrétien government has promised to make the judicial appointment process more open to public scrutiny, and there are indications that the consultative committees may have a recruitment role as well.

The provincial governments in British Columbia, Alberta, Ontario, Quebec, and Newfoundland have been the most successful in abolishing patronage in their judicial appointment procedures. Beginning in the 1970s, these governments established judicial selection committees (often called judicial councils)—usually composed of a combination of lawyers, judges, and lay persons—to assist in the provincial judicial appointment process.[12] These committees consider not only the names submitted by the attorney general, but they also actively seek well-qualified candidates. In Ontario, for example, the Judicial Appointments Advisory Committee, established in 1988 under chair Peter Russell, advertises for lawyers to apply for vacant judicial positions. After interviewing the most promising candidates, the committee draws up a short list of the most qualified candidates and presents the list to the attorney general. The committee bases its recommendations on the applicants' "professional excellence, . . . community involvement and social awareness. It does not, however, attach any importance to candidates' political connections."[13]

An issue related to judicial selection is judicial promotion—or elevation, as judges prefer to call it. This refers to the promotion of a lower court judge to a higher court, or the appointment of a junior judge to an administrative position such as chief judge or justice. It should be noted that some consider it improper for the government to promote judges from lower courts to higher ones. The reasoning is that, if promotions were common, judges might decide cases in order to please the authority with the power to grant the promotion (the federal minister of justice), and thereby abandon their impartiality. In fact, only 4 percent of federally appointed judges in the three central provinces appointed between 1905 and 1970 were elevated from the Provincial Court.[14] However, it is more common for judges to be elevated from a superior trial court to an appeal court, and this practice raises some concerns about impartiality. About half of the appeal court judges in the three Central Canadian provinces between 1905 and 1970 had been promoted,[15] and all but one (Justice John Sopinka) of the current Supreme Court of Canada judges were promoted from the lower appeal courts.

Russell has noted that little is known about what factors are taken into account by the political authorities when deciding to promote judges.[16] The consultative committees on federal judicial appointments established in 1988 do not have a mandate to review the files of judges being considered for promotions; these decisions are made solely by the prime minister (for the Supreme Court and the chief justiceships) or the minister of justice. This raises the question of whether it is appropriate for such important decisions to be left to the sole discretion of one or two individuals. In no other profession are promotions so discretionary.

Training

For most of Canada's history, it has been assumed that judges need no training other than a legal education and several years of experience practising law. This approach, which is usual in common law countries, contrasts with civil law jurisdictions such as France or Italy, where would-be judges must graduate from a specialized training program. After graduation, the newly trained judicial specialists apply for junior judgeships and then are promoted up the judicial hierarchy by other judges according to merit.

In 1971, Parliament established the Canadian Judicial Council to "improve the quality of judicial service" in courts staffed by federally appointed judges. The council, which is composed of all chief and associate chief judges and justices in these courts (totalling thirty-five judges in 1993), has both an educational and disciplinary role. With regard to judicial education, the council conducts several week-long seminars each year on such subjects as judgment writing and the impact of important Supreme Court precedents. As well, the Canadian Institute for the Administration of Justice (an organization composed of judges, lawyers, and academics, established in 1974 to promote judicial research and education) runs an annual one-week seminar for new judges, with the support of the Canadian Judicial Council. The provincial judicial councils or judges' associations run similar seminars for Provincial Court judges.

It is clear that although judicial education has improved dramatically during the past two decades, it remains a "patchwork quilt," to use the words of the former chief justice of Ontario, William Howland.[17] To promote more comprehensive judicial education, the National Judicial Institute was established in Ottawa in 1987. It is jointly financed by the federal and provincial governments and has a mandate "to design and coordinate educational services for both federally- and provincially-appointed judges."[18] The institute has organized frequent "early orientation" seminars for new judges, among other activities, to supplement existing training sessions.

Impartiality

In common or civil law countries that adhere to a liberal political ideology, which stresses the maximization of individual freedom, the limitation of governmental powers through laws enacted by representative legislatures, and equality in the application of the law, judges are expected to be as impartial and independent as possible. Impartiality implies that judges must hear a case with an open mind, without being biased in advance toward any of the litigants. Of course, absolute impartiality is a human impossibility, but the more impartiality that can be demonstrated by judges, the more respectable will be the adjudicative process. A number of practices have developed to promote judicial impartiality, such as the presumption that judges will disqualify themselves if a litigant is a family member or associate, the prohibition against judges holding a second job, and the expectation that judges will, upon appointment, resign from associations that are likely to litigate or that advocate particular courses in public policy (such as political parties).

The most important principle that has developed to promote judicial impartiality, however, is judicial independence. Judicial independence implies an absence of relationships between judges and others (particularly those in the executive and legislative branches of government) that could influence the decision-making process. For example, if the cabinet could decide on an individual judge's salary, or could fire a judge, judicial independence would be compromised. If anyone tries to influence a judicial decision outside of the regular adjudicative process, the result is a violation of judicial independence. Judicial independence is considered an important constitutional principle in Canada. With regard to criminal and quasi-criminal cases, independence and impartiality are now protected by the Charter of Rights. Section 11(d) states that persons accused of offences have a right to an independent and impartial judge.

The Supreme Court of Canada has defined the "essential conditions" for the existence of judicial independence in an extraordinary case decided in 1985.[19] In 1981, Walter Valente was charged with dangerous driving after a fatal accident. The case reached the Provincial Court in Ontario not long after the Charter of Rights came into effect in 1982. As a strategy for keeping his client out of jail, Valente's lawyer argued that the Provincial Court judge had no jurisdiction to hear the case because he was not independent, as required by the Charter. The lawyer maintained that this lack of independence was caused primarily by the fact that Provincial Court judges do not have the same constitutional safeguards for their independence as those possessed by superior court judges.

The Supreme Court of Canada ruled against Valente. The court held that a judge is independent if three conditions are met. First, judges must have "security of tenure," which means that they cannot be fired because the government disagrees with their decisions. A judge may be removed only after a judicial inquiry recommends such action. Second, a judge must have "financial security," or a legislated right to a salary, so that the cabinet cannot secretly manipulate a judge by raising or lowering his or her salary. Third, judges must have "institutional independence," or the ability to make administrative decisions that could affect judicial decision making. The Supreme Court ruled that Provincial Court judges in Ontario met all three conditions.

To promote judicial independence, judges in Canada are given appointments that continue until the mandatory retirement age. Under extraordinary circumstances, a judge may be dismissed, but not by a cabinet minister or legislature acting alone. There must be a judicial inquiry into allegations of wrongdoing, and the inquiry must recommend dismissal before the judge can be removed. A judge cannot be dismissed for making an error in law, but only for inappropriate behaviour such as taking a bribe, making disrespectful remarks to litigants, or not fulfilling court-related duties. The reason why a judge may not be removed for an error in law is that vengeful litigants with adequate financial resources, disappointed with a judicial decision, might harass a judge by pressing for his or her removal. To avoid such situations, a judge might be inclined to decide in favour of well-known "troublemakers."

Discipline and Accountability

Judicial independence is essential for the promotion of impartiality, but it occasionally may be abused. The antidotes against abuse of judicial power are not well known. Persons who feel that a judge has engaged in inappropriate behaviour may complain to one of the judicial councils: to a provincial judicial council regarding provincially appointed judges or to the Canadian Judicial Council regarding federally appointed judges. The composition of the provincial judicial councils varies from province to province, but it usually consists of senior judges or a combination of judges, lawyers, and lay persons. With the Canadian Judicial Council becoming better known, the number of complaints received has increased from 47 during the 1987–88 fiscal year to 127 in 1992–93. Few have produced enough evidence to warrant a judicial inquiry, and the council has never recommended the removal of a federally appointed judge.

The most notorious of inquiries into the conduct of provincially appointed judges was the November 1993 inquiry into complaints of sexual harassment against Ontario Provincial Court Division judge Walter Hryciuk. Madame Justice Jean MacFarland recommended Hryciuk's removal because of rude remarks and behaviour directed at several women. She concluded that such behaviour was unprofessional and made it impossible for Hryciuk to appear impartial. Hryciuk has applied for a judicial review of these findings.

There are two other important mechanisms for promoting judicial accountability. Chief judges and justices exercise a certain amount of authority over the junior judges, although this authority is very limited because of judicial independence. Second, law journals publish articles that analyze and criticize judicial decisions. These journals are widely read by judges. Like playwrights, judges appreciate good reviews, and it may be that the journals help to encourage high-quality judgments.

Many courts in the United States have developed a system whereby trial lawyers may evaluate the performance of judges by filling out periodic evaluation forms, much as students evaluate the performance of their professors through class evaluation forms.[20] To date, Canadian judges have generally not been receptive to such procedures, just as Canadian professors resisted student appraisals twenty years ago. Whether judicial appraisals are instituted in Canada will likely depend on whether any courts are willing to experiment with the procedure.

THE DECISION-MAKING PROCESS

Trial Courts

The trial courts are the courts that hear cases for the first time. Trial court judges, whether federally or provincially appointed, sit alone, although they may be assisted by juries in determining the facts in more serious criminal and civil cases. (Under the Charter of Rights, persons charged with a criminal offence who are liable to at least five years in prison if convicted have a right to trial by jury.) Another important function of judges in criminal cases is the sentencing of those found guilty. Some have suggested that because judges are rarely trained in criminology, their role should be limited to adjudication, and the sentencing function should be delegated to specialized sentencing boards composed of experts in corrections.

Peter McCormick and I interviewed forty-one federally and provincially appointed trial court judges in Alberta and asked all of them to describe the decision-making process in trials. We found that the judges adopted one of four different approaches to decision making. We labelled these approaches *improvisation, strict formalism, pragmatic formalism,* and *intuition.* Following are typical responses associated with each of these approaches:

1. **Improvisors** (10 percent of the judges): "There is no single process of making a decision because cases present too much variety. Nevertheless, different judges would probably come to the same decision about the same case."
2. **Strict Formalists** (22 percent of the judges): "The making of judicial decisions often revolves around highly technical and objective questions requiring little in the way of a conscious formal intellectual process for their application. Going though the correct procedures always produces the correct decision."

3. **Pragmatic Formalists** (44 percent of the judges): "There is a conscious, understandable process that all judges should follow in reaching a judicial decision. This process can be formulated in terms of a 'check list' of items that must be answered, or a 'shifting balance' between the weight of the arguments of the two sides, or 'water rising' to a specific level. However, even if the proper procedures are followed, different judges could reach different conclusions in the hard cases."

4. **Intuitivists** (24 percent of the judges): "The process of a judicial decision is best described in terms of a 'gut-feeling' about the trial as a whole, a "key moment" in a trial around which everything revolves, or arriving at a feeling of what the most fair outcome should be, and then putting together the rationale that justifies reaching the outcome."[21]

What these responses illustrate is that there is no consensus about the thought processes that trial judges should follow when deciding cases. Although adjudication is intended to be as objective as possible, there is always a subjective element that cannot be eliminated. Nor should it: judging is an art and a human process.

Appeal Courts

Courts that are specifically established as appeal courts hear cases in panels of three judges or more. This is because appeal courts frequently have to decide difficult questions about the meaning of the law about which reasonable judges could differ. Thus, it is thought that several heads are likely to make better decisions than a single head. Provincial appeal courts usually sit in panels of three judges, although the court itself is usually composed of many more judges than this—for example, eleven in Alberta and sixteen in Ontario. For more complex cases, a panel of five is sometimes struck. Membership on the panels and assignment of cases to panels is determined by the chief justice, although he or she may sometimes take into consideration the preferences of the regular appeal court judges.

The Supreme Court of Canada

In a complex court structure like Canada's, there are often several levels of court above the court in which a case was originally heard, so that more than one appeal is possible. For a second or third appeal, the right to appeal is sometimes limited to cases in which judges grant permission to appeal, which is known as leave to appeal. Very few litigants have a right to appeal to the Supreme Court of Canada. Those who do include litigants whose cases involve a serious criminal offence where the provincial court of appeal rendered a non-unanimous decision about a point of law, or where the appeal court had reversed the decision of the trial court, as well as those litigants involved in reference cases. In almost all other cases, litigants must apply to the Supreme Court itself for leave to appeal.

The Supreme Court usually considers the applications for leave to appeal in panels of three. They rely heavily on written submissions that explain the importance of the case, although litigants also make oral presentations. It takes the agreement of two judges out of three to grant leave to appeal. Each year, the court receives about five hundred applications for leave to appeal and grants about 15 percent of them. The court decides about one hundred appeals each year, including cases from appellants granted leave to appeal and cases from appellants with an automatic right to appeal. Between 1987 and 1992, the court decided an average of twenty-eight Charter of Rights cases per year.[22]

Once a case is past the leave to appeal stage, a hearing is scheduled. Often the hearing may be scheduled for almost a year after leave to appeal is granted, although in urgent cases—such as Chantelle Daigle's abortion case—the court may schedule a hearing within a week. The court sits in panels of five, seven, or the full court of nine depending on how the chief justice views the importance of the case. The most common panel size is seven, accounting for about 80 percent of the Supreme Court hearings. Nowadays, hearings typically last no longer than half a day. Lawyers for the various parties are assigned limited times to address the court, usually from thirty minutes to an hour. Small lights on the speaker's podium indicate when counsel's time is up.

As soon as possible after the litigants conclude their arguments, the judges in the panel meet privately in a conference. Beginning with the most recently appointed judge, the judges explain in turn how they think the case should be decided; this process can take from five minutes to several hours. After all the judges have spoken, it is usually clear whether the judges will be unanimous or whether several different opinions will be written. A judge in the majority group will often volunteer to write the majority opinion; otherwise, the chief justice will ask a judge in this group to write it. After writing a draft of the opinion, the judge circulates it to the other judges on the panel, and each of them may send it back with suggestions for revisions. If the writer cannot accept the revisions, then the other judges may decide to write separate opinions.[23] Opinions that agree with the outcome of the main opinion, but that disagree with the justification for it, are known as separate concurring opinions. Opinions that disagree with the majority result are known as dissenting opinions. From 1984 to 1992, only 59 percent of the Supreme Court's Charter of Rights decisions were unanimous compared with 82 percent of its non-Charter decisions.[24] The judges seem to try particularly hard to render unanimous decisions for cases involving high-profile political controversies, such as the twin decisions on the constitutionality of Quebec's French-only commercial signs provisions. Because the process of consultation among the judges is often a lengthy one, particularly in cases in which the court desires a unanimous judgment, decisions are usually not rendered for several months after the hearing.

DOES OUR JUSTICE SYSTEM NEED REFORM?

The adjudicative process in courts developed over the centuries as a response to the needs of governments to keep order and to be perceived as fair. Over time, court systems have become more and more complex as society expands and more laws are established and as new courts are created to take the pressure off existing courts. Court procedures, originally designed to promote fairness, become increasingly complex as procedural rules are modified over and over again to plug loopholes or to take new conditions into account. The law itself has become increasingly dense, as both statute law and common law have piled up. As a result, the average person often feels lost when confronted with the law and the legal system. Without a lawyer, an encounter with the justice system can seem like being exiled to an alien world with strange customs and an incomprehensible language.

This tendency for court systems to become almost unmanageably complex has given rise to a number of problems. First, some litigants and lawyers have come to view the court system more as the opportunity to play a skillful game of "beat the system" than as a dispute resolution service of last resort. For example, half of a random sample of lawyers in Alberta and Ontario were not opposed to using delay tactics to their clients' advantage in certain situations. A few lawyers even claimed to specialize in delay: they boasted that they could keep a case out of court almost forever through various technical procedures—if they were paid enough. Some judges complained about some large corporations that took cases to court that they had no hope of winning; their strategy was to force their adversary (who could not afford to litigate a case over several years) to agree to a settlement favourable to the corporation. As well, there are numerous cases that end up in court but could be settled more effectively and with less emotional damage through negotiation or mediation. These cases include some disputes between neighbours or family members. Years ago, such disputes were resolved through mediating organizations such as churches or community groups, but with the increasing urbanization and secularization of society, these means are no longer as common.

On the average, criminal cases can take anywhere from three months to three years to go to trial, depending on the location of the court. The courts in the Peel region west of Toronto have been among the slowest in the world, while courts in New Brunswick routinely try almost all of their criminal cases within ninety days.[25] If a criminal trial decision is appealed, it takes an average of one year in Ontario before the appeal case can be heard. An appeal to the Supreme Court of Canada will usually add at least another year to the process. Private law cases tend to take at least 50 percent longer to get through the system than criminal cases. Thus, occasionally a Supreme Court of Canada decision on a private law matter will concern a factual situation that occurred ten years earlier.

Judges tend to be as frustrated as anyone by the misuse of the court system and by unnecessary delays. But to take action to reduce abuses and delays is problematic given the judge's role as an impartial third party and given the principle of judicial independence, which erects a very high fence between judges and the governmental authorities responsible for court administration. As well, provincial attorneys general are often frustrated by problems in judicial administration but are reluctant to introduce reforms because of public apathy, the complexity of the problem, and the fear of violating judicial independence. Ian Scott's initiatives in Ontario represent a glaring exception to this tendency.

Courts evolved as the official dispute-settlement institutions of government, and they developed a particular method of resolving disputes called adjudication. Over time, courts have taken on additional functions. In the eighteenth century, the French political scientist Baron de Montesquieu described England as having three branches of government: the legislature (Parliament), the executive (the cabinet and public service), and the judiciary. He saw these three branches as checking each other's power, and thus preventing the abuse of power by any one branch. With the development of written constitutions, disputes about the meaning of these documents began to be referred to courts because of judges' reputations for impartiality. Because of the increasing complexity of court systems and the law, courts came to be seen by some as weapons that they could manipulate to frustrate their enemies.

Overall, we could summarize the role of courts in our society as four-fold. Judges are official dispute resolvers, guardians against abuse of power, official constitutional philosophers, and sometimes pawns in other people's battles. Court hearings are open so that the public can serve as a kind of monitoring device to ensure that courts are fulfilling the first three functions to the highest possible standards and that the fourth function is kept to a minimum. I would encourage readers to drop in on court proceedings at any level, observe the process, and consider sending their comments—both positive and negative—to the relevant authority: the federal minister of justice or the provincial attorney general with regard to administrative issues not related to adjudication; the Canadian Judicial Council or the provincial judicial council regarding judicial account-ability; or the appropriate chief justice or chief judge regarding administrative matters connected with adjudication.

NOTES

[1] Some of the material that follows was adapted from Peter McCormick and Ian Greene, *Judges and Judging: Inside the Canadian Judicial System* (Toronto: Lorimer, 1990), with permission of the publisher.

[2] Peter Hogg, *Constitutional Law of Canada*, 2nd ed. (Toronto: Carswell, 1985), 183.

[3] See Bob Woodward and Scott Armstrong, *The Brethren* (New York: Avon, 1981).

[4] Peter H. Russell, *The Judiciary in Canada: The Third Branch of Government* (Toronto: McGraw-Hill Ryerson, 1987), ch. 3.

[5] Ibid., 110.

[6] Ibid.; Perry S. Millar and Carl Baar, *Judicial Administration in Canada* (Montreal: McGill-Queen's University Press, 1981); and Thomas Zuber, *Report of the Ontario Courts Inquiry* (Toronto: Queen's Printer, 1987).

[7] Russell, *The Judiciary in Canada*.

[8] Guy Bouthillier, "Matériaux pour une analyse politique des juges de la Cour d'appel," *La Revue Juridique Thémis* (1971): 563.

[9] William J. Klein, "Judicial Recruitment in Manitoba, Ontario and Quebec" (PhD thesis, Department of Sociology, University of Toronto, 1975).

[10] *Report of the Canadian Bar Association Committee on the Appointment of Judges* (Ottawa: Canadian Bar Association, 1985), ch. 6.

[11] Peter H. Russell and Jacob S. Zeigel, "Federal Judicial Appointments: An Appraisal of the First Mulroney Government's Appointments and the New Judiciary Advisory Committees," *University of Toronto Law Journal* 41 (1991): 4–37.

[12] See Peter McCormick, "Judicial Councils for Provincial Judges in Canada," *Windsor Yearbook of Access to Justice* 6 (1986): 160.

[13] Russell and Zeigel, "Federal Judicial Appointments," 32–33.

[14] Klein, "Judicial Recruitment," 312.

[15] Ibid.

[16] Russell, *The Judiciary in Canada*, 140–41.

[17] Canadian Judicial Council, *Annual Report 1987–1988* (Ottawa: Canadian Judicial Council, 1988), 6.

[18] Ibid.

[19] *Valente v. The Queen et al.,* [1985] 2 Supreme Court Reports, 673. For more detailed commentaries on this case, see Ian Greene, *The Charter of Rights* (Toronto: Lorimer, 1981), 148–50, and Ian Greene, "The Doctrine of Judicial Independence Developed by the Supreme Court of Canada," *Osgoode Hall Law Journal* 26 (1988): 177.

[20] Russell, *The Judiciary in Canada*, 189.

[21] Peter McCormick and I elaborate on these decision-making models in *Judges and Judging*.

[22] F.L. Morton, Peter Russell, and Troy Riddell, "The Canadian Charter of Rights and Freedoms: A Descriptive Analysis of the First Decade" (paper presented at the 16th World Congress of the International Political Science Association, Berlin 21–25 Aug. 1994), table 11.

[23] Madame Justice Bertha Wilson, "Decision-Making in the Supreme Court," *University of Toronto Law Journal* 36 (1986): 227.

[24] Morton, Russell, and Riddell, "Canadian Charter of Rights and Freedoms," table 11.

[25] Carl Baar, "Notes for an Address to the McLaughlin College Public Lecture Series" (York University, 16 Nov. 1989).

SUGGESTED READING

Gall, Gerald. *The Canadian Legal System*. 3rd ed. Toronto: Carswell, 1990.
A lay guide to the Canadian legal/judicial system written by a lawyer. Topics include the sources of law, a comparison of the common law and civil law approaches, the role of lawyers and judges in court, and some of the basic concepts of administrative law.

McCormick, Peter. *Canada's Courts*. Toronto: Lorimer, 1994.
An analysis of the role of courts in Canada from a political science perspective. McCormick summarizes his own extensive research on judicial impact and judicial decision making and provides original insights into the nature of courts.

McCormick, Peter, and Ian Greene. *Judges and Judging*. Toronto: Lorimer, 1990.

An analysis of the backgrounds and decision-making strategies of judges at all levels of court in Canada. With the aid of interviews with judges in Alberta and Ontario, and retired Supreme Court of Canada judges, the authors attempt to demythologize the judicial system by considering who judges are and how they make their decisions.

Millar, Perry S., and Carl Baar. *Judicial Administration in Canada*. Montreal: McGill-Queen's University Press, 1981.

The standard text on judicial administration in Canada. This book is not only a useful guide to court administrators, but also an important source for all who desire a better understanding of such important court-related issues as the constitutional constraints on court unification or strategies for improving the efficiency of the flow of cases through the courts.

Morton, F.L. *Law, Politics and the Judicial Process in Canada*. 2nd ed. Calgary: University of Calgary Press, 1993.

A book of readings covering all the benchmarks concerning the relation between law and politics in Canada. Topics covered include the rule of law, *stare decisis*, judicial review, interest-group litigation, judicial policy making, judicial independence, and judicial selection.

Russell, Peter H. *The Judiciary in Canada: The Third Branch of Government*. Toronto: McGraw-Hill Ryerson, 1987.

The most comprehensive analysis of the Canadian judiciary available. The book is written from a political science perspective so that the implications of judicial organization for the Canadian political system receive careful treatment. After considering alternatives, Russell promotes the concept of a unified trial court in each province, as well as the use of non-partisan selection committees for judicial recruitment.

R.H. Wagenberg

ISSUES IN MUNICIPAL GOVERNMENT

The metropolitan governing structures of Toronto and Montreal each have responsibility for more people than any province except Ontario, Quebec, and British Columbia. Metropolitan Vancouver encompasses more people than six of Canada's ten provinces. Yet when students are introduced to the government and politics of Canada, scant attention is usually paid to the municipalities and their role in governing. Citizens seem to confirm this implied lack of importance by voting in much smaller numbers in municipal elections than they do at the federal or provincial levels. Nonetheless, municipal governments have a crucial impact on the lives of their residents: the elected and administrative officials of the cities, towns, counties, and districts of Canada are responsible for determining policies and delivering vital services to their residents.

Political scientists study power, and because municipalities do not share constitutional power, as do the federal and provincial governments of Canada, they have been considered minor players. The only mention of municipalities in the Constitution Act, 1867, is in section 92(8), which mandates the exclusive powers of the provinces over "Municipal Institutions in the Province." Thus, the very existence, let alone the responsibilities, of municipalities is a question for provincial determination. Provinces retain tight control over the functions and finances of local governments. When constitutional questions are debated, municipal governments are not invited to take part as much as some might wish. Major economic policies are not discussed with the leaders of the cities where a majority of Canadians live. The same is true of social policy or environmental concerns. Students of government as well as average citizens might be excused for not spending too much time thinking about government and politics in the cities and towns of Canada when it is Ottawa and the provincial capitals that make the major decisions and attract the heavyweight politicians. But if one reflects not on the constitutional subservience of municipalities but rather on the question of their role in the quality of life of most Canadians, then there emerge some very good reasons for being concerned with municipal government.

Having their garbage collected and disposed of in an environmentally safe manner on a regular basis is of considerably greater immediate importance to most Canadians than is the question of the purchase of helicopters as part of federal defence policy. Effective snow removal to allow traffic movement is more on people's minds in winter than the propriety of the notwithstanding clause in the Canadian Charter of Rights and Freedoms. The installation of sewer systems to prevent basement flooding concerns more Canadians across the country than does the issue of Senate reform. More Canadians turn out for council meetings in cities and towns to speak on planning matters that affect their neighbourhoods than would dream of attending the meetings of parliamentary task forces that occasionally travel the land looking for citizen input. This is not to minimize the importance of the national issues, but, as important as those issues are, they are somewhat remote and lack the immediacy of the local problems that continually affect people's daily lives. Yet, despite the importance of municipal governments, our attention is directed away from their day-to-day business by the concentration of the news media on international, national, and, to a lesser degree, provincial events.

Another set of factors that may discourage interest in local government is its greater complexity and variety of forms. It is somewhat ironic that the parliamentary system with its responsible prime minister and cabinet, a feature of the federal and provincial governments that is considered to be fundamental to our political heritage, is not considered to be appropriate for our local governments. Since our understanding of politics is so involved with the parliamentary tradition, we might be forgiven for thinking that local institutions that do not use these traditions are not "real" governments. Political parties have not been part of the municipal scene in most places in Canada, and where they are they still do not operate in the same way as those at the federal and provincial levels. Even more fundamental is the degree to which the feeling exists that political parties have no legitimate place in local politics. This point of view is implicitly founded on the notion that the business of local government is not really political. Such a view, of course, can mask the decidedly political colour of civic stances, decisions, and priorities. A business model of local government, for instance, merely fails to address this aspect of its operation.

MUNICIPAL ORGANIZATION

Because the parliamentary system has not been the model for local government, a number of alternative approaches have been allowed to develop. There are five alternative systems, and two or more of them may exist in a small geographical area. Thus, a person may live in a town that has one system of local government and commute to work in a city that has another system. Confusion about how municipal government works surely must be encouraged by this variety. The five systems are council–committee, council–chief administrative officer, council–commission, council–board of control, and council–executive committee.[1] The *council–committee* system is widely used in smaller towns. In this system, several committees of council exercise administrative control over specific departments (e.g., the parks and recreation committee oversees the parks and recreation department). In larger population centres, this system has lost its appeal because councils feel they should be involved in policy making rather than administration. The *council–chief administrative officer* (or council–manager) system places all administrative responsibility in the hands of the appointed chief administrative officer (CAO), who is in turn answerable to council. The model is very much based on business practices, with the CAO being the general manager and the elected council being the board of directors. This system fits the view that municipal government is largely about technical matters that should be decided without political interference. The *council–commission* system used in some places on the Prairies has the same philosophy as the council–CAO system, but rather than one administrator there are a few, each with responsibility over a range of departments. The *council–board of control* system used to be required in all Ontario cities with a population of over 100 000. Now it exists at the option of the community. In this model, usually four persons are elected at large in a city, and together with the mayor they compose a board that has responsibility for the budget and can exercise wide influence over other policies as well. They also sit on and vote with the elected council. Finally, the *council–executive committee* system has gained favour in large municipalities. It has the closest resemblance to cabinet government, although it falls far short of that system in that it does not create a political executive responsible to a legislature and does not involve a government and opposition. The members of the executive committee include the mayor and three to five councillors selected by the elected council from among its members. Each of the councillors has some responsibility for one or more departments.

It is possible that a community may choose to have elements from more than one system—a board of control and a chief administrative officer, for example. The result of this variety is confusion about the nature of authority and responsibility in the municipal system. For instance, local governments have mayors who are popularly elected by the voters at large—that is, by all the voters of the community. This system gives the mayor a degree of political influence that may allow for considerable power to affect policy. Nonetheless, the mayor is not like a prime minister or premier who is the head of a political party that controls a legislature and who can choose party colleagues to form a cabinet to govern under his or her general direction. Instead, the mayor may well be faced with council members who harbour views other than her or his own, and may often be on the losing side of important issues. While a politically astute mayor may benefit from having a wider popular mandate, receiving greater media attention, having ongoing contact with the senior bureaucrats, chairing council meetings, and having some opportunities to help or hinder members of council, in the final analysis he or she is powerless to force colleagues to adopt similar views.[2] Yet citizens of communities, with their understanding of how federal and provincial governments work, are prone to blame the head of government. Thus, a mayor will often have to take the blame for policies that he or she has not supported. The municipal electorate may in all likelihood have no idea how individual members of council voted on particular issues, and there are rarely party labels to help citizens assess credit or blame for policies or situations. It seems clear that this lack of ability to simply judge responsibility in local government has something to do with the lack of interest and poor voter turnout in municipal elections.

The problems do not end there. A variety of structures dividing responsibility among different local government mechanisms complicates things even further. There are county, regional, and metropolitan governments that divide the responsibilities for delivering municipal services to Canadians. A number of communities may be gathered under one government to deliver services such as policing, planning, major sewer systems and sewage treatment facilities, and social assistance, while the various localities continue to provide other services such as fire protection, parks and recreation, and garbage collection, to name a few. These arrangements are normally referred to as two-tier local governments. Typically, the council of the upper tier is drawn from members of the lower tier rather than there being separate elections for each level. More recently, some regional governments in Ontario, including Metropolitan Toronto, have adopted direct elections for the upper tier, but that remains the exception rather than the rule. Direct election may make citizens more aware of their upper-tier local governments, and the councillors elected to them will be more interested in the wider issues of the region rather than in the more narrow ones of localities. Again, however, there is a degree of complexity that makes it hard to determine responsibility for local government decisions.

The growth of urban populations has resulted in the filling up of core cities, and as people have spilled over their boundaries there has been an integration of the countryside into the life of the city. While farmland may still be extensive beyond the city boundaries (although the loss of prime farmland is a growing concern), the people living beyond the city are mostly tied to the urban economy. Over recent decades, various provincial governments have sought to reorganize municipal government so that the costs and benefits of municipal services are fairly distributed among municipal taxpayers. In doing so, a concern is to deal with the concept of *externalities*—that is, the enjoyment of benefits by people who do not pay for them and the imposition of costs on people who do not get all the benefits. A variety of reorganization schemes have been adopted across the country to try to address the problems of growth and equity. In New Brunswick, for instance, there was a reorganization in the 1960s that shifted most education, health, and welfare functions to the province. This allowed the creation of greater uniformity in the services available to municipalities regardless of the wealth of their citizens. In Ontario, reorganization, first in Toronto and then in other regions, was more concerned with managing growth on the basis of planning for larger areas. The result was controversial, as many people resented the loss of traditional municipal boundaries to which they had some loyalties. By the mid-1970s, the backlash was sufficient to halt the trend toward full regionalization. In 1989, a proposal to eliminate separate local governments for communities with populations under 4000 also met resistance.

The ongoing debate in various provinces about the appropriate boundaries and powers of municipalities can do little to help voters understand the system. Provinces can act unilaterally to take powers away from local governments or to saddle them with responsibilities they might rather not have. Whereas federal and provincial politicians are reasonably sure of the arena in which they play and the rules of the games, the same cannot be said as confidently of municipal politicians.

There is one more major complicating factor at the municipal level: the existence of a variety of so-called *special purpose bodies*. Of these, the most important are boards of education. Special purpose bodies are elected or appointed groups that have responsibilities for an aspect of local government and are not subservient to the municipal government. These bodies vary from province to province, as does their relationship with the municipal government. For instance, the municipal government may or may not have representation on the special purpose body. In most provinces, the municipal council has no authority over boards of education. These bodies are separately elected, and their expenditures can consume as much as half of the local property tax revenue. Thus, municipal governments that collect the property taxes for educational as well as other municipal purposes are often the targets of citizen anger for taxation to fund activities over which municipal governments have no control. Concerned local residents who wish to follow local government have in effect two or more governments to monitor. In provinces where there are both public and denominational school boards, the problems are further magnified.

School boards, police commissions, utilities commissions, library boards, and the like have long historical roots and were most often based on the desire to remove their area of responsibility from politics. This is but another reflection of the attitude that local politics is not like politics elsewhere and that local matters should be decided in a non-political manner. Yet few people have suggested that provincial education ministries be separated from provincial governments and that Canadians elect separate provincial educational legislatures. Even where, at the provincial or federal levels, appointed commissions are given important responsibilities, they are made to report to a minister who is in turn responsible to the legislative body. At the local level, elected municipal governments are often maligned because of the activities of a variety of other local bodies (elected and appointed) over which they have little or no control. Where these special purpose bodies have some function that includes several communities (for instance, a regional conservation authority), one may make some argument for their existence. When the functions of such institutions are within the boundaries of a municipality for which there is an elected municipal government to serve the citizens, it is more difficult to provide a rationale that conforms to the democratic ideals we apply to other levels of Canadian government.

ELECTED BODIES

Elected Special Purpose Bodies

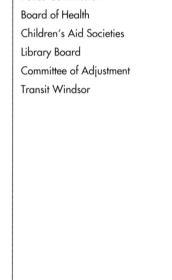

City Council	Public School Board	Separate School Board	Utilities Commission
Mayor, elected at large 10 Councillors, 2 elected per ward	15 members, 3 elected per ward	(15–12 elected in wards, plus 3 representatives of French rate payers)	Mayor + 4 elected at large

CITY ADMINISTRATOR

APPOINTED SPECIAL PURPOSE BODIES

Municipal Department
• Building
• Clerk
• Convention and Visitors Bureau
• Development Commission
• Finance
• Fire
• Huron Lodge (Home for Seniors)
• Legal
• Parks and Recreation
• Personnel
• Planning
• Property and Housing
• Public Works
• Social Services
• Traffic Engineering

Police Commission
Board of Health
Children's Aid Societies
Library Board
Committee of Adjustment
Transit Windsor

*Figure 1: Municipal Government, City of Windsor, Ontario
The Electorate (Divided into 5 Wards)*

Thus, Canadians have allowed their municipal institutions to develop in a way that has discouraged interest and participation in government at the local level. To summarize, the reasons for this development are constitutional subservience; the absence of the parliamentary form in municipal government; a lack of media attention; the complexity and variety of municipal organization; the multiplicity of local governments within a geographical area; and the existence of many special purpose bodies.

SUPPLYING AND PAYING FOR MUNICIPAL SERVICES

The foregoing discussion has attempted to indicate some of the reasons why municipal government has been accorded limited importance in the public mind. Balanced against these factors is the obvious reality of the provision of a variety of crucial public services by local governments. Sometimes these services are mandated by provincial legislation, and local governments act as administrators of policies over which they have little influence. In other areas, local governments have considerable scope for independent action, although there is almost always some provision for provincial review or, just as crucially, dependence on provincial financing. These restrictions will be addressed later. Now it is necessary to look at some of the issues in which local government plays a significant role.

Planning and development is the area on which much of the literature on local government concentrates. Here municipal governments, under the umbrella of provincial planning legislation, can exercise considerable scope in adopting their official plans, passing zoning by-laws governing land use, and granting re-zoning applications for particular properties. There is a certain irony in the fixation on planning and development by students of municipal government who seek to elevate interest and knowledge in the subject yet, in doing so, discount the importance of other major municipal activities. There is absolutely no doubt that planning is a crucial municipal policy field, and it has an impact on other issue areas. Nevertheless, if one were to look at the agendas of municipal councils—and their committees where they exist—and to investigate the activities of municipal councillors, one would find that planning and development issues occupy only a portion of these policy agendas. Thus, before engaging in further discussion of the planning and development policy field, it may be useful to look at some other municipal questions.

What probably concerns municipal electors most is the level of property taxation that they will be expected to pay to support municipal services. In this regard, electors are not much different at the local level than they are as provincial or federal citizens. The annual setting of the mill rate, like the adoption of the budgets of the senior governments, creates more interest than all but the most extraordinary of other events. The budget process at the municipal level is much more public than it is at other levels of government. The budget is not just handed down by the equivalent of a finance minister and adopted by a pliant majority without debate. Rather, it is prepared by municipal administrators, with the degree of input by elected councillors dependent on the type of municipal system of the city or town. When the budget is submitted to the council, there is normally a lengthy debate over the course of several special budget meetings. Media coverage usually concentrates on the percentage increase proposed and perhaps on some items sure to generate public debate, such as councillors adopting a pay raise for themselves. The public is often involved, usually to lobby councils to provide expenditures for their favourite causes. This may especially be the case where councils provide grants to local artistic groups, marching bands, and other private interests in need of public funding. There is a tremendous variety in this process around the country, and the financial situation of any particular community may fluctuate year to year. Property owners are more interested than renters in this process because they are the ones who will receive a tax notice. In earlier times in most of Canada, only property owners could vote in municipal elections, it being thought that others had no stake in municipal government. While that is no longer the situation, it is the case that property taxes are buried in the rent people pay rather than noted separately, and thus may generate less concern for renters. Where rent control exists, however, and a process of rent review determines increases, landlords will certainly use a property tax increase to justify rent increases, and this will no doubt sensitize more people to the importance of the annual municipal budget.

While local taxpayers are concerned with their own property tax bill, they are less aware of the fact that approximately half of the revenue available to municipalities across Canada is supplied by their provincial government. The federal government's subsidies to local governments are minimal. Accordingly, municipal politicians were generally pleased by the job creation program of the Chrétien government, which pledged funds for municipal infrastructure improvements. Most provincial grants are conditional—that is, they are provided to subsidize a specific service. Only unconditional grants allow the municipality to spend the money as it sees fit. Thus, local governments are obviously constrained in their budget decisions by the availability of provincial grants. Local priorities are not necessarily uppermost in the minds of provincial authorities when they construct their budgets, and this can present local politicians with difficult decisions about which services and projects can be undertaken. The amount of unconditional grant money available will likely have an impact on whether, and by how much, the local property tax burden will have to increase.

Taxes on residential, commercial, and industrial property supply the bulk of self-generated revenue for local governments, along with taxes on businesses themselves in addition to that on the property they occupy. The other major source of revenue comes from water and utility charges and smaller sums derived from fines, licences, and investments. Property taxes are based on the assessed value of a property, and thus the assessment process is a key factor in the tax system of local governments. The provinces are equally divided between those that leave assessment to the municipalities and those that make it a provincial function. While all provinces have legislation to guide the assessment process, those provinces that administer the process themselves seek greater uniformity in the application of assessment between municipalities as well as within them. The assessment process is complicated and attempts to make it fair are ongoing. In Ontario, for instance, the process of market value assessment has been applied across the province to achieve more up-to-date and equitable evaluations. Nonetheless, as of 1994, it has not been applied in Metropolitan Toronto because its impact on different constituents of the regional municipality is highly controversial. The amount of property tax that is levied on the taxpayer is determined by applying the mill rate to the assessed value of the property. A mill is one-tenth of a cent, and thus $1000 of assessment taxed at a rate of 1 mill would yield $1. If a property were assessed at $10 000 and the mill rate was 100, then the property tax payable would be $1000. Thus, municipal taxpayers have two concerns: the assessed value of their property (and any changes that might be made to that assessment) and the percentage by which the mill rate may rise in a year. It should be kept in mind that the mill rate in most of Canada is determined by the decision of a board of education as well as by a municipal government.

This system of municipal finance has raised a number of concerns. For one thing its complexity, especially the assessment process, is daunting for most citizens. Once understood, however, there are two major issues: its adequacy to provide the necessary finance for local services and its fairness. If a community is growing in terms of the development of new homes, offices, stores, and factories, then the additional assessment can provide sufficient revenue with little or no increase in the mill rate. If there is little growth, then either services must be curtailed or the property tax rate must be raised, perhaps significantly. This situation can create a vicious circle, as high property taxation may discourage the new development that might mitigate further tax increases and allow better services. Uneven local taxation and uneven local services are common problems across the country.

The question of fairness arises because the property tax can be regressive—that is, not based on the ability to pay. While one might argue that people who are better off live in larger homes, in better neighbourhoods, and thus pay higher property taxes, that is not universally the case. Other situations are common, such as retired people on reduced income having to continue to pay the same (or higher) property taxes as they did when they were earning more. People who are unemployed or who lose income for whatever reason get no break in property taxes. Businesses continue to pay property taxes regardless of their profitability in any particular year. When property taxes were raised for services that applied mainly to property, the concept of the user paying might have been appropriate. Now, however, the property tax pays for a share of a variety of services (for example, education, public health, social assistance, culture, and recreation) that do not apply directly to one's property.

Abandonment of the property tax system because of its unfairness is not imminent. Nonetheless, local governments would like to curtail the increasing burden of property tax by developing alternative sources of income. The best of these would be a percentage of the income tax and corporate tax paid to the province. Manitoba made a start at this in 1976. Other provinces have allowed municipalities to levy a variety of taxes, such as amusement taxes. Still, the essential problem remains: municipalities are dependent on regressive property taxes that must be increased yearly unless the community grows substantially.

To a considerable degree, concern for minimizing the growing tax burden is the impetus for what Andrew Sancton calls *boosterism*.[3] This term refers to attempts to foster the image of the city as a good place in which to live, invest, and visit as a tourist or conventioneer. Boosterism finds its institutional expression in municipal agencies dedicated to economic development and to the development of tourism. In the past, these functions may have been the responsibility of the local board of trade or chamber of commerce, and in smaller communities it may remain so with the financial support of the municipal government. In the medium and larger cities of Canada, boosterism has emerged as a major responsibility of local governments. It is no longer acceptable to leave the prospects of economic growth, and with it increased assessment bases as well as jobs, to the senior governments and the private economy.

In terms of municipal policies, the quest for economic development has a variety of manifestations. In the area of planning, it may mean a willingness to grant favourable rezoning decisions that allow major projects to go forward. These decisions can be controversial and can change the face of a city. (I will return to this question in the discussion of planning.) Municipalities may acquire tracts of land for industrial parks and service these lands with water, electricity, roads, and sewers to make them available for industrial development. The aim is not to make money on property development but rather to sell as cheaply as possible to people who can be enticed to one's municipality. Decisions on the provision of major services such as roads or sewers can often be affected by whether those services will attract new industries and possibly induce present ones to stay or expand. The competition between communities for growth in their assessment bases makes the provision of adequate services an issue of prime importance and may at times create conflict between those needs and the demands of local citizens for a variety of other amenities in their own neighbourhoods.

Boosterism can also be seen in the push for a variety of public buildings like civic centres, convention halls, arenas, art galleries, museums, and concert halls. As often as not, the reason for these facilities is based on the contribution they will make to attracting tourists and conventions. They are, of course, also responses to local groups who want the facilities to enhance the local quality of life or at least that part of life in which they have an interest. In communities that are growing and prosperous, these public buildings are monuments to civic pride and the visions of politicians. In our largest cities, these facilities can be literally Olympic in stature. Public opinion will usually be divided on the need for, or at least the scope of, many of these public undertakings. The selling of these projects to the public is very much based on the boosterism syndrome, which holds that one's municipality must compete with others for a place in the sun.

The issues of municipal taxation and the quest for economic development are directly related to the taxpayer's pocketbook. There are also various issues that, although they have financial implications, are of concern to municipal governments because of their substance. The importance of problems varies from province to province and even community to community within provinces. The size of the municipality, for instance, will likely have a major impact on whether traffic problems, municipal public transit, or policing are important problems. On the other hand, educational and environmental questions may be relevant regardless of size. The next section will discuss some of those issues.

EDUCATION—THE OTHER MUNICIPAL GOVERNMENT

The literature on local government tends to say little about school boards and problems in education. Yet the cost of education to local taxpayers in most provinces is significant and in some municipalities may account for as much as half of all local expenditures. It is true that in all provinces the provincial department of education plays a dominant role in setting educational policy. Nonetheless, locally elected school boards almost everywhere play a crucial role in administering these policies and have the capacity to make important decisions for their communities. The building and location of new schools are matters of great concern to local citizens, and such decisions are essentially local ones. In Ontario, the existence of a public school system and a Roman Catholic school system has occasioned a degree of competition for students, especially at the high school level, that is played out locally. The extension of full funding to Roman Catholic high schools in the late 1980s created in some municipalities the need for the public and Roman Catholic school boards to bargain over facilities. For some communities, this became perhaps the dominant local political issue. In Quebec, the school boards became the focus for the provincial government's language policies. Anglophone boards especially were expected by their local supporters to preserve traditional rights. In British Columbia, in 1983, the introduction of a financially stringent budget by the provincial government placed several school boards in a politically contentious position with the province over the question of local control. The foregoing examples are only a few of the instances in which local school boards have become the focus of real political controversy.

School boards can become the focus of public concern not only about the quality of education but also about a variety of public issues that have an educational aspect. The question of race relations within schools can create the need for school boards to develop policies that may arouse considerable public debate. To the degree that school boards have some flexibility in curriculum, the introduction of course segments on the Native peoples of Canada and on the place of non-European immigrants, beginning with Black United Empire Loyalists, has become a feature of education in some localities in Canada. The efficacy of integrating students with physical or mental disabilities into the educational mainstream is another question that places school board members on the front lines of policy on a developing social concern. Advocates on both sides of this question can create a politically sensitive situation. The AIDS epidemic has led to local policy debate over the use of curriculum to educate students about the dangers of the disease. The availability of condoms in schools, first mandated by one school board in British Columbia, in 1989, continues to raise controversy in many localities across Canada. A furor over a teacher with AIDS in Nova Scotia presented a school board with a difficult political situation in 1988, and until the public educates itself about the disease and becomes less terrified of its victims this is not likely to be the only such case in Canada.

The examples cited above are some of the more widespread problems that Canadian local educational governments have faced, but in communities across Canada there may be specific questions that school boards face. These are political problems involving disputes about contending views on policy, and they involve questions of expenditure of locally raised taxes. It has become increasingly important for Canadians to have an understanding of, and concern about, the behaviour of the locally elected officials who are responsible for this aspect of local government.

POLICING

Policing is another area that has occupied a great deal of public attention but is rarely considered as a local government problem in the traditional sense. There has been a widespread attitude that policing should be isolated from politics rather than made a subject of political direction. Nonetheless, local special purpose bodies known as police commissions, or some similar designation, have budgetary and other policy control over local police forces. Like school boards, these commissions are independent of the municipal council, but unlike school boards in most provinces they may have some councillors who can bring the perspective of council to the deliberation on police matters.

In communities across Canada, there has been a growing concern for public safety and the problem of crime. The availability and efficiency of policing services in many communities raise questions of budget and operational procedures just as does the delivery of any other municipal service. However, the power invested in police forces and their relations with the public make the service they deliver a much more sensitive question than other municipal functions. A major concern is the method of dealing with complaints (especially alleged racism) about police behaviour. Traditionally, this has been done internally, with police investigating complaints within their own departments and police commissions making the determination on cases. In Ontario, that procedure has been augmented by a provincial office of the police complaints commissioner to monitor complaints and a special investigations unit to deal with instances involving extreme force, shootings, or death. The latter body is especially controversial and unpopular with police. The resolution of the ancient question "Who is to guard the guardians?" is far from satisfactorily resolved in Canada.

As immigration has changed the composition of the Canadian population, especially in the largest cities, the relations between almost completely white police forces and citizens who are not white has become at times an explosive issue. Native Canadians have registered concerns about the treatment accorded to members of their community in cities across Canada. The late 1980s saw a number of incidents and subsequent commissions that revealed serious problems in this area. The Donald Marshall inquiry into the false conviction and imprisonment of Marshall, a Mi'kmaq Indian in Sydney, Nova Scotia, raised questions not only about the police procedures in that case but also about the entire administration of justice in the province. Representatives of both Native and Black citizens' groups used the opportunity to air their long-standing grievances over discriminatory treatment. Both Metropolitan Toronto and Montreal witnessed the fatal shootings of Blacks by police during apprehension and arrest, which inflamed feelings in the Black community. The police shooting of an Aboriginal Canadian in Winnipeg gave rise to an inquiry into the Manitoba justice system and relations between the police force and members of the Native community in the late 1980s. In Alberta, Indian bands raised questions regarding the investigations by police of deaths among their members. The police argue that racial considerations have no place in their actions. Investigations and inquiries can only begin to seek a resolution to a festering problem that will not disappear in a short period, as Canadian cities witness a degree of racial tension from which the majority population thought they were free. These instances are only the most publicized examples of a problem that is of crucial interest, especially to minority groups in municipalities across Canada. Issues of racism and policy are a local government problem to the degree that the staffing, discipline, and general direction of police forces are matters directed by an appointed local body funded mainly by the municipal government. While police commissions were set up because of a desire to keep police functions out of politics, the concerns that members of communities have about police in fact raise highly political issues, and the solutions that they seek will have to be the result of local (and provincial) political activity.

ENVIRONMENTAL ISSUES

Environmental issues have achieved prominence in municipal affairs in the last third of the twentieth century. A main cause of the pollution in Canadian rivers and lakes has been the flow of untreated sewage into bodies of water adjacent to the population centres. As late as 1989, 80 percent of Quebec municipalities did not have sewage treatment facilities. The city of Victoria, British Columbia, attracted widespread criticism for discharging raw sewage into coastal waters and, even in the early 1990s, appeared reluctant to adopt expensive pollution-control methods.

Major efforts to deal with environmental degradation began in Ontario and elsewhere in the 1960s. Large-scale expenditures were involved in building the facilities necessary to treat water before it returned to rivers and lakes. Provincial financial support was necessary for this effort, and some federal subsidies were available as well. Nonetheless, once facilities were built, municipalities were responsible for the operation of plants that required personnel and large quantities of chemicals for the treatment of waste. Growth of housing and industry necessitated the building of sewer systems and sometimes the expansion of treatment plants. In built-up areas, the use of septic tanks for new development was often forbidden, and the extension of sewer systems to replace septic tanks often became an expensive responsibility for municipal governments. This could often be a major issue as municipalities expanded into their own previously undeveloped areas or took over neighbouring smaller (previously rural) communities. Not surprisingly, the building of major sewer systems and sewage treatment plants was often thought to be an argument for the establishment of regional governments.

Solid waste presents another environmental challenge to local governments. For the average person, garbage was something put out once a week and collected by a municipal employee (or contractor) who then made it disappear. However, it reappeared in landfills out in the countryside, and the people living near those sites were never happy about it. As these dumps have filled up, their neighbours have sought to have them closed rather than expanded. People in other areas where sites have been identified as suitable for landfilling have almost always rebelled against the idea. This predictable reaction has become known as the NIMBY syndrome— that is, "Not in my backyard." It represents a classic case of externalities in that a rural community has to accept the costs (a landfill) of a problem (tons of garbage) created in an urban municipality. The balancing of costs and benefits in these circumstances is a very difficult problem. Nonetheless, the garbage must be dealt with somehow.

Recycling represents the best solution because it not only reduces the amount of garbage to be landfilled but also saves resources by reusing materials. The co-operation of the public is vital for recycling because separating the reusable materials before collection—that is, at home—is crucial to a feasible system. In the best of all environmentally sound worlds, people would create less waste to start with and would compost their food wastes for their gardens. However, in the congested urban world of many Canadians, the most that can reasonably be hoped for is that people will separate their newspapers, glass, and metal products for collection. Optimists believe that as much as half of all garbage can be recycled, thus reducing the need for landfilling.

Another alternative to landfilling involves the incineration of garbage. Some of the methods proposed for burning wastes would create commercially valuable quantities of power that could be used by municipalities and industry. The technology for this approach is already in use, more in Europe and the United States than in Canada, and it is simple and cheap. From an environmental point of view, however, there is concern that burning waste materials can create toxic emissions that harm air quality. People in urban areas are not usually enthusiastic about having large incinerators in their communities. As with many municipal policy questions, one person's solution is another person's problem.

The disposal of industrial waste products, many of them highly toxic, presents a particularly difficult problem to municipalities. Industries provide the employment that may be the basis for a community's existence, yet they pose a serious threat to the environment in which the community's citizens live. No acceptable solution to this problem has yet emerged. Industrial and household waste is a municipal problem whose resolution is both expensive and politically contentious.

DEVELOPMENT AND MUNICIPAL POLITICS

The foregoing discussions of taxation, economic development policies, education, policing, and the environment have been presented to demonstrate that municipal governments have important policy agendas that include much more than land-use planning. It is true that various aspects of municipal policy may be very closely tied to land-use planning questions, but nevertheless much of municipal government involves political debate having little reference to the development of property. That is why the literature that reduces municipal government to little more than the relationship between large property developers and compliant municipal politicians and administrators is really a caricature of city politics. To say that is not to dismiss the importance of the property development industry or to deny that, depending on time and place, it can be the major question of municipal politics. The huge developments in the downtowns of major Canadian cities have a major impact on the faces of those cities, their lifestyle, their traffic, even their climate. Private developers seek intensive use of property to maximize their profits, while the goal of municipal planners is to create a cityscape more conducive to the enjoyment of a better quality of life for urban dwellers. It seems apparent that in too many instances the goals of the developer have trampled over those of the planner.

The large economic power of huge development companies obviously gives them major influence with municipal governments. Those firms can employ architects, planners, traffic consultants, and other professionals who offer their own version of proper planning to oppose that of municipal planning departments if there are differences of opinion. The development industry provides campaign contributions to municipal candidates who will likely support development proposals. These factors seem to confirm the view that the development industry has inordinate influence over the land-use planning process and that the views of others, such as citizens groups, are shut out.

There is another side to this question that is just as serious, and it has to do with the attitudes of mayors and councils across the country. Simply put, they tend to favour large-scale development and do not need much convincing by developers. Boosterism leads them to seek out development. The relationship between assessment and their ability to provide services without large tax increases makes a large development an attractive proposition. Certainly, seeking out industrial development—and the bigger the factory, the better—is a top priority of municipal politicians. In their quest for development, councils by and large have the approval of their electors, while the local media act as a cheering section.

Where individual home-owners who are organized in their communities do have some influence is with changes to their neighbourhood. Usually this revolves around the rejection of any variation from the norm of single-family dwellings. While citizen groups may have little impact on the land-use planning of the downtown cores of their cities, they may achieve considerable influence over planning issues closer to their own concerns. The introduction of housing that is more affordable for lower-income groups—which usually means more intensive land use in the form of apartments, townhouses, duplexes, or single-family dwellings on small lots—is typically opposed by neighbourhoods (sometimes even entire municipalities) on the grounds that it will alter the nature of their community, depress property values, increase traffic, overcrowd schools, and have various other negative effects. In these instances, attempts by developers to use land intensively are often thwarted by middle-class home-owners who oppose the development. Unfortunately for those seeking affordable housing, their interests are represented by developers and builders who can easily be attacked as greedy business people who are trying to undermine the character of someone's neighbourhood. When the developer is a government agency or a sponsor of co-operative housing, the opposition can be even more shrill because of the prospect that the proposed housing will be inhabited by subsidized tenants.

The land-use planning process in Canadian communities is complex and often leads to political confrontation. The relationships between land-use decisions and the financial health of the community, between the boosterism of elected officials and civic organizations, and between the economic power of large development firms and the determination of single-family home-owners to maintaining the standard of housing in their neighbourhoods may all conspire to thwart what some might think is proper land-use planning. It should not be surprising that various groups will not abandon what they perceive to be their interests to satisfy concepts that municipal planners and social activists prescribe for a better community. Planning decisions, however, have long-term ramifications, and it is crucial that municipal politicians do not allow any short-run interests to dictate policies that may drastically affect the future of their community.

Only a few of the many issues that confront local governments have been touched on in this chapter. Beyond these and other concerns that municipal councils and other local bodies must confront, there is a growing tendency to use municipal governments as sounding boards for questions that are outside of municipal jurisdiction. The relative ease with which one may appear before a council and the potential for media coverage (many councils have their meetings televised on local cable stations) attract many groups to use the opportunity to foster their cause. Thus, requests to have councils proclaim "Right to Life Week" or "Gay Pride Day," or to declare a municipality a "Nuclear Free Zone," are attempts to have municipal legislators take a stand on and help to legitimize various points of view on essentially non-municipal matters. It is questionable how useful it is for municipal councillors to expend considerable emotional energy on matters over which they have no jurisdiction, especially when one considers the degree of provincial control they must confront even in their own municipal concerns.

MUNICIPAL POLITICIANS AND ELECTIONS

Throughout the foregoing discussion of local government problems, reference has been made to the need for local politicians to make policy decisions. What will follow is a brief discussion of who these people are and the processes by which they get into office. To generalize about the backgrounds of local elected officials can be a problem because of the variety of communities and of positions available. Well over half of Canadians live in twenty-five cities with populations of over 100 000, yet the elected representatives in these cities do not make up even 10 percent of the total number of elected local politicians in Canada. Beyond that, the substantial number of elected school board trustees would not necessarily have the same kinds of backgrounds as members of municipal councils. The picture one might encounter of the typical urban councillor may be considerably different than that of the large majority of elected local representatives.

As is the case with MPs and provincial legislators, municipal councillors are disproportionately business and professional people. Lawyers might constitute 10 percent to 15 percent of councillors, a significant percentage, but considerably less than the typical 25 percent or more in the House of Commons. Self-employed business people, managers, and other professionals constitute the bulk of council members. This situation fuels the view that municipal government is run in the interests of the local business community and that non-political services to property, as well as pro-development characteristics of most local governments, derive from this circumstance. The reform era of the 1960s and 1970s may have brought to councils other people to challenge the prevailing views, but these new councillors were also professionals such as teachers, professors, and social workers. Urban councillors do not mirror the population of their communities in terms of occupations, incomes, education, ethnicity (where there is ethnic diversity), or sex. With regard to the last, as we have seen in chapter 13, local councils have a somewhat higher percentage of women than the House of Commons or provincial legislatures, but it is certainly nowhere near 50 percent.[4]

Widespread social attitudes and entrenched inequalities give rise to this situation. For women and visible minorities, historical impediments to entry into political life have been fundamental. The prominence of the business and professional class reflects the continued support for a capitalist economy by a majority of Canadians and a respect for those who have been successful in that economy. Economic success, for instance, means having the financial resources and contacts that make political success more likely than it is for those who do not have these resources. A majority of councillors do not have to be convinced, let alone bought off, to agree that the ethic of business, growth, development, and private enterprise will lead to the best outcomes for their community.

Elections to municipal councils differ from federal and provincial elections in a variety of ways. First of all there are fixed terms, and the election dates are established by law. The three-year term is now most common, although shorter terms used to be the norm. Second, the major political figure, the mayor, is elected directly by the entire electorate rather than taking office by virtue of leadership of a victorious political party. This is the case even where local party organizations have developed or the national parties are involved in the contest. Of the national parties, only the NDP is a regular and open participant in municipal elections, and even that party contests in only a few large cities. For the most part, the national parties are content to provide some financial support and campaign workers for selected party members who run as independents like the other candidates. Financial support from the state (in its local guise) is not available to local candidates, unlike their federal and provincial counterparts, nor can contributors claim their donations as a tax credit. Limits on expenditures and disclosure of sources of campaign contributions are not imposed consistently across Canada and, even where they are imposed, they are recent innovations that are not rigidly enforced.

The absence of political parties at the local level has a variety of effects. Candidates are self-selected rather than chosen by political parties in a nomination process. Municipal candidates are usually on their own in terms of getting campaign funds. This raises the question of donations from particular sources, especially those interested in land-use planning and development. Competition is less intense, and acclamations,[5] especially in smaller communities, are common. At the federal and provincial levels, uncontested elections are almost non-existent. Accountability is difficult to establish because candidates run on their own names and records. Thus, the municipal electorate does not have a party position to use as a standard for decision. Voting turnouts are lower in municipal elections because the party mechanisms that organize voters to participate are not present for the most part.

That political parties have not developed a local presence is testament to the widespread attitude that municipal government is somehow non-political. "There is no Progressive Conservative, Liberal, or New Democratic Party way to fill a pothole," goes the old cliché. But this ignores the reality that not all potholes in all parts of a city may be filled at the same time. Whose will get priority? Beyond that, limited resources mean that devoting funds to fix potholes may reduce spending on other services that are demanded by other interests. While the technical question of how best to fill a pothole may be non-political, other aspects of the pothole issue may be highly political and can evoke different attitudes that may be best represented by political parties. In Europe, participation of political parties at the local level is a well-established democratic practice.

Another example of thinking that exists at the municipal level but is absent elsewhere is the preference for at-large elections[6] rather than ward (smaller geographical districts) representation. Except for Vancouver, the ward system has won out in larger and medium-sized Canadian cities, but many municipal voters still do not like the idea, and smaller town and township elections are still on an at-large basis. The argument most cited to support the at-large system is that it encourages an appreciation of the general interests of the community rather than more parochial neighbourhood concerns. Those who make that argument do not follow up its logic by insisting, for instance, that all their provincial legislators be elected at large to pursue province-wide interests rather than narrow constituency concerns. And would not national unity best be served by electing to the House of Commons 295 representatives committed to national interests rather than the petty concerns of their localities? Advocates of at-large elections would counter that the limited geography and the feeling of community in municipalities creates common interests rather than conflict. Such arguments are but another example of the prevalence of attitudes that seek to de-politicize municipal government.

More could be said about the processes of local politics, elections, candidates, and the behaviour of elected and appointed officials. Appointed officials, the bureaucracy, have great influence over municipal government, as they do at the other levels. The point of this chapter has not been, however, to describe local government in a complete way, but rather to argue that local governments play an important role in the lives of Canadians. Moreover, local governments deal with political problems, and the tendency to try to de-politicize the local government process is inconsistent with a concern for democratic processes and participation.

Notes

[1] D.J.H. Higgins, *Local and Urban Politics in Canada* (Toronto: Gage, 1989), 148–64.

[2] Andrew Sancton, "Mayors as Political Leaders" in *Leaders and Leadership in Canada*, ed. Maureen Mancuso, Richard Price, and R.H. Wagenberg (Toronto: Oxford University Press, 1994), ch. 10.

[3] Andrew Sancton, "Canadian City Politics in Comparative Perspective" in *City Politics in Canada*, ed. Warren Magnusson and Andrew Sancton (Toronto: University of Toronto Press, 1983), 293.

[4] See Higgins, *Local and Urban Politics*, 361–65, for reference to some studies on representation.

[5] Acclamations result when only one person seeks an office and is thus "acclaimed" without the necessity of holding an election.

[6] At-large elections for municipal councils are those in which the entire council is elected for the entire community. If there is a ten-member council, each voter gets to vote for ten candidates, and the top ten vote-getters are elected.

SUGGESTED READING

Cameron, David M. "Provincial Responsibilites for Municipal Government." *Canadian Public Administration* 23, 2 (1980): 222–35.
A thoughtful article discussing the purposes of municipal government.

Feldman, Lionel, ed. *Politics and Government of Urban Canada*. 4th ed. Toronto: Methuen, 1981.
A collection of readings covering various aspects of local politics and government.

Higgins, D.J.H. *Local and Urban Politics in Canada*. Toronto: Gage, 1986.
An excellent text offering a comprehensive description and analysis of urban government and politics.

Magnusson, Warren, and Sancton, Andrew, eds. *City Politics in Canada*. Toronto: University of Toronto Press, 1983.
Essays on the politics of Montreal, Toronto, Ottawa-Hull, Halifax, Vancouver, Winnipeg, and Edmonton provide the basis for comparative analysis.

T.A. Keenleyside

CANADA AND THE WORLD

Canada's role in world affairs is usually accorded little attention in introductions to the study of Canadian government and politics. Nonetheless, foreign policy is an extremely important aspect of the study of public policy in Canada and has its own expanding and varied literature. This chapter has three main purposes. First, it sets out four of the central reasons why global affairs are important to Canada: peace and security; economic growth and independence; the environment; and social justice. Second, it briefly discusses how Canadian policy in these areas has evolved over the years. Third, it comments on the contemporary challenges confronting Canada in each of these areas and suggests policy responses to these problems.

PEACE AND SECURITY
The Problem

For all countries, the effective management of their relations with other states is important, in that ensuring their security vis-à-vis potential aggressors is necessary for the successful attainment of their domestic goals. Conflict requires the diversion of scarce resources from economic, social, environmental, and other programs that enhance the quality of life to generally unproductive but costly military purposes. Further, defeat at the hands of other powers risks the complete collapse of a state's capacity to realize its goals, the destruction of its culture and values, and perhaps the loss of sovereignty itself. All states, then, inevitably concern themselves with international relations to maximize their security in an uncertain world.

For a country like Canada, there are arguably particular security reasons for becoming involved in global politics. It shares a continent-wide border with the world's only superpower and is situated between the United States and Russia, both principal nuclear powers. This geographical reality leaves Canada highly vulnerable should the United States fail to manage its international relationships in a peaceful manner. At the same time, having a close partnership with the United States based on geography, related histories, similar cultures, and shared values, Canada has an opportunity, bilaterally and through its international institutional involvement, to influence, however modestly, the shaping of American policy on a wide range of international issues. Canada can thus affect, to a greater degree than might otherwise be the case, the prospects for enhanced global stability. Finally, Canada is dependent on international commerce for its well-being to a far greater degree than most countries. Tension and conflict in world politics tend to be accompanied by tariff wars and other disruptions to the normal flow of goods and services, jeopardizing the stable economic order so central to Canada's welfare. This economic concern furnishes an additional reason for active internationalism on Canada's part in the interests of attaining global peace and security.

The Response

Since World War II, Canada has pursued peace and security—the first and paramount goal of foreign policy—by two broad means: military alliance commitments, and support, particularly via the United Nations, for international mediation of disputes, peacekeeping, arms control, and disarmament. Commencing with the Ogdensburg Agreement of 1940 and the creation of the Permanent Joint Defence Board to plan the defence of North America during World War II, Canada has been bound militarily to the United States. This co-operation climaxed in 1958 with the creation of the North American Air Defence Command (NORAD), now known as the North American Aerospace Command, a bilateral pact that principally protects the continent against a bomber attack. Under NORAD, Canada and the United States devised an integrated command structure for continental air defence, built and staffed radar stations in the Canadian North in order to detect conventional air strikes, and developed the capacity to intercept and shoot down attacking bombers.

In addition to bilateral security arrangements, Canada has been a participant in the North Atlantic Treaty Organization (NATO) since its inception in 1949. NATO is a multilateral pact that joins Canada and the United States together with a number of Western European countries in mutual obligations to assist each other in the event that any member is a victim of external aggression. Under NATO, Canada had forces stationed in Europe from 1951 to 1994. Until the sudden collapse in 1989 of the ideological divide between Eastern and Western Europe, these forces were intended to help protect Western Europe against advances by the Soviet bloc—encroachments that, it was feared, could endanger the security of Canada and the United States. Now NATO is moving tentatively toward a wider mandate of helping to preserve the security of all the states of Europe.

Canada was a strong supporter immediately after World War II of the idea of using the United Nations to guarantee the security of members through the collective application of economic and military sanctions against would-be aggressors. When deadlock between the United States and the Soviet Union ended the prospects of the organization's functioning effectively in this fashion, not only did Canada turn to the above-mentioned alliances, but it also became involved in new, secondary UN roles related to fostering international peace and stability—United Nations observer and peacekeeping forces. These operations have been designed to monitor cease-fire agreements in regional conflicts principally in the Third World, oversee the withdrawal of combatants, and ensure the preservation of peace and order thereafter. Since, historically, one of the purposes of such missions was to prevent limited regional conflicts from escalating to larger wars into which the United States and the Soviet Union might be drawn at the risk of nuclear holocaust, the great powers had to be excluded from participation. By contrast, Canada, possessing well-trained and highly disciplined forces with a variety of specialized skills necessary for the success of peacekeeping, was well suited for this activity. As a consequence, performing UN observer and peacekeeping duties was, and continues to be in the post–Cold War era, one of Canada's central contributions to fostering global security. Canada has been involved at some stage in virtually every UN peacekeeping operation, a unique record among member states. Some 80 000 Canadians have served abroad in peacekeeping functions, more soldiers than any other country.

Similarly, from the creation of the original ten-nation UN Committee on Disarmament to its current participation in the forty-nation Conference on Disarmament, Canada has been actively involved since World War II in fostering global security through its support of arms-control measures. As a state that voluntarily chose after the war to eschew the development of an independent nuclear arsenal and instead maintain only modest military capabilities, Canada necessarily plays a secondary role in arms-control deliberations and the attendant agreements. Nevertheless, it has made a contribution of some significance, especially in the technical area of verifying states' adherence to the terms of agreements in such fields as nuclear non-proliferation, the abolition of chemical weapons, and the partial banning of underground nuclear tests.

The Contemporary Challenges

Since 1989, the international system has undergone dramatic changes that have simultaneously generated hopes for a more peaceful and orderly world and precipitated new threats to global security. The most promising development was the collapse of the Soviet empire over the 1989–91 period. This development marked the end of the Cold War and the emergence of nascent democratic governments and market economies throughout much of Eastern Europe and the former Soviet Union. There have been hopeful political changes in recent years in the Third World as well, with several states in Africa and Latin America in particular making progress toward meaningful participatory democracy and respect for the rule of law. If the contention that democracies do not usually resolve their differences with other states by military means is valid, then these developments may presage a more secure global community. Certainly, they have facilitated major reductions in the nuclear and conventional forces of the two major military powers, the United States and Russia, as well as their initiation of moratoria on nuclear testing.

The new atmosphere of co-operation between old Cold War adversaries has also precipitated a revival of the United Nations, since the organization is no longer effectively paralyzed by a deadlocked Security Council. Perhaps most significant for the long term has been the resurgence of the role of United Nations peacekeeping. From 1987 to 1993, thirteen new operations were launched, as many as throughout the entire previous history of the United Nations, reflecting perhaps growing prospects of this organization serving as the principal guarantor of a secure global order.

The very number of new UN operations discloses, however, that the passing of the Cold War has not brought the end of conflict, but has, in fact, created new threats to peace. The lifting of the iron hand of the Kremlin from the backs of its former republics and satellites has unleashed nationalistic forces and pent-up ethnic animosities that are embroiling the successor states of the Soviet empire in costly and bloody conflicts. These in turn are jeopardizing the capacity of these states for democratic evolution, already made difficult by the precarious nature of their economies and the anger and frustration of their peoples at the hardships they are being forced to endure in the transition to capitalism. Anarchy or a reversion to authoritarianism, with the attendant risk of renewed confrontations with old enemies, threatens the fragile new ties being built between East and West. At the same time, the end of the Cold War has removed some of the restraints that held Third World states together, albeit often under repressive rule. The result has been an increase in ethnic conflict and civil war, adding to the global flood of refugees, forestalling economic development, and delaying attention to environmental decay, problems that enhance the risks to regional and global security. Under these circumstances, the continuing presence as of 1993 of roughly 45 000 nuclear weapons, some of them in the hands of successor states to the Soviet Union that lack effective safety systems and dismantling capabilities, is a major cause of concern. All in all, the euphoria of 1989, when many people felt that the world was embarking on what would be a protracted era of peace, has given way, if not to pessimism, at least to new anxieties and even nostalgia for the Cold War era and an international order that, if not liked, was at least understood.

The security challenges confronting Canada in the present era are substantial, but the opportunities to have an impact may be limited. Broadly speaking, there are four areas that require particular attention. One is aiding the transition to democracy and capitalism in Eastern Europe and the former Soviet Union, recognizing that if the forces of reaction triumph, the world could slide into a new cold war. Despite the risks, more needs to be done by way of technical assistance, food aid, and credits as well as capital contributions to the European Bank for Reconstruction and Development. Additional people-to-people linkages should be forged in the areas of industry, education, science, the arts, sports, and even the military. The private sector must be encouraged to be more aggressive in seeking trade and investment opportunities. Canada needs to press other Western states to redouble their own co-operative efforts so that this hopeful moment for building trust and mutual dependence across the former Cold War divide is not lost.

A second area of focus for Canadian security policy should be pushing for advances related to arms control and disarmament. An urgent priority in this respect is renewal of the Nuclear Non-Proliferation Treaty in 1995 and obtaining the adherence of such non-signatories as India, Pakistan, and Israel. International Atomic Energy safeguards need to be enhanced by the introduction of surprise inspections of nuclear facilities to ensure that they are not being used for military purposes. Canada must work assiduously for a comprehensive nuclear test ban treaty. Here its principal contribution is likely to be helping to develop a seismic monitoring network so that the treaty's adherents will have confidence that any illegal underground tests will be detected. Canada should encourage the United States and Russia to stabilize their nuclear arsenals at much lower levels than the 11 000 weapons each currently envisaged for early in the next century. Finally, Canada must work to check the mushrooming sale of arms to developing countries. While it has only a modest military industry itself, Canada ranks seventh or eighth as an arms producer. When beneficial to its own economic interests, Canada has been ready to pursue arms exports to states that are at risk of becoming embroiled in regional conflict.

A third area of attention is the reshaping of old and the building of new regional security institutions. This is perhaps most urgent in Europe. While in 1989 it looked as if the need for NATO would shortly disappear, new threats to security in Europe suggest that, with a revised mandate and gradually expanding membership (to include many if not all of the Cold War adversaries), the alliance may be required for some time to come. Its new, principal priority is the development of flexible, mobile forces able to respond rapidly to ethnic violence and civil war in Europe and to support United Nations or other peacekeeping missions operating in the region. There is also a place for Canada in strengthening the institutions of the Conference on Security and Co-operation in Europe, currently the only organization embracing virtually all of the countries of Europe plus Canada and the United States. It is, along with NATO, one of the key organizations that can play a creative role in cementing new relationships between East and West across a broad range of issues.

In the above three areas, Canada's future role is likely to be relatively limited, confined largely to diplomatic pressure on more powerful states to pursue policies consistent with Canada's own security interests. However, in the fourth area, strengthening of the United Nations, the key global institution, Canada is well positioned to play a substantial part. As indicated above, given the new co-operative environment in the Security Council, the UN has assumed major new security responsibilities in recent years—from traditional peacekeeping to enforcement actions, as in the Gulf War. The variety and complexity of UN operations are also expanding as recent missions in Cambodia, Somalia, and the former Yugoslavia demonstrate. In addition to the classic function of supervising cease-fires, UN forces are assuming responsibility for ensuring the safe delivery of emergency food and medical supplies, protecting human rights, providing for the relief and resettlement of refugees, monitoring elections, and helping to build civil administrations in newly emerging states and those recovering from civil war. Canada is eminently suited to the task of helping to meet the expanding activities of the United Nations in all these areas, and that is reflected in the fact that it is currently providing roughly 10 percent of the UN's peace-keeping forces. To ensure that it continues to be in a position to make such a contribution, the organization, training, and equipping of the Canadian armed forces should be undertaken with support to the United Nations principally in mind. Canada should also explore opportunities for strengthening the UN's capacity to undertake its expanded security functions. It could, for instance, consider establishing an international training centre for peacekeeping operations where armed forces and civilians from other countries frequently chosen for such missions would train with Canadians. Leadership is needed in seeking solutions to the perennial problems related to authorization, command, control, logistics, financing, and the status of peacekeeping forces in the host countries.

In sum, the contribution that Canada can make to global stability in the first three areas discussed above is likely to be limited. However, at the United Nations, and especially in the theatre of peacekeeping, it has been at centre stage. The old actor has willingly accepted the accolades showered on it by a grateful international audience for its past performances, but Canada must not rest on its laurels. The peacekeeping part must still be played and plumbed to new depths to meet the challenges of the future in the quest for international peace and security.

ECONOMIC GROWTH AND INDEPENDENCE

The Problem

Maximizing domestic economic growth is another goal that leads states into international activity. Like security, the attainment of wealth is central to a country's capacity to provide the advanced level of services demanded by its citizens. Some states, endowed with natural resources and large populations with sophisticated skills, are capable of generating economic growth essentially by internal means. However, almost all states rely to a certain degree on trade with other countries and on inward and outward flows of capital and technical knowledge to maximize their economic potential. The search for economic growth thus inevitably leads countries to interact with each other.

Canada is one of those states particularly reliant on international economic relations for its well-being. It ranks second after Germany in its dependence on international trade for the creation of national wealth, and the jobs of roughly one-third of Canadians are linked in some way to trade.

This reliance is principally a product of Canada's small population base. The domestic market has a limited absorptive capacity for the natural resources and manufactured products that Canada produces. They must, therefore, be sold abroad in order for Canada to be able to purchase the variety of goods and services that it does not itself produce but that are important to a high standard of living. Possessing a small and scattered population of traditionally cautious investors, Canada has also not always been able to generate (or effectively organize) the large amounts of capital required for the high-cost projects related to exploiting its natural resources and developing a sophisticated manufacturing sector. Canada thus has often looked outside its borders for its capital needs. These have been readily met by foreign investors who have been anxious to gain access to Canadian resources, have seen Canada as a politically and economically stable country in which to do business, and have used the building of branch plants as a means of circumventing the tariff barriers that Canada erected after Confederation to protect the development of domestic industries.

While economic considerations have served to push Canada into international affairs, at the same time a variety of circumstances have led to a situation where most Canadian economic activity takes place with just one country, the United States. Geographic isolation with the American giant on the North American continent is the principal explanation. Canada's distance from other markets and the presence of trading blocs from which, as a North American country, Canada has been excluded have rendered it more often than not uncompetitive outside North America. These problems of geography have been compounded by Canada's small domestic market, which has frequently denied its producers the economies of scale that would enable them to price their goods low enough to appeal to buyers in distant countries. At the same time, Canadian suppliers are situated close to the enormous American market. Transportation costs and extended delivery times are not major obstacles. As well, the United States is hungry for Canadian resources and other products and has an almost boundless absorptive capacity. Further, the two countries share the same language and similar cultures and tastes. Naturally they have been drawn to each other economically, and as a result they share the largest trading relationship between any two countries in the world. However, Canada is much more dependent upon this trade than is the United States. Roughly 75 percent of Canada's combined exports and imports are with the United States, while the latter's trade with Canada accounts for only about 20 percent of its world trade. Canada's greater dependence is compounded by the fact that almost one-third of its gross national product is derived from foreign trade while in the case of the United States the figure is less than 10 percent. Similarly, for the reasons already indicated, Canada has relied heavily on inflows of American capital to finance its economic growth.

Ironically, international commerce is of vital importance to Canada's economic growth and its capacity to meet the needs and demands of its citizens, but at the same time, in the view of many, Canada's economic over-reliance on the United States poses threats to its independence. Trade and investment ties with the United States mean that Canada is highly vulnerable to fluctuations in American economic performance and to decisions made by American boards of directors, often in response to American governmental policies rather than Canadian ones. Historically, it has also meant that Canada could be coerced, by threats to the disruption of the free flow of goods, services, and capital, into pursuing policies compatible with American rather than Canadian interests. Finally, the gradual process toward closer economic integration with the United States poses the ultimate danger of loss of Canadian sovereignty, as new forms of collaboration are introduced until the point of political union itself is reached. In short, Canada faces the paradox of necessarily being drawn into international relations to achieve the economic growth its citizens expect, while creating in the process challenges to its independence.

The Response

Recognizing the importance of foreign trade to its economic prosperity, Canada has long made efforts to enlarge its market opportunities abroad. It has, for example, engaged in vigorous bilateral and multilateral diplomatic efforts to reduce the tariff and non-tariff barriers to international commerce. Early on, it developed a strong trade commissioners service to support the efforts of Canadian business in securing foreign markets. In 1982, this service was integrated into the Department of External Affairs, and in 1989 the department changed its name to External Affairs and International Trade Canada (now Foreign Affairs and International Trade), moves that manifested the importance Ottawa attaches to commerce in its foreign policy. The government has also adopted a variety of incentive schemes to help Canadian businesses expand their activities abroad, underwriting certain costs and risks associated with attempting to penetrate distant markets.

Canada has long recognized the potentially serious implications of its heavy economic (as well as cultural and military) reliance upon the United

States. It was not until the early 1970s, however, that the government of Pierre Trudeau officially adopted the strategy of attempting to reduce Canadian dependence upon the United States by diversifying economic and other relations and by implementing policies designed to achieve a higher level of Canadian ownership of the economy. The Trudeau years saw intensive efforts to cultivate expanded relations with a number of countries that seemed to offer sound prospects as countervailing economic partners. These included China, Japan, the member states of the Association of Southeast Asian Nations, the Soviet Union, Saudi Arabia, and Brazil.

A variety of domestic economic (and cultural) measures were taken in response to the perceived American challenge to Canadian sovereignty. Two are particularly important to note. In 1973, the Trudeau government created the Foreign Investment Review Agency to screen foreign takeovers of Canadian firms, the establishment of wholly new enterprises in Canada by foreign investors, and the expansion of existing subsidiaries to ensure that investments were of significant benefit to Canada. In 1980, the Liberals adopted the National Energy Program, designed to achieve two broad goals: 51 percent Canadian ownership in the oil and gas industry and self-sufficiency of supply by 1990. These and other interventionist measures of the Trudeau years were intensely disliked in the United States, where they were perceived as artificial impediments to free market forces, and they sparked considerable friction in Canadian–American relations.

By the 1980s it was clear that the policy of attempting to diversify Canada's trade relations was not working effectively. While substantial absolute increases in Canadian trade with other markets occurred over the Trudeau period, in relative terms Canada was considerably more dependent upon trade with the United States at the end of this era than at the outset. The traditional impediments to extra-continental trade had conspired to undermine the efforts of the government. Moreover, by the 1980s there was considerable anxiety in Ottawa over a growing climate of American protectionism, which was seen as jeopardizing future growth in Canadian exports to that market, especially if the Canadian dollar significantly appreciated in value. Securing assured access to the United States market by some form of bilateral agreement became the new solution to assuring Canada's future prosperity. Thus, by the time the Mulroney government came to power in 1984, a comprehensive free trade deal was being touted by many not only as central to sustaining Canadian economic growth, but as an instrument for enhancing Canadian independence, in that expanding wealth was necessary for Canada to sustain social, cultural, and other programs that gave it an identity distinct from that of the United States.

It was argued that the increased productivity of Canadian industry, stream-lined by the demands of free trade and now benefiting from economies of scale, would be better able to penetrate distant markets, bringing about the diversification of trade long sought as a means of preserving Canadian sovereignty.

The Mulroney government also took a different view of foreign invest-ment, arguing that Canada needed more, not less, of it to sustain its eco-nomic growth. The real risk was seen in capital moving offshore to resource-rich countries where production costs were lower. A free trade deal with the United States was thus favoured in part because it was antici-pated that it would lead to new capital inflows by investors confident about opening plants in Canada given the prospect of ready access to the entire North American market.

Starting in 1984, the Mulroney government undertook a major rever-sal of Canadian policies related to economic growth and independence. The Conservatives dismantled the Foreign Investment Review Agency and replaced it with Investment Canada (a body designed principally to seek out, rather than control, new capital inflows), largely disbanded the National Energy Program, and, most importantly, negotiated the Canada–United States Free Trade Agreement (CUSFTA), which went into operation on 1 January 1989. In 1992, a trilateral North American Free Trade Agreement (NAFTA) was concluded, adding Mexico, and hence an additional 85 million people, to this free trade zone. NAFTA came into effect on 1 January 1994. In short, a strikingly new approach to Canada's traditional, interrelated goals of achieving economic growth and preserving independence was pursued by the Conservatives from 1984 to 1993.

The Contemporary Challenges

Whatever the inclinations of the Liberal government elected in October 1993, a reversal of the broad direction of international economic policy pursued over the past decade is highly improbable. For better or worse, Canada will have to live with the CUSFTA and NAFTA and the constraints they impose on Canadian policy making. The impact of the former has naturally been much greater on the Canadian economy than on that of the United States, given this country's far heavier reliance on this bilateral trading relationship. Accordingly, the private sector in Canada has been making much more substantial adjustments to cope with the new trad-ing environment. That process has already gone too far to be reversed;

any unravelling of the agreement would be highly disruptive and would create such uncertainty among businesses in Canada and abroad about investment decisions as to seriously affect Canadian economic performance. If Canada cannot disentangle itself from the CUSFTA, it is equally enmeshed in NAFTA; entering the latter was necessary to protect Canada from the effects of the United States having free trade agreements with both Canada and Mexico while they lacked an agreement with each other. Under such circumstances, there would have been a strong incentive for capital in North America to flow to the United States, the only base with ready access to the entire North American market.

Whatever they think about the two trade pacts, Canadians must learn to live with the CUSFTA and NAFTA. It is imperative that Canadian firms move swiftly and creatively in adapting to these agreements, reorganizing their operations and increasing their productivity so as to be able to effectively penetrate the North American and other markets. Expanding Canada's economic relations with countries other than the United States and Mexico is particularly important lest, as a result of the CUSFTA and NAFTA, the level of its interaction with the rest of the world should shrink to the point where Canada is no longer treated seriously by extra-continental countries as a sovereign entity separate from the United States.

The relatively successful conclusion at the end of 1993 to the multilateral trade negotiations under the auspices of the General Agreement on Tariffs and Trade (GATT) provides a welcome opportunity for Canadian export expansion. Significant gains were made in the removal of tariff and non-tariff barriers to trade in manufactures, semi-processed goods, agricultural products, and services that should prove of benefit to Canada if the opportunities are pursued aggressively.

To facilitate the expansion and diversification of exports, it is critical that Ottawa develop an industrial policy that identifies economic sectors and individual Canadian firms that have the potential to be "winners" internationally. The government must then provide support in those areas and to those specific firms deemed to have the greatest long-term prospects for global competitiveness. Unfortunately, the policy instruments available to Canada in its pursuit of an industrial strategy have considerably narrowed in recent years: such measures as selective tax incentives, subsidies, and most strictures on foreign investment would violate terms of the CUSFTA, NAFTA, and GATT. To a certain degree, therefore, Canada seems destined to have to pay the price for not following the pattern of Japan and Europe and adopting, prior to the recent surge toward regional and global trade liberalization, an industrial policy that would have prepared it for the intensely competitive global markets it faces today. Nevertheless, there are still a number of initiatives that can be taken. More public funds can and should be directed toward research on industrial technological innovation. In co-operation with the provinces, educational reform and job-retraining schemes must be introduced to shape a work force suited to the needs of Canada's most promising industries. Consideration might be given to expanding the facilities of the Export Development Corporation in the provision of credit at competitive rates and insurance for Canadian exports. Incentive schemes, like the Program for Export Market Development funded by the Department of Foreign Affairs and International Trade, might be usefully expanded and more trading conferences organized to persuade business leaders to explore new market outlets and to approach them as long-term propositions, not short-term means of disposing of surplus products developed for North American consumers. Efforts might be made to develop Canadian trading companies, along the lines of those in Japan, to help smaller Canadian firms overcome the costs and other impediments associated with attempting, in distant and often exotic areas, to market, ship, and store their goods. Finally, there seems to be a call for a shift in Canadian diplomatic resources, from Europe, where Canadian exports have been in relative decline over recent decades, to Asia, whose share of Canada's export market has increased over the same period.

In short, Canada's situation today cries out for global involvement and a new focus on the traditional foreign policy goal of forging extra-continental links as one of the surest means of achieving economic growth and preserving Canadian independence.

THE ENVIRONMENT

The Problem

For decades the international community largely ignored the warning signs of humankind's degradation of the global environment in the rush toward industrial development. Now the signals of the incompatibility of our modern way of life with the very survival of the planet have become too obvious and grave to be ignored. Depletion of the ozone layer threatens a major increase in the incidence of cancer. Emissions from coal- and oil-burning plants, automobiles, and other sources, and the destruction of the tropical rain forests, are increasing the carbon dioxide in the atmosphere and contributing to a global warming trend that may turn vast tracts of arable land into arid deserts. The world's variety of flora and fauna are also jeopardized by these developments. Acid rain has been ravaging the lakes and forests of North America and Europe. Effluent from industrial plants and the run-off of pesticides from farmers' fields is poisoning the world's supply of fresh water. Oil spills and the dumping of sewage, garbage, and nuclear waste are polluting the oceans, and over-fishing is robbing future generations of a vital and traditional source of protein. The threats to the environment are numerous, and suddenly the world's leaders, prodded by their concerned publics, are starting to pay attention to them. Sustainable development is the new buzzword, and the environment now appears likely to be a dominant issue on the international agenda for the remainder of this century and well into the next. Pollution recognizes no state boundaries, and environmental issues must be confronted jointly in the mutual interests of all. These concerns propel all states toward collaborative international involvement.

For Canada there are particular reasons to be concerned. Possessing the longest coastline of any country in the world, including ecologically fragile Arctic waters, and being one of the world's leading fishing nations, it is inevitably concerned with the pollution of the oceans and the depletion of fish stocks. The Great Lakes, which Canada shares with the United States, supply 40 percent of the world's fresh water and are the principal source of drinking water for nearly forty million people. Yet this vital resource is seriously threatened by chemical and other pollutants. Finally, before the initiation of abatement programs in the late 1980s, smokestacks and exhaust pipes in North America were spewing into the air millions of tonnes a year of sulphur dioxide and nitrogen oxides, leading to acid rain. Roughly half the damage caused to Canada's forests and lakes has come from such emissions originating in the United States. Faced with these and other problems, it is not surprising that Canada was one of the first countries to give serious consideration to environmental issues in its foreign policy.

The Response

In a major review of foreign policy in 1970, the Liberal government of Pierre Trudeau set a harmonious natural environment as a basic goal. Since that time, a number of important initiatives related to that end have been undertaken. In 1969, a giant American tanker, the *Manhattan,* traversed the Northwest Passage, thereby demonstrating the feasibility of transporting oil from the southern slopes of Alaska through the Canadian

Arctic to supply eastern American consumers. The voyage was not only a challenge to Canada's control over the Northwest Passage: it also raised the risk of oil spills in Arctic waters—spills that, under permafrost conditions, could do irreparable ecological damage. In response, Canada passed the Arctic Waters Pollution Prevention Act, asserting its jurisdiction, for purposes of controlling pollution one hundred miles out to sea from the islands of the Arctic archipelago. Under the act, Canada claimed the right to set standards regarding the hulls of vessels plying Arctic waters and to board and inspect such ships. In 1977, Canada declared a two-hundred-mile fisheries zone off its coasts, assuming responsibility for regulating stocks within these waters. Nevertheless, it continued to have disagreements with a number of countries regarding the size of the annual catch, inside and outside this zone, that was compatible with the long-term health of the ocean fisheries. In sum, controversies related to protecting the oceans and their resources for future generations have formed an important dimension of Canadian foreign policy in recent years.

With respect to the degradation of its lakes and forests, Canada has been active bilaterally on the diplomatic front with the United States. In 1972 and 1978, the two countries entered into Great Lakes Water Quality agreements, the latter of which set standards on effluent emissions into the lakes. A new agreement in 1987 extended the scope of the clean-up beyond obvious sources of toxic waste to include secondary contaminants. This pact also committed both governments to move toward zero discharge of waste. Throughout the 1970s and early 1980s, Canada also engaged in protracted diplomatic efforts to curb North Dakota's Garrison Diversion project because of its concerns that it would seriously pollute rivers and lakes in Manitoba, cause springtime flooding, and damage the valuable Lake Winnipeg fishery. In the end, under pressure from Canada and more particularly the anti-Garrison environmental lobby in the United States, the project was halted.

At one time, the thorniest bilateral environmental issue was that of acid rain. In August 1980, at the end of the Carter administration, a Canada–United States memorandum of intent was signed, committing both countries to begin the process of negotiating an air quality agreement. However, throughout the ensuing Reagan presidency, the United States resisted making any progress on this issue, stubbornly insisting that there was insufficient evidence of the environmental damage caused by acid rain. While the administration agreed to spend additional funds on research, it refused to consider new air pollution controls or to commit itself to emission standards. The Bush administration adopted a more forthcoming attitude, and eventually Congress passed a clean-air bill committing the United States to a ten-million-ton reduction in sulphur dioxide emissions by early in the twenty-first century. Subsequently, Washington entered into an accord with Canada, setting limits on cross-border emissions.

Some environmental issues of concern to Canada go well beyond the continent and its adjacent waters. Thus, in 1987 and 1989, Canada was an active participant in the Montreal and London conferences on the ozone layer and a strong supporter of the agreements negotiated to curtail the emission of substances that deplete the ozone. It was also a leading player in the 1992 United Nations Conference on the Environment and Development in Rio de Janeiro and ratified the Conventions on Biological Diversity and Climate Change that emanated from that important meeting. Given its varied environmental concerns, Canada can be expected to play an active diplomatic role in dealing with these issues in the future.

The Contemporary Challenges

The principal challenge of the 1990s posed by the environmental problems plaguing the Earth is to transform the words of states' leaders into deeds. The rhetorical emphasis of late has to some degree been a calculated response of politicians sensitive to public opinion polls, to the perceived concerns of their electorates. This has been as true in Canada as elsewhere. There is no assurance that, without sustained societal pressure, the necessary concrete action will be taken.

The circumstances are, however, right for meaningful international action. The scientific evidence of the threats is overwhelming, and the public is increasingly informed about environmental issues. Further, the former Soviet bloc countries have begun to take environmental concerns seriously. Even many developing countries, long concerned that the effect of international environmental regulation would be to condemn them forever to the poverty of pre-industrial societies, have started to recognize the urgent need for co-operative action. However, it will take the leadership of countries like Canada to ensure that an adequate regime of international regulation is put in place. Devising agreed-upon international standards is only the first step. It must be followed by the establishment of effective means of monitoring and enforcement.

On the environmental issues of specific concern to Canada, intensive diplomatic activity is necessary to protect its interests, but at the same time Canada must match its demands on others by redoubled efforts of its own. For instance, Canada has had legitimate grievances against other countries that for years have overfished the Atlantic continental shelf, but former catches by Canadian fishers beyond what the stocks could support and misrepresentations of the sizes of catches also contributed to the problem. In the 1990s, Canada has at last taken serious unilateral conservation measures despite the short-term hardships curtailed catches have meant for those employed in the Atlantic fishery. At the time of writing, there were hopeful signs of a more co-operative attitude on the part of European countries in terms of adhering to the quotas set by the Northwest Atlantic Fisheries Organization. With respect to the Great Lakes Water Quality agreements, while over the years the United States has lagged behind Canada in getting on with the clean-up, both countries and their respective provinces and states have been dilatory in moving toward the goal of zero discharge. No timetable has been set for achieving this goal and no specific commitments have been made regarding the expenditure of funds. Canada and the United States have also lagged behind countries like West Germany, France, and Japan in adopting the sophisticated technology necessary to safeguard the cleanliness of their lakes and rivers. Bolder initiatives are required if the bilateral agreements to improve the quality of shared bodies of water are to have real meaning.

As indicated earlier, considerable progress has now been made on the bilateral issue of reducing sulphur dioxide emissions. However, this is only one of many substances polluting the environment. Commitments covering other contaminants are needed from Canada, the United States, and other countries. At the same time, there is a need to reduce still further the emission levels of sulphur dioxide.

At the multilateral level, an important priority for Canada is to ensure that the agreements reached at the Earth Summit in Rio de Janeiro are effectively implemented. In 1993, Canada was elected to the UN's new Commission on Sustainable Development, and it must now use this position not only to ensure that there is effective follow-up to the Rio Conference, but to press states to strengthen their commitments to sound forest management, protection of marine resources, preservation of a diversity of plant and animal species, and reduction of emissions that are causing global warming and depleting the ozone layer. In order to be taken seriously, Canada must be prepared to take more assertive measures to put its own house in order. For example, on a per capita basis, among the industrialized countries, it remains the worst emitter of carbon (carbon dioxide is the major contributor to the greenhouse effect). Canada has also been lax in insisting on rigorous environmental impact assessments of large-scale capital projects.

One of the most important contributions that Canada can make to the environment is through its assistance to developing countries to help them resolve their own problems. This entails not only targeting aid directly at combating pollution, but selecting for support developmental projects that are compatible with long-term environmental integrity. Finally, it must not be forgotten that the presence and testing of nuclear and chemical weapons pose potentially cataclysmic threats to the environment. This third area of foreign policy thus intersects with that of peace and security on the critical issue of arms control and disarmament.

SOCIAL JUSTICE

The Problem

The foreign policy theme of social justice has, in effect, two interrelated dimensions: improving the economic well-being of the disadvantaged peoples of the world and enhancing the degree of respect shown by governments for the basic rights of their citizens. The attention of politicans to this theme, like that of the environment, is partly a result of societal pressure. To a certain degree, the peoples of Western developed countries have recognized that their obligation to improve the lot of the less affluent within their own societies (as reflected in their support of progressive tax systems and social programs that redistribute wealth) extends to the poor of the Third World. Hence, they have supported modest levels of economic aid to developing countries. Similarly, their lives enhanced by the respect generally shown by their governments for a range of fundamental rights of the individual, citizens of Western countries have protested the gross and persistent repression of other states and turned to their own governments for a response. To some degree, too, the focus on international social justice has stemmed from a sense that it is an integral part of justice within Western democracies themselves. This lofty motive was reflected in 1970 when, in its review of Canadian foreign policy, the Trudeau government asserted that a truly just society could not be created within Canada unless the country was prepared to play its part in building a more just society globally.

Arguably, however, the theme of social justice has found a place in the foreign policy of states largely for reasons related to national interests more narrowly defined. Greater prosperity in the Third World provides new trade and investment opportunities for developed states. For a country like Canada, highly dependent on international trade but often uncompetitive in distant markets, an aid program heavily tied to the provision of Canadian goods and services offers Canadian firms new outlets abroad out of which long-term commercial relationships may develop. Politically, aid to Third World countries has been perceived as a means of enhancing stability and reducing the risks of regional conflicts, of winning friends and allies, and of buying support in general for the goals of one's own state. In the case of Canada, in the late 1960s and 1970s, a sizeable aid program was launched in francophone Africa to discourage these countries from supporting Quebec's aspirations of developing an international status of its own. More recently, it has come to be understood that providing aid to developing countries is necessary to elicit their support in addressing global environmental problems.

Enhancing respect for basic human rights around the world arguably also serves the political and economic interests of developed democracies like Canada. The end result of harsh repression is often civil unrest and revolution and the creation of unstable conditions that may tempt foreign states to intervene, leading to wars that damage global peace and security. Likewise, states that respect basic rights make better long-term trade and investment partners than countries where violations of human rights serve to perpetuate underdevelopment, inequality, and a concomitant climate of uncertainty, inimical to the secure conduct of business activity.

A variety of selfish as well as altruistic considerations have, then, led Western states, including Canada, into international involvement in the purported pursuit of social justice, whether or not that is really their goal.

The Response

With regard to Third World development, Canada steadily increased its aid disbursements from the launching of its aid program in 1950 to the beginning of the 1990s. From a very modest technical assistance program at the outset, Canada reached the point where its annual aid disbursements amounted to roughly $3 billion for a wide range of purposes. The period from 1968 to 1989 in particular witnessed a rapid rise in Canadian aid. Because this rise occurred over years in which there was a lagging effort on the part of other donors, including the United States and Britain, Canada became an increasingly important development partner for Third World countries, especially those of the Commonwealth and francophone Africa. In relative terms as well, Canadian aid increased over the initial years of this period. In 1961, Canadian assistance amounted to only .19 percent of Canada's gross national product, but by the 1975–76 fiscal year, the figure had reached an all-time high of .56. Thereafter, however, while the dollar value of Canadian aid continued to climb, measured as a percentage of GNP, Canada's performance began to slip.

The terms of Canadian aid have also been generous. Loans to Third World countries had been offered at 0 or 3 percent interest with repayments over thirty or fifty years, but in 1986 Canada shifted to an all-grant program. Canada has shown less largesse in terms of untying its aid to enable recipient states to use Canadian funds to purchase goods and services wherever desired based on price and/or quality. However, a reasonable proportion of Canadian aid is now provided on an untied basis through multilateral channels, and in 1987 Canada reduced the tying provisions for its bilateral aid (exclusive of food aid) to 50 percent for the countries designated by the United Nations as least developed and for all African recipients south of the Sahara. Elsewhere, two-thirds of bilateral aid must be spent on goods and services from Canada.

Canada has also initiated some creative ventures related to development. For instance, it operates a program of matching grants to non-governmental organizations that, through private agencies in Third World countries, support developmental projects targeted at the most disadvantaged. Further, in 1970, it created the International Development Research Centre, which, operating with an international board of governors, has directed funds at research in the Third World itself on grassroots developmental problems. Outside the field of foreign aid, Canada's contributions to Third World development have been less significant. However, in 1973 it did establish a relatively modest tariff preference scheme for developing countries to facilitate their exports to Canada.

With respect to human rights observance, Canada has long been active at the multilateral level in efforts to define the meaning of human rights, establish conventions setting out agreed-upon norms of behaviour, and put in place machinery for monitoring violations. Canada was an active participant in the drafting of several agreements: the UN's Universal Declaration of Human Rights; the conventions and declarations on genocide, torture, and disappearance; the elimination of discrimination based on race, religion, and sex; and the UN covenants on economic, social, and cultural rights and civil and political rights. Further, it has been heavily involved in the various UN commissions, committees, and working groups concerned with the implementation of these multilateral accords. In 1993, it was an active participant in the moderately successful World Conference on Human Rights in Vienna, pressing other reluctant delegations to accept a declaration affirming the universality and indivisibility of human rights. Finally, Canada has used meetings of the Commonwealth, la Francophonie, the Organization of American States, and the follow-up conferences to the 1975 Helsinki Conference on European Security and Co-operation to press for improved human rights observance in developing countries, South Africa, and Eastern Europe.

Bilaterally, Canada has used quiet diplomacy to encourage improved human rights observance, and in some instances it has applied modest economic and other strictures against states guilty of serious and protracted human rights abuses. A creative undertaking in 1990 was the establishment in Montreal of the International Centre for Human Rights and Democratic Development. In co-operation with various agencies of the Canadian government, the centre is responsible for initiating international projects in such areas as strengthening judicial institutions, improving legal and police training, establishing human rights offices and ombudsmen, and developing democratic election procedures.

The Contemporary Challenges

International social justice is still only a hope, not a reality. The initiatives of Canada and other countries have been of some help to the oppressed and disadvantaged, but they are not nearly enough, and the efficacy of the action taken has often been undermined by the mix of motives driving foreign policy in this area.

After almost forty-five years of developmental endeavours, large segments of the world's population still lack the basic requisites of a decent life: adequate nutrition, health care, shelter, and education. It is estimated that over one billion people in developing countries live in abject poverty, struggling to stay alive on 1.4 percent of the world's income. Moreover, by 1990, the developing countries had accumulated an external debt of $1.4 trillion (US). As a result, revenues for development are drained away in repayments to developed countries while budget cuts and other structural adjustments further reduce the capacity of Third World nations to meet the basic needs of their citizens.

The situation with respect to human rights is almost as bleak. Amnesty International annually documents a variety of serious human rights abuses, in well over one hundred countries, including such practices as torture, disappearances, arbitrary arrest and protracted detention without trial, and extra-judicial killings. Despite a hopeful trend toward democratic government and greater respect for human rights since the late 1980s, a large proportion of the world's population clearly lives in a climate of constant terror where intimidation and violence, perpetrated by those in authority, or agents acting on their behalf, are regular features of daily life. In sum, the challenges facing any country serious about international social justice are, indeed, daunting.

There is cause to be concerned about the nature of Canada's developmental effort over the 1990s. For the 1989–95 period, as part of the effort to reduce the deficit, Ottawa has slashed $4.5 billion from its originally intended aid expenditures. The aid program has had to bear a disproportionate share of the government's cuts in spending. In the past, Canada had committed itself on a number of occasions to meeting relatively modest targets of aid-giving, ranging from .6 to 1 percent of GNP in the form of aid. While these goals were never reached, they nevertheless served as an indication of intent as well as a benchmark against which to measure Canadian performance. At the time of writing, Canada seems to have abandoned these targets altogether and is at risk of dropping below .40 percent of GNP by mid-decade. Reversing the current downward trend in Canada's developmental effort is one of the principal tasks that must be pursued by the government of Jean Chrétien to preserve the legitimacy of Canada's purported commitment to social justice.

In theory, Canada concentrates its aid on countries that are at "the lower end of the development scale" and on "the critical problems of their poor majority." In fact, less than one-quarter of Canadian aid flows to the forty-two least-developed countries, as classified by the United Nations, making Ottawa one of the least generous donors to low-income developing states. Over the period 1988–89 to 1990–91, only five of Canada's top twenty aid recipients were in the least developed group. In addition, according to the United Nations Development Program, only a very modest proportion of Canadian assistance actually goes to meeting basic human needs. A reorientation of Canadian aid toward human resource development in the world's most disadvantaged nations is thus called for. It will require strong societal pressure to bring this about, for there are forces at work pushing Canada in a different direction. In particular, these arise from the temptation in an intensely competitive international trading environment to channel aid toward projects and states of commercial promise to Canada.

The impact of selfish interests on the extent to which Canada makes a meaningful contribution to social justice is even more starkly apparent with respect to Canada's non-aid contributions to development. The tariff preference scheme for developing countries that Canada put into effect in 1973 offered only modest cuts and it excluded from its purview many of the products that developing countries are most interested in exporting to Canada, including textiles and footwear. It also has other built-in safeguards against injury to Canadian producers. In addition, Canada has long applied quantitative restrictions against the import of commodities like textiles and clothing, and the number of products and developing countries subject to such restraints on exporting to Canada has increased. It is noteworthy that only 12 percent of Canada's imports come from developing countries, compared to 40 percent for the United States and 48 percent for Japan. Canada has also exhibited little generosity in the negotiation of commodity price stabilization agreements that would provide developing countries with better and more stable prices for the staple exports on which they often depend. To a significant degree, the meaningfulness of Canada's commitment to social justice over the 1990s will be measured by the degree to which it pursues more generous policies outside the area of traditional aid, including seeking solutions to the debt crisis of the Third World.

The complex area of human rights requires of Canada a careful blend of persuasion and subtle pressure. There are clear limits to its capacity to influence the internal affairs of other countries, and inappropriate actions could do more harm than good. What seems particularly called for is an end to the inconsistency and symbolism that has often characterized Canadian policy in the past. Canada has been far more inclined to take punitive action against states with which it has limited economic and political relations than against where its commercial, developmental, and political-strategic interests are substantial. Policy has thus been based not on careful, objective assessments of the relative severity of human rights violations in different countries, but on calculations of the impact of initiatives on Canada's own interests. Canadian actions, therefore, often appear not only inconsistent, but hypocritical. Moreover, when Canada has applied strictures against gross violators of human rights, it has not always been clear that its actions were in response to human rights abuses, and sanctions frequently have been so insubstantial as to be of little consequence. Greater consistency, transparency, and effectiveness are all required in the future. At the same time, there must be a readiness on Canada's part to commit the resources necessary for effective human rights monitoring and the identification and implementation of projects that can make a positive contribution to improved human rights observance.

The challenges to the attainment of social justice are numerous and complex, and the commitment of Canada, based as it is on a mixture of altruistic and selfish motives, is unclear. Under the circumstances, its accomplishments are likely to be limited without sustained pressure from an informed public that believes in the right of all inhabitants of the Earth to lives of dignity and worth.

CONCLUSION

The four areas of foreign policy discussed in this chapter only partly explain the factors that impel Canada toward a role in world affairs and make the study of foreign policy an important dimension of Canadian politics. There are many others. They include, for instance, the need for a middle power like Canada to reach out to the world in order to sustain at home a vigorous culture and standards of excellence in such fields as education, science, and industrial technology. The desire of Canada's different ethnic groups to maintain ties with their homelands and the particular interest of Quebec in links with la Francophonie in order to help nurture the French language and culture in North America are other important factors pressing Canada into international relationships. There is also an enhanced sense of national identity to be derived from Canada's making a large and constructive contribution to global affairs. The four dimensions discussed above provide, however, the principal explanations for Canada's international involvement, and the actions pursued by Canada indicate the variety and complexity of Canadian foreign policy. The four themes also illustrate that there are imposing international problems that Canada must contend with in the years ahead. They ensure that foreign policy will remain an important aspect of the study of Canadian government and politics, offering exciting challenges to students concerned not only about the future of Canada, but about the wider international community.

SUGGESTED READING

Canada Among Nations, various editors and publishers (1985–).
   An annual volume of essays surveying issues in Canadian foreign policy since 1984.

"Canada and the New World Order," *International Journal* 47, 3 (Summer 1992).

A good collection of articles, mostly by distinguished Canadian academics, exploring some of the contemporary challenges facing Canadian foreign policy.

Granatstein, J.L., ed. *Canadian Foreign Policy: Historical Readings*. 2nd ed. Toronto: Copp Clark Pitman, 1992.

A useful collection of essays and government documents pertaining to different periods of Canadian foreign policy.

Holmes, John, and Norman Hillmer, eds. *Making a Difference? Canada's Foreign Policy in a Changing World Order*. Toronto: Lester Publishing, 1992.

Retrospective but also forward-looking essays on subjects of long-term importance in Canadian foreign policy, drawn from a 1991 conference celebrating sixty years of Canadian foreign policy independence.

Nossal, Kim Richard. *The Politics of Canadian Foreign Policy*. Scarborough, ON: Prentice-Hall, 1989.

An introductory text focusing on the domestic and international context in which Canadian foreign policy takes place, and on the institutions involved in the policy-making process (rather than on the substance of Canadian policy).

INDEX